Bargaining Theory with Applications

The first unified and systematic treatment of the modern theory of bargaining, presented together with many examples of how that theory is applied in a variety of bargaining situations.

Abhinay Muthoo provides a masterful synthesis of the fundamental results and insights obtained from the wide-ranging and diverse (game theoretic) bargaining theory literature. Furthermore, he develops new analyses and results, especially on the relative impacts of two or more forces on the bargaining outcome. Many topics — such as inside options, commitment tactics and repeated bargaining situations — receive their most extensive treatment to date. In the concluding chapter, he offers pointers towards future research.

Bargaining Theory with Applications is a textbook for graduate students in economic theory and other social sciences and a research resource for scholars interested in bargaining situations.

Abhinay Muthoo is Professor of Economics at the University of Essex. He was educated at the London School of Economics and the University of Cambridge. Professor Muthoo has published papers on bargaining theory and game theory, among other topics, in journals such as *Review of Economic Studies*, *Journal of Economic Theory*, *Games and Economic Behavior* and *Economic Journal*.

Bargaining Theory with Applications

ABHINAY MUTHOO

University of Essex

CAMBRIDGE
UNIVERSITY PRESS

PUBLISHED BY THE PRESS SYNDICATE OF THE UNIVERSITY OF CAMBRIDGE
The Pitt Building, Trumpington Street, Cambridge, United Kingdom

CAMBRIDGE UNIVERSITY PRESS
The Edinburgh Building, Cambridge CB2 2RU, UK   www.cup.cam.ac.uk
40 West 20th Street, New York NY 1011-4211, USA   www.cup.org
10 Stamford Road, Oakleigh, Melbourne 3166, Australia
Ruiz de Alarcón 13, 28014 Madrid, Spain

First Published 1999

Printed in the United Kingdom at the University Press, Cambridge

Typeface Computer Modern 11pt   *System* LATEX2e   [Typeset by the author]

A catalogue record for this book is available from the British Library

Library of Congress cataloguing in publication data applied for

ISBN 0 521 572258 hardback
ISBN 0 521 576474 paperback

To my parents

Contents

Preface

Ariel Rubinstein's contribution to bargaining theory in Rubinstein (1982) captured the imagination of the economics profession. The origins of most papers in the wide-ranging and diverse literature that has since developed can be traced back to that seminal paper; even those papers that cannot have probably been inspired by the literature that has. At the same time as the development of the *theory* of bargaining, applied economic theorists have used models from this literature to construct models of a variety of economic phenomena that had hitherto not been studied at all, or not been studied properly. There is now a large literature that contains *applications* of that bargaining theory.

With the exception of John Nash's path-breaking contributions to bargaining theory in Nash (1950, 1953), much of the material in this book is based upon and/or inspired by the literature (theoretical and applied) that has developed since 1982.

I have written this book with two main objectives in mind. Firstly, from a *theoretical* perspective, I synthesize, and organize into a coherent and unified picture, the main fundamental results and insights obtained from the bargaining theory literature. The chapters are organized around the main forces that determine the bargaining outcome. I not only analyse the impact on the bargaining outcome of each force, but I also often analyse the relative impacts of two or more forces. And, secondly, from an *applied* perspective, I show how the theory can be fruitfully applied to a variety of economic phenomena.

In order to achieve the first of the two objectives stated above, I have had to take stock of, and reflect upon, the bargaining theory literature. In the process of doing so, it has been necessary to conduct some new analyses (not contained in the literature) — especially in order to develop an understanding of the *relative* impacts of two or more forces on the bargaining outcome.

Since this book provides a unified treatment of bargaining theory and contains new results, it is part textbook and part research monograph. As such this book should be useful not only to graduate students and professional applied economic and political theorists interested in bargaining situations (that arise in many areas of economics and politics), but also to bargaining and game theorists. This book can be used to learn bargaining theory and to improve one's understanding of it. Furthermore, it should help researchers apply that theory and/or construct their own models of the specific real-life bargaining situations that interest them.

Chapter 1 introduces some basic issues and provides an outline of the book. The theory and application of bargaining are developed in Chapters 2–10. The final (concluding) chapter, Chapter 11, draws attention to some of the main omissions and weaknesses of the theory developed in this book, and identifies specific avenues and topics for future research in the further development of the theory and application of bargaining.

Acknowledgements

I began working on this book in October 1995, after much encouragement from Ariel Rubinstein. I owe my greatest debt to him for several reasons, besides that. Firstly, of course, because of his written contributions, which have not only made this book possible, but have influenced my own work and thinking on the subject. Secondly, because I have had the privilege of discussing bargaining theory with him ever since I was a graduate student at the University of Cambridge. I have learned a great deal and obtained much insight from our discussions.

Ken Binmore has also played an important role in my work and thinking, both through his important and insightful contributions and through our discussions. He also provided encouragement to write this book.

While writing the book, I have accumulated many debts. Many friends and colleagues made very detailed comments on several chapters that led me to substantially revise them. They include Roy Bailey (Chapters 1, 2–4 and 11), Craig Brett (Chapters 1, 5, 6 and 11), Vince Crawford (Chapter 8), Martin Cripps (Chapters 2 and 3), Leonardo Felli (Chapter 10), Shinsuke Kambe (Chapters 7–9), Ben Lockwood (Chapters 5 and 6), Martin Osborne (Chapters 3, 4, 7 and 8) and Anders Poulsen (Chapters 3 and 7).

Craig Brett, Roy Bailey, Ken Binmore, Vince Crawford, Osvaldo Feinstein, Drew Fudenberg, Oliver Hart, Jim Malcomson, Martin Osborne, Alvin Roth and Ariel Rubinstein provided me with some helpful advice and/or comments on some aspects of the book.

Without access to LaTeX, I think I would not have written this book. I owe much gratitude to Roy Bailey, who (a few years earlier) introduced me to this amazing software package, helped me learn it, and, while writing the book, helped me when I had queries on how to do this or that. Craig Brett also kindly provided some help in this latter respect.

Patrick McCartan was the economics editor at CUP for much of the time while I was writing the book, before he moved on to head the CUP journals department. Patrick's enthusiasm for the book and general support gave me much encouragement. The anonymous referees (organized by Patrick) provided me with some very useful specific and general comments. Ashwin Rattan, who succeeded Patrick as the CUP economics editor, very kindly and efficiently steered the completed typescript through the various (editing and production) stages at the Press. It has been a pleasure to work with the staff at CUP.

Last, but certainly not least, my family provided me with much encouragement and support.

Abhinay Muthoo
University of Essex

1   Preliminaries

1.1   Bargaining Situations and Bargaining

Consider the following situation. Individual S owns a house that she values at £50,000 (which is the minimum price at which she would sell it). Individual B values this house at £70,000 (which is the maximum price at which she would buy it). If trade occurs — that is, if individual S sells the house to individual B — at a price that lies between £50,000 and £70,000, then both the seller (individual S) and the buyer (individual B) would become better off. This means that in this situation the two individuals have a common interest to trade. But, at the same time, they have conflicting interests over the price at which to trade: the seller would like to trade at a high price, while the buyer would like to trade at a low price. Any exchange situation, such as the one just described, in which a pair of individuals (or, organizations) can engage in mutually beneficial trade but have conflicting interests over the terms of trade is a bargaining situation.

Stated in general and broad terms, a *bargaining situation* is a situation in which two *players*[1] have a common interest to co-operate, but have conflicting interests over exactly how to co-operate. To put it differently, the players can mutually benefit from reaching agreement on an outcome from a set of possible outcomes (that contains two or more elements), but have

---

[1]A 'player' can be either an individual, or an organization (such as a firm, or a country).

conflicting interests over the set of outcomes.

There are two main reasons for studying bargaining situations. The first, practical, reason is that many important and interesting human (economic, social and political) interactions are bargaining situations. As mentioned above, exchange situations (which characterize much of human economic interaction) are bargaining situations. In the arena of social interaction, a married couple, for example, are involved in many bargaining situations throughout their relationship. In the political arena, a bargaining situation exists, for example, when no single party on its own can form a government (such as when there is a hung parliament); the party that has obtained the most votes will typically find itself in a bargaining situation with one of the other parties. The second, theoretical, reason for studying bargaining situations is that understanding such situations is fundamental to the development of the economic theory of markets.

The main issue that confronts the players in a bargaining situation is the need to reach agreement over exactly how to co-operate — before they actually co-operate (and obtain the fruits of that co-operation). On the one hand, each player would like to reach some agreement rather than disagree and not reach any agreement. But, on the other hand, each player would like to reach an agreement that is as favourable to her as possible. It is thus conceivable that the players will strike an agreement only after some costly delay, or indeed fail to reach any agreement — as is witnessed by the history of disagreements and costly delayed agreements in many real-life bargaining situations (as exemplified by the occurrences of trade wars, military wars, strikes and divorce).

Bargaining is any process through which the players *on their own* try to reach an agreement. This process is typically time consuming and involves the players making offers and counteroffers to each other. If the players get a third party to help them determine the agreement, then this means that agreement is not reached via bargaining (but, for example, via some arbitration process). The theory developed in this book concerns bargaining situations in which the outcome is determined entirely via some bargaining process. The role of arbitrators and mediators in helping the players reach agreement is briefly discussed in the final chapter.

A main focus of any theory of bargaining is on the *efficiency* and *distribution* properties of the outcome of bargaining. The former property relates to the possibility that the bargaining outcome is not Pareto efficient. As indicated above, this could arise, for example, either because the players fail to reach an agreement, or because they reach an agreement after some costly delay. Examples of costly delayed agreements include: when a wage agreement is reached after lost production due to a long strike, and when a peace settlement is negotiated after the loss of life through war. The distribution property, on the other hand, relates to the issue of exactly how the fruits of co-operation are divided between the players (or, to put it differently, how the gains from trade are divided). The theory developed in this book determines the roles of various forces on the bargaining outcome (and, in particular, on these two properties). As such it addresses the issue of what determines a player's *bargaining power*.

1.2   Outline of the Book

A basic, intuitive, observation is that if the bargaining process is frictionless — by which I mean, in particular, that neither player incurs any cost during the bargaining process — then each player may continuously demand (without incurring any cost) that agreement be struck on terms that are most favourable to her. For example, in the exchange situation described at the beginning of Section 1.1, the seller may continuously demand that trade take place at the price of £69,000, while the buyer may continuously demand that trade take place at the price of £51,000. It may therefore be argued that the outcome of a frictionless bargaining process is indeterminate, since the players may have no incentive to compromise and reach an agreement. Consequently, it would seem hopeless to construct a theory of bargaining — that determines the outcome of bargaining in terms of the primitives of the bargaining situation (such as the set of possible agreements and the players' preferences over this set) — based on frictionless bargaining processes.

Fortunately, in most real-life bargaining situations the bargaining process is not frictionless. A basic source of the cost incurred by a player while bargaining — that provides some friction in the bargaining process — comes from the twin facts that bargaining is time consuming and time is valuable to the player. Rubinstein's bargaining model — which is the subject of study in Chapter 3 — is a formal exploration of the role of the players' discount rates (that represent their values for time) in a time-consuming, offer-counteroffer process. It is shown that, indeed, the players will reach an (immediate) agreement if and only if time is valuable to at least one of the two players. Furthermore, a number of other fundamental results and insights are obtained from the study of this model, including those concerning the role of the *relative* magnitude of the players' discount rates on the terms of the agreement. It is worth pointing out that these results (and many others derived in the book) — although, in hindsight, are rather intuitive — were not obtainable without formally modelling the bargaining process. I should also emphasize here (although this will become clear in Chapter 3) that Rubinstein's bargaining model provides the basic framework that is extended and/or adapted (in several later chapters) to address the roles of various other forces.

Another basic source of the cost incurred by a player while bargaining comes from the possibility that the negotiations might randomly and exogenously breakdown in disagreement. Even if the probability of such an occurrence is small, it nevertheless provides some friction in the bargaining process — and as such may provide appropriate incentives to the players to compromise and reach an agreement. The role of such an exogenous risk of breakdown is studied in Chapter 4. I also explore the interplay of this force with the players' discount rates, and study their relative impacts on the bargaining outcome.

In many bargaining situations the players may have access to outside options and/or inside options. For example, in the exchange situation described above the seller may have a non-negotiable (fixed) price offer on the house from a different buyer, and she may derive some utility while she lives in the house. The former is her outside option, while the latter her inside option. I should emphasize that when, and if, the seller exercises her outside option, the negotiations between individuals B and S terminate *forever* in disagreement. In contrast, the seller's inside option describes her (flow) utility while she *temporarily* disagrees with individual B over the price at which to trade. The role of outside options is studied in Chapter 5, while the role of inside options in Chapter 6. I also study the interplay amongst the players' discount rates, outside options, inside options and an exogenous risk of breakdown.

An important set of questions addressed in Chapters 3–6 are *why, when and how* to apply Nash's bargaining solution, where the latter is described and studied in Chapter 2. It is shown that under some circumstances, when appropriately applied, Nash's bargaining solution describes the outcome of a variety of bargaining situations. These results are especially important and useful in applications, since it is often convenient for applied economic theorists to describe the outcome of a bargaining situation — which may be one of many ingredients of their economic models — in a *simple* (and tractable) manner.

The procedure of bargaining constitutes the rules of the bargaining process, and includes matters such as who makes offers and when. It seems self-evident that the bargaining outcome will depend on the bargaining procedure. I study the impact that various specific procedural features have on the bargaining outcome in Chapter 7. However, the thorny issue of what or who determines the procedure is left unanswered. In the final chapter, I return to this difficult issue.

The role of bargaining tactics is taken up in Chapter 8, where the focus is on a particular type of tactic, known as the commitment tactic. The basic model studied here establishes a number of fundamental results and insights. In particular, it formalizes the notion that (in bargaining situations) weakness can often be a source of strength. An important aspect of many bargaining processes is the making of claims followed by concessions, which leads me to also study wars of attrition based bargaining models.

In Chapter 9 I study the role of asymmetric information. In particular, I explore whether or not the presence of asymmetric information necessarily implies that the bargaining outcome is inefficient. Furthermore, I explore the impact that asymmetric information has on the players' respective bargaining powers.

In the preceding chapters the focus is on 'one-shot' bargaining situations. In Chapter 10 I study 'repeated' bargaining situations in which the players have the opportunity to be involved in a sequence of (possibly different and/or interdependent) bargaining situations. After studying repeated bargaining models, I explore whether or not the players might wish to commit themselves to a long-term relationship by writing a long-term contract. I then explore the notion that in such repeated bargaining situations a player might build a reputation for being a particular type of bargainer.

In Chapters 2–10 I develop a theory of bargaining, and apply that theory to a variety of bargaining situations. I should emphasize that the focus is on *fundamentals*. Furthermore, the models studied are particularly simple, so as to bring out the main fundamental results and insights in a simple but rigorous manner. I conclude in Chapter 11, where I describe some of the main omissions and weaknesses of the theory developed in this book. In particular, I identify potential avenues and topics for future research. Furthermore, I offer some comments on the role of bargaining experiments.

1.3   The Role of Game Theory

A bargaining situation is a game situation in the sense that the outcome of bargaining depends on *both* players' bargaining strategies: whether or not an agreement is struck, and the terms of the agreement (if one is struck), depends on both players' actions during the bargaining process. It is therefore natural to study bargaining situations using the methodology of game theory. Indeed, almost all of the bargaining models studied in this book are game-theoretic models. In particular, a bargaining situation is modelled as an extensive-form game. When there is no asymmetric information, I characterize its Nash equilibria if the bargaining game is static and its subgame perfect equilibria if it is dynamic. On the other hand, when there is asymmetric information, I characterize its Bayesian Nash equilibria if it is static and its perfect Bayesian equilibria if it is dynamic.

Although — as I briefly discuss in the final chapter — there are several important weaknesses with the game-theoretic methodology, as it currently stands, its strengths are considerable. In particular, it is currently the best available tool with which one can formalize the phenomena under consideration, and conduct a deep, insightful and rigorous investigation of the role of various forces on the bargaining outcome.

1.4   Further Remarks

Most of the models studied in this book are dynamic games with perfect information. As indicated above, I use the subgame perfect equilibrium concept to analyse these models. Although, therefore, readers should have some basic knowledge of the subgame perfect equilibrium concept, it is not necessary to have taken a course in game theory in order to understand much of the material in this book.[2]

In order to make the theory as widely accessible as possible, and so as to develop a relatively deeper understanding of it, I adopt several simplifying assumptions, and focus attention primarily on bargaining situations that can be represented as involving the partition of a cake (or, 'surplus') of fixed size. When it is deemed worthwhile to do so, I generalize the results.

Since a significant proportion of the material in this book is based upon and/or inspired by the literature, it may perhaps be misleading for me to ascribe the material directly to the authors concerned. Hence, I provide appropriate acknowledgements to the relevant literature at the end of each chapter, under the heading 'Notes'.

---

[2]It might nevertheless be of interest for some readers to refer to a game theory text. Fudenberg and Tirole (1991), Myerson (1991), van Damme (1991) and Osborne and Rubinstein (1994) are fairly formal, while Binmore (1992) and Gibbons (1992) are much less so.

2 The Nash Bargaining Solution

2.1 Introduction

A bargaining solution may be interpreted as a formula that determines a unique outcome for each bargaining situation in some class of bargaining situations. In this chapter I study the bargaining solution created by John Nash.[1] The Nash bargaining solution is defined by a fairly simple formula, and it is applicable to a large class of bargaining situations — these features contribute to its attractiveness in applications. However, the most important of reasons for studying and applying the Nash bargaining solution is that it possesses sound strategic foundations: several plausible (game-theoretic) models of bargaining vindicate its use. These strategic bargaining models will be studied in later chapters where I shall address the issues of why, when and how to use the Nash bargaining solution.

A prime objective of the current chapter, on the other hand, is to develop a thorough understanding of the definition of the Nash bargaining solution, which should, in particular, facilitate its characterization and use in any application.

In the next section I define and characterize the Nash bargaining solution of a specific bargaining situation in which two players bargain over the par-

---

[1]Nash's bargaining solution and the concept of a Nash equilibrium are unrelated concepts, other than the fact that both concepts are the creations of the same individual.

tition of a cake (or 'surplus') of fixed size. Although this type of bargaining situation is not uncommon, a main purpose of this section is to introduce — in a relatively simple and concrete context — some of the main concepts involved in defining Nash's bargaining solution. Section 2.3 contains two applications of the Nash bargaining solution — one is to bribery and the control of crime, and the other to optimal asset ownership.

Having mastered the concepts and results in Section 2.2, it should prove relatively easier to understand Section 2.4, where I define and characterize the Nash bargaining solution in its general form, which is somewhat abstract. Section 2.5 contains three further applications of the Nash bargaining solution — one is to union-firm negotiations, the second to team production under moral hazard, and the third extends the application to bribery and the control of crime studied in Section 2.3.1.

Section 2.6 shows that the Nash bargaining solution is the only possible bargaining solution that satisfies four properties. Although these properties are commonly referred to as axioms, one could debate whether or not any of these properties are axiomatic. In any case, this 'axiomatic' foundation is interesting and provides some insights into Nash's bargaining solution. A key insight is that the Nash bargaining solution may be influenced by the players' attitudes towards risk.

It is argued in Section 2.7 that the definition of the Nash bargaining solution stated in Sections 2.2 and 2.4 fails to provide it with a natural interpretation. An alternative (but equivalent) definition is stated in Section 2.7 which suggests that the Nash bargaining solution may be interpreted as a stable bargaining convention.

Section 2.8 defines and characterizes the asymmetric Nash bargaining solutions. These generalizations of the Nash bargaining solution possess a facility to take into account additional factors of a bargaining situation that may be deemed relevant for the bargaining outcome.

2.2   Bargaining over the Partition of a Cake

Two players, A and B, bargain over the partition of a cake of size π, where $\pi > 0$. The set of possible agreements is $X = \{(x_A, x_B) : 0 \leq x_A \leq \pi$ and $x_B = \pi - x_A\}$, where x_i is the share of the cake to player i $(i = A, B)$. For each $x_i \in [0, \pi]$, $U_i(x_i)$ is player i's utility from obtaining a share x_i of the cake, where player i's utility function $U_i : [0, \pi] \rightarrow \Re$ is strictly increasing and concave. If the players fail to reach agreement, then player i obtains a utility of d_i, where $d_i \geq U_i(0)$. There exists an agreement $x \in X$ such that $U_A(x) > d_A$ and $U_B(x) > d_B$, which ensures that there exists a mutually beneficial agreement.

The utility pair $d = (d_A, d_B)$ is called the *disagreement point*. In order to define the Nash bargaining solution of this bargaining situation, it is useful to first define the set Ω of *possible utility pairs* obtainable through agreement. For the bargaining situation described above, $\Omega = \{(u_A, u_B) :$ there exists $x \in X$ such that $U_A(x_A) = u_A$ and $U_B(x_B) = u_B\}$.

Fix an arbitrary utility u_A to player A, where $u_A \in [U_A(0), U_A(\pi)]$. From the strict monotonicity of U_i, there exists a unique share $x_A \in [0, \pi]$ such that $U_A(x_A) = u_A$; i.e., $x_A = U_A^{-1}(u_A)$, where U_A^{-1} denotes the inverse of U_A.[2] Hence

$$g(u_A) \equiv U_B(\pi - U_A^{-1}(u_A))$$

is the utility player B obtains when player A obtains the utility u_A. It immediately follows that $\Omega = \{(u_A, u_B) : U_A(0) \leq u_A \leq U_A(\pi)$ and $u_B = g(u_A)\}$; that is, Ω is the graph of the function $g : [U_A(0), U_A(\pi)] \rightarrow \Re$.

The *Nash bargaining solution* (NBS) of the bargaining situation described above is the unique pair of utilities, denoted by (u_A^N, u_B^N), that solves the following maximization problem

$$\max_{(u_A, u_B) \in \Theta} (u_A - d_A)(u_B - d_B),$$

where $\Theta \equiv \{(u_A, u_B) \in \Omega : u_A \geq d_A$ and $u_B \geq d_B\} \equiv \{(u_A, u_B) : U_A(0) \leq u_A \leq U_A(\pi), u_B = g(u_A), u_A \geq d_A$ and $u_B \geq d_B\}$.

The maximization problem stated above has a unique solution, because the maximand $(u_A - d_A)(u_B - d_B)$ — which is referred to as the Nash product — is continuous and strictly quasiconcave, g is strictly decreasing and concave (as stated below in Lemma 2.1), and the set Θ is non-empty.[3] Figure 2.1 illustrates the NBS. Since $u_A^N > d_A$ and $u_B^N > d_B$, in the NBS the players reach agreement on $(x_A^N, x_B^N) = (U_A^{-1}(u_A^N), U_B^{-1}(u_B^N))$.

---

[2] It should be noted that the inverse U_A^{-1} is a strictly increasing and convex function, whose domain is the closed interval $[U_A(0), U_A(\pi)]$ and range is the closed interval $[0, \pi]$.

[3] In fact, there exists a continuum of utility pairs $(u_A, u_B) \in \Theta$ such that $u_A > d_A$ and $u_B > d_B$.

Lemma 2.1. *g is strictly decreasing and concave.*

Proof. In the Appendix.   □

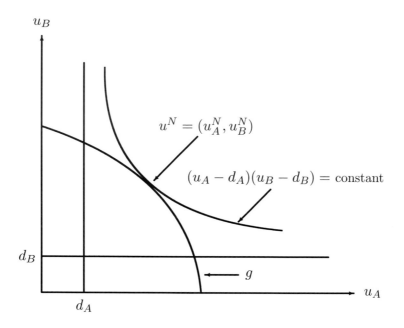

Figure 2.1: u^N is the Nash bargaining solution of the bargaining situation in which the set Ω of possible utility pairs obtainable through agreement is the graph of g, and d is the disagreement point.

2.2.1   Characterization

The following result provides a characterization of the NBS of the bargaining situation described above, when g is differentiable.

Proposition 2.1. *In the bargaining situation described above, if g is differentiable, then the Nash bargaining solution is the unique solution to the following pair of equations*

$$-g'(u_A) = \frac{u_B - d_B}{u_A - d_A} \quad \text{and} \quad u_B = g(u_A),$$

where g' denotes the derivative of g.

Proof. Since the NBS is such that $u_A^N > d_A$ and $u_B^N > d_B$, it may be characterized by finding the value of u_A that maximizes $(u_A - d_A)(g(u_A) - d_B)$. The proposition follows immediately from the first-order condition. $\square$

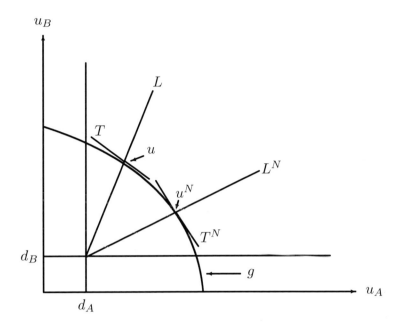

Figure 2.2: When g is differentiable, the NBS is the unique point on the graph of g where the slope of the line L^N is equal to the absolute value of the slope of the unique tangent T^N.

It is instructive, and useful in some applications, to note the following geometric characterization of the NBS — which is valid when g is differentiable and follows from Proposition 2.1. The NBS is the unique point u^N on the graph of g with the property that the slope of the line joining the points u^N and d is equal to the absolute value of the slope of the unique tangent to the graph of g at u^N. This is illustrated in Figure 2.2. Consider any point u on the graph of g to the left of u^N. The slope of the line L joining points d and u has increased relative to the slope of the line L^N, while the absolute value of the slope of the tangent T to the graph of g at u has decreased relative to the absolute value of the slope of the tangent T^N. Therefore, the slope of L is strictly greater than the absolute value of the slope of T. By a symmetric argument, it follows that the slope of the line joining the point d with a point on the graph of g to the right of the NBS is strictly less than the absolute value of the slope of the tangent to the graph of g at that point.

The result contained in the following corollary to Proposition 2.1 may be useful in applications.

Corollary 2.1. *In the bargaining situation described above, if g is differentiable, then the share x_A^N of the cake obtained by player A in the Nash bargaining solution is the unique solution to the equation*

$$\frac{U_A(x_A) - d_A}{U_A'(x_A)} = \frac{U_B(\pi - x_A) - d_B}{U_B'(\pi - x_A)},$$

and player B's share in the NBS is $x_B^N = \pi - x_A^N$.

Proof. The result follows immediately from Proposition 2.1 after differentiating g (with respect to u_A) and noting that $U_i(x_i) = u_i$ and $x_i = U_i^{-1}(u_i)$. $\qquad\square$

I now provide a characterization of the NBS when g is not assumed to be differentiable. However, since g is concave, it is differentiable 'almost everywhere'. But, it is possible that the NBS is precisely at a point where g is not differentiable.[4] Since g is concave, its left-hand and right-hand derivatives exist. Let $g'(u_A-)$ and $g'(u_A+)$ respectively denote the left-hand and right-hand derivatives of g at u_A. Since g is concave, $g'(u_A-) \geq g'(u_A+)$. The following result is straightforward to establish, and is illustrated in Figure 2.3.

Proposition 2.2. *In the bargaining situation described above, if g is not differentiable at the Nash bargaining solution, then there exists a number k, where $g'(u_A^N-) \geq k \geq g'(u_A^N+)$, such that the Nash bargaining solution is the unique solution to the following pair of equations*

$$-k = \frac{u_B - d_B}{u_A - d_A} \quad and \quad u_B = g(u_A).$$

As is illustrated in Figure 2.3, the NBS is the unique point u^N on the graph of g with the property that the slope of the line L^N joining u^N and d is equal to the absolute value (namely, $-k$) of the slope of *some* tangent T^N to the graph of g at u^N.

---

[4]Chapter 8 studies a model of bargaining in which this is the case.

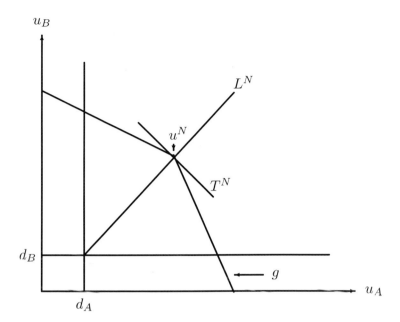

Figure 2.3: When g is not differentiable, the NBS is the unique point on the graph of g where the slope of the line L^N is equal to the absolute value of the slope of *some* tangent T^N.

Remark 2.1 (Comparative-Statics). The following results may be established by using the geometric characterizations of the NBS, as illustrated in Figures 2.2 and 2.3. Since the NBS of the bargaining situation described above depends upon the disagreement point, I emphasize this by writing the NBS as $(u_A^N(d), u_B^N(d))$. Let d and d' denote two alternative disagreement points such that $d_i' > d_i$ and $d_j' = d_j$ $(j \neq i)$. If g is differentiable at $u_A^N(d)$, then $u_i^N(d') > u_i^N(d)$ and $u_j^N(d') < u_j^N(d)$. If, on the other hand, g is not differentiable at $u_A^N(d)$, then $u_i^N(d') \geq u_i^N(d)$ and $u_j^N(d') \leq u_j^N(d)$.

2.2.2 Examples

Example 2.1 (Split-The-Difference Rule). Suppose $U_A(x_A) = x_A$ for all $x_A \in [0, \pi]$ and $U_B(x_B) = x_B$ for all $x_B \in [0, \pi]$. This means that for each $u_A \in [0, \pi]$, $g(u_A) = \pi - u_A$, and $d_i \geq 0$ $(i = A, B)$. Applying Proposition 2.1, it follows that

$$u_A^N = \frac{1}{2}\left(\pi - d_B + d_A\right) \quad \text{and} \quad u_B^N = \frac{1}{2}\left(\pi - d_A + d_B\right).$$

Thus

$$x_A^N = d_A + \frac{1}{2}\left(\pi - d_A - d_B\right) \quad \text{and} \quad x_B^N = d_B + \frac{1}{2}\left(\pi - d_A - d_B\right),$$

which may be given the following interpretation. The players agree first of all to give player i $(i = A, B)$ a share d_i of the cake (which gives her a utility equal to the utility she obtains from not reaching agreement), and then they split equally the remaining cake $\pi - d_A - d_B$. Notice that player i's share x_i^N is strictly increasing in d_i and strictly decreasing in d_j $(j \neq i)$.

Example 2.2 (Risk Aversion). Suppose $U_A(x_A) = x_A^\gamma$ for all $x_A \in [0, \pi]$, where $0 < \gamma < 1$, $U_B(x_B) = x_B$ for all $x_B \in [0, \pi]$ and $d_A = d_B = 0$. This means that for each $u_A \in [0, \pi]$, $g(u_A) = \pi - u_A^{1/\gamma}$. Applying Corollary 2.1, it follows that

$$x_A^N = \frac{\gamma \pi}{1 + \gamma} \quad \text{and} \quad x_B^N = \frac{\pi}{1 + \gamma}.$$

As γ decreases, x_A^N decreases and x_B^N increases. In the limit, as $\gamma \to 0$, $x_A^N \to 0$ and $x_B^N \to 1$. Player B may be considered risk neutral (since her utility function is linear), while player A risk averse (since her utility function is strictly concave), where the degree of her risk aversion is decreasing in γ. Given this interpretation of the utility functions, it has been shown that player A's share of the cake decreases as she becomes more risk averse.

2.3 Applications

2.3.1 Bribery and the Control of Crime

An individual C decides whether or not to steal a fixed amount of money π, where $\pi > 0$. If she steals the money, then with probability ζ she is caught by a policeman P. The policeman is corruptible, and bargains with the criminal over the amount of bribe b that C gives P in return for not reporting her to the authorities.

     The set of possible agreements is the set of possible divisions of the stolen money, which (assuming money is perfectly divisible) is $\{(\pi - b, b) : 0 \leq b \leq \pi\}$. The policeman reports the criminal to the authorities if and only if they fail to reach agreement. In that eventuality, the criminal pays a monetary fine. The disagreement point $(d_C, d_P) = (\pi(1 - \nu), 0)$, where $\nu \in (0, 1]$ is the penalty rate. The utility to each player from obtaining x units of money is x.

The bargaining situation described here is a special case of Example 2.1, and thus it immediately follows that the NBS is $u_C^N = \pi[1 - (\nu/2)]$ and $u_P^N = \pi\nu/2$. The bribe associated with the NBS is $b^N = \pi\nu/2$. Notice that, although the penalty is never paid to the authorities, the penalty rate influences the amount of bribe that the criminal pays the corruptible policeman.

Given this outcome of the bargaining situation, I now address the issue of whether or not the criminal commits the crime. The expected utility to the criminal from stealing the money is $\zeta\pi[1 - (\nu/2)] + (1 - \zeta)\pi$, because with probability ζ she is caught by the policeman (in which case her utility is u_C^N) and with probability $1 - \zeta$ she is not caught by the policeman (in which case she keeps all of the stolen money). Since her utility from not stealing the money is zero, the crime is not committed if and only if $\pi[1 - (\zeta\nu/2)] \leq 0$. That is, since $\pi > 0$, the crime is not committed if and only if $\zeta\nu \geq 2$. Since $\zeta < 1$ and $0 < \nu \leq 1$ implies that $\zeta\nu < 1$, for any penalty rate $\nu \in (0, 1]$ and any probability $\zeta < 1$ of being caught, the crime is committed. This analysis thus vindicates the conventional wisdom that if penalties are evaded through bribery, then they have no role in preventing crime.[5]

2.3.2 Optimal Asset Ownership

Consider a situation with two managers, A and B, and two physical assets α_A and α_B. Manager i knows only how to use asset α_i. There are three possible ownership structures: (i) manager A owns asset α_A and manager B owns asset α_B, which is referred to as non-integration, (ii) manager A owns both assets, which is referred to as type-A integration, and (iii) manager B owns both assets, which is referred to as type-B integration. Denote by Γ_i the set of assets that manager i owns. Thus, $\Gamma_i \in \{\{\alpha_i\}, \{\alpha_A, \alpha_B\}, \{\emptyset\}\}$, where $\{\emptyset\}$ means that manager i owns neither of the two assets. The analysis below determines the optimal ownership structure.[6]

---

[5]The application studied here will be taken up in Section 2.5.3.

[6]The analysis is based on the idea that the ownership structure affects the disagreement point in the bargaining situation that the managers find themselves in. This, in turn, influences the respective levels of asset-specific investments in human capital made by

Given an ownership structure, the managers play the following two-stage game. At the first stage, asset-specific investments in human capital are simultaneously made by the managers. Since manager i knows only how to use asset α_i, and may (at the second stage) work with this asset, her investment may be thought of as improving her knowledge of this asset.[7] Let $E_i \geq 0$ denote the level of such investment made by manager i. The cost of such investment $C_i(E_i)$ is incurred by manager i at this stage.

The second stage involves determining whether or not the managers co-operate (by using the two assets and their respective human capital) in the creation of a cake. If they agree to co-operate, then the two assets are combined with their respective human capital in the most productive manner to generate a cake whose size $\Pi_A(E_A)+\Pi_B(E_B)$ depends on the levels of the investments made at the first stage. The set of possible agreements is the set of partitions of this cake. If and only if the managers fail to reach agreement, each manager goes her own way taking with her the assets that she owns. The payoff $d_i \geq 0$ that manager i obtains in that eventuality depends on E_i and Γ_i, which I emphasize by writing it as $d_i(E_i; \Gamma_i)$. The utility to a manager from obtaining a share x of the cake is equal to x. Assume that for any ownership structure and for any investment pair, $\Pi_A(E_A) + \Pi_B(E_B) > d_A(E_A; \Gamma_A) + d_B(E_B; \Gamma_B)$, which ensures that gains from co-operation exist.

The Bargaining Outcome

For any ownership structure and any investment pair, the bargaining situation described here is a special case of Example 2.1. Hence, it follows that the NBS is

$$u_A^N = \frac{1}{2}\Big[\Pi_A(E_A) + \Pi_B(E_B) - d_B(E_B; \Gamma_B) + d_A(E_A; \Gamma_A)\Big]$$

$$u_B^N = \frac{1}{2}\Big[\Pi_A(E_A) + \Pi_B(E_B) - d_A(E_A; \Gamma_A) + d_B(E_B; \Gamma_B)\Big].$$

the managers, and consequently, the size of the 'gains from co-operation'. The optimal ownership structure is one that maximizes such gains from co-operation.

[7]It is implicitly being assumed that at this stage, whatever the ownership structure might be, manager i has the opportunity to improve her knowledge of asset α_i.

Investments

In order to determine the investment levels, I adopt the following assumptions. For each i, Π_i is twice continuously differentiable, strictly increasing and strictly concave, C_i is twice continuously differentiable, strictly increasing and convex, d_i is twice continuously differentiable, increasing and concave in E_i, $\Pi_i'(0) > 2C_i'(0)$ and $\Pi_i'(E_i) - C_i'(E_i)$ converges to a strictly negative number as E_i tends to plus infinity.

Given an ownership structure, the utility to manager i if she chooses E_i and manager j ($j \neq i$) chooses E_j is $P_i(E_i, E_j) = u_i^N - C_i(E_i)$. Partially differentiating P_i with respect to E_i, it follows that $\partial P_i(E_i, E_j)/\partial E_i = [\Pi_i'(E_i) + d_i'(E_i; \Gamma_i)]/2 - C_i'(E_i)$. Given the assumptions stated above, it follows that manager i's investment level E_i^* is the unique solution[8] to $[\Pi_i'(E_i) + d_i'(E_i; \Gamma_i)]/2 = C_i''(E_i)$. Letting (E_A^N, E_B^N), (E_A^A, E_B^A) and (E_A^B, E_B^B), respectively, denote the pairs of investment levels under non-integration, type-A integration and type-B integration, it follows that for each i

$$\frac{1}{2}\left[\Pi_i'(E_i^N) + d_i'(E_i^N; \{\alpha_i\})\right] = C_i'(E_i^N) \qquad (2.1)$$

$$\frac{1}{2}\left[\Pi_i'(E_i^i) + d_i'(E_i^i; \{\alpha_A, \alpha_B\})\right] = C_i'(E_i^i) \qquad (2.2)$$

$$\frac{1}{2}\left[\Pi_i'(E_i^j) + d_i'(E_i^j; \{\emptyset\})\right] = C_i'(E_i^j), \qquad (2.3)$$

where $j \neq i$.

The Optimal Ownership Structure

For any pair of investment levels $E = (E_A, E_B)$, the surplus is $S(E_A, E_B) = \Pi_A(E_A) + \Pi_B(E_B) - C_A(E_A) - C_B(E_B)$. The first best investment levels (E_A^F, E_B^F) maximize the surplus, and hence, they constitute the unique solution to the first-order conditions $\Pi_A'(E_A^F) = C_A'(E_A^F)$ and $\Pi_B'(E_B^F) = C_B'(E_B^F)$. I shall compare the four pairs of investment levels under the following assumption: for each i and for any E_i

$$\Pi_i'(E_i) > d_i'(E_i; \{\alpha_A, \alpha_B\}) \geq d_i'(E_i; \{\alpha_i\}) \geq d_i'(E_i; \{\emptyset\}). \qquad (2.4)$$

---

[8]Notice that E_i^* is manager i's strictly dominant investment level: i.e., for any E_i and E_j, $P_i(E_i^*, E_j) > P_i(E_i, E_j)$.

A key result can now be put forth: for each i

$$E_i^F > E_i^i \geq E_i^N \geq E_i^j \quad (j \neq i), \tag{2.5}$$

where the first (resp., second) weak inequality is strict if the first (resp., second) weak inequality in (2.4) is strict. A formal proof of (2.5) is rather trivial to write down, and hence I omit it. Instead, it is far more illuminating to illustrate the result using Figure 2.4.[9]

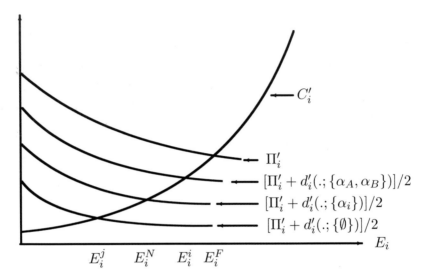

Figure 2.4: Manager i's first best investment level is strictly greater than her investment level when she owns both assets, which, in turn, is greater than her investment level when she owns only asset α_i, which, in turn, is greater than her investment level when she owns neither of the two assets.

Under any ownership structure there is under-investment relative to the first best levels of investment. The intuition for this result is straightforward: for any ownership structure manager i obtains strictly less than the full marginal benefit $\Pi_i'(E_i)$ from her investment, and, hence, she invests strictly less than her first best investment level. Furthermore, relative to non-integration, type-A integration increases manager A's investment level, but decreases manager B's investment level. Symmetrically, relative to non-integration, type-B integration increases manager B's investment level, but

---

[9]The shapes and relative positions of the various curves shown in Figure 2.4 follow from the assumptions made above.

decreases manager A's investment level. Hence, integration of either type has a benefit and a cost. The optimal ownership structure balances such costs and benefits.

The surpluses generated under the three ownership structures are $S(E^N)$, $S(E^A)$ and $S(E^B)$. The optimal ownership structure is the one that produces the largest surplus. It has been noted above that this maximized surplus is strictly less than the first best surplus $S(E^F)$ generated by the first best investment levels. I now determine the nature of the optimal ownership structure in two potentially interesting scenarios.

First consider the case when the two assets are 'independent' in the following sense: the assets α_A and α_B are said to be independent if and only if for each i and for any E_i, $d_i'(E_i; \{\alpha_A, \alpha_B\}) = d_i'(E_i; \{\alpha_i\})$. It follows from (2.1) and (2.2) that for each i, $E_i^N = E_i^i$. Hence, since (by (2.5)) $E_j^N \geq E_j^i$ ($j \neq i$), it follows that the surplus under non-integration is greater than or equal to the surplus under type-i integration ($i = A, B$).[10] Therefore, manager i should own asset α_i. The intuition behind this result is straightforward. Since ownership of asset α_j does not affect manager i's investment level, but may instead decrease manager j's investment level, surplus may therefore decrease if manager i owns asset α_j. Consequently, the optimality of the non-integration ownership structure when α_A and α_B are independent.

Now consider the case when the two assets are 'strictly complementary' in the following sense: the assets α_A and α_B are said to be strictly complementary if and only if for some i ($i = A$ or $i = B$) and for any E_i, $d_i'(E_i; \{\alpha_i\}) = d_i'(E_i; \{\emptyset\})$. It follows from (2.1) and (2.3) that $E_i^N = E_i^j$ ($j \neq i$). Hence, since (by (2.5)) $E_j^j \geq E_j^N$, it follows that the surplus under type-j integration is greater than or equal to the surplus under non-integration. The intuition behind this result is straightforward. Since ownership by manager i of asset α_i on its own does not affect manager i's investment level, surplus could therefore be increased by transferring the ownership of asset α_i to manager j (as this would then induce manager j to increase her investment level). Consequently, the non-optimality of the non-integration ownership structure under strict complementarity. In gen-

---

[10]Notice that I am appealing to the fact that S is strictly increasing over $[0, E_A^F] \times [0, E_B^F]$, and that the investment levels under any ownership structure are strictly below the first best investment levels.

eral, however, it is not possible to determine which of the two integration type ownership structures (type-A or type-B) is optimal.

2.4 A General Definition

A *bargaining problem* is a pair (Ω, d), where $\Omega \subset \Re^2$ and $d \in \Re^2$. I interpret Ω as a set of possible utility pairs obtainable through agreement, and the *disagreement point* $d = (d_A, d_B)$ as the utility pair obtainable if the players fail to reach agreement.[11] Attention will be restricted to bargaining problems which satisfy the conditions stated below in Assumptions 2.1 and 2.2.

Assumption 2.1. The Pareto frontier Ω^e of the set Ω is the graph of a concave function, denoted by h, whose domain is a closed interval $I_A \subseteq \Re$. Furthermore, there exists $u_A \in I_A$ such that $u_A > d_A$ and $h(u_A) > d_B$.[12]

Assumption 2.2. The set Ω^w of *weakly* Pareto efficient utility pairs is closed.[13]

Notice that (by the definition of the Pareto frontier) h is strictly decreasing. The set of all bargaining problems which satisfy Assumptions 2.1 and 2.2 is denoted by Σ. That is, $\Sigma \equiv \{(\Omega, d) : \Omega \subset \Re^2, d \in \Re^2$ and the pair (Ω, d) satisfies Assumptions 2.1 and 2.2 $\}$.

Definition 2.1. The *Nash bargaining solution* (NBS) is a function $f^N : \Sigma \to \Re^2$, defined as follows. For each bargaining problem (Ω, d) that satisfies Assumptions 2.1 and 2.2, the NBS $f^N(\Omega, d) \equiv (f_A^N(\Omega, d), f_B^N(\Omega, d))$ is the unique solution to the following maximization problem

$$\max_{(u_A, u_B) \in \Theta} (u_A - d_A)(u_B - d_B),$$

where $\Theta \equiv \{(u_A, u_B) \in \Omega^e : u_A \geq d_A$ and $u_B \geq d_B\} \equiv \{(u_A, u_B) : u_A \in I_A, u_B = h(u_A), u_A \geq d_A$ and $u_B \geq d_B\}$.

---

[11]If $(u_A, u_B) \in \Omega$, then this means that there exists an agreement which gives player i $(i = A, B)$ a utility $u_i \in \Re$.

[12]A utility pair $(u_A, u_B) \in \Omega^e$ if and only if $(u_A, u_B) \in \Omega$ and there does not exist another utility pair $(u'_A, u'_B) \in \Omega$ such that $u'_A \geq u_A$, $u'_B \geq u_B$ and for some i, $u'_i > u_i$.

[13]A utility pair $(u_A, u_B) \in \Omega^w$ if and only if $(u_A, u_B) \in \Omega$ and there does not exist another utility pair $(u'_A, u'_B) \in \Omega$ such that $u'_A > u_A$ and $u'_B > u_B$. Notice that $\Omega^e \subseteq \Omega^w$.

The maximization problem stated above has a unique solution, because the maximand $(u_A - d_A)(u_B - d_B)$ — which is referred to as the Nash product — is continuous and strictly quasiconcave, and because Assumption 2.1 implies that h is strictly decreasing and concave, and the set Θ is nonempty. It should be noted that the NBS has the property that $f_i^N(\Omega, d) > d_i$ $(i = A, B)$.

Fix an arbitrary bargaining problem $(\Omega, d) \in \Sigma$. The NBS of this bargaining problem will lie on the graph of h. Let $I_A \equiv [\underline{u}_A, \bar{u}_A]$, where $\bar{u}_A \geq \underline{u}_A$. The range of h is $h(I_A) = \{u_B \in \Re : \text{there exists } u_A \in I_A \text{ such that } u_B = h(u_A)\}$. It follows from Assumption 2.1 that $h(I_A) = [\underline{u}_B, \bar{u}_B]$, where $h(\underline{u}_A) = \bar{u}_B \geq \underline{u}_B = h(\bar{u}_A)$. Furthermore, Assumption 2.1 implies that $d_A < \bar{u}_A$ and $d_B < \bar{u}_B$. However, the possibility that for some i ($i = A$ or $i = B$ or $i = A, B$) $d_i < \underline{u}_i$ is not ruled out by Assumption 2.1.

If $d_A \in I_A$ and $d_B \in h(I_A)$ — which (from the above discussion) means that $d_i \geq \underline{u}_i$ $(i = A, B)$ — then the NBS is illustrated in Figure 2.1 *with g replaced by h.*[14] In particular, the NBS lies in the interior of the graph of h; that is, $f_A^N(\Omega, d) \in (\underline{u}_A, \bar{u}_A)$ and $f_B^N(\Omega, d) \in (\underline{u}_B, \bar{u}_B)$. However, if for some i ($i = A$ or $i = B$ or $i = A, B$) $d_i < \underline{u}_i$, then it is possible (but not necessary) that the NBS is at one of the two corners of the graph of h; that is, the NBS $f^N(\Omega, d)$ may equal either $(\underline{u}_A, \bar{u}_B)$ or $(\bar{u}_A, \underline{u}_B)$ — as is illustrated in Figure 2.5.

Remark 2.2. A bargaining problem (Ω, d) — upon which the NBS is defined — is an abstract concept. Although this is valuable in some respects and it enhances the applicability of the NBS, it is nevertheless helpful to interpret the concept of a bargaining problem in terms of the following basic elements of a bargaining situation: (i) the set X of possible *physical* agreements, (ii) the 'disagreement' outcome D — which is the outcome, or event, that occurs if the players fail to reach agreement, and (iii) the players' utility functions $U_A : X \cup \{D\} \to \Re$ and $U_B : X \cup \{D\} \to \Re$. A bargaining problem (Ω, d) may then be derived from these elements as follows: $\Omega = \{(u_A, u_B) : \text{there exists } x \in X \text{ such that } U_A(x) = u_A \text{ and } U_B(x) = u_B\}$ and $d = (U_A(D), U_B(D))$.

---

[14]It should be noted that in the specific bargaining situation studied in Section 2.2 the Pareto frontier $\Omega^e = \Omega$, the set of possible utility pairs obtainable through agreement — and, hence, Ω^e is the graph of g. In contrast, in an arbitrary bargaining problem $(\Omega, d) \in \Sigma$ the Pareto frontier $\Omega^e \subseteq \Omega$ — that is, it need not equal Ω.

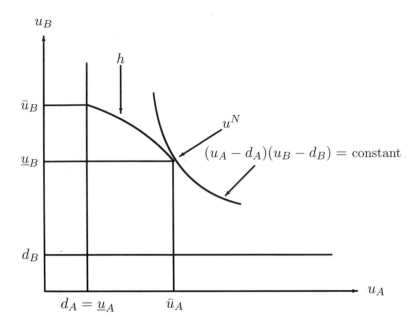

Figure 2.5: If $d_B < \underline{u}_B$, then the NBS may be at the right-hand corner of the graph of h — that is, $u^N = (\bar{u}_A, \underline{u}_B)$.

2.4.1   Characterization

It is straightforward to extend Proposition 2.1 to any bargaining problem $(\Omega, d) \in \Sigma$ such that h is differentiable and $d_i \geq \underline{u}_i$ $(i = A, B)$ — as is done in the following proposition.[15]

Proposition 2.3. *For any bargaining problem $(\Omega, d) \in \Sigma$ such that h is differentiable and $d_i \geq \underline{u}_i$ $(i = A, B)$, the NBS is the unique solution to the following pair of equations*

$$-h'(u_A) = \frac{u_B - d_B}{u_A - d_A} \quad and \quad u_B = h(u_A).$$

As is also discussed in the context of the specific bargaining situation studied in Section 2.2 (cf. Figure 2.2), Proposition 2.3 implies that, for any bargaining problem specified in the proposition, the NBS is the unique point u^N on the graph of h with the property that the slope of the line joining

---

[15]It should be noted that this proposition is not valid if for some i ($i = A$ or $i = B$ or $i = A, B$) $d_i < \underline{u}_i$, because (as discussed above and illustrated in Figure 2.5) it is possible that the NBS may then be at one of the two corners of the graph of h.

the points u^N and d is equal to the absolute value of the slope of the unique tangent to the graph of h at u^N — which is illustrated in Figure 2.2, *but with g replaced by h.*

A similar geometric characterization applies to the NBS of any bargaining problem $(\Omega, d) \in \Sigma$, even if it does not satisfy the additional hypotheses stated in Proposition 2.3. Fix an arbitrary bargaining problem $(\Omega, d) \in \Sigma$, and let (u_A^N, u_B^N) be the NBS, which lies on the graph of h. The NBS has the following geometric property. The slope of the line joining the points u^N and d — which equals $(u_B^N - d_B)/(u_A^N - d_A)$ — is greater than or equal to $-h'(u_A^N-)$ *if $u_A^N > \underline{u}_A$* and is less than or equal to $-h'(u_A^N+)$ *if $u_A^N < \bar{u}_A$*. Notice that this geometric property is similar to that stated in Proposition 2.2.

In some applications the bargaining problem (Ω, d) is such that the Pareto frontier Ω^e of the set Ω of possible utility pairs obtainable through agreement is the graph of the linear function $h(u_A) = s - u_A$, where $s > 0$. The NBS of such a bargaining problem may be derived from Proposition 2.3, and is stated in the following corollary.

Corollary 2.2 (Split-The-Difference Rule). *For any $(\Omega, d) \in \Sigma$ such that $h(u_A) = s - u_A$, where $s > 0$, and $d_i \geq \underline{u}_i$ $(i = A, B)$, the NBS (u_A^N, u_B^N) is*

$$u_A^N = d_A + \frac{1}{2}\left(s - d_A - d_B\right) \quad and \quad u_B^N = d_B + \frac{1}{2}\left(s - d_A - d_B\right).$$

Corollary 2.2 may be given the following interpretation. The players are bargaining over the partition of s units of (transferable) utility, and they agree first of all to give each other the utilities (d_A and d_B) that they would, respectively, obtain from not reaching agreement, and then they split equally the remaining utility $s - d_A - d_B$.

2.5 Applications

2.5.1 Union-Firm Negotiations

A firm and its union bargain over the wage rate w and the employment level L. The set of possible agreements is the set of wage-employment pairs (w, L) such that $w \geq w_u$, $R(L) - wL \geq 0$ and $L \leq L_0$, where $w_u \geq 0$

is the rate of unemployment benefit, $R(L)$ is the revenue obtained by the firm if it employs L workers, and L_0 is the size of the union. $R(0) = 0$ and R is strictly increasing and strictly concave. The constraint $w \geq w_u$ captures the fact that no worker works at a wage rate that lies below the rate of unemployment benefit, while the constraint $R(L) - wL \geq 0$ captures the fact that the firm prefers to close down rather than receive a negative profit, where its profit from a pair (w, L) is $R(L) - wL$. It is assumed that the firm cannot employ more than L_0 workers. Thus, the set of possible agreements is $X = \{(w, L) : w \geq w_u, L \leq L_0 \text{ and } R(L) - wL \geq 0\}$. If the players fail to reach agreement, then the firm shuts down and the L_0 workers become unemployed. If agreement is reached on $(w, L) \in X$, then the profit to the firm is $\Pi(w, L) = R(L) - wL$, and the union's utility is $U(w, L) = wL + (L_0 - L)w_u$, which constitutes the total income received by its members. Since $R(0) = 0$, the profit to the firm if the parties fail to reach agreement is zero. The union's utility in that eventuality is $w_u L_0$, since its L_0 members become unemployed. Hence, the disagreement point $d = (w_u L_0, 0)$.

The Pareto frontier Ω^e of the set of possible utility pairs obtainable through agreement may be derived by solving the following maximization problem: $\max_{(w,L) \in X} \Pi(w, L)$ subject to $U(w, L) \geq \bar{u}$, where $\bar{u}$ is some constant greater than or equal to $w_u L_0$. At the unique solution to this problem $L = L^*$, where L^* is the first best employment level, namely $R'(L^*) = w_u$.[16] Thus, a utility pair $(u, \pi) \in \Omega^e$ only if the employment level $L = L^*$. The Pareto frontier Ω^e is therefore the graph of the function h defined as follows. For each utility level of the union $u \in [w_u L_0, s]$, $h(u) = s - u$, where $s \equiv R(L^*) + (L_0 - L^*)w_u$.

Applying Corollary 2.2, it follows that the NBS is $\pi^N = (s - w_u L_0)/2$ and $u^N = w_u L_0 + (s - w_u L_0)/2$. The wage-employment pair (w^N, L^N) associated with the NBS is now derived. It has been shown above that at the NBS the employment level $L^N = L^*$. The wage rate w^N may be derived from $\pi^N = R(L^*) - w^N L^*$. After substituting for π^N and s, it follows that $w^N = [w_u + (R(L^*)/L^*)]/2$. The wage rate is therefore equal to the average of the rate of unemployment benefit and the average revenue. However, since $R'(L^*) = w_u$, the wage rate is equal to the average of the marginal and average revenues.

---

[16] It is assumed that $L^* \leq L_0$ and $R(L^*) - w_u L^* > 0$.

2.5.2 Moral Hazard in Teams

The output produced by a team of two players, A and B, depends on their respective individual effort levels: output $Q = 2e_A^{1/2} e_B^{1/2}$, where $e_i > 0$ is player i's effort level. The cost to player i of effort level e_i is $C_i = \alpha_i e_i^2/2$, where $\alpha_i > 0$.

The effort levels are not verifiable, and, thus, cannot be contracted upon — the players can only contract upon the output level, which is verifiable. Before the players simultaneously choose their respective effort levels they bargain over the output sharing rule. The set of possible agreements is $X = (0,1)$, where $x \in X$ is the share of the output obtained by player A and $1 - x$ is the share of the output obtained by player B. If the players reach agreement on $x \in X$, then they simultaneously choose their respective effort levels $e_A > 0$ and $e_B > 0$, and, consequently, player i obtains a profit of $x_i Q - C_i$, where $x_i = x$ if $i = A$ and $x_i = 1 - x$ if $i = B$. If the players fail to reach agreement, then player i receives no output and incurs no cost — and, hence, the disagreement point $d = (0,0)$.

I first derive the Nash equilibrium of the simultaneous-move game in effort levels, for each possible agreement $x \in X$. Fix an arbitrary $x \in X$. Since $x_i Q - C_i$ is strictly concave in e_i, the unique Nash equilibrium e_A^* and e_B^* is the unique solution to the following first-order conditions

$$xe_A^{-1/2} e_B^{1/2} = \alpha_A e_A \quad \text{and} \quad (1-x)e_A^{1/2} e_B^{-1/2} = \alpha_B e_B.$$

Thus, after solving for e_A and e_B, it follows that

$$e_A^* = \frac{x^{3/4}(1-x)^{1/4}}{\alpha_A^{3/4} \alpha_B^{1/4}} \quad \text{and} \quad e_B^* = \frac{x^{1/4}(1-x)^{3/4}}{\alpha_A^{1/4} \alpha_B^{3/4}}.$$

After substituting for these Nash equilibrium values of e_A and e_B, it follows that the players' (equilibrium) profits if agreement is reached on $x \in X$ are

$$U_A(x) = \beta x^{3/2}(1-x)^{1/2} \quad \text{and} \quad U_B(x) = \beta x^{1/2}(1-x)^{3/2}$$

where $\beta = 3/2(\alpha_A \alpha_B)^{1/2}$.

Notice that U_A is strictly increasing on the open interval $(0, 3/4)$, achieves a maximum at $x = 3/4$ and is strictly decreasing on the open interval $(3/4, 1)$, and U_B is strictly increasing on the open interval $(0, 1/4)$, achieves a maximum at $x = 1/4$ and is strictly decreasing on the open interval $(1/4, 1)$.

This implies that the Pareto frontier of the set of possible utilities obtainable through agreement is $\Omega^e = \{(u_A, u_B) : \text{there exists an } x \in [1/4, 3/4] \text{ such that } U_A(x) = u_A \text{ and } U_B(x) = u_B\}$.

The bargaining problem (Ω, d) described here satisfies Assumptions 2.1 and 2.2, and hence I use Definition 2.1 to derive the NBS of this bargaining problem.[17] Definition 2.1 implies that the agreement x^N obtained in the NBS is the unique solution to the following maximization problem: $\max_{x \in [1/4, 3/4]} U_A(x) U_B(x)$. It immediately follows from the first-order condition to this problem that $x^N = 1/2$. Hence, the NBS — which is shown in Figure 2.6 — is $(u_A^N, u_B^N) = (U_A(1/2), U_B(1/2))$.

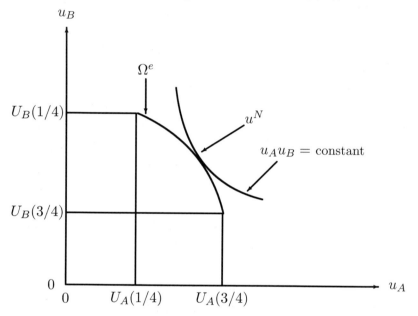

Figure 2.6: The NBS of the bargaining problem associated with the bargaining situation that the two team members find themselves in when bargaining over the output sharing rule under moral hazard.

For any values of α_A and α_B, in the NBS the output is split equally between the two players. This means that for any values of α_A and α_B, $C_A(e_A^*) = C_B(e_B^*)$, which, in turn, implies that the two players obtain iden-

---

[17]Notice that the domain of the graph of h — which is Ω^e — is $I_A = [U_A(1/4), U_A(3/4)]$. Hence, since $d_i < \underline{u}_i$ $(i = A, B)$ — where $\underline{u}_A = U_A(1/4)$ and $\underline{u}_B = U_B(3/4)$ — Proposition 2.3 is inapplicable.

tical profits. Thus, even if $\alpha_A > \alpha_B$ (which implies that player A's effort is relatively more costly, and $e_A^* < e_B^*$), the costs incurred by the players are identical and their respective profits are identical.

2.5.3 Bribery and the Control of Crime: An Extension

An implicit assumption underlying the application studied in Section 2.3.1 is that individual C (the criminal) has limited liability in the sense that the maximal possible bribe which the policeman P can obtain equals the amount π of stolen money (i.e., $b \leq \pi$), and the maximal possible penalty that the authorities can impose equals the amount π of stolen money (i.e., $\nu \leq 1$). It is thus perhaps not surprising that — as is shown in Section 2.3.1 — for any penalty rate $\nu \leq 1$ and any probability $\zeta < 1$ of being caught, C finds it profitable to commit the crime.

I now remove this limited liability assumption, by only requiring that the bribe $b \geq 0$ and the penalty rate $\nu > 0$ — hence, I now allow for the possibility that the bribe and the penalty exceed the amount π of stolen money.[18] If agreement is reached on b, then C's payoff is $\pi - b$ and P's payoff is b. Hence, the Pareto frontier of the set of possible utility pairs is the graph of a function h defined as follows: for each $u_C \leq \pi$, $u_P = h(u_C) = \pi - u_C$. The disagreement point $(d_C, d_P) = (\pi(1 - \nu), 0)$.

Applying Corollary 2.2 — notice that $\underline{u}_C = -\infty$ and $\underline{u}_P = 0$ — it follows that the NBS is $u_C^N = \pi[1 - (\nu/2)]$ and $u_P^N = \pi\nu/2$. The bribe is $b^N = \pi\nu/2$. Although this is also the NBS obtained in Section 2.3.1, there is now no upper bound on ν — which means that if $\nu > 2$ then C's payoff is negative. From the arguments used in Section 2.3.1, it follows that the crime is not committed if and only if $\zeta\nu \geq 2$. Hence, for any $\zeta < 1$, if the penalty rate is sufficiently large — in particular, if $\nu > 2/\zeta$ — then the crime is not committed. Thus, in contrast to the conclusion arrived at in Section 2.3.1, this analysis successfully challenges the conventional wisdom that if penalties are evaded through bribery then they have no role in preventing crime.[19]

---

[18]If the bribe $b > \pi$, then the difference $b - \pi$ may be financed by C in several ways, including from her current (and possibly future) wealth and by payment in kind. If the penalty $\pi\nu > \pi$, then the difference $\pi(\nu - 1)$ may be interpreted as the monetary equivalent of a prison sentence.

[19]The analysis here seems relatively more plausible compared to the analysis of Section

2.6 Axiomatic Foundation

It is now shown that the NBS is the only bargaining solution that satisfies the four properties (or, axioms) stated below.[20] This axiomatization provides a justification for using the NBS. However, whether or not such a justification is convincing depends on the plausibility or otherwise of these axioms.

Risk: A Key Idea

As indicated in Remark 2.2 above, the elements of a bargaining situation that may be relevant in defining a bargaining problem (and hence the NBS) are the set of possible agreements, the disagreement outcome and the players' utility functions. While bargaining the players may perceive that there is some *risk* that the negotiations may break down in a *random* manner. Hence the players' attitudes towards risk is another element that may be relevant for the outcome of bargaining. For example, it seems intuitive that if player A is averse to risk while player B is not, then player A may be willing to reach an agreement that is relatively more favourable to player B (cf. Example 2.2).

The axiomatization of the NBS is based on this additional element, namely, the players' attitudes towards risk. As is well known, von Neumann and Morgenstern's theory of expected utility deals with situations in which a player has to act under conditions of risk. In order to appeal to that theory, a player's utility function is interpreted as her *von Neumann–Morgenstern utility function*. Her attitude towards risk is captured, or expressed, by the shape of her utility function — if it is strictly concave (resp., strictly convex) then she is risk averse (resp., risk loving), and if it is linear then she is risk neutral.

The Axiomatization

Fix a bargaining problem $(\Omega, d) \in \Sigma$. As in Remark 2.2, one may interpret the two elements Ω and d of this problem as being derived from the set X of possible agreements, the disagreement outcome D and the utility functions

---

2.3.1, because it may be unreasonable to assume that the criminal has limited liability. The application studied here will be taken up in Section 5.3.3.

[20]A bargaining solution is a function $f : \Sigma \rightarrow \Re^2$ such that for each $(\Omega, d) \in \Sigma$, $f(\Omega, d) \in \Omega \bigcup \{d\}$. Nash's bargaining solution f^N is stated in Definition 2.1.

U_A and U_B. Now consider another bargaining situation with the same set X of agreements and the same disagreement outcome D but with different utility functions $\widehat{U}_A$ and $\widehat{U}_B$, where $\widehat{U}_i = \alpha_i U_i + \beta_i$ for some $\alpha_i > 0$ and $\beta_i \in \Re$ $(i = A, B)$. The disagreement point d' and the set Ω' of possible utility pairs obtainable through agreement of this (new) bargaining situation are as follows

$$d' = (\alpha_A d_A + \beta_A, \alpha_B d_B + \beta_B) \tag{2.6}$$

$$\Omega' = \{(\alpha_A u_A + \beta_A, \alpha_B u_B + \beta_B) : (u_A, u_B) \in \Omega\}. \tag{2.7}$$

Since (Ω, d) satisfies Assumptions 2.1 and 2.2, (Ω', d') satisfies Assumptions 2.1 and 2.2, and, hence, $(\Omega', d') \in \Sigma$. This new bargaining situation is, in effect, identical to the one originally specified, since (by construction) both U_i and $\widehat{U}_i$ represent player i's preferences.[21] The first axiom emphasizes this point by describing how, given any bargaining solution $f : \Sigma \to \Re^2$, the solutions to these two bargaining problems should be related.

Axiom 2.1 (Invariance to Equivalent Utility Representations). Fix $(\Omega, d) \in \Sigma$ and a bargaining solution $f : \Sigma \to \Re^2$. Now consider $(\Omega', d') \in \Sigma$, where d' and Ω' are respectively defined by (2.6) and (2.7), with $\alpha_i > 0$ and $\beta_i \in \Re$. Then, for $i = A, B$, $f_i(\Omega', d') = \alpha_i f_i(\Omega, d) + \beta_i$.

Axiom 2.1 is motivated by the viewpoint that it is the players' preferences, and not the particular utility functions which represent them, that are 'basic'. The agreements associated with the bargaining solution in these two (related) bargaining problems should be identical. Thus, although the bargaining solution of these two problems may differ, they should be related in the manner specified. This axiom seems reasonable. However, the next axiom, which requires that the bargaining solution for each bargaining problem be Pareto efficient, is not as easy to justify. In many bargaining situations players fail to reach agreement. For example, strikes and trade wars are examples of phenomena that contribute to the inefficiency of the bargaining outcome. However, in some bargaining situations, this may be a plausible axiom.

---

[21]Since a player's preferences satisfy the von Neumann–Morgenstern expected utility theory, her von Neumann–Morgenstern utility function is unique only up to a positive affine transformation. For an excellent account of this theory, see Luce and Raiffa (1957, Chapter 2).

Axiom 2.2 (Pareto Efficiency). Fix $(\Omega, d) \in \Sigma$ and a bargaining solution $f : \Sigma \to \Re^2$. There does not exist a utility pair $(u_A, u_B) \in \Omega \bigcup \{d\}$ such that $u_A \geq f_A(\Omega, d)$, $u_B \geq f_B(\Omega, d)$ and for some i ($i = A$ or $i = B$), $u_i > f_i(\Omega, d)$.

The next axiom seems easy to justify. (Ω, d) is said to be *symmetric* if $d_A = d_B(= d)$, and $(x, y) \in \Omega$ if and only if $(y, x) \in \Omega$.

Axiom 2.3 (Symmetry). Fix $(\Omega, d) \in \Sigma$ and a bargaining solution $f : \Sigma \to \Re^2$. If (Ω, d) is symmetric, as defined above, then $f_A(\Omega, d) = f_B(\Omega, d)$.

Of the four axioms, the last is the most problematic. I discuss the axiom after formally stating it.

Axiom 2.4 (Independence of Irrelevant Alternatives). Fix a bargaining solution $f : \Sigma \to \Re^2$, $(\Omega_1, d_1) \in \Sigma$ and $(\Omega_2, d_2) \in \Sigma$ such that $d_1 = d_2$, $\Omega_2 \subset \Omega_1$ and $f(\Omega_1, d_1) \in \Omega_2$. Then, for $i = A, B$, $f_i(\Omega_1, d_1) = f_i(\Omega_2, d_2)$.

This axiom considers two bargaining problems in which the disagreement points are identical, the set of possible utilities in one problem is strictly contained in the set of possible utilities of the other problem, and the bargaining solution of the latter problem is an element of the former set. It states that the bargaining solutions to such related problems should be identical. The motivation for this axiom can be put forth in the following manner. Suppose the bargainers agree on the element x_1 when the set X of agreements consists of three elements, namely x_1, x_2 and x_3, and when the disagreement outcome is D. Now consider another bargaining situation in which the players have to agree on an element from a subset Y of this set X, that contains the element x_1 agreed to in the preceding bargaining situation. For example, suppose $Y = \{x_1, x_2\}$. And, moreover, the disagreement outcome is the same, namely, D. The argument is that since x_1 was agreed to over x_2 and x_3 in the original bargaining situation, and since the disagreement outcome is the same in the new bargaining situation, x_1 should be agreed to (again) over x_2, despite the fact that x_3 is no longer available. Indeed, x_3 is 'irrelevant'. At an intuitive level, this may seem persuasive. However, it can be interpreted as an axiom about the process of negotiation, which is not modelled here. In some negotiation processes the outcome may be influenced by such apparently 'irrelevant' alternatives. For example, an outcome based on some compromise may be influenced by such alternatives. Hence, as is the case with the other axioms, especially Axiom 2.2, one needs to study plausible game-theoretic models of bargaining in order to assess the circumstances under which this axiom is and is not plausible.

Notice that Axioms 2.2 and 2.3 are concerned with the outcome of a particular bargaining problem, while Axioms 2.1 and 2.4, on the other hand, are not about the outcome of any particular bargaining problem, but concern the relationship between the outcomes of two somewhat related bargaining problems. I now establish the remarkable result that the Nash bargaining solution is the *unique* bargaining solution that satisfies Axioms 2.1 to 2.4.

Proposition 2.4. *A bargaining solution* $f : \Sigma \to \Re^2$ *satisfies Axioms 2.1 to 2.4 if and only if* $f = f^N$, *Nash's bargaining solution.*

Proof. In the Appendix. $\square$

Although the four 'axioms' may not be axiomatic, and although Axiom 2.4 in particular is somewhat problematic, this proposition provides the NBS with an interesting justification.[22]

2.7 An Interpretation

Although the definition of the NBS — in terms of a maximization problem — is convenient in applications, its interpretation is unclear. How should the maximization of the product of the players' utilities be interpreted? The axiomatization discussed in the preceding section provides a justification for the maximization of the Nash product: it follows from Axioms 2.1–2.4 by logical deduction. Thus, an *indirect* way to interpret Definition 2.1 is to interpret the four axioms. In this section I state an alternative (but equivalent) definition of the NBS that has a natural interpretation. This alternative definition, however, is relatively more complex, and, hence, it is not as attractive for applications.

Unlike Definition 2.1, which is in terms of the players' utilities, the following definition of the NBS is in terms of the 'physical' agreement struck. Furthermore, it is based explicitly on the players' attitudes towards risk.

---

[22]It can be shown that none of the four axioms is superfluous: by dropping any one of these axioms, there is an alternative bargaining solution that satisfies the other three axioms (cf. Osborne and Rubinstein (1990, pp. 20–23)).

Definition 2.2. For any bargaining situation as defined by X, D, U_A and U_B — where X is the set of physical agreements, D the disagreement outcome, and U_A and U_B the players' von Neumann–Morgenstern utility functions — such that the induced bargaining problem (Ω, d) (as defined in Remark 2.2 above) satisfies Assumptions 2.1 and 2.2, the agreement $x^* \in X$ is an *ordinal* NBS if for any $i = A, B$, any $x \in X$ and any probability $p \in [0, 1]$

$$(1 - p)U_i(x) + pU_i(D) > U_i(x^*) \Rightarrow (1 - p)U_j(x^*) + pU_j(D) > U_j(x),$$

where $j \neq i$.

In Lemma 2.2 below, it is shown that x^* is an ordinal NBS if and only if the utility pair $(U_A(x^*), U_B(x^*))$ is the NBS. This means that Definitions 2.1 and 2.2 are equivalent. It also implies that an ordinal NBS exists for any bargaining situation that satisfies Assumptions 2.1 and 2.2. Furthermore, the ordinal NBS is unique if and only if there exists a unique $x \in X$ such that $(U_A(x), U_B(x)) = (u_A^N, u_B^N)$.

I now discuss the interpretation of the NBS prompted by this alternative definition. It involves interpreting the NBS as a stable (bargaining) convention.

In any bargaining situation the players often put forward arguments of various kinds supporting the implementation of specific agreements. The ordinal NBS is interpreted as that agreement which is immune to a particular class of arguments. In that sense it may be interpreted as a conventional agreement, where the convention is stable in a particular manner.

Suppose that x^* is the conventional agreement, but player i puts forth an argument supporting the implementation of some alternative agreement x. More importantly, the argument involves a 'risk of breakdown': with probability p this argument forces bargaining to terminate, in which case the disagreement outcome occurs. However, with probability $1 - p$ the argument 'wins': that is, the alternative agreement x is implemented. It is assumed that

$$(1 - p)U_i(x) + pU_i(D) > U_i(x^*),$$

for otherwise player i would not put forth this argument. Now suppose that player j ($j \neq i$) puts forth a counterargument insisting on implementing the conventional agreement x^*. However, in putting forth this counterargument, it is perceived that with probability p bargaining terminates in disagreement and with probability $1 - p$ this counterargument wins. If

$$(1 - p)U_j(x^*) + pU_j(D) > U_j(x),$$

then player j puts forth this counterargument to player i's initial argument against the convention. Hence, if the conventional agreement satisfies Definition 2.2, then the convention is protected from arguments (or, objections) put forth by player i.

Lemma 2.2. *Fix a bargaining situation as defined by X, D, U_A and U_B such that Assumptions 2.1 and 2.2 are satisfied. Without loss of generality, assume that $U_A(D) = U_B(D) = 0$.[23] The agreement $x^* \in X$ is an ordinal NBS if and only if for all $x \in X$*

$$U_A(x^*)U_B(x^*) \geq U_A(x)U_B(x).$$

Proof. In the Appendix. □

2.8 Asymmetric Nash Bargaining Solutions

The NBS depends upon the set Ω of possible utility pairs and the disagreement point d. However, the outcome of a bargaining situation may be influenced by other forces (or, variables), such as the tactics employed by the bargainers, the procedure through which negotiations are conducted, the information structure and the players' discount rates. However, none of these forces seem to affect the two objects upon which the NBS is defined, and yet it seems reasonable not to rule out the possibility that such forces may have a significant impact on the bargaining outcome. I now state generalizations of the NBS which possess a facility to take into account additional factors that may be deemed relevant for the bargaining outcome.

Definition 2.3. For each $\tau \in (0, 1)$, an *asymmetric* (or, *generalized*) Nash bargaining solution is a function $f_\tau^N : \Sigma \to \Re^2$, defined as follows. For each

---

[23]Since U_i is a von Neumann–Morgenstern utility function, one can always normalize utilities so that the disagreement point is at the origin.

$(\Omega, d) \in \Sigma$, $f_\tau^N(\Omega, d)$ is the unique solution to the following maximization problem

$$\max_{(u_A, u_B) \in \Theta} (u_A - d_A)^\tau (u_B - d_B)^{1-\tau},$$

where Θ is stated in Definition 2.1.

For each $\tau \in (0, 1)$, an asymmetric NBS f_τ^N satisfies Axioms 2.1, 2.2 and 2.4. Furthermore, any bargaining solution that satisfies Axioms 2.1, 2.2 and 2.4 is an asymmetric NBS for some value of τ. Unless $\tau = 1/2$, an asymmetric NBS does not satisfy Axiom 2.3. If, on the other hand, $\tau = 1/2$, then the asymmetric NBS is *identical* to the NBS.[24] I now state two useful characterizations of any asymmetric NBS, which follow trivially from Proposition 2.3 and Corollary 2.2.

Proposition 2.5. *For any $\tau \in (0, 1)$ and any bargaining problem $(\Omega, d) \in \Sigma$ such that h is differentiable and $d_i \geq \underline{u}_i$ $(i = A, B)$, the asymmetric NBS is the unique solution to the following pair of equations*

$$-h'(u_A) = \left(\frac{\tau}{1 - \tau}\right) \left[\frac{u_B - d_B}{u_A - d_A}\right] \quad \text{and} \quad u_B = h(u_A).$$

Corollary 2.3 (Split-The-Difference Rule). *For any $\tau \in (0, 1)$ and any $(\Omega, d) \in \Sigma$ such that $h(u_A) = s - u_A$, where $s > 0$, and $d_i \geq \underline{u}_i$ $(i = A, B)$, the asymmetric NBS (u_A^N, u_B^N) is*

$$u_A^N = d_A + \tau \left(s - d_A - d_B\right) \quad \text{and} \quad u_B^N = d_B + (1 - \tau)\left(s - d_A - d_B\right).$$

Notice that as τ increases, player A's utility increases while player B's utility decreases. Corollary 2.3 may be given the following interpretation. The players are bargaining over the partition of s units of (transferable) utility, and they agree first of all to give each other the utilities (d_A and d_B) that they would, respectively, obtain from not reaching agreement, and then players A and B, respectively, obtain a fraction τ and $1 - \tau$ of the remaining utility $s - d_A - d_B$.

---

[24]Strategic models of bargaining studied in later chapters provide guidance on what elements of a bargaining situation determine the value of τ.

2.9   Appendix: Proofs

Proof of Lemma 2.1

First I establish that g is strictly decreasing. Fix an arbitrary pair u_A^1 and u_A^2 of utilities to player A such that $u_A^1 > u_A^2$, where $u_A^1 \in [U_A(0), U_A(\pi)]$ and $u_A^2 \in [U_A(0), U_A(\pi)]$. Since U_A^{-1} is strictly increasing, $U_A^{-1}(u_A^1) > U_A^{-1}(u_A^2)$. This implies that $\pi - U_A^{-1}(u_A^1) < \pi - U_A^{-1}(u_A^2)$, and hence, since U_B is strictly increasing, $g(u_A^1) > g(u_A^2)$. I now establish that g is concave. Fix an arbitrary pair u_A^1 and u_A^2 of utilities to player A such that $u_A^1 > u_A^2$, where $u_A^1 \in [U_A(0), U_A(\pi)]$ and $u_A^2 \in [U_A(0), U_A(\pi)]$, and fix an arbitrary number $\alpha \in [0, 1]$. Since U_B is concave

$$U_B(x_B^3) \geq \alpha U_B(x_B^1) + (1 - \alpha)U_B(x_B^2), \tag{2.8}$$

where $x_B^1 = \pi - U_A^{-1}(u_A^1)$, $x_B^2 = \pi - U_A^{-1}(u_A^2)$ and $x_B^3 = \alpha[\pi - U_A^{-1}(u_A^1)] + (1 - \alpha)[\pi - U_A^{-1}(u_A^2)]$. Furthermore, since U_A^{-1} is convex, $U_A^{-1}(u_A^3) \leq \alpha U_A^{-1}(u_A^1) + (1 - \alpha)U_A^{-1}(u_A^2)$, where $u_A^3 = \alpha u_A^1 + (1 - \alpha)u_A^2$. Hence, it follows that

$$\pi - U_A^{-1}(u_A^3) \geq x_B^3. \tag{2.9}$$

Consequently, since U_B is strictly increasing, it follows from (2.8) and (2.9) that $g(u_A^3) \geq \alpha g(u_A^1) + (1 - \alpha)g(u_A^2)$, which establishes that g is concave.

Proof of Propostion 2.4

I first show that the NBS satisfies Axioms 2.1–2.4. Consider Axiom 2.1. By definition, for any $u \in \Theta$, $(u_A^N - d_A)(u_B^N - d_B) \geq (u_A - d_A)(u_B - d_B)$. Which is if and only if for any $u \in \Theta$, $\alpha_A \alpha_B(u_A^N - d_A)(u_B^N - d_B) \geq \alpha_A \alpha_B(u_A - d_A)(u_B - d_B)$. Which, in turn, is if and only if for any $v \in \widehat{\Theta}$, $(v_A^N - d_A')(v_B^N - d_B') \geq (v_A - d_A')(v_B - d_B')$, where $\widehat{\Theta} = \{(v_A, v_B) : \exists u \in \Theta \text{ s.t. } v_i = \alpha_i u_i + \beta_i\}$ and $v_i^N = \alpha_i u_i^N + \beta_i$. Hence, the NBS satisfies Axiom 2.1. By definition, the NBS satisfies Axiom 2.2. Now consider Axiom 2.3, and a bargaining problem that is symmetric. By the definition of symmetry, $(u_A^N, h(u_A^N)) \in \Theta$ implies that $(h(u_A^N), u_A^N) \in \Theta$. Since the maximand $(u_A - d)(u_B - d)$ is a symmetric function, $(h(u_A^N), u_A^N)$ maximizes $(u_A - d)(u_B - d)$ over the set Θ. But since the maximizer is unique, $u_A^N = h(u_A^N)$. Hence, the NBS satisfies Axiom 2.3. Finally, consider Axiom 2.4. Since the disagreement points in the two related bargaining problems are identical, the Nash products of these problems are identical. Hence, since $f^N(\Omega_1, d_1) \in \Omega_2$ and $(\Omega_2 \subset \Omega_1$ implies) $\Theta_2 \subseteq \Theta_1$, $f^N(\Omega_1, d_1)$ maximizes $(u_A - d_A)(u_B - d_B)$ over the set Θ_1 only if $f^N(\Omega_1, d_1)$ maximizes $(u_A - d_A)(u_B - d_B)$ over the set Θ_2.

I now establish that no other bargaining solution satisfies Axioms 2.1–2.4. Suppose f is a bargaining solution that satisfies Axioms 2.1–2.4. I shall show that $f = f^N$. Fix $(\Omega, d) \in \Sigma$. It needs to be shown that for $i = A, B$, $f_i(\Omega, d) = f_i^N(\Omega, d)$.

Since $u_i^N > d_i$, define for each i, $\alpha_i = 1/2(u_i^N - d_i)$ and $\beta_i = -d_i/2(u_i^N - d_i)$. Given (Ω, d) and these values for α_A, α_B, β_A and β_B, define (Ω', d'), where d' and Ω' are respectively defined by (2.6) and (2.7). It is easy to verify that for each i, $d_i' = 0$ and $\alpha_i u_i^N + \beta_i = 1/2$ — the values of α_i and β_i are constructed to ensure these two conclusions (i.e., in order to shift the disagreement point d to the origin and the NBS to the point $(1/2, 1/2)$). Since both f and f^N satisfy Axiom 2.1, and since $\alpha_i > 0$, it follows that $f_i(\Omega', 0) = \alpha_i f_i(\Omega, d) + \beta_i$ and $f_i^N(\Omega', 0) = \alpha_i f_i^N(\Omega, d) + \beta_i$. Hence, $f(\Omega, d) = f^N(\Omega, d)$ if and only if $f(\Omega', 0) = f^N(\Omega', 0)$. Thus, since $f^N(\Omega', 0) = (1/2, 1/2)$, it needs to be shown that $f(\Omega', 0) = (1/2, 1/2)$.

Since $f^N(\Omega', 0) = (1/2, 1/2)$, and since Ω' satisfies Assumptions 2.1 and 2.2, it follows that $1/2 \in I_A$ and $h(1/2) = 1/2$. I now argue that for any $u_A \in I_A$, $h(u_A) \leq 1 - u_A$. Suppose, to the contrary, there exists $u_A' \in I_A$ such that $h(u_A') > 1 - u_A'$. Since h is concave, any point $(u_A, h(u_A))$ on the graph of h between points $(1/2, 1/2)$ and $(u_A', h(u_A'))$ has the property that $h(u_A) > 1 - u_A$. Hence, there exists a point $(u_A'', h(u_A''))$ such that $u_A'' h(u_A'') > 1/4$. Since $u_A'' > 0$ and $h(u_A'')) > 0$, this contradicts the established fact that $f^N(\Omega', 0) = (1/2, 1/2)$.

This result implies that $Q = \{(u_A, u_B) : u_A + u_B \leq 1\}$ contains the set Ω'. By Axioms 2.2 and 2.3, it follows that $f(Q, 0) = (1/2, 1/2)$. Consequently, by Axiom 2.4, it follows that $f(\Omega', 0) = (1/2, 1/2)$.

Proof of Lemma 2.2

I first establish the *if* part. Suppose, to the contrary, that for all x,

$$U_A(x^*)U_B(x^*) \geq U_A(x)U_B(x),$$

but that there exists an i, x and p such that $(1 - p)U_i(x) > U_i(x^*) \implies U_j(x) \geq (1 - p)U_j(x^*)$. Since $U_A(D) = U_B(D) = 0$, there exists an x

such that $U_A(x) > 0$ and $U_B(x) > 0$, which implies that $U_A(x^*) > 0$ and $U_B(x^*) > 0$. Hence, $(1-p)U_i(x) > U_i(x^*)$ implies that $(1-p)U_i(x)U_j(x^*) > U_i(x^*)U_j(x^*)$. This, in turn, implies (from my supposition) that $(1-p)U_j(x^*) > U_j(x)$, which is a contradiction. I now establish the *only if* part. Suppose that x^* is such that for any i, x and p, $(1-p)U_i(x) > U_i(x^*) \implies (1-p)U_j(x^*) > U_j(x)$. Consider an arbitrary x such that $U_A(x) > 0$, $U_B(x) > 0$ and for some i, $U_i(x) > U_i(x^*)$.[25] This means that for any $(1-p) > U_i(x^*)/U_i(x)$, $(1-p) > U_j(x)/U_j(x^*)$, which implies that $U_i(x^*)/U_i(x) \geq U_j(x)/U_j(x^*)$, and, hence, crossmultiplication gives the desired conclusion.

2.10   Notes

The Nash bargaining solution was proposed in John Nash's seminal paper, Nash (1950), where he provided the axiomatization discussed in Section 2.6. Binmore (1992, pp. 180–195) discusses additional properties of the asymmetric NBS, and contains a proof of the result, mentioned in Section 2.8, that any bargaining solution which satisfies Axioms 2.1, 2.2 and 2.4 is an asymmetric NBS for some value of τ. Both Osborne and Rubinstein (1990, pp. 9–27) and Binmore (1992, pp. 165–195) contain excellent expositions of the Nash bargaining solution.

For further elaboration on the applications in Sections 2.3.1/2.5.3 and 2.5.1 respectively, see Basu, Bhattacharya and Mishra (1992) and McDonald and Solow (1981). The application in Section 2.3.2 is based upon Hart (1995, pp. 34–49), which is a simple exposition of the ideas of Grossman and Hart (1986) and Hart and Moore (1990) — concerning the theory of the firm. For an alternative analysis of the phenomenon studied in Section 2.3.2 — based upon the *outside option principle* (which I describe in Chapter 5) — see de Meza and Lockwood (1998). The application in Section 2.5.2 is based upon Nandeibam (1996), who studies a general version of this problem of team production under moral hazard, but uses Rubinstein's bargaining model — which is studied in the next chapter — rather than the NBS.

The interpretation of the NBS discussed in Section 2.7 is due to Rubinstein, Safra and Thomson (1992).

---

[25]For any other x it is trivially the case that $U_A(x^*)U_B(x^*) \geq U_A(x)U_B(x)$.

3 The Rubinstein Model

3.1 Introduction

In this chapter I study Rubinstein's model of bargaining. A key feature of this model is that it specifies a rather attractive procedure of bargaining: the players take turns to make offers to each other until agreement is secured. This model has much intuitive appeal, since making offers and counteroffers lies at the heart of many real-life negotiations.

Rubinstein's model provides several insights about bargaining situations. One insight is that frictionless bargaining processes are indeterminate. A bargaining process may be considered 'frictionless' if the players do not incur any costs by haggling (i.e., by making offers and counteroffers) — in which case there is nothing to prevent them from haggling for as long as they wish. It seems intuitive that for the players to have some incentive to reach agreement they should find it costly to haggle. Another insight is that a player's bargaining power depends on the relative magnitude of the players' respective costs of haggling, with the absolute magnitudes of these costs being irrelevant to the bargaining outcome.

An important reason for the immense influence that Rubinstein's model has had, and continues to have, is that it provides a basic framework, which can be adapted, extended and modified for the purposes of application. This will become evident in several later chapters of this book.

In the next section I describe and analyse a simple version of Rubinstein's model in which two players are bargaining over the partition of a cake (or 'surplus') of fixed size. The analysis involves characterizing the unique subgame perfect equilibrium of this game-theoretic model. I study a fairly simple version of the model, because my objective in this section is to present the main arguments in a simple, but rigorous, manner. A discussion of the properties of the unique subgame perfect equilibrium and of the value and interpretation of the model respectively are contained in Sections 3.2.3 and 3.2.4. An application to a bilateral monopoly market is studied in Section 3.3.

In some applications of Rubinstein's model the set of possible agreements and the players' utility functions may be relatively more complex than what is assumed in Section 3.2. Hence, in Section 3.4, I study a general version of Rubinstein's model. The method of analysing this generalization is similar to that of the simple version. Section 3.5 contains an application to a two-person exchange economy.

Under a (plausible) condition, the unique subgame perfect equilibrium payoff pair of Rubinstein's model is identical to an asymmetric Nash bargaining solution of an appropriately defined bargaining problem. This remarkable result, which is the subject of discussion in Sections 3.2.3 and 3.4.3, provides a compelling justification for the use of Nash's bargaining solution.

3.2   The Basic Alternating-Offers Model

Two players, A and B, bargain over the partition of a cake of size π (where $\pi > 0$) according to the following, alternating-offers, procedure. At time 0 player A makes an offer to player B. An offer is a proposal of a partition of the cake. If player B accepts the offer, then agreement is struck and the players divide the cake according to the accepted offer. On the other hand, if player B rejects the offer, then she makes a counteroffer at time $\Delta > 0$. If this counteroffer is accepted by player A, then agreement is struck. Otherwise, player A makes a counter-counteroffer at time 2Δ. This process of making offers and counteroffers continues until a player accepts an offer.

A precise description of this bargaining procedure now follows. Offers are made at discrete points in time: namely, at times $0, \Delta, 2\Delta, 3\Delta, \ldots, t\Delta, \ldots,$

where $\Delta > 0$. An offer is a number greater than or equal to zero and less than or equal to π. I adopt the convention that an offer is the share of the cake to the proposer, and, therefore, π minus the offer is the share to the responder. At time $t\Delta$ when t is even (i.e., $t = 0, 2, 4, \dots$) player A makes an offer to player B. If player B accepts the offer, then the negotiations end with agreement. On the other hand, if player B rejects the offer, then Δ time units later, at time $(t+1)\Delta$, player B makes an offer to player A. If player A accepts the offer, then the negotiations end with agreement. On the other hand, if player A rejects the offer, then Δ time units later, at time $(t+2)\Delta$, player A makes an offer to player B, and so on. The negotiations end if and only if a player accepts an offer.

The payoffs are as follows. If the players reach agreement at time $t\Delta$ ($t = 0, 1, 2, \dots$) on a partition that gives player i ($i = A, B$) a share x_i ($0 \leq x_i \leq \pi$) of the cake, then player i's payoff is $x_i \exp(-r_i t\Delta)$, where $r_i > 0$ is player i's discount rate. On the other hand, if the players perpetually disagree (i.e., each player always rejects any offer made to her), then each player's payoff is zero.

This completes the description of the basic alternating-offers game. For notational convenience, define $\delta_i \equiv \exp(-r_i \Delta)$, where δ_i is player i's discount factor. Notice that $0 < \delta_i < 1$.

The subgame perfect equilibrium (SPE) concept will be employed to characterize the outcome of this game. In particular, answers to the following questions will be sought. In equilibrium, do the players reach agreement or do they perpetually disagree? In the former case, what is the agreed partition and at what time is agreement struck?

3.2.1 The Unique Subgame Perfect Equilibrium

How should one proceed to characterize the subgame perfect equilibria of this game? Notice that, since this is an infinite horizon game, one cannot use the backwards induction method. I shall proceed as follows. First, I shall characterize the unique SPE that satisfies the two properties stated below. Then, I shall show that it is the unique SPE of this game, which means that there does not exist a SPE which fails to satisfy these two properties.

Consider a SPE that satisfies the following two properties:[1]

---

[1] At this point I do not claim that such an equilibrium exists. The argument that

Property 3.1 (No Delay). Whenever a player has to make an offer, her equilibrium offer is accepted by the other player.

Property 3.2 (Stationarity). In equilibrium, a player makes the same offer whenever she has to make an offer.

Given Property 3.2, let x_i^* denote the equilibrium offer that player i makes whenever she has to make an offer. Consider an arbitrary point in time at which player A has to make an offer to player B. It follows from Properties 3.1 and 3.2 that player B's equilibrium payoff from rejecting any offer is $\delta_B x_B^*$. This is because, by Property 3.2, she offers x_B^* after rejecting any offer, which, by Property 3.1, is accepted by player A. Perfection requires that player B accept any offer x_A such that $\pi - x_A > \delta_B x_B^*$, and reject any offer x_A such that $\pi - x_A < \delta_B x_B^*$. Furthermore, it follows from Property 3.1 that $\pi - x_A^* \geq \delta_B x_B^*$. However, $\pi - x_A^* \not> \delta_B x_B^*$; otherwise player A could increase her payoff by instead offering x_A' such that $\pi - x_A^* > \pi - x_A' > \delta_B x_B^*$. Hence

$$\pi - x_A^* = \delta_B x_B^*. \tag{3.1}$$

Equation 3.1 states that player B is indifferent between accepting and rejecting player A's equilibrium offer. By a symmetric argument (with the roles of A and B reversed), it follows that player A is indifferent between accepting and rejecting player B's equilibrium offer. That is

$$\pi - x_B^* = \delta_A x_A^*. \tag{3.2}$$

Equations 3.1 and 3.2 have a unique solution, namely

$$x_A^* = \mu_A \pi \qquad \text{and} \qquad x_B^* = \mu_B \pi, \quad \text{where} \tag{3.3}$$

$$\mu_A = \frac{1 - \delta_B}{1 - \delta_A \delta_B} \qquad \text{and} \qquad \mu_B = \frac{1 - \delta_A}{1 - \delta_A \delta_B}. \tag{3.4}$$

The uniqueness of the solution to equations 3.1 and 3.2 means that there exists at most one SPE satisfying Properties 3.1 and 3.2. In that SPE, player A always offers x_A^* and always accepts an offer x_B if and only if $\pi - x_B \geq \delta_A x_A^*$, and player B always offers x_B^* and always accepts an offer

---

follows derives some further properties of such an equilibrium. I shall subsequently be in a position to claim the existence of such an equilibrium.

x_A if and only if $\pi - x_A \geq \delta_B x_B^*$, where x_A^* and x_B^* are defined in (3.3). It is straightforward to verify, as is done below in the proof of Proposition 3.1, that this pair of strategies is a subgame perfect equilibrium.

Proposition 3.1. *The following pair of strategies is a subgame perfect equilibrium of the basic alternating-offers game:*
- *player A always offers x_A^* and always accepts an offer x_B if and only if $x_B \leq x_B^*$,*
- *player B always offers x_B^* and always accepts an offer x_A if and only if $x_A \leq x_A^*$,*
where x_A^* and x_B^* are defined in (3.3).

Proof. I shall show that player A's strategy — as defined in the proposition — is optimal at any point in the game, given that player B uses the strategy described in the proposition. Consider any point in time $t\Delta$ (where t is an arbitrary even number) when player A has to make an offer to player B. If she uses the strategy described in the proposition, then her payoff is x_A^*. Consider any alternative strategy for player A, where x_A^t denotes the offer she makes at time $t\Delta$. If $x_A^t \leq x_A^*$, then, since player B accepts such an offer, deviation to this alternative strategy is not profitable. Now suppose that $x_A^t > x_A^*$. In this case player B rejects the offer made at time $t\Delta$. Since player B always rejects any offer that gives player A a share greater than x_A^* and always offers x_B^*, player A's payoff from this alternative strategy is less than or equal to $\max\{\delta_A(\pi - x_B^*), \delta_A^2 x_A^*\}$. Using (3.2), it follows that deviation to this alternative strategy is not profitable.

Now consider any point in time $t\Delta$ (where t is an arbitrary odd number) when player A has to respond to an offer made by player B. I have established above that at time $(t+1)\Delta$ it is optimal for player A to use the strategy described in the proposition. It therefore follows that it is optimal for her to accept an offer x_B if and only if $\pi - x_B \geq \delta_A x_A^*$.

By a symmetric argument (with the roles of A and B reversed), it follows that player B's strategy — as defined in the proposition — is optimal at any point in the game, given that player A uses the strategy described in the proposition. □

Proposition 3.1 characterizes the unique SPE that satisfies Properties 3.1 and 3.2. The following theorem states that this SPE is the unique SPE of the basic alternating-offers game. This means that there does not exist a SPE which fails to satisfy Properties 3.1 and 3.2.

Theorem 3.1. *The subgame perfect equilibrium described in Proposition 3.1 is the unique subgame perfect equilibrium of the basic alternating-offers game.*

Proof. In Section 3.2.2 below. □

In the unique SPE, agreement is reached at time 0, and the SPE is Pareto efficient. Since it is player A who makes the offer at time 0, the shares of the cake obtained by players A and B in the unique SPE are x_A^* and $\pi - x_A^*$, respectively, where $x_A^* = \mu_A \pi$ and $\pi - x_A^* = \delta_B \mu_B \pi$.

The equilibrium share to each player depends on both players' discount factors. In particular, the equilibrium share obtained by a player is strictly increasing in her discount factor, and strictly decreasing in her opponent's discount factor. Notice that if the players' discount rates are identical (i.e., $r_A = r_B = r > 0$), then player A's equilibrium share $\pi/(1 + \delta)$ is strictly greater than player B's equilibrium share $\pi\delta/(1+\delta)$, where $\delta \equiv \exp(-r\Delta)$. This result suggests that there exists a 'first-mover' advantage, since if $r_A = r_B$ then the only asymmetry in the game is that player A makes the first offer, at time 0. However, note that this first-mover advantage disappears in the limit as $\Delta \to 0$: each player obtains one-half of the cake.

As is evident in the following corollary, the properties of the equilibrium shares (when $r_A \neq r_B$) are relatively more transparent in the limit as the time interval Δ between two consecutive offers tends to zero.

Corollary 3.1. *In the limit, as $\Delta \to 0$, the shares obtained by players A and B respectively in the unique SPE converge to $\eta_A \pi$ and $\eta_B \pi$, where*

$$\eta_A = \frac{r_B}{r_A + r_B} \quad and \quad \eta_B = \frac{r_A}{r_A + r_B}.$$

Proof. For any $\Delta > 0$

$$\mu_A = \frac{1 - \exp(-r_B\Delta)}{1 - \exp(-(r_A + r_B)\Delta)}.$$

Since when $\Delta > 0$ *but small*, $\exp(-r_i\Delta) = 1 - r_i\Delta$, it follows that when $\Delta > 0$ but small, $\mu_A = r_B\Delta/(r_A + r_B)\Delta$ — that is, $\mu_A = r_B/(r_A + r_B)$. The corollary now follows immediately. □

In the limit, as $\Delta \to 0$, the relative magnitude of the players' discount rates critically influence the equilibrium partition of the cake: the equilibrium share obtained by a player depends on the ratio r_A/r_B. Notice that even in the limit, as both r_A and r_B tend to zero, the equilibrium partition depends on the ratio r_A/r_B. The following metaphor nicely illustrates the message contained in Corollary 3.1. In a boxing match, the winner is the relatively stronger of the two boxers; the absolute strengths of the boxers are irrelevant to the outcome.

3.2.2   Proof of Theorem 3.1

The strategy of the proof of Theorem 3.1 is as follows. I shall first establish that the payoffs to each player in any two subgame perfect equilibria are identical. Notice that this result does not rule out the possibility that there exists more than one subgame perfect equilibrium. However, given this result, I shall then establish Theorem 3.1. The central argument rests on exploiting the stationary structure that underlies the alternating-offers game: any two subgames that begin with player i's offer are 'strategically equivalent', in the sense that the strategic structures of such subgames are identical. This means that the sets of subgame perfect equilibria in such subgames are identical. Hence, the sets of SPE payoffs to player i in such subgames are identical. Let G_i denote the set of SPE payoffs to player i in any subgame beginning with player i's offer. Formally, $G_i \equiv \{u_i :$ there exists a SPE in any subgame beginning with player i's offer that gives player i a payoff equal to $u_i\}$. I shall derive the result (that the payoffs to each player in any two SPE are identical) by showing that the maximum and minimum values of G_i are identical. Let M_i and m_i respectively denote the maximum and minimum payoffs that player i obtains in any SPE of any subgame beginning with her offer.

Remark 3.1. To be precise, M_i denotes the supremum of G_i, and m_i its infimum. This is because, at this point, I do not rule out the possibility that G_i is an open set; that is, there may not exist a SPE (in any subgame beginning with player i's offer) that gives player i a payoff exactly equal to M_i. However, since G_i is bounded, there will exist a SPE that does give player i a payoff which is arbitrarily close to M_i; hence M_i denotes the supremum, rather than the maximum.[2] Similar remarks apply to m_i.

Lemmas 3.1, 3.3 and 3.4 (stated below) establish several relationships amongst the four unknowns, namely, amongst M_A, m_A, M_B and m_B. Lemma 3.2 is an intermediate result.

Lemma 3.1. *(i)* $m_A \geq \pi - \delta_B M_B$ *and (ii)* $m_B \geq \pi - \delta_A M_A$.

Proof. In any SPE player B accepts any offer x_A such that $\pi - x_A > \delta_B M_B$. Hence, there does not exist $u_A \in G_A$ such that $u_A < \pi - \delta_B M_B$; otherwise player A could increase her payoff by offering x'_A such that $u_A < x'_A < \pi - \delta_B M_B$. Therefore, for any $u_A \in G_A$, $u_A \geq \pi - \delta_B M_B$. Hence, $m_A \geq \pi - \delta_B M_B$.[3] $\square$

Lemma 3.2. *(i) For any* $u_B \in G_B$, $\pi - \delta_B u_B \in G_A$ *and (ii) for any* $u_A \in G_A$, $\pi - \delta_A u_A \in G_B$.

Proof. Fix an arbitrary $u_B \in G_B$; let σ denote the SPE that supports the payoff u_B to player B, and let player A's payoff in this SPE be denoted by v_A. Now fix an arbitrary subgame beginning with player A's offer, and consider the following pair of strategies. Player A begins by making the offer $x'_A = \pi - \delta_B u_B$. Player B accepts an offer x_A if and only if $x_A \leq x'_A$. If any offer is rejected, then play proceeds according to σ. I claim that this pair of strategies is a SPE. Player B's response behaviour is optimal and credible. Player A's initial offer is optimal provided she does not benefit by making an offer greater than x'_A. This is true provided $\pi - \delta_B u_B \geq \delta_A v_A$, which holds since $u_B + v_A \leq \pi$. Hence, it follows that $\pi - \delta_B u_B \in G_A$. $\square$

Lemma 3.3. *(i)* $m_A \leq \pi - \delta_B M_B$ *and* $M_A \geq \pi - \delta_B m_B$, *and (ii)* $m_B \leq \pi - \delta_A M_A$ *and* $M_B \geq \pi - \delta_A m_A$.

Proof. If $m_A > \pi - \delta_B M_B$, then there exists $u_B \in G_B$ such that $m_A > \pi - \delta_B u_B$, which contradicts Lemma 3.2(i). Similarly, if $M_A < \pi - \delta_B m_B$, then there exists $u_B \in G_B$ such that $M_A < \pi - \delta_B u_B$, which contradicts Lemma 3.2(i). $\square$

---

[2] It should be noted that Proposition 3.1 implies that G_i is non-empty.

[3] By a symmetric argument (with the roles of A and B reversed) part (ii) of the lemma can be proven. For the same reason, in the proofs of Lemmas 3.2–3.4 below I shall only establish the first parts of each of these lemmas.

Lemma 3.4. (i) $M_A \leq \pi - \delta_B m_B$ and (ii) $M_B \leq \pi - \delta_A m_A$.

Proof. Fix an arbitrary subgame beginning with player A's offer. The set of SPE in this subgame can be partitioned into types: (i) equilibria in which player A's initial offer is accepted, and (ii) equilibria in which player A's initial offer is rejected. Note that, in any SPE, player B rejects any offer $x_A > \pi - \delta_B m_B$. Hence, in any type (i) SPE, player A's payoff $u_A \leq \pi - \delta_B m_B$. Now consider any type (ii) SPE. Once, in such an equilibrium, player A's offer is rejected the game begins with player B's offer. In any SPE in such subgames, the sum of the equilibrium payoffs v_A and u_B to the players is less than or equal to π. This implies that $v_A \leq \pi - m_B$. Hence, in any type (ii) SPE, player A's payoff $u_A = \delta_A v_A \leq \delta_A(\pi - m_B)$. In summary, for any $u_A \in G_A$, $u_A \leq \max\{\pi - \delta_B m_B, \delta_A(\pi - m_B)\}$. Part (i) now follows since $\max\{\pi - \delta_B m_B, \delta_A(\pi - m_B)\} = \pi - \delta_B m_B$. □

Combining Lemmas 3.1, 3.3 and 3.4, it follows that

$$M_A = \pi - \delta_B m_B \tag{3.5}$$

$$m_A = \pi - \delta_B M_B \tag{3.6}$$

$$M_B = \pi - \delta_A m_A \tag{3.7}$$

$$m_B = \pi - \delta_A M_A. \tag{3.8}$$

Solving these equations for M_A, m_A, M_B and m_B, it follows that the payoffs to each player in any two SPE are identical:

Proposition 3.2. $M_A = m_A = \mu_A \pi$ and $M_B = m_B = \mu_B \pi$, where μ_A and μ_B are defined in (3.4).

Notice that $M_A = m_A = x_A^*$ and $M_B = m_B = x_B^*$, where x_A^* and x_B^* are defined in (3.3). Theorem 3.1 follows immediately once it is shown (using the result contained in Proposition 3.2) that in any SPE Property 3.1 is satisfied. The argument is by contradiction. Thus, suppose there exists a SPE in which some player's equilibrium offer, say player A's, is rejected. From Proposition 3.2, the SPE payoff to player A in this subgame is x_A^*. Now, given my supposition, $x_A^* \leq \delta_A(\pi - x_B^*)$; this is because after player A's offer is rejected her SPE payoff in the subgame beginning with player B's offer is not greater than $\pi - x_B^*$. Since $\pi - x_B^* = \delta_A x_A^*$, it follows that $x_A^* \leq \delta_A^2 x_A^*$, which is a contradiction. This result, combined with Proposition

3.2, implies that in any SPE Property 3.2 is satisfied. In particular, the offer that player i $(i = A, B)$ always makes is x_i^*. Hence, Theorem 3.1 is proven.

3.2.3 Properties of the Equilibrium

Uniqueness and Efficiency

It has been shown that if $r_A > 0$ and $r_B > 0$, then the basic alternating-offers game has a unique SPE, which is Pareto efficient. As I now show, if, on the other hand, $r_A = r_B = 0$, then there exists many (indeed, a continuum) of subgame perfect equilibria, including equilibria which are Pareto inefficient. Fix an arbitrary number $x^* \in [0, \pi]$, and consider the following pair of strategies:

• Player A always offers $x_A = x^*$ and always accepts an offer x_B if and only if $x_B \leq \pi - x^*$.

• Player B always offers $x_B = \pi - x^*$ and always accepts the offer x_A if and only if $x_A \leq x^*$.

It is easy to verify that if $r_A = r_B = 0$, then this pair of strategies is a subgame perfect equilibrium. Hence, if $r_A = r_B = 0$, then any partition of the cake agreed to at time 0 can be supported in a SPE.[4] It is instructive to see why the pair of strategies described above is not a subgame perfect equilibrium if at least one player has a strictly positive discount rate. Suppose, for example, $r_B > 0$. Consider a subgame that begins with player B having to decide whether or not to accept an offer x_A such that $\delta_B(\pi - x^*) < \pi - x_A < \pi - x^*$. Notice that such an offer exists since $r_B > 0$ implies that $\delta_B < 1$. According to her strategy described above, player B rejects such an offer, and her payoff is $\delta_B(\pi - x^*)$. This means that she can profitably deviate to an alternative strategy in which she accepts this offer, because her payoff from such an alternative strategy is $\pi - x_A$. I have thus shown that player B's plan to reject the offer x_A is not credible.[5]

---

[4] It is straightforward to construct an SPE in which agreement is reached on an arbitrary partition at an arbitrary time. The main ingredients of such a construction are as follows. Along the path of play before agreement is secured, say at time $t\Delta$ (where $t \geq 1$), each player insists on receiving the whole cake. If neither player deviates from this path of play, then at time $t\Delta$ play proceeds according to the SPE stated above. But if a player deviates from the path of play at any time before $t\Delta$, then immediately play proceeds according to the SPE (described above) in which she receives no share of the cake.

[5] Notice that this argument is valid even if $r_A = 0$. It is, in fact, easy to verify that

If $r_A = r_B = 0$, then neither player cares about the time at which agreement is struck. This means that the players do not incur any costs by haggling (i.e., by making offers and counteroffers) — which characterizes, what may be called, a 'frictionless' bargaining process. One important message, therefore, of the basic alternating-offers model is that frictionless bargaining processes are indeterminate. This seems intuitive, because, if the players do not care about the time at which agreement is struck, then there is nothing to prevent them from haggling for as long as they wish. On the other hand, frictions in the bargaining process may provide the players with some incentive to reach agreement.

The importance of the concept of perfection — the requirement that each player's actions should always be credible — is illustrated by the following result. For any $r_A \geq 0$ and $r_B \geq 0$, the pair of strategies described above is a Nash equilibrium.[6] Hence, even if $r_A > 0$ and $r_B > 0$, the alternating-offers game has many (indeed, a continuum) of Nash equilibria.

Bargaining Power

It seems reasonable to assume that the share of the cake obtained by a player in the unique SPE reflects her 'bargaining power'. Thus, a player's bargaining power is decreasing in her discount rate, and increasing in her opponent's discount rate. Why does being relatively more patient confer greater bargaining power? To obtain some insight into this issue, I now identify the cost of haggling to each player, because it is intuitive that a player's bargaining power is decreasing in her cost of haggling, and increasing in her opponent's cost of haggling.

In the alternating-offers game, if a player does not wish to accept any particular offer and, instead, would like to make a counteroffer, then she is free to do so, but she has to incur a 'cost': this is the cost to her of waiting Δ time units. The smaller is her discount rate, the smaller is this cost. That is why being relatively more patient confers greater bargaining power.

Notice that even if both players' costs of haggling become arbitrarily small in absolute terms (for example, as $\Delta \to 0$), the equilibrium partition

---

Proposition 3.1 and Theorem 3.1 are valid for any $r_A \geq 0$ and $r_B \geq 0$ such that $r_A + r_B > 0$.

[6]This is trivial to verify. For example, given player B's strategy, deviation by player A to any alternative strategy does not give her a payoff greater than x^*.

depends on the relative magnitude of these costs (as captured by the ratio r_A/r_B).

Relationship with Nash's Bargaining Solution

It is straightforward to verify that the limiting, as $\Delta \to 0$, SPE payoff pair $(\eta_A \pi, \eta_B \pi)$ — as stated in Corollary 3.1 — is identical to the asymmetric Nash bargaining solution of the bargaining problem (Ω, d) with $\tau = \eta_A$, where $\Omega = \{(u_A, u_B) : 0 \le u_A \le \pi \text{ and } u_B = \pi - u_A\}$ and $d = (0,0)$ — where the asymmetric Nash bargaining solution is stated in Definition 2.3.[7]

This remarkable result — which is generalized in Corollary 3.4 — provides a strategic justification for Nash's bargaining solution. In particular, it provides answers to the questions of *why*, *when* and *how* to use Nash's bargaining solution. The asymmetric Nash bargaining solution is applicable because the bargaining outcome that it generates is identical to the (limiting) bargaining outcome that is generated by the basic alternating-offers model. However, it should only be used when Δ is arbitrarily small, which may be interpreted as follows: it should be used in those bargaining situations in which the *absolute* magnitudes of the frictions in the bargaining process are small. Furthermore, it should be defined on the bargaining problem (Ω, d), where Ω is the set of instantaneous utility pairs obtainable through agreement, and d is the payoff pair obtainable through perpetual disagreement. The following definition is useful.

Definition 3.1 (Impasse Point). The payoff pair obtainable through perpetual disagreement — that is, the payoffs obtained by the players if each player always rejects any offer made to her — is called the *impasse point*, which is denoted generically by $(\mathcal{I}_A, \mathcal{I}_B)$.

---

[7] As has been noted in Section 2.8 (immediately after Definition 2.3), for any bargaining problem $(\Omega, d) \in \Sigma$, if $\tau = 1/2$ then the asymmetric Nash bargaining solution of (Ω, d) is identical to the Nash bargaining solution of (Ω, d), where the Nash bargaining solution is stated in Definition 2.1. Hence, it follows from the above result that, in the limit, as $\Delta \to 0$, the unique SPE payoff pair of the basic alternating-offers model converges to the Nash bargaining solution of the bargaining problem (Ω, d) if and only if the players' discount rates are identical (i.e., $r_A = r_B$). This result makes sense, because (unlike an asymmetric Nash bargaining solution) the Nash bargaining solution embodies a symmetry axiom that would not be satisfied if the players have different discount rates.

In the basic alternating-offers model studied above, the impasse point $(\mathcal{I}_A, \mathcal{I}_B) = (0,0)$. It has been shown here that *the disagreement point in Nash's bargaining solution should be identified with the impasse point* of the basic alternating-offers model.[8] Finally, it should be noted that since the parameter τ in Nash's set-up reflects the 'bargaining power' of player A relative to that of player B, and $1 - \tau$ reflects the 'bargaining power' of player B relative to that of player A, it is plausible that $\tau = \eta_A$ and $1 - \tau = \eta_B$.

3.2.4 The Value and Interpretation of the Alternating-Offers Model

The basic alternating-offers game is a stylized representation of the following two features that lie at the heart of most real-life negotiations:

- Players attempt to reach agreement by making offers and counteroffers.
- Bargaining imposes costs on both players.

As such the game is useful because it provides a basic framework upon which one can build richer models of bargaining — this is shown in later chapters where, for example, I shall study extensions of this game that incorporate other important features of real-life negotiations. Furthermore, since this game is relatively plausible and tractable, it is attractive to embed it (or, some extension of it) in larger economic models. An important value, therefore, of the basic alternating-offers game is in terms of the insights that its extensions deliver about bargaining situations, and also in terms of its usefulness in applications.

Another important contribution of this model is that it provides a justification for the use of Nash's bargaining solution. Furthermore, as is shown in later chapters, its extensions can guide the application of the Nash bargaining solution in relatively more complex bargaining situations.

The basic alternating-offers model incorporates several specific assumptions that I now interpret. First, I shall interpret the (infinite horizon) assumption that the players may make offers and counteroffers forever. Is this assumption plausible, especially since players have finite lives? I now argue that, when properly interpreted, this modelling assumption is com-

---

[8]As will be shown in Corollary 3.4 and in later chapters, this result turns out to be fairly general and robust.

pelling. The assumption is motivated by the observation that a player can always make a counteroffer immediately after rejecting an offer. This observation points towards the infinite horizon assumption, and against the finite horizon assumption.[9] Suppose, for example, a seller and a buyer are bargaining over the price of some object, and have to reach agreement within a single day. The players' strategic reasoning (and hence their bargaining behaviour) is typically influenced by their perception that after any offer is rejected there is room for at least one more offer. This suggests that the infinite horizon assumption is an appropriate *modelling* assumption — notwithstanding the *descriptive* reality that bargaining ends in finite time.

The time interval Δ between two consecutive offers is a parameter of the game, and it is assumed that $\Delta > 0$. I now argue that attention should, in general, focus on arbitrarily small values of Δ. The argument rests on the observation that since waiting to make a counteroffer is costly, a player will wish to make her counteroffer immediately after rejecting her opponent's offer. Unless there is some good reason that prevents her from doing so, the model with Δ arbitrarily small is the most compelling and least artificial. Why not then set $\Delta = 0$? There are two reasons for not doing so. The straightforward reason is that it does take some time, albeit very small, to reject an offer and make a counteroffer. The subtle reason is that such a model fails to capture any friction in the bargaining process. The model with $\Delta > 0$, on the other hand, does contain frictions — as captured by the players' positive costs of haggling. To further illustrate the difference between the model with $\Delta = 0$ and the model with Δ strictly positive but arbitrarily small, notice the following. In the limit as $\Delta \to 0$ the relative magnitude of the players' costs of haggling is well defined, but if $\Delta = 0$ then this relative magnitude is undetermined (since zero divided by zero is meaningless). This difference is of considerable significance, since, as I argued above, it is intuitive that the equilibrium partition depends critically on the players' relative bargaining powers — as captured by the relative magnitude of the players' costs of haggling — and not so much on absolute

---

[9]The finite horizon version of the alternating-offers game begs the following question. Why should the players stop bargaining after some exogenously given number of offers have been rejected? Since they would prefer to continue bargaining, somehow they have to be prevented from doing so. What, or who, prevents them from continuing to attempt to reach agreement? Unless a convincing answer is provided, the finite horizon assumption is implausible.

magnitudes.[10]

The discount factor may be interpreted more broadly as reflecting the costs of haggling — it need not be given a literal interpretation. For example, set $r_A = r_B = r$. The literal interpretation is that r is the players' common discount rate. An alternative interpretation is that r is the rate at which the cake (or, 'gains from trade') shrinks. For example, when bargaining over the partition of an ice cream, discounting future utilities is an insignificant factor. The friction in this bargaining process is that the ice cream is melting, where the rate r at which the ice cream is melting captures the magnitude of this friction.

3.3   An Application to Bilateral Monopoly

Consider a market for some intermediate good with a single seller S and a single buyer B. If the buyer buys a quantity q at a price p, then the profits to the players are as follows

$$\Pi_B(p, q) = R(q) - pq \tag{3.9}$$

$$\Pi_S(p, q) = pq - C(q), \tag{3.10}$$

where $R(q)$ is the revenue obtained by the buyer by transforming the quantity q of the input into some output and then selling the output on some final good market, and $C(q)$ is the cost to the seller of producing the quantity q of the input. Assume that $R(0) = 0$, $R'(q) > 0$, $R''(q) < 0$, $C(0) = 0$, $C'(q) > 0$, $C''(q) > 0$ and $R'(0) > C'(0)$.

The players bargain over the price and quantity of trade according to the alternating-offers procedure. An offer is a pair (p, q), where $p \geq 0$ and $q \geq 0$. If the seller and the buyer reach agreement at time $t\Delta$ on a pair (p, q), then player i's $(i = B, S)$ payoff is $\Pi_i(p, q) \exp(-r_i t\Delta)$. On the other hand, if the players perpetually disagree, then each player's payoff is zero.

Bilateral Monopoly Equilibrium

Consider a SPE that satisfies Properties 3.1 and 3.2. Let (p_i^*, q_i^*) denote the equilibrium offer that player i makes whenever she has to make an offer.

---

[10]In the limit as $\Delta \to 0$ the first-mover advantage disappears — hence this is an additional reason for focusing on arbitrarily small values of Δ.

Furthermore, let $V_i^* \equiv \Pi_i(p_i^*, q_i^*)$.

It follows from Properties 3.1 and 3.2 that the buyer's payoff from rejecting any offer is $\delta_B V_B^*$. Perfection requires that the buyer accept any offer (p_S, q_S) such that $\Pi_B(p_S, q_S) > \delta_B V_B^*$, and reject any offer (p_S, q_S) such that $\Pi_B(p_S, q_S) < \delta_B V_B^*$. Furthermore, Property 3.1 implies that $\Pi_B(p_S^*, q_S^*) \geq \delta_B V_B^*$. However, $\Pi_B(p_S^*, q_S^*) \not> \delta_B V_B^*$; for otherwise, the seller could increase her profit by offering a slightly higher price (i.e., by instead offering a pair (p_S', q_S^*) where p_S' is slightly greater than p_S^*). Hence

$$\Pi_B(p_S^*, q_S^*) = \delta_B V_B^*. \tag{3.11}$$

Furthermore, optimality requires that the seller's equilibrium offer (p_S^*, q_S^*) maximize her profit $\Pi_S(p_S, q_S)$ subject to $\Pi_B(p_S, q_S) = \delta_B V_B^*$.[11] This implies that

$$q_S^* = q^e, \tag{3.12}$$

where q^e is the unique solution to $R'(q) = C'(q)$. Using (3.11), it follows that

$$V_S^* = \pi - \delta_B V_B^*, \qquad \text{where} \tag{3.13}$$
$$\pi = R(q^e) - C(q^e). \tag{3.14}$$

By a symmetric argument (with the roles of B and S reversed), it follows that

$$\Pi_S(p_B^*, q_B^*) = \delta_S V_S^* \tag{3.15}$$
$$q_B^* = q^e \tag{3.16}$$
$$V_B^* = \pi - \delta_S V_S^*. \tag{3.17}$$

---

[11]Suppose, to the contrary, that there exists a pair (p_S', q_S') such that $\Pi_S(p_S', q_S') > \Pi_S(p_S^*, q_S^*)$ and $\Pi_B(p_S', q_S') = \delta_B V_B^*$. Notice that the buyer is indifferent between accepting and rejecting the offer (p_S', q_S'). If, in equilibrium, the buyer accepts the offer (p_S', q_S'), then the seller can increase her profit by instead offering the pair (p_S', q_S'). Suppose, on the other hand, that, in equilibrium, the buyer rejects the offer (p_S', q_S'). In that case, the seller can increase her profit by instead offering the pair (p_S'', q_S') where p_S'' is slightly lower than p_S' (i.e., p_S'' is such that $\Pi_S(p_S'', q_S') > \Pi_S(p_S^*, q_S^*)$ and $\Pi_B(p_S'', q_S') > \delta_B V_B^*$).

Equations 3.13 and 3.17 have a unique solution, namely

$$V_B^* = \frac{\pi(1 - \delta_S)}{1 - \delta_B \delta_S} \tag{3.18}$$

$$V_S^* = \frac{\pi(1 - \delta_B)}{1 - \delta_B \delta_S}. \tag{3.19}$$

Hence, since $V_i^* \equiv \Pi_i(p_i^*, q_i^*)$, it follows (using (3.9), (3.10), (3.12), (3.14) and (3.16)) that

$$p_B^* = \frac{\delta_S(1 - \delta_B)}{1 - \delta_B \delta_S}\left(\frac{R(q^e)}{q^e}\right) + \frac{1 - \delta_S}{1 - \delta_B \delta_S}\left(\frac{C(q^e)}{q^e}\right) \tag{3.20}$$

$$p_S^* = \frac{1 - \delta_B}{1 - \delta_B \delta_S}\left(\frac{R(q^e)}{q^e}\right) + \frac{\delta_B(1 - \delta_S)}{1 - \delta_B \delta_S}\left(\frac{C(q^e)}{q^e}\right). \tag{3.21}$$

I have established that there exists at most one SPE that satisfies Properties 3.1 and 3.2. In this SPE:

• The buyer always offers the pair (p_B^*, q_B^*) and always accepts an offer (p_S, q_S) if and only if $\Pi_B(p_S, q_S) \geq \delta_B V_B^*$, where p_B^*, q_B^* and V_B^* are respectively defined in (3.20), (3.16) and (3.18).

• The seller always offers the pair (p_S^*, q_S^*) and always accepts an offer (p_B, q_B) if and only if $\Pi_S(p_B, q_B) \geq \delta_S V_S^*$, where p_S^*, q_S^* and V_S^* are respectively defined in (3.21), (3.12) and (3.19).

It is easy to verify (by a straightforward adaptation of the proof of Proposition 3.1) that this pair of strategies is a subgame perfect equilibrium. Here I shall verify that the buyer's strategy is optimal at any point in time $t\Delta$ when she has to make an offer, given the seller's strategy. If she uses the strategy stated above, then her payoff is V_B^*. Consider any alternative strategy for the buyer, where (p_B^t, q_B^t) denotes the offer she makes at time $t\Delta$. If this offer is such that $\Pi_S(p_B^t, q_B^t) \geq \delta_S V_S^*$, then, since the seller accepts such an offer and since (p_B^*, q_B^*) maximizes $\Pi_B(p_B, q_B)$ subject to $\Pi_S(p_B, q_B) \geq \delta_S V_S^*$, deviation to this alternative strategy is not profitable. Now suppose that the offer is such that $\Pi_S(p_B^t, q_B^t) < \delta_S V_S^*$. In this case the seller rejects the offer made at time $t\Delta$. Since the seller always rejects any offer (p_B, q_B) such that $\Pi_S(p_B, q_B) < \delta_S V_S^*$ and always offers (p_S^*, q_S^*), the buyer's payoff from this alternative strategy is less than or equal to $\max\{\delta_B \Pi_B(p_S^*, q_S^*), \delta_B^2 V_B^*\}$, where V_B^* is the maximum value of $\Pi_B(p_B, q_B)$

subject to $\Pi_S(p_B, q_B) \geq \delta_S V_S^*$. Using (3.11), it follows that deviation to this alternative strategy is not profitable.

Through a straightforward adaptation of the arguments in Section 3.2.2, it can be proven that this SPE is the unique subgame perfect equilibrium of the bilateral monopoly model (cf. Theorem 3.2, below).

Properties of the Bilateral Monopoly Outcome

In the unique SPE, the equilibrium quantity traded q^e maximizes the surplus (or, gains from trade) $R(q) - C(q)$. This suggests that the bilateral monopoly equilibrium is Pareto efficient — that is, there does not exist another outcome which makes at least one player strictly better off without making any player worse off. I now show that an outcome is Pareto efficient if and only if agreement is reached at time 0 on a pair (p, q) such that $q = q^e$. First, notice that an outcome in which agreement is reached at time $t\Delta$ where $t \geq 1$ on a pair (p, q) is not Pareto efficient, because (due to discounting) both players are better off with the outcome in which agreement is reached at time 0 on the same pair (p, q). The set of Pareto efficient pairs (p, q) is then derived by maximizing $\Pi_S(p, q)$ subject to $\Pi_B(p, q) \geq \alpha$, where α is some arbitrary number. At the optimum, the constraint binds. Thus, after substitution, it immediately follows that a pair (p, q) is a solution to this constrained maximization problem if and only if $q = q^e$.

The equilibrium trade price is p_B^* if the buyer makes the offer at time 0, and p_S^* if the seller makes the offer at time 0. In the limit as $\Delta \to 0$ it does not matter who makes the offer at time 0, since, as $\Delta \to 0$, both p_B^* and p_S^* converge to the same price p^*, where

$$p^* = \frac{r_B}{r_B + r_S}\left(\frac{R(q^e)}{q^e}\right) + \frac{r_S}{r_B + r_S}\left(\frac{C(q^e)}{q^e}\right).$$

Notice that the equilibrium trade price is a convex combination of the equilibrium average revenue and average cost. Thus, the equilibrium trade price is unrelated to the equilibrium marginal cost $C'(q^e)$. The intuition behind this result is straightforward: the seller and the buyer set quantity to the level which maximizes the gains from trade $R(q) - C(q)$, and use the price as an instrument to divide the generated surplus $R(q^e) - C(q^e)$. Thus, for example, if the ratio r_B/r_S is close to zero (which means that the buyer is significantly more patient than the seller), then p^* is close to the equilibrium average cost, which implies that the seller's equilibrium profit is close to zero while the buyer receives most of the generated surplus.

Comparing (3.18)–(3.19) with (3.3)–(3.4), one may interpret the equilibrium payoffs in this bilateral monopoly model as the equilibrium shares the players obtain when bargaining over a cake of size $R(q^e) - C(q^e)$.

3.4 A General Model

I now study a general version of Rubinstein's model. Let X denote the set of possible agreements.[12] Two players, A and B, bargain according to the alternating-offers procedure in which an offer is an element from the set X. If the players reach agreement at time $t\Delta$ on $x \in X$, then player i's $(i = A, B)$ payoff is $U_i(x) \exp(-r_i t\Delta)$, where $U_i : X \to \Re$ is player i's utility function. For each $x \in X$, $U_i(x)$ is the instantaneous utility player i obtains from agreement x. If the players perpetually disagree (i.e., each player always rejects any offer made to her), then each player's payoff is zero.

The set of possible utility pairs $\Omega = \{(u_A, u_B) :$ there exists $x \in X$ such that $U_A(x) = u_A$ and $U_B(x) = u_B\}$ is the set of instantaneous utility pairs obtainable through agreement. Thus, the set of possible utility pairs obtainable through agreement at time $t\Delta$ is $\Omega^t = \{(u_A \delta_A^t, u_B \delta_B^t) : (u_A, u_B) \subset \Omega\}$. It should be noted that $\Omega^0 = \Omega$.

The *Pareto frontier* Ω^e of the set Ω is a key concept in the analysis of the subgame perfect equilibria. A utility pair $(u_A, u_B) \in \Omega^e$ if and only if $(u_A, u_B) \in \Omega$ and there does not exist another utility pair $(u_A', u_B') \in \Omega$ such that $u_A' \geq u_A$, $u_B' \geq u_B$ and for some i, $u_i' > u_i$. In order to study the subgame perfect equilibria, I do not need to make any assumptions directly about X, U_A and U_B. The assumptions I make (stated below in Assumption 3.1) are about the Pareto frontier of Ω. However, since this concept is derived from X, U_A and U_B, Assumption 3.1 does indirectly restrict the nature of these three objects.[13]

---

[12]The set of agreements in the basic alternating-offers model is the set of partitions of the cake, namely, $\{(x_A, x_B) : 0 \leq x_A \leq \pi$ and $x_A + x_B = \pi\}$, and the set of agreements in the bilateral monopoly model is $\{(p, q) : p \geq 0$ and $q \geq 0\}$.

[13]For example, Assumption 3.1 implies that X has a continuum of elements — thus, X

Assumption 3.1. The Pareto frontier Ω^e of the set Ω is the graph of a concave function, denoted by ϕ, whose domain is an interval $I_A \subseteq \Re$ and range an interval $I_B \subseteq \Re$, with $0 \in I_A$, $0 \in I_B$ and $\phi(0) > 0$.

It should be noted that Assumption 3.1 implies that $\Omega^e = \{(u_A, u_B) : u_A \in I_A \text{ and } u_B = \phi(u_A)\}$. Notice that (by the definition of the Pareto frontier) ϕ is a strictly decreasing function. Denote by ϕ^{-1} the inverse of ϕ. By Assumption 3.1, it follows that ϕ^{-1} is a strictly decreasing and concave function from I_B to I_A, with $\phi^{-1}(0) > 0$. It should be noted that for any $u_A \in I_A$, $\phi(u_A)$ is the maximum utility player B receives subject to player A receiving a utility of at least u_A. Similarly, for any $u_B \in I_B$, $\phi^{-1}(u_B)$ is the maximum utility player A receives subject to player B receiving a utility of at least u_B.

It can be verified that Assumption 3.1 is satisfied in the basic alternating-offers model and in the bilateral monopoly model. In the former model $u_B = \phi(u_A) = \pi - u_A$ where $I_A = [0, \pi]$ and $I_B = [0, \pi]$, and in the latter model $u_S = \phi(u_B) = \pi - u_B$ where $I_B = (-\infty, R(q^e)]$ and $I_S = [-C(q^e), +\infty)$.

3.4.1 The Subgame Perfect Equilibria

Consider a SPE that satisfies Properties 3.1 and 3.2. Let x_i^* denote the equilibrium offer that player i makes whenever she has to make an offer. Furthermore, let $V_i^* \equiv U_i(x_i^*)$ and $W_i^* \equiv U_i(x_j^*)$ $(j \neq i)$.

It follows from Properties 3.1 and 3.2 that player B's payoff from rejecting any offer is $\delta_B V_B^*$. Perfection requires that player B accept any offer x_A such that $U_B(x_A) > \delta_B V_B^*$, and reject any offer x_A such that $U_B(x_A) < \delta_B V_B^*$. Furthermore, Property 3.1 implies that $W_B^* \geq \delta_B V_B^*$. I now establish that player B is indifferent between accepting and rejecting player A's equilibrium offer.[14] That is,

$$W_B^* = \delta_B V_B^*. \tag{3.22}$$

Suppose, to the contrary, that $W_B^* > \delta_B V_B^*$. Since $\delta_B V_B^* \geq 0$ and $\phi(0) \geq W_B^*$,[15] Assumption 3.1 ensures the existence of an agreement $x_A' \in X$ such

---

is not a finite or a countably infinite set.

[14]The formal arguments presented below — which establish (3.22)–(3.24) — may be illustrated using a diagram that depicts the graph of ϕ^{-1}.

[15]$V_B^* \geq 0$, because player B can guarantee a payoff of zero by always offering $x_B'' \in$

that $U_B(x'_A) = u'_B$ and $U_A(x'_A) = \phi^{-1}(u'_B)$, where $W^*_B > u'_B > \delta_B V^*_B$. Player B accepts x'_A. Since ϕ^{-1} is strictly decreasing, $\phi^{-1}(u'_B) > \phi^{-1}(W^*_B)$. Hence $\phi^{-1}(u'_B) > V^*_A$, because $\phi^{-1}(W^*_B) \geq V^*_A$. A contradiction is thus obtained, because player A can increase her payoff by instead offering x'_A.

I now establish that player A's equilibrium offer x^*_A maximizes her utility $U_A(x_A)$ subject to $U_B(x_A) = \delta_B V^*_B$. That is

$$V^*_A \geq U_A(x_A) \text{ for all } x_A \in X \text{ such that } U_B(x_A) = \delta_B V^*_B. \tag{3.23}$$

Suppose, to the contrary, there exists an $x'_A \in X$ such that $U_A(x'_A) > V^*_A$ and $U_B(x'_A) = \delta_B V^*_B$. Since $V^*_A \geq 0$ and $\phi^{-1}(\delta_B V^*_B) \geq U_A(x'_A)$, Assumption 3.1 ensures the existence of an agreement $x''_A \in X$ such that $U_A(x''_A) = u''_A$ and $U_B(x''_A) = \phi(u''_A)$, where $U_A(x'_A) > u''_A > V^*_A$. Since ϕ is strictly decreasing, $\phi(U_A(x'_A)) < \phi(u''_A)$. Hence $\phi(u''_A) > \delta_B V^*_B$, because $U_A(x'_A) \leq \phi^{-1}(\delta_B V^*_B)$ implies $\phi(U_A(x'_A)) \geq \delta_B V^*_B$. Therefore, player B accepts x''_A. A contradiction is thus obtained, because player A can increase her payoff by instead offering x''_A.

It immediately follows from (3.23) that

$$V^*_A = \phi^{-1}(\delta_B V^*_B). \tag{3.24}$$

By a symmetric argument (with the roles of A and B reversed), it follows that

$$W^*_A = \delta_A V^*_A \tag{3.25}$$

$$V^*_B \geq U_B(x_B) \text{ for all } x_B \in X \text{ such that } U_A(x_B) = \delta_A V^*_A \tag{3.26}$$

$$V^*_B = \phi(\delta_A V^*_A). \tag{3.27}$$

I now show that equations 3.24 and 3.27 have a unique solution in V^*_A and V^*_B. Furthermore, I shall show that this unique solution is such that $0 < V^*_A < \phi^{-1}(0)$ and $0 < V^*_B < \phi(0)$. Define, for each $V_A \in I_A$

$$\Gamma(V_A) \equiv \phi(V_A) - \delta_B \phi(\delta_A V_A). \tag{3.28}$$

X such that $(U_A(x''_B), U_B(x''_B)) = (\phi^{-1}(0), 0)$ and always rejecting any offer $x_A \in X$. Similarly, $V^*_A \geq 0$, $W^*_A \geq 0$ and $W^*_B \geq 0$. Now suppose, to the contrary, that $W^*_B > \phi(0)$. Using Assumption 3.1, this implies that $W^*_B \in I_B$ and $\phi^{-1}(W^*_B) < 0$. Since $V^*_A \leq \phi^{-1}(W^*_B)$, it follows that $V^*_A < 0$, which is a contradiction. Similarly, $V^*_B \leq \phi(0)$, $V^*_A \leq \phi^{-1}(0)$ and $W^*_A \leq \phi^{-1}(0)$.

Assumption 3.1 implies that Γ is strictly decreasing and continuous, $\Gamma(0) > 0$ and $\Gamma(\phi^{-1}(0)) < 0$. The desired conclusions follow immediately.

The uniqueness of the solution to equations 3.24 and 3.27 means that in any SPE that satisfies Properties 3.1 and 3.2 the players' equilibrium payoffs are uniquely defined. Let Z_i denote the set of maximizers of $U_i(x_i)$ subject to $U_j(x_i) = \delta_j V_j^*$ ($j \neq i$). Assumption 3.1 ensures that Z_i, which is a subset of X, is non-empty. However, Assumption 3.1 does not rule out the possibility that Z_i contains more than one element.[16] The following proposition characterizes the set of all subgame perfect equilibria that satisfy Properties 3.1 and 3.2.

Proposition 3.3. *For any $x_A^* \in Z_A$ and $x_B^* \in Z_B$, the following pair of strategies is a subgame perfect equilibrium of the general Rubinstein model:*
• Player A always offers x_A^* and always accepts an offer x_B if and only if $U_A(x_B) \geq \delta_A V_A^*$.
• Player B always offers x_B^* and always accepts an offer x_A if and only if $U_B(x_A) \geq \delta_B V_B^*$.

Proof. The proof involves a minor adaptation of the proof of Proposition 3.1. Here I verify that player B's strategy is optimal at any point in time $t\Delta$ when she has to make an offer, given player A's strategy. If she uses the strategy stated above, then her payoff is V_B^*. Consider any alternative strategy for player B, where $x_B^t \in X$ denotes the offer she makes at time $t\Delta$. If this offer is such that $U_A(x_B^t) \geq \delta_A V_A^*$, then, since player A accepts such an offer and since x_B^* maximizes $U_B(x_B)$ subject to $U_A(x_B) \geq \delta_A V_A^*$, deviation to this alternative strategy is not profitable. Now suppose that the offer is such that $U_A(x_B^t) < \delta_A V_A^*$. In this case player A rejects the offer made at time $t\Delta$. Since player A always rejects any offer x_B such that $U_A(x_B) < \delta_A V_A^*$ and always offers x_A^*, player B's payoff from this alternative strategy is less than or equal to $\max\{\delta_B W_B^*, \delta_B^2 V_B^*\}$, where V_B^* is the maximum value of $U_B(x_B)$ subject to $U_A(x_B) \geq \delta_A V_A^*$. Using (3.22), it follows that deviation to this alternative strategy is not profitable. $\square$

If Z_A contains a unique element and Z_B contains a unique element, then the SPE described in Proposition 3.3 is the unique SPE that satisfies

---

[16]Given Assumption 3.1, a sufficient condition which ensures that Z_i contains a unique element is as follows: for any $u_A \in I_A$ and any utility pair $(u_A, \phi(u_A)) \in \Omega^e$ there exists a unique element x of X such that $U_A(x) = u_A$ and $U_B(x) = \phi(u_A)$.

Properties 3.1 and 3.2.[17] If, on the other hand, for some i ($i = A$ or $i = B$) Z_i contains more than one element, then there exists more than one SPE satisfying these two properties — although in any such SPE each player receives the same payoff.

I now establish the main results about the set of subgame perfect equilibria. It is useful (especially for future reference) to state the results in two theorems.

Theorem 3.2. *If Z_A contains a unique element and Z_B contains a unique element, then the unique subgame perfect equilibrium described in Proposition 3.3 is the unique subgame perfect equilibrium of the general Rubinstein model.*

Proof. The proof involves a straightforward adaptation of the proof of Theorem 3.1 — and is contained in Section 3.4.4 below. □

Theorem 3.3. *If for some i ($i = A$ or $i = B$) Z_i contains more than one element, then there exists more than one subgame perfect equilibrium in the general Rubinstein model, which may be characterized as follows. Whenever player i ($i = A, B$) has to make an offer, she offers an element from the set Z_i, and she accepts an offer x_j ($j \neq i$) if and only if $U_i(x_j) \geq \delta_i V_i^*$.*

Proof. The proof is in Section 3.4.4, below.[18] □

In any SPE, agreement is reached at time 0. Since it is player A who makes the offer at time 0, her equilibrium payoff is V_A^* and player B's equilibrium payoff is $\phi(V_A^*)$. The equilibrium payoff pair is Pareto efficient.[19] The result stated in the following corollary implies that each player's unique SPE payoff is strictly increasing in her discount factor, and strictly decreasing in her opponent's discount factor. Thus, the more patient a player is relative to her opponent, the higher is her unique SPE payoff.

---

[17]Z_A contains a unique element if and only if there exists a unique element x_A^* of X such that $U_A(x_A^*) = V_A^*$ and $U_B(x_A^*) = \phi(V_A^*)$. Z_B contains a unique element if and only if there exists a unique element x_B^* of X such that $U_B(x_B^*) = V_B^*$ and $U_A(x_B^*) = \phi^{-1}(V_B^*)$.

[18]It should be noted that the differences between any two subgame perfect equilibria are insignificant, because any two elements of the set Z_A (resp., Z_B) generate the same payoff pair, namely, $(V_A^*, \phi(V_A^*))$ (resp., $(\phi^{-1}(V_B^*), V_B^*)$).

[19]If player B makes the first offer at time 0, then her equilibrium payoff is V_B^* and player A's equilibrium payoff is $\phi^{-1}(V_B^*)$.

Corollary 3.2. V_A^* *is strictly increasing in δ_A and strictly decreasing in δ_B.*

Proof. For any pair of discount factors δ_A and δ_B, V_A^* is the unique number at which the function Γ — defined in (3.28) — is equal to zero. It can be shown, using Assumption 3.1, that for any $V_A \in I_A$, $\Gamma(V_A)$ is strictly increasing in δ_A and strictly decreasing in δ_B. The desired conclusions follow immediately. $\square$

3.4.2 Small Time Intervals

I argued in Section 3.2.4 that, in general, attention should be focused on arbitrarily small values of Δ. Hence, I now characterize the unique SPE payoffs in the limit as $\Delta \to 0$.[20]

Corollary 3.3. *In the limit, as $\Delta \to 0$, the payoff pairs $(V_A^*, \phi(V_A^*))$ and $(\phi^{-1}(V_B^*), V_B^*)$ converge to the unique solution of the following maximization problem*

$$\max_{u_A, u_B} (u_A)^{\eta_A} (u_B)^{\eta_B}$$

subject to $(u_A, u_B) \in \Omega^e$, $u_A \geq 0$ and $u_B \geq 0$, where η_A and η_B are defined in Corollary 3.1.

Proof. For notational convenience, define for each $u_A > 0$ and $u_B > 0$

$$N(u_A, u_B) = (u_A)^{\widehat{\eta}_A} (u_B)^{\widehat{\eta}_B},$$

where $\widehat{\eta}_A = \ln \delta_B/(\ln \delta_A + \ln \delta_B)$ and $\widehat{\eta}_B = 1 - \widehat{\eta}_A$. Using (3.24) and (3.27), and noting that $\widehat{\eta}_A \ln \delta_A = \widehat{\eta}_B \ln \delta_B$, it follows that $N(V_A^*, \phi(V_A^*)) = N(\phi^{-1}(V_B^*), V_B^*)$. Furthermore, (3.24) implies that $V_A^* > \phi^{-1}(V_B^*)$. Thus, as is illustrated in Figure 3.1, the two distinct utility pairs $(V_A^*, \phi(V_A^*))$ and $(\phi^{-1}(V_B^*), V_B^*)$ lie on the graph of the function $N(u_A, u_B) = N(V_A^*, \phi(V_A^*))$ and on the graph of the function ϕ. From (3.24) and (3.27), it follows that as $\Delta \to 0$, $V_A^* - \phi^{-1}(V_B^*) \to 0$ and $V_B^* - \phi(V_A^*) \to 0$. Hence, since, as $\Delta \to 0$, $\widehat{\eta}_A \to \eta_A$ and $\widehat{\eta}_B \to \eta_B$, the pairs $(V_A^*, \phi(V_A^*))$ and $(\phi^{-1}(V_B^*), V_B^*)$ converge to the unique solution of the maximization problem defined in the corollary. $\square$

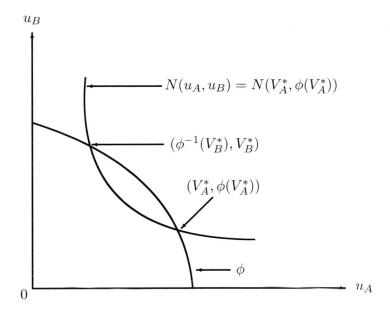

Figure 3.1: An illustration of the proof of Corollary 3.3.

Let (u_A^*, u_B^*) denote the unique solution to the maximization problem stated in Corollary 3.3, and $x^* \in X$ be such that $U_i(x^*) = u_i^*$ $(i = A, B)$. Although such a limiting (as $\Delta \to 0$) SPE agreement exists, it should be noted that Assumption 3.1 does not rule out the possibility that there exists more than one such limiting SPE agreement. Of course, any limiting SPE agreement generates the payoff pair (u_A^*, u_B^*).

It is useful to note — and this follows immediately from Corollary 3.3 — that x^* is a solution to the following maximization problem

$$\max_{x \in X}(U_A(x))^{\eta_A}(U_B(x))^{\eta_B}.$$

3.4.3 Relationship with Nash's Bargaining Solution

I now show that the limiting, as $\Delta \to 0$, SPE payoff pair (u_A^*, u_B^*) is identical to an asymmetric Nash bargaining solution of an appropriately defined

---

[20] As is shown in Corollary 3.3, in the limit as $\Delta \to 0$ a player's equilibrium payoff does not depend on which player makes the first offer at time 0; in this limit, a first-mover advantage does not exist.

bargaining problem — the latter bargaining solution is stated in Definition 2.3. I first state this remarkable result, which is an immediate consequence of Corollary 3.3, and then I shall discuss it.

Corollary 3.4 (Relationship with Nash's Bargaining Solution). *In the limit, as $\Delta \to 0$, the unique SPE payoff pair in Rubinstein's model converges to the asymmetric Nash bargaining solution of the bargaining problem (Ω, d) with $\tau = \eta_A$, where $\Omega = \{(u_A, u_B) : \text{there exists } x \in X \text{ such that } U_A(x) = u_A \text{ and } U_B(x) = u_B\}$, $d = (0,0)$ and η_A is defined in Corollary 3.1.*

Proof. First note that since the Pareto frontier Ω^e of the set Ω (where Ω is as stated in the corollary) satisfies Assumption 3.1, the bargaining problem (Ω, d) (where $d = (0,0)$) satisfies Assumptions 2.1 and 2.2. The desired result follows immediately by noting from Definition 2.3 that the asymmetric NBS of the bargaining problem (Ω, d) with $\tau = \eta_A$ is identical to the unique solution of the maximization problem stated in Corollary 3.3. $\square$

As has been noted in Section 2.8 (immediately after Definition 2.3), for any bargaining problem $(\Omega, d) \in \Sigma$, if $\tau = 1/2$ then the asymmetric Nash bargaining solution of (Ω, d) is identical to the Nash bargaining solution of (Ω, d), where the Nash bargaining solution is stated in Definition 2.1. Hence, it follows from Corollary 3.4 that in the limit, as $\Delta \to 0$, the unique SPE payoff pair in Rubinstein's model converges to the Nash bargaining solution of the bargaining problem (Ω, d) if and only if the players' discount rates are identical (i.e., $r_A = r_B$), where (Ω, d) is as defined in Corollary 3.4. This result makes sense, because (unlike an asymmetric Nash bargaining solution) the Nash bargaining solution embodies a symmetry axiom that would not be satisfied if the players have different discount rates.

The remarkable result contained in Corollary 3.4, which generalizes the result discussed in Section 3.2.3, provides a strategic justification for Nash's bargaining solution. In particular, it provides answers to the questions of *why*, *when* and *how* to use Nash's bargaining solution. The asymmetric Nash bargaining solution is applicable because the bargaining outcome that it generates is identical to the (limiting) bargaining outcome that is generated by Rubinstein's model. However, it should only be used when Δ is arbitrarily small, which may be interpreted as follows: it should be used in those bargaining situations in which the *absolute* magnitudes of the frictions in the bargaining process are small. Furthermore, it should be defined on the bargaining problem (Ω, d), where Ω is the set of instantaneous utility pairs obtainable through agreement and $d = (0, 0)$.

In Rubinstein's model studied here, the *impasse point* $(\mathcal{I}_A, \mathcal{I}_B) = (0, 0)$, where the impasse point is the payoff pair obtainable through perpetual disagreement (cf. Definition 3.1). It has been shown here that *the disagreement point in Nash's bargaining solution should be identified with the impasse point* of Rubinstein's model. Finally, it should be noted that since the parameter τ in Nash's set-up reflects the 'bargaining power' of player A relative to that of player B, and $1 - \tau$ reflects the 'bargaining power' of player B relative to that of player A, it is plausible that $\tau = \eta_A$ and $1 - \tau = \eta_B$.

3.4.4 Proof of Theorems 3.2 and 3.3

The strategy of the proof is similar to that of Theorem 3.1. Let G_i denote the set of SPE payoffs to player i in any subgame beginning with player i's offer, and let M_i and m_i respectively be the supremum and infimum of G_i. The following lemma establishes a preliminary result.

Lemma 3.5. *For any $u_A \in G_A$, $0 \le u_A \le \phi^{-1}(0)$, and for any $u_B \in G_B$, $0 \le u_B \le \phi(0)$.*

Proof. Since player A can guarantee a payoff of zero by always offering $x'_A \in X$ such that $(U_A(x'_A), U_B(x'_A)) = (0, \phi(0))$ and always rejecting any offer $x_B \in X$, it follows that $u_A \ge 0$ (for all $u_A \in G_A$). By a symmetric argument, it can be shown that $u_B \ge 0$ (for all $u_B \in G_B$). Now suppose, to the contrary, that for some $u_A \in G_A$, $u_A > \phi^{-1}(0)$. Using Assumption 3.1, this implies that $u_A \in I_A$ and $\phi^{-1}(u_A) < 0$. Let v_B denote the equilibrium payoff to player B in the SPE (of the subgame beginning with player A's offer) that supports the payoff u_A to player A. Since $v_B \le \phi^{-1}(u_A)$, it follows that $v_B < 0$. A contradiction is thus obtained, because player B can guarantee a payoff of zero. By a symmetric argument, it can be shown that $u_B \le \phi(0)$ (for all $u_B \in G_B$). $\square$

Lemma 3.6. *(i) $m_A \ge \phi^{-1}(\delta_B M_B)$ and (ii) $m_B \ge \phi(\delta_A M_A)$.*

Proof. In any SPE player B accepts any offer x_A such that $U_B(x_A) > \delta_B M_B$.[21] Hence, there does not exist $u_A \in G_A$ such that $u_A < \phi^{-1}(\delta_B M_B)$; otherwise player A could increase her payoff by offering x'_A such that $U_A(x'_A) = u'_A$ and $U_B(x'_A) = \phi(u'_A)$, where $u_A < u'_A < \phi^{-1}(\delta_B M_B)$. Therefore, for any $u_A \in G_A$, $u_A \geq \phi^{-1}(\delta_B M_B)$. Hence, $m_A \geq \phi^{-1}(\delta_B M_B)$.[22]   □

Lemma 3.7. *(i) For any $u_B \in G_B$, $\phi^{-1}(\delta_B u_B) \in G_A$ and (ii) for any $u_A \in G_A$, $\phi(\delta_A u_A) \in G_B$.*

Proof. Fix an arbitrary $u_B \in G_B$; let σ denote the SPE that supports the payoff u_B to player B, and let player A's payoff in this SPE be denoted by v_A. Now fix an arbitrary subgame beginning with player A's offer, and consider the following pair of strategies. Player A begins by making the offer x'_A such that $U_B(x'_A) = \delta_B u_B$ and $U_A(x'_A) = \phi^{-1}(\delta_B u_B)$.[23] Player B accepts an offer x_A if and only if $U_B(x'_A) \geq \delta_B u_B$. If any offer is rejected, then play proceeds according to σ. I claim that this pair of strategies is a SPE. Player B's response behaviour is optimal and credible. Player A's initial offer is optimal provided she does not benefit by making an offer x_A such that $U_B(x_A) < \delta_B u_B$. This is true provided $\phi^{-1}(\delta_B u_B) \geq \delta_A v_A$, which holds since $v_A \leq \phi^{-1}(u_B)$. Hence, it follows that $\phi^{-1}(\delta_B u_B) \in G_A$.   □

Lemma 3.8. *(i) $m_A \leq \phi^{-1}(\delta_B M_B)$ and $M_A \geq \phi^{-1}(\delta_B m_B)$, and (ii) $m_B \leq \phi(\delta_A M_A)$ and $M_B \geq \phi(\delta_A m_A)$.*

Proof. If $m_A > \phi^{-1}(\delta_B M_B)$, then there exists $u_B \in G_B$ such that $m_A > \phi^{-1}(\delta_B u_B)$, which contradicts Lemma 3.7(i). Similarly, if $M_A < \phi^{-1}(\delta_B m_B)$, then there exists $u_B \in G_B$ such that $M_A < \phi^{-1}(\delta_B u_B)$, which contradicts Lemma 3.7(i).   □

Lemma 3.9. *(i) $M_A \leq \phi^{-1}(\delta_B m_B)$ and (ii) $M_B \leq \phi(\delta_A m_A)$.*

Proof. Fix an arbitrary subgame beginning with player A's offer. The set of SPE in this subgame can be partitioned into types: (i) equilibria in which

---

[21]Notice that Lemma 3.5 implies $0 \leq \delta_B M_B \leq \phi(0)$. This, in turn, implies $\delta_B M_B \in I_B$ and $0 \leq \phi^{-1}(\delta_B M_B) \leq \phi^{-1}(0)$.

[22]By a symmetric argument (with the roles of A and B reversed) part (ii) of the lemma can be proven. For the same reason, in the proofs of Lemmas 3.7–3.9 below I shall only establish the first parts of each of these lemmas.

[23]Lemma 3.5 implies that $\delta_B u_B \in I_B$, and hence such an offer does exist.

player A's initial offer is accepted, and (ii) equilibria in which player A's initial offer is rejected. Note that, in any SPE, player B rejects any offer x_A such that $U_B(x_A) < \delta_B m_B$. Hence, in any type (i) SPE, player A's payoff $u_A \leq \phi^{-1}(\delta_B m_B)$. Now consider any type (ii) SPE. Once, in such an equilibrium, player A's offer is rejected the game begins with player B's offer. In any SPE in such subgames the equilibrium payoffs v_A and u_B to the players are such that $v_A \leq \phi^{-1}(u_B)$. This implies that $v_A \leq \phi^{-1}(m_B)$. Hence, in any type (ii) SPE, player A's payoff $u_A = \delta_A v_A \leq \delta_A \phi^{-1}(m_B)$. In summary, for any $u_A \in G_A$, $u_A \leq \max\{\phi^{-1}(\delta_B m_B), \delta_A \phi^{-1}(m_B)\}$. Part (i) now follows since $\max\{\phi^{-1}(\delta_B m_B), \delta_A \phi^{-1}(m_B)\} = \phi^{-1}(\delta_B m_B)$. $\square$

Combining Lemmas 3.6, 3.7 and 3.9, it follows that

$$M_A = \phi^{-1}(\delta_B m_B) \tag{3.29}$$

$$m_A = \phi^{-1}(\delta_B M_B) \tag{3.30}$$

$$M_B = \phi(\delta_A m_A) \tag{3.31}$$

$$m_B = \phi(\delta_A M_A). \tag{3.32}$$

It immediately follows from the result that equations 3.24 and 3.27 have a unique solution that

$$M_A = m_A = V_A^* \quad \text{and } M_B = m_B = V_B^*. \tag{3.33}$$

Using (3.33), I now establish that in any SPE Property 3.1 is satisfied. Suppose, to the contrary, there exists a SPE in which some player's equilibrium offer, say player A's, is rejected. The SPE payoff to player A in this subgame is V_A^*. Now, given my supposition, $V_A^* \leq \delta_A \phi^{-1}(V_B^*)$; this is because after player A's offer is rejected her SPE payoff in the subgame beginning with player B's offer is not greater than $\phi^{-1}(V_B^*)$. It follows that $V_A^* < \delta_A \phi^{-1}(\delta_B V_A^*)$, which is a contradiction. This result, combined with (3.33), implies that whenever player i $(i = A, B)$ has to make an offer, she offers an element from Z_i. Theorems 3.2 and 3.3 are thus proven.

3.5 An Application to a Two-Person Exchange Economy

Consider an exchange economy with two individuals (or, players), A and B, and two (perfectly divisible) goods, namely, bread and wine. Player A

owns one unit of bread and player B owns one unit of wine. The set of possible agreements is $X = \{(x_B, y_B) : 0 \le x_B \le 1 \text{ and } 0 \le y_B \le 1\}$, where x_B and y_B are respectively the quantities of bread and wine obtained by player B, and $1 - x_B$ and $1 - y_B$ are respectively the quantities of bread and wine obtained by player A. If agreement is reached on $x \in X$ at time $t\Delta$, then player A's payoff is $U_A(x_A, y_A) \exp(-rt\Delta)$, where $x_A = 1 - x_B$ and $y_A = 1 - y_B$, and player B's payoff is $U_B(x_B, y_B) \exp(-rt\Delta)$, where $r > 0$ denotes the players' common discount rate. Player i's instantaneous utility function $U_i : [0,1] \times [0,1] \to \Re$ is concave, and is strictly increasing in each of its arguments. Furthermore, $U_i(x_i, y_i) = 0$ if either $x_i = 0$ or $y_i = 0$. Finally, if the players perpetually disagree, then player i's payoff is zero.

The Pareto frontier Ω^e of the set Ω of instantaneous utility pairs obtainable through agreement may be derived by maximizing one player's utility subject to the other player receiving a minimum utility level. Define for each $u_A \ge 0$, $\phi(u_A) = \max U_B(x)$ subject to $x \in X$ and $U_A(1 - x_B, 1 - y_B) \ge u_A$. Since U_i is concave, it follows from the 'Theorem of the Maximum under Convexity restrictions' (cf. Sundaram (1996, Theorem 9.17)) that ϕ is a concave function of u_A, and hence, (since U_i is strictly increasing and there exists $x \in X$ such that $U_i(x) = 0$), Assumption 3.1 is satisfied — with $I_A = [0, U_A(1,1)]$, $I_B = [0, U_B(1,1)]$ and $\phi(0) = U_B(1,1) > 0$. This means that the analysis and results contained in Section 3.4 may be applied to characterize the SPE of the alternating-offers bargaining game between players A and B.

I shall characterize the SPE in the limit, as $\Delta \to 0$. It follows from Corollary 3.3 that in the limit, as $\Delta \to 0$, a SPE agreement (or, resource allocation) $x^* \in X$ is a solution to the following maximization problem

$$\max_{x \in X} U_A(1 - x_B, 1 - y_B) U_B(x).$$

Assuming U_i is differentiable in its arguments, the first-order conditions characterize the solution. Thus, (x_B^*, y_B^*) is the unique solution to the following pair of equations

$$U_A(1 - x_B, 1 - y_B) \frac{\partial U_B}{\partial x_B} = U_B(x_B, y_B) \frac{\partial U_A}{\partial x_A}$$

$$U_A(1 - x_B, 1 - y_B) \frac{\partial U_B}{\partial y_B} = U_B(x_B, y_B) \frac{\partial U_A}{\partial y_A}.$$

Notice that these equations imply that at (x_B^*, y_B^*)

$$\frac{\partial U_B/\partial x_B}{\partial U_B/\partial y_B} = \frac{\partial U_A/\partial x_A}{\partial U_A/\partial y_A}.$$

That is, in the limiting Rubinsteinian bargaining equilibrium, the players' marginal rates of substitution between the two goods are equal. This, of course, is the condition that characterizes a Pareto-efficient resource allocation.

3.6   Notes

The model studied in this chapter is due to Rubinstein (1982). It has been assumed that each player discounts future utilities according to a constant discount rate. For an analysis of the model when the players' time preferences are allowed to take other structures, see Osborne and Rubinstein (1990, Chapter 3). Despite the many expositions of Rubinstein's model, the original Rubinstein (1982) paper is still a delight to read. This classic paper in economic theory contains ideas which have yet to be fully explored.

The relationship with Nash's bargaining solution (discussed in Sections 3.2.3 and 3.4.3) was first discovered in Binmore (1987), which contains a number of interesting extensions and generalizations of Rubinstein's model. Some of these extensions are only briefly explored by him and await a fuller investigation.

The idea of addressing the issue of the uniqueness of the SPE payoffs by characterizing the suprema and infima of the sets of SPE *payoffs* to each of the two players is due to Shaked and Sutton (1984), who adapt and simplify the original proof contained in Rubinstein (1982). I should emphasize that this 'method of proof' should be applied with care in any extension/application of Rubinstein's model. Although its use in Rubinstein's model turns out to be rather straightforward (especially since the method generates four equations in four unknowns), it should be noted that the method may only generate upper bounds on the suprema and lower bounds on the infima — this point is illustrated in several of the later chapters.

4　Risk of Breakdown

4.1　Introduction

While bargaining the players may perceive that the negotiations might break down in a *random* manner for one reason or another. A potential cause for such a *risk of breakdown* is that the players may get fed up as negotiations become protracted, and thus walk away from the negotiating table. This type of human behaviour is random, in the sense that the exact time at which a player walks away for such reasons is random. Another possible cause for the existence of a risk of breakdown is that 'intervention' by a third party results in the disappearance of the 'gains from co-operation' that exists between the two players. For example, while two firms bargain over how to divide the returns from the exploitation of a new technology, an outside firm may discover a superior technology that makes their technology obsolete. Another example is as follows: while a corruptible policeman and a criminal are bargaining over the bribe, an honest policeman turns up and reports the criminal to the authorities.

In the next section I analyse a simple modification of the basic alternating-offers model — studied in Section 3.2 — in which the risk of breakdown is a main force that influences the bargaining outcome. It will be shown that the players' payoffs when (and if) negotiations break down and their respective degrees of risk aversion are crucial determinants of the bargaining outcome.

Section 4.3 contains an application to the problem of tax collection when the tax inspector is corruptible.

Section 4.4 extends the model studied in Section 4.2 in order to investigate the relative impacts of discounting and a risk of breakdown on the bargaining outcome. An application to price determination while searching is contained in Section 4.5.

The results in Sections 4.2 and 4.4 are derived in the context of a bargaining situation in which the players are bargaining over the partition of a cake (or 'surplus') of fixed size. In Section 4.6 I study a generalization of the model analysed in Section 4.4 to a bargaining situation in which the set X of possible agreements can take any form, subject to satisfying a slightly modified version of Assumption 3.1.

The issue of whether or not Nash's bargaining solution can be justified in bargaining situations with a risk of breakdown is addressed in Section 4.2.2, while the same issue in bargaining situations with a risk of breakdown *and* discounting is addressed in Section 4.4.1 — see also Section 4.6. Furthermore, the issues of when and how to apply Nash's bargaining solution are also addressed.

4.2   A Model with a Risk of Breakdown

Two players, A and B, bargain over the partition of a cake of size π (where $\pi > 0$) according to the alternating-offers procedure, but with the following modification: immediately after any player rejects any offer at any time $t\Delta$, with probability p (where $0 < p < 1$) the negotiations break down in disagreement, and with probability $1 - p$ the game proceeds to time $(t+1)\Delta$ — where the player makes her counteroffer.

The payoffs are as follows. If the players reach agreement at time $t\Delta$ ($t = 0, 1, 2, 3, \ldots$, and $\Delta > 0$) on a partition that gives player i a share x_i ($0 \le x_i \le \pi$) of the cake, then her payoff is $U_i(x_i)$, where $U_i : [0, \pi] \to \Re$ is her (von Neumann–Morgenstern) utility function.[1] It is assumed that U_i is

---

[1]Unlike in the model studied in Section 3.2, in the above described bargaining procedure the players have to make decisions in the face of risk. Hence, I interpret each player's utility function as her von Neumann–Morgenstern utility function. Furthermore, I shall assume that the players do not discount future utilities, because my objective here is to focus upon the role of a risk of breakdown on the bargaining outcome. In Section 4.4 I shall

strictly increasing and concave. If negotiations break down in disagreement at time $t\Delta$, then player i obtains a payoff of b_i, where $U_i(0) \le b_i < U_i(\pi)$. The payoff pair (b_A, b_B) is called the *breakdown point*.

Since $b_i \in [U_i(0), U_i(\pi))$, there exists a number $z_i \in [0, \pi)$ such that $U_i(z_i) = b_i$; that is, $z_i = U_i^{-1}(b_i)$, where U_i^{-1} denotes the inverse of U_i. Assume that $z_A + z_B < \pi$, which ensures that there exist mutually beneficial partitions of the cake.

If the players perpetually disagree (i.e., each player always rejects any offer made to her), then player i's payoff is

$$pb_i \sum_{t=0}^{\infty} (1-p)^t,$$

which equals b_i. Thus, it follows from Definition 3.1 that the *impasse point* $(\mathcal{I}_A, \mathcal{I}_B) = (b_A, b_B)$. The following lemma is an immediate consequence of the observation that player i can guarantee a payoff of b_i by always asking for a share z_i and always rejecting all offers.

Lemma 4.1. *In any subgame perfect equilibrium of any subgame of the model with a risk of breakdown, player i's $(i = A, B)$ payoff is greater than or equal to b_i.*

It is assumed that as the time interval Δ between two consecutive offers decreases, the probability of breakdown p between two consecutive offers decreases, and that $p \to 0$ as $\Delta \to 0$.

4.2.1 The Unique SPE when both Players are Risk Neutral

The following proposition characterizes the unique subgame perfect equilibrium on the assumption that $U_A(x_A) = x_A$ for all $x_A \in [0, \pi]$ and $U_B(x_B) = x_B$ for all $x_B \in [0, \pi]$. It should be noted that this implies that $z_i = b_i$ $(i = A, B)$.

Proposition 4.1 (Risk Neutral Players). *If for any $i = A, B$ and any $x_i \in [0, \pi]$, $U_i(x_i) = x_i$, then the unique subgame perfect equilibrium of the model with a risk of breakdown is as follows:*
- *player A always offers x_A^* and always accepts an offer x_B if and only if $x_B \le x_B^*$,*

---

study the interplay of discounting and a risk of breakdown on the bargaining outcome.

- *player B always offers x_B^* and always accepts an offer x_A if and only if $x_A \leq x_A^*$, where*

$$x_A^* = b_A + \frac{1}{2-p}\Big(\pi - b_A - b_B\Big) \quad and$$

$$x_B^* = b_B + \frac{1}{2-p}\Big(\pi - b_A - b_B\Big).$$

Proof. The proof involves a straightforward adaptation of the arguments in Sections 3.2.1 and 3.2.2. In particular, in any SPE that satisfies Properties 3.1 and 3.2 player i is indifferent between accepting and rejecting player j's $(j \neq i)$ equilibrium offer. That is

$$\pi - x_A^* = pb_B + (1-p)x_B^* \quad and$$

$$\pi - x_B^* = pb_A + (1-p)x_A^*.$$

The unique solution to these two equations is stated in the proposition. This means that there exists at most a unique SPE that satisfies Properties 3.1 and 3.2, which is described in the proposition. Using an argument similar to that contained in the proof of Proposition 3.1, it can be verified that the pair of strategies described in the proposition is a subgame perfect equilibrium. Through a slight modification of the arguments presented in Section 3.2.2, it can be shown that there does not exist another subgame perfect equilibrium.[2]   □

    In the unique SPE, agreement is reached at time 0, and the bargaining outcome is Pareto efficient: in equilibrium, the negotiations do not break down in disagreement. Since player A makes the first offer, at time 0, the unique SPE share to player A is x_A^* and to player B is $\pi - x_A^*$, where x_A^* is defined in Proposition 4.1. Notice that player i's share is strictly increasing in b_i, and strictly decreasing in b_j. If $b_A = b_B$, then $x_A^* > \pi - x_A^*$, which suggests that player A has a first-mover advantage. However, this first-mover advantage disappears in the limit as $\Delta \to 0$: each player obtains one-half of the cake (since $p \to 0$ as $\Delta \to 0$, and $b_A = b_B$).

---

[2]A key modification involves replacing the terms $\delta_i M_i$ and $\delta_i m_i$ respectively with $pb_i + (1-p)M_i$ and $pb_i + (1-p)m_i$, which are respectively the maximum and minimum SPE payoffs that player i obtains if she rejects any offer — since, after rejecting any offer, with probability p the negotiations break down, and since the players do not discount future utilities.

As I argued in Section 3.2.4, attention should in general be focused upon arbitrarily small values of Δ. I therefore obtain the following corollary to Proposition 4.1.

Corollary 4.1 (Split-The-Difference Rule). *In the limit, as $\Delta \to 0$, the unique SPE shares of the cake to players A and B respectively converge to*

$$b_A + \frac{1}{2}\left(\pi - b_A - b_B\right) \quad and \quad b_B + \frac{1}{2}\left(\pi - b_A - b_B\right).$$

The friction in the bargaining process underlying the above described game arises from the risk that negotiations break down between two consecutive offers, which is captured by the probability p. As the absolute magnitude of this friction becomes arbitrarily small — and thus the common cost of haggling to the players becomes arbitrarily small — the limiting equilibrium partition of the cake, which is independent of who makes the first offer, may be interpreted as follows. The players agree first of all to give player i $(i = A, B)$ a share b_i of the cake (which gives her a payoff equal to the payoff she obtains when, and if, negotiations break down), and then they split equally the remaining cake $\pi - b_A - b_B$.

4.2.2 The Unique SPE with Risk Averse Players

I now study the model on the assumption that U_i is a strictly increasing and concave function. In any SPE that satisfies Properties 3.1 and 3.2 player i is indifferent between accepting and rejecting player j's $(j \neq i)$ equilibrium offer. That is

$$U_B(\pi - x_A^*) = pb_B + (1 - p)U_B(x_B^*) \quad \text{and} \tag{4.1}$$
$$U_A(\pi - x_B^*) = pb_A + (1 - p)U_A(x_A^*). \tag{4.2}$$

Lemma 4.1 requires that

$$x_A^* \geq z_A \tag{4.3}$$
$$x_B^* \geq z_B \tag{4.4}$$
$$\pi - x_A^* \geq z_B \tag{4.5}$$
$$\pi - x_B^* \geq z_A. \tag{4.6}$$

I now show that there exists a unique pair (x_A^*, x_B^*) that satisfies (4.1)–(4.6), and that it has the property that

$$z_A < x_A^* < \pi - z_B \quad \text{and} \quad z_B < x_B^* < \pi - z_A. \qquad (4.7)$$

Using (4.1) and (4.2), define for each i

$$\widehat{\Gamma}_i(x_i) = U_j(\pi - x_i) - pb_j -$$

$$(1-p)U_j\left(\pi - U_i^{-1}\left(pb_i + (1-p)U_i(x_i)\right)\right), \qquad (4.8)$$

where $j \neq i$. It is easy to verify that $\widehat{\Gamma}_i(z_i) > 0$, $\widehat{\Gamma}_i(\pi) < 0$ and $\widehat{\Gamma}_i$ is strictly decreasing and continuous in x_i on the open interval (z_i, π). Hence, since (4.1)–(4.4) imply (4.5)–(4.6), the desired conclusions follow immediately. The following proposition characterizes the unique SPE.

Proposition 4.2. *Let (x_A^*, x_B^*) be the unique pair that satisfies (4.1)–(4.6). The unique subgame perfect equilibrium of the model with a risk of breakdown is as follows:*
* *player A always offers x_A^* and always accepts an offer x_B if and only if $x_B \leq x_B^*$.*
* *player B always offers x_B^* and always accepts an offer x_A if and only if $x_A \leq x_A^*$.*

Proof. Since there exists a unique pair that satisfies (4.1)–(4.6), there exists at most a unique SPE that satisfies Properties 3.1 and 3.2, which is described in the proposition. It is easy to verify — using an argument similar to that contained in the proof of Proposition 3.1, and (4.7) — that the pair of strategies described in the proposition is a subgame perfect equilibrium. Through a slight modification of the arguments presented in Section 3.4.2, it can be shown that there does not exist another subgame perfect equilibrium. □

In the unique SPE, agreement is reached at time 0, and the bargaining outcome is Pareto efficient: in equilibrium, the negotiations do not break down in disagreement. The unique SPE share to player A is x_A^* and to player B is $\pi - x_A^*$, where x_A^* is defined in Proposition 4.2. Since, for each x_A, $\widehat{\Gamma}_A(x_A)$ — as defined in (4.8) — is strictly increasing in b_A and strictly decreasing in b_B, it follows that player i's SPE share of the cake is strictly increasing in b_i, and strictly decreasing in b_j.

If $U_A \equiv U_B$ and $b_A = b_B$, then, since $\widehat{\Gamma}_A \equiv \widehat{\Gamma}_B$, $x_A^* = x_B^*$. This implies, using (4.1) and (4.7), that $x_A^* > \pi - x_A^*$, which suggests that player A has a first-mover advantage. However, this first-mover advantage disappears in the limit as $\Delta \to 0$: each player obtains one-half of the cake.

The following corollary to Proposition 4.2 characterizes the SPE in the limit as $\Delta \to 0$.[3]

Corollary 4.2. *In the limit, as $\Delta \to 0$, the payoff pairs $(U_A(x_A^*), U_B(\pi - x_A^*))$ and $(U_A(\pi - x_B^*), U_B(x_B^*))$ converge to the unique solution of the following maximization problem*

$$\max_{(u_A, u_B) \in \Theta} (u_A - b_A)(u_B - b_B),$$

where $\Theta = \{(u_A, u_B) : U_A(0) \le u_A \le U_A(\pi), u_B = g(u_A), u_A \ge b_A$ and $u_B \ge b_B\}$, and where for each $u_A \in [U_A(0), U_A(\pi)]$, $g(u_A) = U_B(\pi - U_A^{-1}(u_A))$.

Proof. The proof is similar to that of Corollary 3.3. For notational convenience, define for each $u_A > b_A$ and $u_B > b_B$

$$N(u_A, u_B) = (u_A - b_A)(u_B - b_B).$$

Using (4.1) and (4.2), it can be shown that $N(U_A(x_A^*), U_B(\pi - x_A^*)) = N(U_A(\pi - x_B^*), U_B(x_B^*))$. Furthermore, from (4.2) and (4.7) it follows that $U_A(x_A^*) > U_A(\pi - x_B^*)$.[4] As is illustrated in Figure 4.1, it follows that the two distinct utility pairs $(U_A(x_A^*), U_B(\pi - x_A^*))$ and $(U_A(\pi - x_B^*), U_B(x_B^*))$ lie on the graph of the function $N(u_A, u_B) = N(U_A(x_A^*), U_B(\pi - x_A^*))$, and on the graph of the function g defined in the corollary — where the set Ω of possible utility pairs obtainable through agreement is the graph of the function g (cf. Section 2.2, where it is shown — in Lemma 2.1 — that g is strictly decreasing and concave). From (4.1) and (4.2), it follows that as $\Delta \to 0$, $U_A(x_A^*) - U_A(\pi - x_B^*) \to 0$ and $U_B(x_B^*) - U_B(\pi - x_A^*) \to 0$.

---

[3]As is shown in Corollary 4.2, in the limit, as $\Delta \to 0$, a player's SPE payoff does not depend on which player makes the first offer at time 0; in this limit a first-mover advantage does not exist.

[4]Suppose, to the contrary, that $U_A(x_A^*) \le U_A(\pi - x_B^*)$. Using (4.2), it follows that $x_A^* \le z_A$, which contradicts (4.7).

Hence, both payoff pairs $(U_A(x_A^*), U_B(\pi - x_A^*))$ and $(U_A(\pi - x_B^*), U_B(x_B^*))$ converge to the unique solution of the maximization problem defined in the corollary.   □

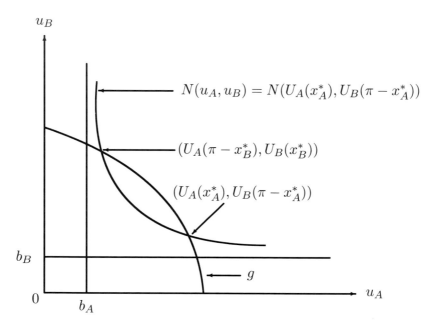

Figure 4.1: An illustration of the proof of Corollary 4.2.

It follows immediately from Corollary 4.2 and the definition of the Nash bargaining solution (as stated in Section 2.2) that in the limit, as $\Delta \to 0$ (and, hence, as $p \to 0$), the unique SPE payoff pair converges to the Nash bargaining solution of the bargaining problem (Ω, d), where the set of possible utility pairs $\Omega = \{(u_A, u_B) : U_A(0) \le u_A \le U_A(\pi) \text{ and } u_B = g(u_A)\}$ and the disagreement point $d = (b_A, b_B)$. Thus, the disagreement point in Nash's set-up should be identified with the impasse point of the model with a risk of breakdown. Furthermore, the Nash bargaining solution is applicable when the friction in the bargaining process (namely, the risk of breakdown) is arbitrarily small.

4.3   An Application to Corruption in Tax Collection

A corruptible tax inspector I and a citizen C bargain over the income to be reported and the bribe, given that the citizen's true income is $y \in [0,1]$. While bargaining there is a possibility — considered a random event — that an honest superior of the tax inspector turns up and asks her to immediately report the citizen's income.

An agreement between the tax inspector and the citizen is a pair (m, b), with the interpretation that I certifies to the government that the true income of C is m, and C pays I a bribe of b. Immediately after the inspector submits an income report m, I and C face two possible outcomes. With probability $1 - \gamma$ the report is not audited, and I and C respectively obtain $\omega + \lambda(m)T(m) + b$ and $y - T(m) - b$ amounts of money, where ω is the inspector's wage and $\lambda(m)T(m)$ is her commission on the reported tax liability $T(m)$. On the other hand, with probability γ the report is audited (which reveals to the government the citizen's true income), and I and C respectively obtain $\omega + \lambda(y)T(y) + b - f_I(m, y)$ and $y - T(y) - b - f_C(m, y)$ amounts of money, where $f_i(m, y)$ is the monetary fine paid by player i ($i = C, I$) if the true income is y and the reported income is m.

Assume that $0 < \gamma < 1$, the wage $\omega \geq 0$, the tax liability $T(x) \in [0, x]$ and the commission rate $\lambda(x) \in [0, 1]$ (for any income x), the penalties are monotonic, namely, for any $y \in [0, 1]$, $f_i(m_1, y) \geq f_i(m_2, y)$ for all $m_1 < m_2 \leq y$ and for all $m_1 > m_2 \geq y$, with $f_I(y, y) = f_C(y, y) = 0$, and for any y and any m, $f_I(m, y) \leq \omega + \lambda(y)T(y)$ and $f_C(m, y) \leq y - T(y)$. Furthermore, assume that the players are risk neutral: the utility to each player from receiving x amount of money is x.

Define for each true income $y \in [0, 1]$ and any reported income $x \in [0, 1]$

$$\alpha_I(x) = \omega + \gamma\lambda(y)T(y) + (1 - \gamma)\lambda(x)T(x) - \gamma f_I(x, y)$$
$$\alpha_C(x) = y - \gamma T(y) - (1 - \gamma)T(x) - \gamma f_C(x, y).$$

Thus, the expected amounts of money obtained by the two players from agreement on a pair (m, b) are $x_I = \alpha_I(m) + b$ and $x_C = \alpha_C(m) - b$.

If negotiations break down, which occurs with probability p after any offer is rejected — since with this probability an honest superior of the inspector turns up and asks her to immediately submit an income report

— then the inspector (unilaterally) chooses an income report $n \in [0, 1]$ that maximizes her expected amount of money $\alpha_I(n)$ subject to $\alpha_C(n) \geq 0$. Assume that this maximization problem has a solution, which is denoted by n^*. Thus, the expected amounts of money obtained by the two players when (and if) negotiations break down are $b_I = \alpha_I(n^*)$ and $b_C = \alpha_C(n^*)$.

The Bargaining Outcome

For each true income y, define $S(m, y) = \alpha_I(m) + \alpha_C(m)$. Assume that there exists an income report which maximizes $S(m, y)$, and denote it by m^*. It is easy to verify that an agreement (m, b) is Pareto efficient only if $m = m^*$. To simplify the argument, assume that at the beginning of the bargaining process the players agree that the inspector reports m^* if they reach agreement on the bribe.[5] To ensure that the expected money obtained by each player is non-negative, it is assumed that the bribe $b \in [-\alpha_I(m^*), \alpha_C(m^*)]$. One may now model the negotiations using the model with a risk of breakdown, where the risk neutral players bargain over the partition of $S(m^*, y)$ amount of money with b_C and b_I defined above.[6] If the inspector obtains a share x_I of this pot of money, then this means that the bribe $b = x_I - \alpha_I(m^*)$.

I now characterize the unique SPE bribe b^* in limit, as $\Delta \to 0$ (i.e., when the risk of an honest superior turning up is arbitrarily small). Applying Corollary 4.1, it follows that

$$b^* = \frac{1}{2}\Bigg[(1 - \gamma)\Big[[1 + \lambda(n^*)]T(n^*) - [1 + \lambda(m^*)]T(m^*)\Big] +$$

$$\gamma\Big[f_I(m^*) - f_C(m^*) + f_C(n^*) - f_I(n^*)\Big]\Bigg].$$

---

[5]This assumption is without loss of generality, because it can be shown by extending the arguments presented in Section 4.2.1 — as is done in Section 4.6 — that in the unique SPE of a general version of the model with a risk of breakdown, the players agree on a Pareto-efficient agreement. It may be noted that this result follows essentially from the result that the unique SPE in Rubinstein's model is Pareto efficient.

[6]It follows, by definition, that $S(m^*, y) \geq S(n^*, y)$, which implies that $S(m^*, y) \geq b_C + b_I$. Furthermore (by assumption) $b_C \geq 0$ and (since the inspector has the option to report the truth) $b_I \geq 0$.

In equilibrium, agreement is reached at time 0. The equilibrium income reported by the inspector is m^* and the equilibrium bribe paid by the citizen to the inspector is b^*. The income report n^* (which is submitted if negotiations break down) critically influences the level of the equilibrium bribe. It does not, however, influence the income reported in equilibrium, because that is chosen to maximize the gains from collusion. Since n^* influences the breakdown point, it influences the equilibrium partition of the gains from collusion through its influence on the equilibrium bribe.

If, for example, the tax schedule T is strictly increasing, then $m^* < y$ means that taxes are evaded. Corruption, on the other hand, takes place if some bribe is paid. From the expression above for the equilibrium bribe, it is clear that penalties may influence the level of corruption. However, notice that if $m^* < y < n^*$, then an increase in the penalty on I for under-reporting increases the bribe, while an increase in the penalty on I for over-reporting decreases the bribe. This suggests that it is over-reporting (or extortion) that needs to be penalized heavily to discourage corruption.

Optimal Policy

I now characterize the optimal government policy — namely, the tax schedule T, reward system ω and λ, and penalty functions f_C and f_I that maximize the government's expected revenue. Attention is restricted to policies that induce truthful reporting: for any true income $y \in [0,1]$, the income reported in the unique SPE $m^* = y$. Any such evasion-proof policy satisfies the following (evasion-proofness) condition[7]

$$\text{For all } y, \quad S(y,y) \geq S(m,y) \quad \text{for all } m.$$

For any evasion-proof policy, the government's expected revenue is the expected value of $[1 - \lambda(y)]T(y) - \omega$.[8]

I now maximize the government's expected revenue subject to the evasion-proofness condition. It is optimal to set the penalities, for any $m \neq y$, to their maximal admissible levels. Thus, for any y and m such that

---

[7]This restriction is without loss of generality, because Hindriks, Keen and Muthoo (1998), who study this model, show that for any policy such that for some y, $m^* \neq y$, there exists another policy which is evasion-proof and revenue-equivalent.

[8]Assume that the distribution of income in society is such that the expectation of $[1 - \lambda(y)]T(y) - \omega$ w.r.t y is well defined.

$m \neq y$, $f_I(m,y) = \omega + \lambda(y)T(y)$ and $f_C(m,y) = y - T(y)$. This implies that the evasion-proofness condition becomes the requirement that for all y, $(1 - \gamma)[1 - \lambda(m)]T(m) \geq [1 - \lambda(y)]T(y) - \gamma(\omega + y)$ for all m. Since $T(m)[1 - \lambda(m)] \geq 0$ (for all m) and $T(0)[1 - \lambda(0)] = 0$, this implies $\gamma(\omega + y) \geq [1 - \lambda(y)]T(y)$. Maximizing the government's expected revenue then requires setting the RHS of this latter inequality to its maximum level — that is, $\gamma(\omega + y) = [1 - \lambda(y)]T(y)$. The government's expected revenue then becomes the expected value of $\gamma y - (1 - \gamma)\omega$, which, since $\omega \geq 0$, is maximized by setting $\omega = 0$.

It has thus been established that any policy which has the following features is evasion-proof and maximizes the government's expected revenue: for all y, $\gamma y = [1 - \lambda(y)]T(y)$, $\omega = 0$, and for all y and m such that $m \neq y$, $f_I(m,y) = \lambda(y)T(y)$ and $f_C(m,y) = y - T(y)$. The maximized expected revenue to the government is γy^e, where y^e denotes the expectation of y.

The most striking aspect of the optimum is that revenue-maximization places very few restrictions on either the tax schedule or the commission structure. Nevertheless, the result implies that the average tax rate $T(y)/y$ be no less than the probability of audit γ, and the commission rate no greater than $1 - \gamma$. What is very substantially restricted, however, is the relationship between T and λ. It is perfectly possible, for example, for the government to raise the maximum revenue by implementing a tax schedule that is progressive in the sense that the average tax rate rises with income; but in order to do so it must also implement a reward structure such that the commission rate λ also increases with the income reported. By the same token, a constant commission rate is optimal only if tax liabilities are proportional to income.

An optimal policy — with the above stated features — is corruption-proof if and only if for all y, the equilibrium bribe $b^* = 0$. From the expression above for the equilibrium bribe b^*, it thus follows that an optimal policy is corruption-proof if and only if for all y, $n^* = y$.

I now show that there exists an optimal policy which is not corruption-proof. Assume that the probability of audit $\gamma < 1/2$, and consider the optimal policy in which $T(y) = ty$, where $t \in (\gamma, 1 - \gamma)$, and $\lambda(y) = 1 - \gamma/t$. For any true income $y > 0$, $\alpha_I(n = y/t) > \alpha_I(n \leq y)$ and $\alpha_C(n = y/t) = 0$. Hence, for any $y > 0$, $n^* > y$. The impact of the possibility of extortion is now self-evident: if there is some possibility that the citizen is subjected to extortion, then an optimal policy need not eliminate corruption.

It is intuitive that the inspector's incentive to over-report comes from the commission aspect of the policy. Suppose, therefore, that incentive is eliminated by choosing the optimal policy in which for all y, $\lambda(y) = 0$. This, however, implies that $T(y) = \gamma y$. With this optimal policy, $n^* = y$ (for all y). This conclusion is striking: a government that seeks to maximize expected revenue but is averse to evasion and corruption can do no better than use one of the simplest of all policies, involving a proportional tax (at a rate equal to the probability of audit) with a fixed wage contract for inspectors.

4.4   The Effect of Discounting

I now extend the model studied in Section 4.2 by assuming that the players discount future utilities. As in Section 3.2, for notational convenience, define $\delta_i \equiv \exp(-r_i\Delta)$, where $r_i > 0$ is player i's discount rate. To simplify the notation, assume that $U_i(0) = 0$.[9]

If the players perpetually disagree (i.e., each player always rejects any offer made to her), then player i's payoff is

$$pb_i \sum_{t=0}^{\infty}(1-p)^t\delta_i^t, \quad \text{which is equal to} \quad \beta_i = \frac{pb_i}{1-(1-p)\delta_i}.$$

Since $\beta_i \in [0, b_i)$, there exists a number $x_i^b \in [0, b_i)$ such that $U_i(x_i^b) = \beta_i$; that is, $x_i^b = U_i^{-1}(\beta_i)$. Notice that, since $z_A + z_B < \pi$, $x_A^b + x_B^b < \pi$. The following lemma is an immediate consequence of the observation that player i can guarantee a payoff of β_i by always asking for a share x_i^b and always rejecting all offers.

Lemma 4.2. *In any subgame perfect equilibrium of any subgame of the model with a risk of breakdown and discounting, player i's $(i = A, B)$ payoff is greater than or equal to β_i.*

---

[9]This assumption is without loss of generality, because U_i is a von Neumann–Morgenstern utility function. Thus, if $U_i(0) \neq 0$, then one may rescale utilities, and define another von Neumann–Morgenstern utility function $\widehat{U}_i$ such that for each $x_i \in [0, \pi]$, $\widehat{U}_i(x_i) = U_i(x_i) - U_i(0)$, which also represents player i's preferences.

In any SPE that satisfies Properties 3.1 and 3.2 player i is indifferent between accepting and rejecting player j's equilibrium offer. That is

$$U_B(\pi - x_A^*) = pb_B + (1-p)\delta_B U_B(x_B^*) \quad \text{and} \tag{4.9}$$

$$U_A(\pi - x_B^*) = pb_A + (1-p)\delta_A U_A(x_A^*). \tag{4.10}$$

In addition, Lemma 4.2 requires that

$$x_A^* \geq x_A^b \tag{4.11}$$

$$x_B^* \geq x_B^b \tag{4.12}$$

$$\pi - x_A^* \geq x_B^b \tag{4.13}$$

$$\pi - x_B^* \geq x_A^b. \tag{4.14}$$

I now show that there exists a unique pair (x_A^*, x_B^*) that satisfies (4.9)–(4.14), and that it has the property that

$$x_A^b < x_A^* < \pi - x_B^b \quad \text{and} \quad x_B^b < x_B^* < \pi - x_A^b. \tag{4.15}$$

Using (4.9) and (4.10), define for each i

$$\Gamma_i^*(x_i) = U_j(\pi - x_i) - pb_j -$$

$$(1-p)\delta_j U_j\left(\pi - U_i^{-1}\left(pb_i + (1-p)\delta_i U_i(x_i)\right)\right), \tag{4.16}$$

where $j \neq i$. It is easy to verify that $\Gamma_i^*(x_i^b) > 0$, $\Gamma_i^*(\pi) < 0$ and Γ_i^* is strictly decreasing and continuous in x_i on the open interval (x_i^b, π). Hence, since (4.9)–(4.12) imply (4.13)–(4.14), the desired conclusions follow immediately. The following proposition characterizes the unique SPE.

Proposition 4.3. *Let (x_A^*, x_B^*) be the unique pair that satisfies (4.9)–(4.14). The unique subgame perfect equilibrium of the model with a risk of breakdown and discounting is as follows:*
* *player A always offers x_A^* and always accepts an offer x_B if and only if $x_B \leq x_B^*$.*
* *player B always offers x_B^* and always accepts an offer x_A if and only if $x_A \leq x_A^*$.*

Proof. Similar to the proof of Proposition 4.2.   □

In the unique SPE, agreement is reached at time 0, and the bargaining outcome is Pareto efficient: in equilibrium, the negotiations do not break down in disagreement. The unique SPE share to player A is x_A^* and to player B is $\pi - x_A^*$, where x_A^* is defined in Proposition 4.3. Since, for each x_A, $\Gamma_A^*(x_A)$ — as defined in (4.16) — is strictly increasing in b_A and r_B, and strictly decreasing in b_B and r_A, it follows that player i's SPE share of the cake is strictly increasing in b_i and r_j, and strictly decreasing in b_j and r_i.

If $U_A \equiv U_B$, $b_A = b_B$ and $r_A = r_B$, then, since $\Gamma_A^* \equiv \Gamma_B^*$, $x_A^* = x_B^*$. This implies, using (4.9) and (4.15), that $x_A^* > \pi - x_A^*$, which suggests that player A has a first-mover advantage. However, this first-mover advantage disappears as $\Delta \to 0$: each player obtains one-half of the cake.

4.4.1 Small Time Intervals

I now characterize the SPE in the limit as $\Delta \to 0$. Unlike in the model without discounting, in order for this limit to exist it needs to be assumed that the limit of the ratio p/Δ as $\Delta \to 0$ exists, in addition to the assumption that $p \to 0$ as $\Delta \to 0$. Assume that when Δ is small (infinitesimal), $p/\Delta = \lambda$, where $\lambda > 0$.[10] Thus, it follows from the expression above for β_i that when $\Delta > 0$ but small the payoff to player i from perpetual diagreement is

$$\beta_i = \frac{\lambda b_i}{r_i + \lambda - r_i \lambda \Delta},$$

since, when $\Delta > 0$ but small, the discount factor $\delta_i \equiv \exp(-r_i\Delta) = 1 - r_i\Delta$. Hence, in the limit, as $\Delta \to 0$, β_i converges to $\lambda b_i/(r_i + \lambda)$. Thus, the (limiting, as $\Delta \to 0$) *impasse point*

$$(\mathcal{I}_A, \mathcal{I}_B) = \left(\frac{\lambda b_A}{r_A + \lambda}, \frac{\lambda b_B}{r_B + \lambda} \right).$$

Corollary 4.3. *In the limit, as $\Delta \to 0$, the SPE payoff pairs $(U_A(x_A^*), U_B(\pi - x_A^*))$ and $(U_A(\pi - x_B^*), U_B(x_B^*))$ converge to the unique solution of the following maximization problem*

$$\max_{(u_A, u_B) \in \Theta} (u_A - \mathcal{I}_A)^{\sigma_A} (u_B - \mathcal{I}_B)^{\sigma_B},$$

---

[10]Notice that this assumption is implied if, for example, negotiations break down according to a Poisson process at a rate $\lambda > 0$.

where $\Theta = \{(u_A, u_B) : 0 \leq u_A \leq U_A(\pi), u_B = g(u_A), u_A \geq \mathcal{I}_A$ *and* $u_B \geq \mathcal{I}_B\}$, *with* g *defined in Corollary 4.2, the (limiting) impasse point* $(\mathcal{I}_A, \mathcal{I}_B)$ *is defined above,*

$$\sigma_A = \frac{r_B + \lambda}{2\lambda + r_A + r_B} \quad and \quad \sigma_B = \frac{r_A + \lambda}{2\lambda + r_A + r_B}.$$

Proof. The proof is similar to the proofs of Corollaries 3.3 and 4.2. One defines a function N such that for each $u_A > \beta_A$ and $u_B > \beta_B$, $N(u_A, u_B) = (u_A - \beta_A)^{\sigma_A^*}(u_B - \beta_B)^{\sigma_B^*}$, where $\sigma_A^* = [\ln(1-p) + \ln \delta_B]/[2\ln(1-p) + \ln \delta_A + \ln \delta_B]$ and $\sigma_B^* = 1 - \sigma_A^*$. The subsequent argument is similar to the arguments in the proofs of Corollaries 3.3 and 4.2.[11] $\qquad \square$

The following corollary is an immediate consequence of Corollary 4.3 and Definition 2.3.

Corollary 4.4 (Relationship with Nash's Bargaining Solution). *In the limit, as* $\Delta \to 0$, *the unique SPE payoff pair of the model with a risk of breakdown and discounting converges to the asymmetric Nash bargaining solution of the bargaining problem* (Ω, d) *with* $\tau = (r_B + \lambda)/(2\lambda + r_A + r_B)$, *where* $\Omega = \{(u_A, u_B) : 0 \leq u_A \leq U_A(\pi)$ *and* $u_B = U_B(\pi - U_A^{-1}(u_A))\}$ *and* $d = (\mathcal{I}_A, \mathcal{I}_B)$, *with* $\mathcal{I}_i = \lambda b_i/(r_i + \lambda)$ $(i = A, B)$.

When Δ is arbitrarily small, both the probability that negotiations break down in any finite time and the cost of waiting to make a counteroffer are arbitrarily small, and, thus, the friction in the bargaining process is arbitrarily small. It has thus been established that the model with a risk of breakdown and discounting provides a strategic justification for the asymmetric Nash bargaining solution when the friction in the bargaining process is small. The Nash bargaining solution is justified if, in addition, the players' discount rates are identical.

I now emphasize the manner in which Nash's bargaining solution should be applied in bargaining situations when there is a risk of breakdown and the players discount future utilities. With discounting, the *breakdown point* (b_A, b_B) — which is the payoff pair obtainable if negotiations break down at any point in time — is different from the (limiting) *impasse point* $(\mathcal{I}_A, \mathcal{I}_B) = (\lambda b_A/(r_A + \lambda), \lambda b_B/(r_B + \lambda))$ — which is the payoff pair obtainable (in the

---

[11]Note that, as $\Delta \to 0$, $\sigma_A^* \to \sigma_A$ and, as shown above, $\beta_i \to \mathcal{I}_i$.

limit, as $\Delta \rightarrow 0$) if each player always rejects any offer made to her. I have established in Corollary 4.4 that the disagreement point in Nash's set-up should be identified with the (limiting, as $\Delta \rightarrow 0$) impasse point of the model with a risk of breakdown and discounting, and not with the breakdown point. This is rather intuitive, because in any finite time the probability of breakdown is arbitrarily small (in the limit as $\Delta \rightarrow 0$).

The impasse point depends on the breakdown point and on the players' expected discount rates r_A/λ and r_B/λ. Only if these expected discount rates are arbitrarily small should the breakdown point — which, in this case, is identical to the impasse point — be identified with the disagreement point. For example, if discounting is considered an insignificant force relative to the force of a risk of breakdown, then it is appropriate to identify the breakdown point with the disagreement point. On the other hand, if the risk of breakdown is considered insignificant relative to discounting — and thus the model approximates the basic alternating-offers model — then the impasse point (which converges to $(0,0)$ as $\lambda/r_i \rightarrow 0$) should be identified with the disagreement point.

Example 4.1 (Differentiable Utility Functions). Suppose that the utility functions, U_A and U_B, are differentiable. Applying Proposition 2.5 to the result stated in Corollary 4.4, it follows that the unique (limiting, as $\Delta \rightarrow 0$) SPE payoff pair is the unique solution to the following first-order conditions

$$-g'(u_A) = \left(\frac{r_A + \lambda}{r_B + \lambda}\right)\left[\frac{u_B - \mathcal{I}_B}{u_A - \mathcal{I}_A}\right] \quad \text{and} \quad u_B = g(u_A),$$

where $(\mathcal{I}_A, \mathcal{I}_B)$ is defined in Corollary 4.4.

4.4.2 Risk Neutral Players: Split-The-Difference Rule

Suppose that $U_A(x_A) = x_A$ for all $x_A \in [0, \pi]$ and $U_B(x_B) = x_B$ for all $x_B \in [0, \pi]$. Applying Example 4.1, and noting that (with linear utilities) $g(u_A) = \pi - u_A$, it follows that the unique limiting SPE payoffs (and shares) to players A and B respectively are

$$R_A = \mathcal{I}_A + \frac{r_B + \lambda}{2\lambda + r_A + r_B}\left(\pi - \mathcal{I}_A - \mathcal{I}_B\right) \quad \text{and} \tag{4.17}$$

$$R_B = \mathcal{I}_B + \frac{r_A + \lambda}{2\lambda + r_A + r_B}\left(\pi - \mathcal{I}_A - \mathcal{I}_B\right), \tag{4.18}$$

where $(\mathcal{I}_A, \mathcal{I}_B)$ is defined in Corollary 4.4. This limiting SPE partition may be interpreted as follows. The players agree first of all to give player i ($i = A, B$) a share $\mathcal{I}_i$ of the cake (which gives her a payoff equal to her payoff from perpetual disagreement), and then player i ($i = A, B$) obtains a fraction $(r_j + \lambda)/(2\lambda + r_A + r_B)$ of the remaining cake $\pi - \mathcal{I}_A - \mathcal{I}_B$. If $r_A = r_B$, then they split equally the remaining cake; otherwise the relatively more patient player obtains a relatively bigger share of the remaining cake.

It is easy to verify that player i's limiting SPE share is strictly increasing in r_j and strictly decreasing in r_i. The intuition for these results is as follows. An increase in r_j decreases $\mathcal{I}_j$, has no effect on $\mathcal{I}_i$ and increases the fraction $(r_j + \lambda)/(2\lambda + r_A + r_B)$ of any remaining cake obtained by player i. Hence, player i's limiting SPE share increases, because she obtains a bigger slice of a bigger remaining cake. On the other hand, an increase in r_i decreases $\mathcal{I}_i$, has no effect on $\mathcal{I}_j$ and decreases the fraction $(r_j + \lambda)/(2\lambda + r_A + r_B)$ of any remaining cake obtained by player i. Hence, player i's limiting SPE share decreases, because her limiting payoff from perpetual disagreement decreases and she obtains a smaller slice of a smaller remaining cake.

The effect on player i's limiting SPE share as the rate λ at which negotiations break down increases is relatively more complex. In particular, as I show below, it depends on the difference $b_i - b_j$. First notice that as λ increases, both players' limiting payoffs from perpetual disagreement increases. The intuition for this is as follows: an increase in λ decreases the expected time to breakdown, and, hence, the expected discounted value of b_i increases. To simplify the discussion below, set $r_A = r_B = r$.

If $b_A = b_B$, then player i's limiting SPE share is $\pi/2$. Thus, r and λ have no effect on the limiting SPE partition, which makes sense because under these conditions the players have equal bargaining power.

Now suppose that $b_A \neq b_B$. In this case player i's limiting SPE share is

$$\frac{\pi}{2} + \left(\frac{1}{(r/\lambda) + 1}\right)\left[\frac{b_i - b_j}{2}\right],$$

which depends upon the difference $b_i - b_j$ and the expected discount rate r/λ. It follows that player i's limiting SPE share is strictly decreasing in r/λ if $b_i > b_j$, and strictly increasing in r/λ if $b_i < b_j$. This means that the players have conflicting interests over the value of r/λ. If $b_i > b_j$ then player i prefers r small and/or λ large, while player j prefers the opposite.

The intuition is as follows. If $b_i > b_j$, then break down of negotiations is a relatively more desirable event for player i. Thus, as its impact is increased (by decreasing the ratio r/λ), player i's share of the cake increases (and player j's decreases).

4.5   An Application to Price Determination

A buyer B and a seller S are bargaining over the price p at which to trade a unit of some commodity. The von Neumann–Morgenstern utility functions to the players are $U_S(p) = p - c$ and $U_B(p) = v - p$, where $v > c \geq 0$. The seller S has placed an advert in the local newspaper asking a non-negotiable price q_S for the unit of the commodity that she owns. Thus, while bargaining with B, different buyers telephone S according to a Poisson process at a rate λ_S, where $\lambda_S \geq 0$. Similarly, the buyer B has placed an advert in the local newspaper asking to buy a unit of this commodity at a non-negotiable price q_B. Thus, while bargaining with S, different sellers telephone B according to an independent Poisson process at a rate λ_B, where $\lambda_B \geq 0$. When either a different seller telephones B or a different buyer telephones S, the negotiations between B and S break down in disagreement.

In order to study this bargaining situation, I extend (in a simple manner) the model with a risk of breakdown and discounting. Before I describe that extension, two simplifying assumptions are made: the players discount future utilities at a common rate $r > 0$, and Δ is strictly positive but sufficiently small so that $\lambda_B\Delta$ (resp., $\lambda_S\Delta$) is (approximately) the probability that a different seller (resp., buyer) telephones B (resp., S) in the small time interval Δ.

The extension concerns the manner in which negotiations break down. Immediately after any player rejects any offer at any time $t\Delta$, there are four possible events: (i) with probability $\lambda_B\lambda_S\Delta^2$ a different seller telephones B and a different buyer telephones S, (ii) with probability $\lambda_B\Delta(1 - \lambda_S\Delta)$ a different seller telephones B, (iii) with probability $\lambda_S\Delta(1 - \lambda_B\Delta)$ a different buyer telephones S, and (iv) with probability $(1 - \lambda_S\Delta)(1 - \lambda_B\Delta)$ the game proceeds to time $(t + 1)\Delta$, when the player makes her counteroffer.

If either of the first three events, (i)–(iii), occurs, then the negotiations between B and S break down in disagreement. If both players receive telephone calls (event (i)), then they trade at the prices that they respectively advertised. Their payoffs are $b_B = v - q_B$ and $b_S = q_S - c$. If, on the other hand, negotiations break down because exactly one player receives a phone call (events (ii) and (iii)), then the other player waits to receive a phone call. If player i receives a phone call then her payoff is b_i, and player j's payoff — who is left waiting for a phone call — is $\lambda_j b_j/(r + \lambda_j)$.

Indeed, as $\Delta \to 0$, the payoff to player i from perpetual disgreement converges to $\lambda_i b_i/(r + \lambda_i)$. Hence, the (limiting, as $\Delta \to 0$) *impasse point*

$$(\mathcal{I}_A, \mathcal{I}_B) = \left(\frac{\lambda_A b_A}{r + \lambda_A}, \frac{\lambda_B b_B}{r + \lambda_B} \right). \tag{4.19}$$

Assume that $\mathcal{I}_A + \mathcal{I}_B < v - c$; for otherwise, gains from trade do not exist between B and S. Furthermore, without loss of generality, assume that the advertised prices q_B and q_S are greater than or equal to c and less than or equal to v. It should be noted that in the limit, as $\Delta \to 0$, the payoff to player i in any SPE is greater than or equal to $\mathcal{I}_i$.

The Bargaining Outcome

Using arguments similar to those presented in Section 4.4, it can be established that the unique SPE price is p_S^* if S makes the first offer and p_B^* if B makes the first offer, where the pair (p_S^*, p_B^*) is the unique solution to the following pair of equations (which are similar to equations 4.9 and 4.10)

$$v - p_S^* = \lambda_B \Delta b_B + \lambda_S \Delta (1 - \lambda_B \Delta) \mathcal{I}_B + (1 - \lambda_S \Delta)(1 - \lambda_B \Delta)(1 - r\Delta)(v - p_B^*)$$

$$p_B^* - c = \lambda_S \Delta b_S + \lambda_B \Delta (1 - \lambda_S \Delta) \mathcal{I}_S + (1 - \lambda_B \Delta)(1 - \lambda_S \Delta)(1 - r\Delta)(p_S^* - c),$$

where $(\mathcal{I}_A, \mathcal{I}_B)$ is defined in (4.19). It is easy to show that, as $\Delta \to 0$, the unique solution to these equations p_S^* and p_B^* converges to p^*, where

$$v - p^* = \mathcal{I}_B + \frac{1}{2}(v - c - \mathcal{I}_B - \mathcal{I}_S).$$

This means that

$$p^* - c = \mathcal{I}_S + \frac{1}{2}(v - c - \mathcal{I}_B - \mathcal{I}_S).$$

Hence, in the unique limiting SPE (as $\Delta \to 0$) agreement is reached at time 0 on the price p^*. Notice that the limiting SPE outcome reflects the

Split-The-Difference Rule, as illustrated in Section 4.4.2. The players are, in effect, bargaining over the partition of a cake of size $v - c$: they agree first of all to give each other the limiting expected payoffs ($\mathcal{I}_A$ and $\mathcal{I}_B$) that they would, respectively, obtain from perpetual disagreement, and then they split equally the remaining cake.

Equilibrium Advertised Prices

I now determine whether or not the players place such adverts in the local newspaper, and if player i chooses to do so, her advertised price q_i. The cost of placing such an advert is $\epsilon > 0$. The analysis focuses on arbitrarily small values of ϵ. Assume, as seems reasonable, that the rate λ_B at which different sellers call B is strictly increasing in q_B, and the rate λ_S at which different buyers call S is strictly decreasing in q_S. Furthermore, assume that λ_i ($i = B, S$) is differentiable and concave, $\lambda_B(q_B) = 0$ for any $q_B \leq c$, and $\lambda_S(q_S) = 0$ for any $q_S \geq v$.

Before B and S bargain over the price at which to trade — which they do if and only if gains to trade exist — they simultaneously choose whether or not to place an advert in the local newspaper, and, if player i chooses to do so, the price $q_i \in [c, v]$. If both players do not advertise then each player's payoff is $(v - c)/2$ — there is then no risk of breakdown, and the bargaining game boils down to the basic alternating-offers game (studied in Section 3.2). If player i does not advertise, while player j ($j \neq i$) does advertise and sets a price q_j, then (since $q_j \in [c, v]$) $\mathcal{I}_A + \mathcal{I}_B < v - c$ (where, of course, $\mathcal{I}_i = 0$). This means that gains to trade exist between B and S, and hence, from the bargaining outcome derived above, it follows that players i's payoff is $(v - c - \mathcal{I}_j)/2$ and player j's payoff is $(v - c + \mathcal{I}_j)/2 - \epsilon$. Finally, if both players advertise then player i's payoff is $\mathcal{I}_i + \max\{(v - c - \mathcal{I}_B - \mathcal{I}_S)/2, 0\}$.[12]

Let q_i^* denote the unique value of q_i that maximizes $\mathcal{I}_i$ — which is characterized below. It is easy to verify that provided the cost ϵ of placing an advert in the local newspaper is sufficiently small, the above described simultaneous-move game has a unique Nash equilibrium in which player i places an advert in the local newspaper with price $q_i = q_i^*$. Since ϵ is suf-

---

[12]For some pairs (q_B, q_S) of advertised prices, $\mathcal{I}_A + \mathcal{I}_B < v - c$, while, for other pairs, $\mathcal{I}_A + \mathcal{I}_B \geq v - c$. In the former case, the payoffs follow from the bargaining outcome derived above, while for the latter case there do not exist any gains to trade and hence player i's payoff is $\mathcal{I}_i$.

ficiently small, it is perhaps not surprising that in equilibrium both players place adverts. I now characterize this unique pair of advertised prices q_B^* and q_S^* in order to explore their properties. For example, it is interesting to investigate whether or not the equilibrium prices are such that gains to trade do exist between B and S.

Differentiating $\mathcal{I}_i$ w.r.t. q_i, it follows that

$$\frac{\partial \mathcal{I}_i(q_i)}{\partial q_i} = \left(\frac{\lambda_i}{r + \lambda_i}\right) b_i'(q_i) + \left(\frac{r\lambda_i'(q_i)}{(r + \lambda_i)^2}\right) b_i.$$

Since $\mathcal{I}_i$ is concave in q_i, and since

$$\frac{\partial \mathcal{I}_i(c)}{\partial q_i} > 0 \quad \text{and} \quad \frac{\partial \mathcal{I}_i(v)}{\partial q_i} < 0,$$

the price q_i^* set by player i is the unique solution to the first-order condition

$$\left(\frac{\lambda_i}{r + \lambda_i}\right) b_i'(q_i) + \left(\frac{r\lambda_i'(q_i)}{(r + \lambda_i)^2}\right) b_i = 0.$$

Hence, the equilibrium advertised prices q_B^* and q_S^* respectively are the unique solutions to the the following equations

$$\lambda_B(q_B)[r + \lambda_B(q_B)] = (v - q_B)r\lambda_B'(q_B)$$
$$\lambda_S(q_S)[r + \lambda_S(q_S)] = -(q_S - c)r\lambda_S'(q_S).$$

These prices have the property that $c < q_B^* < v$ and $c < q_S^* < v$. The unique solution (q_B^*, q_S^*) to these equations may, in general, be such that either $\mathcal{I}_A + \mathcal{I}_B < v - c$ or $\mathcal{I}_A + \mathcal{I}_B \geq v - c$. This means that, in general, trade may or may not take place between B and S. I now show that in the limit, as $r \to 0$, trade does not take place between B and S.

It is easy to verify that q_B^* is strictly increasing in r, and q_S^* is strictly decreasing in r. In the limit, as $r \to 0$, $q_B^* \to c$, $q_S^* \to v$ and $r/\lambda_i \to 0$. Hence, as $r \to 0$, $\mathcal{I}_i \to b_i$. These results are rather intuitive, because, as $r \to 0$, each player is almost indifferent to the timing at which she receives a phone call from a different trader, and, hence, she sets her most favourable price ($q_B^* \to c$ and $q_S^* \to v$). Although this means that the arrival rate is close to zero, this price maximizes her utility since r is infinitesimal relative to λ_i (and hence her expected discount rate is zero) and since in infinite time she receives a phone call for sure. Therefore, since, in the limit as $r \to 0$, $\mathcal{I}_B + \mathcal{I}_S > v - c$, there do not exist gains to trade between B and S. Hence, each player i waits for a phone call from a different trader who is willing to trade at the advertised (or, posted) price q_i.

4.6   A Generalization

I now extend the model studied in Section 4.4 by assuming — as in Section 3.4 — that the players are bargaining over a set X of possible agreements, where $U_i : X \to \Re$ is player i's (instantaneous) von Neumann–Morgenstern utility function. As in Section 4.4, immediately after any player rejects any offer at any time $t\Delta$, with some probability negotiations break down: assume that player i believes this probability to be p_i, where $p_i = 1 - \exp(-\lambda_i \Delta)$ with $\lambda_i > 0$. Thus, I allow for the possibility that the players have different beliefs about the rate at which negotiations break down in disagreement.

The payoff to player i from perpetual disagreement is

$$\beta_i^* = \frac{p_i b_i}{1 - (1 - p_i)\delta_i}.$$

Similar to Assumption 3.1, assume that the Pareto frontier Ω^e of the set Ω of instantaneous utility pairs obtainable through agreement is the graph of a concave function, denoted by ϕ, whose domain is an interval $I_A \subseteq \Re$ and range an interval $I_B \subseteq \Re$, with $\beta_A^* \in I_A$, $\beta_B^* \in I_B$ and $\phi(\beta_A^*) > \beta_B^*$.

A minor adaptation of the analysis of Sections 3.4.1 and 3.4.4 characterizes the unique SPE of this model. In particular, it follows that $M_A = m_A = V_A^*$ and $M_B = m_B = V_B^*$, where (V_A^*, V_B^*) is the unique pair that satisfies (4.20)–(4.25), stated below.[13]

$$V_A^* = \phi^{-1}(p_B b_B + (1 - p_B)\delta_B V_B^*) \tag{4.20}$$

$$V_B^* = \phi(p_A b_A + (1 - p_A)\delta_A V_A^*) \tag{4.21}$$

$$V_A^* \geq \beta_A^* \tag{4.22}$$

$$V_B^* \geq \beta_B^* \tag{4.23}$$

$$\phi(V_A^*) \geq \beta_B^* \tag{4.24}$$

$$\phi^{-1}(V_B^*) \geq \beta_A^*. \tag{4.25}$$

---

[13]Recall that M_i and m_i are respectively the supremum and infimum of the set of SPE payoffs to player i in any subgame beginning with player i's offer.

In the following corollary — which can be proven along the lines of the proofs of Corollaries 3.3 and 4.3 — I characterize the limit of the unique SPE payoff pair, as $\Delta \to 0$.

Corollary 4.5. *In the limit, as $\Delta \to 0$, the unique SPE payoff pair of the general model with a risk of breakdown and discounting converges to the unique solution of the following maximization problem*

$$\max_{(u_A, u_B) \in \Theta} (u_A - \mathcal{I}_A)^{\sigma_A} (u_B - \mathcal{I}_B)^{\sigma_B},$$

where $\Theta = \{(u_A, u_B) : u_A \in I_A, u_B = \phi(u_A), u_A \geq \mathcal{I}_A$ and $u_B \geq \mathcal{I}_B\}$, and for each $i = A, B$

$$\mathcal{I}_i = \left(\frac{\lambda_i}{r_i + \lambda_i} \right) b_i \quad and \quad \sigma_i = \frac{r_j + \lambda_j}{\lambda_A + \lambda_B + r_A + r_B} \quad (j \neq i).$$

It follows immediately from Corollary 4.5 and Definition 2.3 that the unique SPE payoff pair converges, as $\Delta \to 0$, to the asymmetric Nash bargaining solution of the bargaining problem (Ω, d) with $\tau = \sigma_A$, where Ω is the set of instantaneous utility pairs obtainable through agreement and $d = (\mathcal{I}_A, \mathcal{I}_B)$ with $\mathcal{I}_i$ $(i = A, B)$ and σ_A defined in Corollary 4.5. Thus, as has been shown before (in Sections 3.2.3 and 3.4.3), *the disagreement point in Nash's set-up should be identified with the (limiting, as $\Delta \to 0$) impasse point*, and not with the breakdown point (b_A, b_B).

It may be noted that the Nash bargaining solution is applicable if and only if $r_A + \lambda_A = r_B + \lambda_B$ (since then $\tau = 1/2$). Furthermore, notice that if $\lambda_A = \lambda_B = \lambda$, then the result stated in Corollary 4.5 is similar to that stated in Corollary 4.3.

Suppose discounting is an insignificant force relative to the force of a risk of breakdown. More precisely, consider the limiting SPE, as $r_A \to 0$ and $r_B \to 0$. This means that the limiting impasse point converges to the breakdown point (b_A, b_B), and σ_i converges to $\lambda_j/(\lambda_A + \lambda_B)$. In this limit, therefore, player i's SPE payoff is decreasing in λ_i and increasing in λ_j, which may be interpreted as follows: it pays to be optimistic, in the sense of believing that the rate at which negotiations break down is small.

4.7   Notes

Binmore, Rubinstein and Wolinsky (1986) introduced the idea of a risk of breakdown in the alternating-offers model, and investigated the relationship with Nash's bargaining solution. The analyses in Sections 4.2 and 4.4 are inspired by that paper.

The application studied in Section 4.3 is due to Hindriks, Keen and Muthoo (1998). An interesting application — somewhat similar to that in Section 4.5 — is contained in Rubinstein and Wolinsky (1985), who embed the model studied in Section 4.5 in a model of a decentralized market. Unlike in the application studied in Section 4.5, in Rubinstein and Wolinsky's model the prices q_S and q_B respectively are determined by *bargaining* with a different buyer and a different seller; hence the outcome in any one bargaining situation is determined as part of a 'market equilibrium'. For an excellent exposition of Rubinstein and Wolinsky (1985), see Osborne and Rubinstein (1990, Chapter 6).

5   Outside Options

5.1   Introduction

Consider a situation in which University A and academic economist B bargain over the wage. Moreover, suppose that the academic economist has been offered a job at some alternative (but similar) university at a fixed, non-negotiable, wage w_B. A main objective of this chapter is to investigate the impact of such an 'outside option' on the outcome of bargaining between A and B. Although the academic economist B has to receive at least a wage of w_B if she is to work at University A, it is far from clear, for example, whether the negotiated wage will equal w_B, or strictly exceed w_B. In the next section I study the role of outside options through a simple extension of the basic alternating-offers model studied in Section 3.2. Section 5.3 contains applications to relationship-specific investments, sovereign debt negotiations and bribery and the control of crime.

In contrast to the models studied in Chapter 4, in the model studied in Section 5.2 there is no exogenous risk of breakdown. A player's decision to take up her outside option (and thus, to terminate the negotiations in disagreement) is a *strategic* decision: no random event forces her to opt out. In Section 5.4 I extend the model studied in Section 5.2 by also allowing for a risk of breakdown — and thus I study the relative impacts on the

bargaining outcome of the *breakdown point* and the *outside option point*.[1]
In particular, in Section 5.4.4 I study a general model with outside options
and a risk of breakdown in which the set X of possible agreements can take
any form, subject to satisfying a modified version of Assumption 3.1.

The model studied in Section 5.2 may be interpreted as follows: at least
one of the two players has an outside option, which she has to accept or
reject within a short interval of time, and thus, the players bargain on the
expectation that within a short interval of time either agreement is struck
or outside options are taken up.[2] The two models studied in Section 5.5,
on the other hand, may be interpreted as follows: when negotiations begin
neither player has an outside option, but while bargaining they may search
for an outside option, and when a player obtains an outside option she has
to immediately accept or reject it.

In Section 5.6 I study a model that differs from the model studied in Section 5.2 with respect to the points in the alternating-offers process at which
a player can choose to opt out. It will be suggested that the model studied in
Section 5.2 is suited to situations in which the players are making offers and
counteroffers face-to-face, while the model studied in Section 5.6 is suited
to situations in which the players are bargaining via a telephone/computer.

The issues of why, when and how to use Nash's bargaining solution in
bargaining situations with outside options is addressed in Section 5.2, while
the same issues are addressed in Section 5.4 in the context of bargaining
situations with outside options and a risk of breakdown.

5.2 A Model with Outside Options

Two players, A and B, bargain over the partition of a cake of size π (where
$\pi > 0$) according to the alternating-offers procedure, but with the following
modification. Whenever any player has to respond to any offer, she has
three choices, namely: (i) accept the offer, (ii) reject the offer and make

---

[1]The breakdown point is the payoff pair (b_A, b_B) obtained through an exogenous risk
of breakdown, and the outside option point is the payoff pair (w_A, w_B) obtained when a
player strategically opts out (and the players take up their respective outside options).

[2]Although the game is expected to end in a short interval of time, for reasons discussed
in Section 3.2.4 the infinite-horizon assumption better captures the players' strategic reasoning.

a counteroffer Δ time units later, and (iii) reject the offer and opt out, in which case negotiations terminate in disagreement.

The payoffs are as follows. If the players reach agreement at time $t\Delta$ ($t = 0, 1, 2, 3, \ldots$, and $\Delta > 0$) on a partition that gives player i ($i = A, B$) a share x_i ($0 \le x_i \le \pi$) of the cake, then her payoff is $x_i \exp(-r_i t\Delta)$. If, on the other hand, the players do not reach agreement because a player opts out at time $t\Delta$, then player i takes up her outside option, and obtains a payoff of $w_i \exp(-r_i t\Delta)$, where $w_A < \pi$, $w_B < \pi$ and $w_A + w_B < \pi$. The *outside option point* is the payoff pair (w_A, w_B), where w_i is player i's outside option.[3] Finally, if the players perpetually disagree (i.e., each player always rejects any offer made to her, and never opts out), then each player's payoff is zero. It follows from Definition 3.1 that the *impasse point* $(\mathcal{I}_A, \mathcal{I}_B) = (0, 0)$.

As in Section 3.2, for notational convenience, define $\delta_i \equiv \exp(-r_i \Delta)$. The following proposition characterizes the unique subgame perfect equilibrium of this model.

Proposition 5.1. *The unique subgame perfect equilibrium of the model with outside options and discounting is as follows:*

- *player A always offers x_A^*, always accepts an offer x_B if and only if $x_B \le x_B^*$, and always opts out after receiving an offer $x_B > x_B^*$ if and only if $\delta_A x_A^* \le w_A$,*
- *player B always offers x_B^*, always accepts an offer x_A if and only if $x_A \le x_A^*$, and always opts out after receiving an offer $x_A > x_A^*$ if and only if $\delta_B x_B^* \le w_B$, where*

$$
x_A^* = \begin{cases}
\mu_A \pi & \text{if } w_A \le \delta_A \mu_A \pi \text{ and } w_B \le \delta_B \mu_B \pi \\
\pi - w_B & \text{if } w_A \le \delta_A(\pi - w_B) \text{ and } w_B > \delta_B \mu_B \pi \\
\delta_B w_A + (1 - \delta_B)\pi & \text{if } w_A > \delta_A \mu_A \pi \text{ and } w_B \le \delta_B(\pi - w_A) \\
\pi - w_B & \text{if } w_A > \delta_A(\pi - w_B) \text{ and } w_B > \delta_B(\pi - w_A)
\end{cases}
$$

---

[3]It should be noted that I allow for the possibility that player i's outside option is negative. It is only required that $w_A < \pi$, $w_B < \pi$ and $w_A + w_B < \pi$; for, otherwise, there would not exist mutually beneficial partitions of the cake.

and

$$x_B^* = \begin{cases} \mu_B \pi & \text{if } w_A \leq \delta_A \mu_A \pi \text{ and } w_B \leq \delta_B \mu_B \pi \\ \delta_A w_B + (1 - \delta_A)\pi & \text{if } w_A \leq \delta_A(\pi - w_B) \text{ and } w_B > \delta_B \mu_B \pi \\ \pi - w_A & \text{if } w_A > \delta_A \mu_A \pi \text{ and } w_B \leq \delta_B(\pi - w_A) \\ \pi - w_A & \text{if } w_A > \delta_A(\pi - w_B) \text{ and } w_B > \delta_B(\pi - w_A) \end{cases}$$

with $\mu_A = (1 - \delta_B)/(1 - \delta_A \delta_B)$ *and* $\mu_B = (1 - \delta_A)/(1 - \delta_A \delta_B)$.

Proof. Since the proof involves a minor and straightforward adaptation of the arguments in Sections 3.2.1 and 3.2.2 (which establish Theorem 3.1), I shall only indicate the main changes to those arguments. In any SPE that satisfies Properties 3.1 and 3.2 player i is indifferent between accepting and not accepting player j's $(j \neq i)$ equilibrium offer. That is

$$\pi - x_A^* = \max\{\delta_B x_B^*, w_B\} \quad \text{and}$$
$$\pi - x_B^* = \max\{\delta_A x_A^*, w_A\}.$$

The unique solution to these equations is stated in the proposition. This means that there exists at most a unique SPE that satisfies Properties 3.1 and 3.2, which is described in the proposition.[4] Using an argument similar to that contained in the proof of Proposition 3.1, it can be verified that the pair of strategies described in the proposition is a subgame perfect equilibrium. Finally, through a slight modification of the arguments presented in Section 3.2.2, it can be shown that there does not exist another subgame perfect equilibrium.[5] $\square$

In the unique SPE, agreement is reached at time 0, and the bargaining outcome is Pareto efficient: in equilibrium, the players do not take up their

---

[4]If $w_i = \delta_i x_i^*$, then player i is indifferent between opting out and making a counteroffer when she receives an offer $x_j > x_j^*$. In order to facilitate the statement of the proposition (but without having any affect on the unique SPE path), I implicitly assume that she breaks this indifference in favour of opting out. Without this (tie-breaking) assumption, if $w_i = \delta_i x_i^*$ then there exists other subgame perfect equilibria, which, however, differ only as to how player i breaks the above stated indifference; the SPE path is uniquely defined.

[5]A key modification involves replacing the terms $\delta_i M_i$ and $\delta_i m_i$ respectively with $\max\{\delta_i M_i, w_i\}$ and $\max\{\delta_i m_i, w_i\}$, which respectively are the maximum and minimum SPE payoffs that player i obtains if she does not accept an offer (since, by not accepting an offer, player i can either take up her outside option or make a counteroffer Δ time units later).

respective outside options.[6] However, the presence of the outside options do influence the equilibrium partition of the cake, and this is relatively transparent in the limit as $\Delta \rightarrow 0$. The following corollary is an immediate consequence of Proposition 5.1.[7]

Corollary 5.1 (The Outside Option Principle). *In the limit, as $\Delta \rightarrow 0$, the unique SPE share x_A^* obtained by player A converges to*

$$x_A^{**} = \begin{cases} \eta_A \pi & \text{if } w_A \leq \eta_A \pi \text{ and } w_B \leq \eta_B \pi \\ \pi - w_B & \text{if } w_A \leq \eta_A \pi \text{ and } w_B > \eta_B \pi \\ w_A & \text{if } w_A > \eta_A \pi \text{ and } w_B \leq \eta_B \pi, \end{cases}$$

where $\eta_A = r_B/(r_A + r_B)$ and $\eta_B = r_A/(r_A + r_B)$, and the unique SPE share obtained by player B converges to $\pi - x_A^{**}$.

It is evident from Corollary 5.1 that if each player's outside option is less than or equal to the share she receives in the (limiting) SPE of Rubinstein's model (cf. Corollary 3.1), then the outside options have no influence on the (limiting) SPE partition. On the other hand, if one player's outside option strictly exceeds her (limiting) Rubinsteinian SPE share,[8] then her (limiting) SPE share is equal to her outside option.

Remark 5.1. Consider a modification of the model studied above in which only a single player can choose whether or not to opt out. Thus, as in the above model, a single player i ($i = A$ or $i = B$) can choose whether or not to opt out when responding to any offer, but player j ($j \neq i$) can only choose between accepting and rejecting any offer. It is trivial to verify that the unique SPE and limiting SPE respectively (of this modified version of the model studied above) are as stated in Proposition 5.1 and Corollary 5.1 with $w_j = 0$.[9]

---

[6]This makes sense, since otherwise the gains from trade, as captured by the 'surplus' $\pi - w_A - w_B$, are left unexploited.

[7]It should be noted that in this limit the unique SPE partition does not depend on which player makes the first offer, at time 0.

[8]Notice that, since $w_A + w_B < \pi$, both players' outside options do not exceed their respective (limiting) Rubinsteinian SPE shares.

[9]Notice that this means that the payoff player j receives when player i opts out has no impact on the bargaining outcome; for further discussion on this point, see Remark 5.2.

As I now illustrate, the results derived above capture, in particular, the notion that the players should not be influenced by threats which are not credible. Suppose that University A and academic economist B are bargaining over the wage w when neither player has any outside option. The (instantaneous) utilities to A and B if they reach agreement on wage w are $1 - w$ and w, respectively, and both players discount future utilities at a common rate $r > 0$. Applying Corollary 3.1, it follows that the (limiting) SPE wage $w^* = 0.5$. Now suppose that B has an outside option $w_B > 0$. It seems intuitive that if B's outside option w_B is less than or equal to 0.5, then her threat to opt out is not credible. If she is receiving a wage of 0.5, then getting an alternative job offer with a wage of 0.49, for example, should be useless: University A should ignore any threats made by B to quit. If, on the other hand, the alternative wage exceeds 0.5, then University A has only to exactly match the outside wage offer; there is no need to give more.

Remark 5.2. In the model studied above I implicitly assume that the (instantaneous) utility player i obtains when she opts out is equal to the (instantaneous) utility she obtains when player j opts out (which is equal to her outside option w_i). In some bargaining situations such an assumption may not be valid. It is trivial to verify that the (instantaneous) utility player i obtains when player j opts out has no impact whatsoever on the unique SPE — which is rather intuitive, since player j's decision on whether or not to opt out is not influenced by the utility player i obtains if she opts out.

5.2.1   Relationship with Nash's Bargaining Solution

I now show how to apply the asymmetric Nash bargaining solution in bargaining situations with outside options. First, note that it follows from Corollary 5.1 that in the limit, as $\Delta \to 0$, the unique SPE payoff pair $(x_A^*, \pi - x_A^*)$ converges to the unique solution of the following maximization problem

$$\max_{u_A, u_B} (u_A)^{\eta_A} (u_B)^{\eta_B}$$

subject to $(u_A, u_B) \in \Omega$, $u_A \geq 0$ and $u_B \geq 0$, where

$$\Omega = \{(u_A, u_B) : 0 \leq u_A \leq \pi, u_B = \pi - u_A, u_A \geq w_A \text{ and } u_B \geq w_B\}. \quad (5.1)$$

The result stated in the following corollary is an immediate consequence of this observation and Definition 2.3.

Corollary 5.2 (Relationship with Nash's Bargaining Solution). *In the limit, as $\Delta \to 0$, the unique SPE payoff pair of the model with outside options and discounting converges to the asymmetric Nash bargaining solution of the bargaining problem (Ω, d) with $\tau = r_B/(r_A + r_B)$, where Ω is defined in (5.1) and $d = (0, 0)$.*

As has been shown in Chapters 3 and 4, Nash's bargaining solution is applicable when the friction in the bargaining process is arbitrarily small (i.e., Δ is arbitrarily close to zero). The important point to note here concerns, in particular, how the outside option point should be mapped into the objects upon which Nash's bargaining solution is defined. It should be noted that in the bargaining situation considered above, there are two possible ways in which the players fail to reach agreement: through perpetual disagreement and when a player opts out. As such there are two possible payoff pairs associated with a failure to reach agreement, namely, the impasse point $(\mathcal{I}_A, \mathcal{I}_B) = (0, 0)$ and the outside option point (w_A, w_B).

Corollary 5.2 states that the disagreement point in Nash's set-up should be identified with the impasse point of the model with outside options and discounting. The outside option point, on the other hand, constrains the set Ω of possible utility pairs on which Nash's bargaining solution should be defined — by requiring that each utility pair $(u_A, u_B) \in \Omega$ be such that u_i is at least as high as player i's outside option. I thus emphasize that *the outside option point does not affect the disagreement point.*

5.3 Applications

5.3.1 Relationship-Specific Investments

At date 0 an investor (e.g., a Japanese firm) chooses the level of some investment (e.g., the size of a car plant in Birmingham), with the cost of investment incurred at date 0. At a subsequent date 1, when the cost of investment is sunk, the investor and some second (non-investing) party (e.g., a union) bargain over the partition of a cake whose size depends on the chosen investment level.[10]

More precisely, at date 0 player A chooses the level I of some investment, where $I \geq 0$. The cost of investment I^2 is incurred by player A at date 0. Then, at date 1 player A and a second player B bargain over the partition of a cake of size I according to the basic alternating-offers procedure. The (instantaneous) utility player i obtains from a share x_i of the cake is x_i, and the players discount future utilities at a common rate $r > 0$. Applying Corollary 3.1, it follows that the investment level chosen by player A in the (limiting) SPE is 1/4. Therefore, there is under-investment relative to the first best level of investment — where the first best investment level maximizes the total 'surplus' $I - I^2$. The intuition for this classic under-investment result is as follows. For any investment level, in the (limiting) Rubinsteinian SPE the cake is split equally between the two players. Hence, since player A obtains only one-half of the marginal return on her date 0 investment, she under-invests relative to the first best level.

I now extend the model described above by giving player A the option to sell her investment during the negotiation process with player B. Thus, player A has an outside option: she can recover some fraction ν $(0 \leq \nu \leq 1)$ of the cost of investment incurred at date 0, and, hence, her outside option $w_A = \nu I^2$. The parameter ν captures the degree to which the cost of investment is sunk.

From Remark 5.1, one may apply Corollary 5.1 with $w_B = 0$, and it follows that for each investment level I chosen at date 0, the (limiting) SPE payoff to player A at date 1 is[11]

$$P(I,\nu) = \begin{cases} I/2 & \text{if } \nu I^2 \leq I/2 \\ \nu I^2 & \text{if } \nu I^2 > I/2. \end{cases}$$

Therefore, for each $\nu \in [0,1]$, the unique equilibrium investment level $I^*(\nu)$ which maximizes $P(I,\nu) - I^2$ is 1/4. This suggests that the degree of inefficiency of the equilibrium investment is independent of the degree of sunke-

---

[10]It is assumed that it is impossible to write any kind of binding (long-term) contract at date 0. In particular, the payment to be made by the investor to the union for the latter's cooperation in generating the cake cannot be contracted upon at date 0.

[11]It should be noted that if $w_A < I$, then Corollary 5.1 is applicable. However, if $w_A \geq I$ (which is possible), then player A will certainly opt out — because if $w_A \geq I$, then there does not exist a mutually beneficial partition of the cake. Hence, if $w_A \geq I$, then player A's payoff is w_A.

ness in the cost of investment. Contrary to conventional wisdom, the classic under-investment result appears to have little to do with the sunkeness in the cost of investment. Furthermore, this analysis suggests that the classic under-investment result may not be robust to reasonable specifications of the *ex-post* bargaining game when the investor may, in addition, be able to strategically terminate the negotiations in order to sell her investment and recover, if not all, at least some fraction of the cost of investment.

5.3.2 Sovereign Debt Negotiations

Country B, whose wealth consists of one unit of some domestic commodity β, owes a large amount of some foreign commodity α to a foreign bank A. By trading on international markets, B obtains P units of commodity α for its one unit of commodity β, where $P > 1$. The (instantaneous) utility to B is the sum of the quantities of commodities α and β that it consumes. In the absence of any outside interference, B trades the unit of commodity β for P units of the foreign commodity α, and obtains a utility of P. However, if B fails to reach agreement on some payment to A, then the bank seizes a fraction ν of the country's traded output.

The players bargain over the payment x that B makes to A. If agreement is reached on x, then B trades the unit of its domestic commodity β for P units of the foreign commodity α, and the (instantaneous) utilities to A and B are x and $P - x$, respectively. The players discount future utilities at a common rate $r > 0$.

While bargaining B can choose to opt out, and either consume the entire unit of the domestic commodity β or trade without agreement. In the former case her (instantaneous) utility is 1 and A's utility is zero, while in the latter case her utility is $(1 - \nu)P$ and A's utility is νP — since a fraction ν of her commodity is seized by the foreign bank. Hence, the outside option to B is $w_B = \max\{1, (1 - \nu)P\}$. The foreign bank does not have an outside option: it is only B who can choose whether or not to opt out immediately after receiving any offer from A (cf. Remark 5.1, above).

From Remark 5.1, one may apply Corollary 5.1 with $w_A = 0$, and it follows that the (limiting) SPE payment made by the country to the foreign bank is

$$x_A^{**} = \begin{cases} P/2 & \text{if } P \geq 2 \text{ and } \nu \geq 1/2 \\ P - 1 & \text{if } P < 2 \text{ and } \nu \geq 1 - (1/P) \\ \nu P & \text{if } \nu < 1/2 \text{ and } \nu < 1 - (1/P). \end{cases}$$

Thus, if the gains from international trade $P - 1$ are sufficiently large and the fraction ν of traded output that can be seized is relatively high, then B's threat to consume the unit of its domestic commodity β and her threat to trade without agreement, respectively, are not credible. Hence, agreement involves splitting the total (maximal) size of the cake. However, if the gains from international trade are relatively small and the potential cost of seizure νP relatively large, then country B's threat to consume the domestic commodity is credible. Although, in equilibrium, agreement is reached without this threat having to be carried out, it does affect the equilibrium debt payment. Finally, if $\nu < \min\{1/2, 1 - (1/P)\}$, then B's threat to trade in international markets without a debt agreement is credible. Hence, the equilibrium debt payment equals νP.

A major insight obtained from this analysis is as follows. If $\nu \geq \min\{1/2, 1 - (1/P)\}$, then ν has no effect on the equilibrium debt payment. Thus, for example, if ν is currently above this critical value, then further international trade sanctions (as captured by an increase in ν) have no effect on debt payments. In contrast, it is evident that an increase in the terms of country B's international trade (as captured by an increase in P) always increases debt payments.

It seems reasonable to assume that the value of ν can be (strategically) chosen by the foreign bank. Assuming that ν is chosen before the negotiations begin, and that the bank is committed to its choice, the bank will set ν to maximize the equilibrium payment x_A^{**}.

If $P < 2$, then x_A^{**} is strictly increasing in ν over the closed interval $[0, 1 - (1/P)]$, and equals $P - 1$ for any ν in the interval $(1 - (1/P), 1]$. Hence, if $P < 2$, then any $\nu \in [1 - (1/P), 1]$ is optimal, and implies an equilibrium payment of $P - 1$. If, on the other hand, $P \geq 2$, then x_A^{**} is strictly increasing in ν over the closed interval $[0, 1/2]$, and equals $P/2$ for any ν in the interval $(1/2, 1]$. Hence, if $P \geq 2$, then any $\nu \in [1/2, 1]$ is optimal, and implies an equilibrium payment of $P/2$.

Thus, for any P, it is not necessary for the foreign bank to seize all the traded output in order to maximize the payment. However, the equilibrium payment at the optimum does depend on the value of P. If $P < 2$, then at the optimum the bank captures all of the gains from international trade — it cannot, however, extract any greater amount of payment from Country B. On the other hand, if $P \geq 2$, then they split the cake equally. This implies that the equilibrium payment at the optimal value of ν is strictly increasing in P for all $P > 1$.

5.3.3 Bribery and the Control of Crime Revisited

I now reconsider the bargaining situation (studied in Section 2.5.3) between the corruptible policeman P and the criminal C on the assumption that P can choose to opt out and report C to the authorities, and C can similarly choose to opt out and report herself to the authorities. The outside options are $w_P = 0$ and $w_C = \pi(1 - \nu)$, and the players discount future utilities at a common rate $r > 0$.

Applying Corollary 5.1, it follows that the equilibrium bribe paid by the criminal to the policeman is

$$b^* = \begin{cases} \pi/2 & \text{if } \nu \geq 1/2 \\ \nu\pi & \text{if } \nu < 1/2. \end{cases}$$

The intuition for this equilibrium bribe is as follows. If ν is relatively large, then the criminal's outside option is relatively small, and thus (since the policeman's outside option is zero), the outside options have no influence on the equilibrium bribe. Notice that even if ν is so large that the criminal's outside option is negative, the policeman can only obtain a bribe of $\pi/2$. This is because the criminal's outside option does not determine the credibility of the policeman's threat to opt out and report the criminal (cf. Remark 5.2, above). Indeed, her threat to opt out and report the criminal is never credible, since her outside option is zero. On the other hand, if ν is relatively small, then the criminal's outside option is relatively large, and hence the amount of bribe that the policeman can extract is relatively small: the criminal's equilibrium payoff $\pi - b^*$ is equal to her outside option $\pi(1 - \nu)$.

Given this outcome of the bargaining situation, I reconsider the optimal behaviour of the criminal and compare it with that derived in Section 2.5.3.

Her expected utility from stealing the money is $\zeta(\pi - b^*) + (1 - \zeta)\pi$. Since, for any $\zeta \in (0, 1)$ and $\nu > 0$, $b^* \leq \pi/2$, her expected payoff from stealing the money is greater than or equal to $\pi/2$. Therefore, in equilibrium, for any $\zeta \in (0, 1)$ and $\nu > 0$, the criminal steals the money.

This conclusion, that the instruments ζ and ν have no influence whatsoever on the determination of crime, appears to be rather striking — especially because I have not imposed an upper bound on either the penalty rate ν or the potential bribe b. Yet the result is rather intuitive. No matter how large the penalty rate is, the criminal always evades paying the penalty by giving the corruptible policeman a bribe, whose magnitude is at most equal to half the amount of the money that she stole. Thus, even if the criminal expects to be caught for sure, the crime is profitable. In sharp contrast to the result derived in Section 2.5.3, the current result supports the conventional wisdom that, since a penalty is evaded through bribery, society may as well not institute the penalty.

5.4   The Effect of a Risk of Breakdown

I now extend the model studied in Section 5.2 by allowing for a risk of breakdown — in order to explore how this force interacts with the force of strategic opting out. In particular, I investigate the robustness of the outside option principle (cf. Corollary 5.1) and the split-the-difference rule (cf. Section 4.4.2).

The model analysed here involves the following extension of the model studied in Section 5.2. At any point in time if a player chooses to reject any offer and make a counteroffer (and thus, she chooses neither to accept the offer nor to opt out), then immediately with probability p (where $0 < p < 1$) the negotiations break down in disagreement, while with probability $1 - p$ the player gets to make her counteroffer Δ time units later.

For simplicity of exposition, I assume that the players are risk neutral:[12] the (instantaneous) utility to player i from obtaining a share $x_i \in [0, \pi]$ of the cake is $U_i(x_i) = x_i$. As in Sections 5.2 and 4.4, player i's discount rate is $r_i > 0$. The *outside option point* (w_A, w_B) is the instantaneous utility pair obtainable if either player chooses to strategically opt out, and the *breakdown point* (b_A, b_B) is the instantaneous utility pair obtainable if negotiations

---

[12]This assumption is relaxed in Section 5.4.4.

break down randomly. Assume that $w_A < \pi$, $w_B < \pi$, $w_A + w_B < \pi$, $b_A \in [0, \pi)$, $b_B \in [0, \pi)$ and $b_A + b_B < \pi$ — which ensure that mutually beneficial partitions of the cake exist.

5.4.1 The Unique Subgame Perfect Equilibrium

Through a straightforward adaptation of the arguments in Sections 4.4 and 5.2 (that lead to Propositions 4.3 and 5.1), it can be shown that the unique SPE is as described in Proposition 5.1, but with the pair (x_A^*, x_B^*) different from that stated in the proposition. In Proposition 5.2 below I characterize the limit, as $\Delta \to 0$, of the unique SPE. In deriving this limit I assume (as in Section 4.4.1) that when Δ is small, $p = \lambda\Delta$, where $\lambda > 0$ is the rate at which negotiations randomly break down in disagreement.

Notice — see, for example, Section 4.4.1 - - that the limiting (as $\Delta \to 0$) *impasse point*

$$(\mathcal{I}_A, \mathcal{I}_B) = \left(\frac{\lambda b_A}{r_A + \lambda}, \frac{\lambda b_B}{r_B + \lambda} \right). \tag{5.2}$$

Before proceeding, it should be noted that, unlike in the model with only a risk of breakdown studied in Section 4.2, it is no longer true that player i $(i = A, B)$ can guarantee (in the limit as $\Delta \to 0$) a payoff of $\mathcal{I}_i$ — because player j $(j \neq i)$ can permanently disagree by opting out, in which case player i obtains her outside option w_i. However, since player i can guarantee a payoff (in the limit, as $\Delta \to 0$) of w_i by opting out at the first opportunity, the following counterpart to Lemma 4.2 is obtained.

Lemma 5.1. *In any limiting (as $\Delta \to 0$) subgame perfect equilibrium of any subgame of the model with outside options, discounting and a risk of breakdown, player i's payoff is greater than or equal to w_i.*

Proposition 5.2. *The unique limiting (as $\Delta \to 0$) subgame perfect equilibrium of the model with outside options, discounting and a risk of breakdown is as follows:*
- *player A always offers x_A^*, always accepts an offer x_B if and only if $x_B \leq x_B^*$, and always opts out after receiving an offer $x_B > x_B^*$ if and only if $x_A^* \leq w_A$,*

• *player B always offers x_B^*, always accepts an offer x_A if and only if $x_A \leq$ x_A^*, and always opts out after receiving an offer $x_A > x_A^*$ if and only if $x_B^* \leq w_B$, where*

$$(x_A^*, x_B^*) = \begin{cases} (R_A, R_B) & \text{if } w_A \leq R_A \text{ and } w_B \leq R_B \\ (\pi - w_B, w_B) & \text{if } w_A \leq R_A \text{ and } w_B > R_B \\ (w_A, \pi - w_A) & \text{if } w_A > R_A \text{ and } w_B \leq R_B \end{cases}$$

with R_A and R_B defined in (4.17) and (4.18).

The payoff pair (R_A, R_B) is the limiting SPE payoff pair when the players do not have any outside options. Proposition 5.2 may thus be interpreted as a generalization of the outside option principle (cf. Corollary 5.1) in which the reference point is the pair (R_A, R_B) rather than the pair $(\eta_A \pi, \eta_B \pi)$, where the latter is the limiting SPE payoff pair in the basic alternating-offers model (cf. Corollary 3.1).

If both players' outside options are sufficiently unattractive (i.e., $w_A \leq R_A$ and $w_B \leq R_B$), then the equilibrium partition of the cake is determined by the (limiting, as $\Delta \to 0$) impasse point $(\mathcal{I}_A, \mathcal{I}_B)$, which depends on the breakdown point (b_A, b_B) — thus, in this case the outside options are irrelevant to the bargaining outcome. On the other hand, if player i's outside option is sufficiently attractive (i.e., $w_i > R_i$), then the equilibrium partition of the cake is determined solely by her outside option w_i; the breakdown point has no influence whatsoever on the equilibrium partition, no matter how attractive player j's payoff $\mathcal{I}_j$ from perpetual disagreement might be. For example, if $w_i = \mathcal{I}_j = 0.9\pi$ and $w_j = \mathcal{I}_i = 0$, then players i and j respectively obtain 0.9π and 0.1π units of the cake. The message here is that when some player's outside option is sufficiently attractive, then that outside option has the decisive impact on the equilibrium partition of the cake; the (limiting) impasse point is irrelevant to the bargaining outcome. The intuition for this result follows from the fact that player i can opt out immediately (either at $t = 0$ if $i = B$, or at $t = \Delta$ if $i = A$) and obtain her attractive outside option, which thus leaves player j with her unattractive outside option. Player j cannot obtain the attractive payoff of $\mathcal{I}_j$, because that payoff is obtained if and only if the players perpetually disagree.

It is interesting to note that if player i's outside option $w_i > \pi - \mathcal{I}_j$ (which implies that $w_j < \mathcal{I}_j$), then player j's limiting SPE payoff $\pi - w_i$

is strictly less than $\mathcal{I}_j$ (but strictly greater than w_j). Thus, as indicated in Lemma 5.1, player j cannot guarantee a payoff of $\mathcal{I}_j$, because player i would opt out if player j offers $x_j > \pi - w_i$.

5.4.2 Relationship with Nash's Bargaining Solution

It follows from Proposition 5.2 that if $w_B < \pi - \mathcal{I}_A$ and $w_A < \pi - \mathcal{I}_B$, where $(\mathcal{I}_A, \mathcal{I}_B)$ is defined in (5.2), then the limiting SPE payoff pair – which is (x_A^*, x_B^*) as stated in Proposition 5.2 — is the unique solution of the following maximization problem

$$\max_{u_A, u_B} (u_A - d_A)^{\sigma_A} (u_A - d_B)^{1-\sigma_A}$$

subject to $(u_A, u_B) \in \Omega$, $u_A \geq d_A$ and $u_B \geq d_B$, where

$$\Omega = \{(u_A, u_B) : 0 \leq u_A \leq \pi, u_B = \pi - u_A, u_A \geq w_A \text{ and } u_B \geq w_B\} \quad (5.3)$$
$$d = (\mathcal{I}_A, \mathcal{I}_B) \quad (5.4)$$
$$\sigma_A = (r_B + \lambda)/(2\lambda + r_A + r_B). \quad (5.5)$$

This observation implies the result — stated in Corollary 5.3 below — that if $w_B < \pi - \mathcal{I}_A$ and $w_A < \pi - \mathcal{I}_B$, then the limiting SPE payoff pair is identical to the asymmetric Nash bargaining solution of the bargaining problem (Ω, d) with $\tau = \sigma_A$, where Ω, d and σ_A are defined in (5.3)–(5.5).[13]

On the other hand, if either $w_B \geq \pi - \mathcal{I}_A$ or $w_A \geq \pi - \mathcal{I}_B$, then the bargaining problem (Ω, d), where Ω and d are respectively defined in (5.3) and (5.4), does not satisfy Assumption 2.1 — since there does not exist a utility pair $(u_A, u_B) \in \Omega$ such that $u_A > d_A$ and $u_B > d_B$. Hence, if either $w_B \geq \pi - \mathcal{I}_A$ or $w_A \geq \pi - \mathcal{I}_B$, then Nash's bargaining solution is not defined on this bargaining problem.

Corollary 5.3. *If $w_B < \pi - \mathcal{I}_A$ and $w_A < \pi - \mathcal{I}_B$, where $(\mathcal{I}_A, \mathcal{I}_B)$ is defined in (5.2), then the unique SPE payoff pair of the model with outside options, discounting and a risk of breakdown converges, as $\Delta \to 0$, to the asymmetric Nash bargaining solution of the bargaining problem (Ω, d) with $\tau = \sigma_A$, where Ω, d and σ_A are defined in (5.3)–(5.5).*

---

[13]It should be noted that if $w_A \geq b_A$ and $w_B \geq b_B$, then $w_A < \pi - \mathcal{I}_B$ and $w_B < \pi - \mathcal{I}_A$.

Thus, if for each $i = A, B$, $w_i < \pi - \mathcal{I}_j$ ($j \neq i$) — which would be satisfied if, for example, $w_i \geq b_i$ ($i = A, B$) — then Nash's bargaining solution is applicable. The disagreement point in Nash's framework should be identified with the (limiting, as $\Delta \to 0$) impasse point, while the outside option point appropriately constrains the set of possible utility pairs.

Corollary 5.3 combines the insights contained in Corollaries 4.4 and 5.2. It should be noted that in the bargaining situation considered here, there are three possible ways in which the players fail to reach agreement: through perpetual disagreement, when a player opts out and when negotiations break down in a random manner. As such there are three possible payoff pairs associated with a failure to reach agreement, namely, the impasse point $(\mathcal{I}_A, \mathcal{I}_B)$, the outside option point (w_A, w_B) and the breakdown point (b_A, b_B).

Corollary 5.3 states that the disagreement point in Nash's set-up should be identified with the impasse point. The outside option point affects the set Ω of possible utility pairs on which the Nash solution should be defined — by requiring that each utility pair $(u_A, u_B) \in \Omega$ be such that u_i is at least as high as the instantaneous utility player i obtains from her outside option. The breakdown point, on the other hand, affects the disagreement point through its impact on the impasse point.

5.4.3   The Impact of The Manner of Disagreement

I now focus on bargaining situations in which the breakdown point and the outside option point are identical (i.e., $b_A = w_A$ and $b_B = w_B$). Such bargaining situations may be interpreted as follows: there are two possible manners in which negotiations can terminate in disagreement at any point in time — either a player strategically opts out, or in a random manner when, for example, a player gets fed up and 'walks away from the negotiating table' — but the outcomes are independent of the particular manner in which negotiations terminate in disagreement.

Straightforward computation show that in this case, for each i

$$w_i \lesseqgtr R_i \iff \left(\frac{\lambda + r_A + r_B}{r_j + \lambda} \right) b_i + \left(\frac{\lambda}{r_j + \lambda} \right) b_j \lesseqgtr \pi \quad (j \neq i).$$

It thus follows that $w_A \leq R_A$ and $w_B \leq R_B$ if and only if both players' expected discount rates r_A/λ and r_B/λ are sufficiently small. Hence, from Proposition 5.2, it follows that:

Corollary 5.4 (Split-The-Difference Rule). *Assume $b_A = w_A$ and $b_B = w_B$. For any b_A and b_B there exists numbers $\epsilon_A > 0$ and $\epsilon_B > 0$ such that if $r_A/\lambda < \epsilon_A$ and $r_B/\lambda < \epsilon_B$, then in the limit, as $\Delta \to 0$, the SPE payoffs to players A and B are respectively R_A and R_B, where R_A and R_B are defined in (4.17) and (4.18).*

Corollary 5.4 implies that if either the rate λ at which negotiations break down exogenously is sufficiently high or the players discount future utilities sufficiently little (r_A and r_B are sufficiently small), then the limiting SPE partition is captured by the split-the-difference rule. It can be verified that, on the other hand, if the rate λ at which negotiations break down exogenously is sufficiently low, then the limiting SPE partition is captured by the outside option principle. Therefore, the outside option principle (Corollary 5.1) is robust to a small risk of breakdown, while the split-the-difference rule (cf. Section 4.4.2) is robust to strategic opting out if and only if both players' expected discount rates (r_A/λ and r_B/λ) are sufficiently small.

5.4.4 A Generalization

I now extend the model studied in Section 4.6 by allowing for outside options — player i ($i = A, B$) can choose whether or not to opt out after rejecting any offer made by player j ($j \neq i$), where the outside option point is (w_A, w_B). In addition to the modified version of Assumption 3.1 specified in Section 4.6, assume that there exists an agreement $x \in X$ such that $U_A(x) > w_A$ and $U_B(x) > w_B$.

A minor adaptation of the analysis of Sections 3.4.1 and 3.4.4 characterizes the unique SPE of this model. In particular, it follows that $M_A = m_A = V_A^*$ and $M_B = m_B = V_B^*$, where (V_A^*, V_B^*) is the unique pair that satisfies the following two equations[14]

$$V_A^* = \max\{w_B, \phi^{-1}(p_B b_B + (1 - p_B)\delta_B V_B^*)\}$$
$$V_B^* = \max\{w_A, \phi(p_A b_A + (1 - p_A)\delta_A V_A^*)\}.$$

In the following proposition — which can be proven along the lines of the proof of Proposition 5.2 — I characterize the limit of the unique SPE payoff

---

[14]It should be noted that Lemma 5.1 is valid here, and thus, (4.22)–(4.25) are not necessarily valid in this extension to the model studied in Section 4.6, in which players also have access to outside options.

pair, as $\Delta \to 0$.[15]

Proposition 5.3. *In the limit, as $\Delta \to 0$, the unique SPE payoff pair of the general model with outside options, discounting and a risk of breakdown converges to*

$$(u_A^*, u_B^*) = \begin{cases} (\widehat{u}_A, \widehat{u}_B) & \text{if } w_A \leq \widehat{u}_A \text{ and } w_B \leq \widehat{u}_B \\ (\phi^{-1}(w_B), w_B) & \text{if } w_A \leq \widehat{u}_A \text{ and } w_B > \widehat{u}_B \\ (w_A, \phi(w_A)) & \text{if } w_A > \widehat{u}_A \text{ and } w_B \leq \widehat{u}_B, \end{cases}$$

where $(\widehat{u}_A, \widehat{u}_B)$ is the unique solution to the maximization problem stated in Corollary 4.5.

The following corollary to this proposition parallels the result contained in Corollary 5.3.

Corollary 5.5. *If $w_B < \phi(\mathcal{I}_A)$ and $w_A < \phi^{-1}(\mathcal{I}_B)$, then the unique subgame perfect equilibrium payoff pair in the generalized model with outside options, discounting and a risk of breakdown converge, as $\Delta \to 0$, to the asymmetric Nash bargaining solution of the bargaining problem (Ω, d) with $\tau = \sigma_A$, where $\Omega = \{(u_A, u_B) : u_A \in I_A, u_B = \phi(u_A), u_A \geq w_A$ and $u_B \geq w_B\}$ and $d = (\mathcal{I}_A, \mathcal{I}_B)$ — with $\mathcal{I}_i$ $(i = A, B)$ and σ_A defined in Corollary 4.5.[16]*

5.5   Searching for Outside Options

The model studied in Section 5.2 may be interpreted as follows: at least one of the two players has an outside option, which she has to accept or reject within a short interval of time, and, thus, the players bargain on the expectation that within a short interval of time either agreement is struck or outside options are taken up.[17] The models studied in this section, on the other hand, may be interpreted as follows: when negotiations begin

---

[15]Recall that $p \to 0$ as $\Delta \to 0$.

[16]It should be noted that if $w_A \geq b_A$ and $w_B \geq b_B$, then $w_A < \phi^{-1}(\mathcal{I}_B)$ and $w_B < \phi(\mathcal{I}_A)$.

[17]Although the game is expected to end in a short interval of time, for reasons discussed in Section 3.2.4 the infinite-horizon assumption better captures the players' strategic reasoning.

neither player has an outside option, but while bargaining they may search for an outside option, and when a player obtains an outside option she has to immediately accept or reject it.

The issue of how the bargaining process is interlaced with the search process needs to be given careful consideration, as it may significantly affect the outcome of bargaining. I consider the following two alternative manners in which these two processes are interlaced. In the model studied in Section 5.5.1, a player can search for an outside option if and only if she physically leaves the negotiating table — she cannot negotiate and search at the same time. However, in the model studied in Section 5.5.2, a player receives outside options while sitting at the negotiating table. The latter model may be appropriate when, for example, a player has placed an advert in the local newspaper and receives outside options via the telephone, while the former model may be appropriate if a player has to go to an interview before receiving an outside option.

In order to simplify the analysis, set $\pi = 1$ and assume that only a single player, player B, can search for outside options — which are located according to a Poisson process at a rate $\lambda > 0$. Furthermore, assume that an outside option is a fixed share of a unit size cake. The magnitudes of the outside options located by player B are independent and identically distributed with a continuous cumulative probability distribution F, whose support is the closed interval $[0, 1]$.

As a preliminary observation, it is useful to consider the case in which player B searches for an outside option without ever negotiating with player A. From Search Theory, it is known that her optimal sequential search strategy has the reservation level property: that is, she keeps searching until she locates an outside option whose magnitude is greater than or equal to some predetermined value. Let y denote this predetermined value. Therefore, her expected payoff from this search strategy is

$$P(y) = \frac{\int_y^1 x \, dF(x)}{(r/\lambda) + 1 - F(y)}. \tag{5.6}$$

It is straightforward to show that the optimal predetermined value y^* satisfies

$$y^* = P(y^*). \tag{5.7}$$

The following result states some standard properties about P.

Lemma 5.2. *The function P defined in (5.6) has the following properties: (i) it has a unique fixed point, which is the unique global maximum, denoted by y^*, where $0 < y^* < 1$, and (ii) for any $y \in [0, y^*)$, $P(y) > y$, and for any $y \in (y^*, 1]$, $P(y) < y$.*

Proof. In the Appendix.   □

5.5.1   Searching on the Streets

In the model considered here, player B cannot search and bargain at the same time. The move-structure of the bargaining-search game, denoted by $\mathcal{G}$, is as follows. At time 0, player A makes an offer to player B, who either accepts the offer, or rejects the offer and makes a counteroffer ('RMC') Δ time units later, or rejects the offer and withdraws from the negotiating table in order to search for an outside option ('RS'). If player B chooses 'RS', then she keeps searching until she locates an outside option; during this time neither player has any decisions to make. When player B locates an outside option, she either accepts this outside option ('AOO'), or rejects the outside option and continues searching ('CS'), or rejects the outside option, stops searching and returns to the negotiating table ('RNT'), where it takes her Δ time units to make an offer. If player B chooses 'CS', then the move-structure of the subgame that follows is identical to the move-structure of the subgame that follows player B's decision to 'RS'. Denote this move-structure, of a subgame that begins with player B starting to search, by $\mathcal{G}_N$. The move-structure of a subgame beginning with player i's offer, which is denoted by $\mathcal{G}_i$, is independent of history. In $\mathcal{G}_B$, player B makes an offer, which player A either accepts or rejects.

The payoffs to the players are as follows. The game terminates if either the players reach agreement on the partition of the unit size cake, or player B accepts an outside option, or the players perpetually disagree, or player B searches forever. In the latter two cases each player obtains a payoff of zero. If player B accepts an outside option at time $t \geq 0$ whose magnitude is $y \in [0, 1]$, then her payoff is $y \exp(-rt)$, where $r > 0$ denotes the players' common discount rate, and player A's payoff is zero. If the players reach agreement at time $t \geq 0$ with player i obtaining a share $x_i \in [0, 1]$, then player i's payoff is $x_i \exp(-rt)$.

The Unique Subgame Perfect Equilibrium

The analysis involves a minor adaptation of the arguments in Sections 3.2.1 and 3.2.2. In any SPE that satisfies Properties 3.1 and 3.2 player i is indifferent between accepting and not accepting player j's equilibrium offer. That is

$$1 - x_B^* = \delta x_A^* \quad \text{and} \tag{5.8}$$

$$1 - x_A^* = \max\{\delta x_B^*, \mathcal{Z}_B\}, \tag{5.9}$$

where $\mathcal{Z}_B$ is player B's SPE payoff when she begins to search for an outside option, and it is the unique solution to the following equation

$$\mathcal{Z}_B = \int_0^\infty \left[\exp(-rt) \int_0^1 \max\{\delta x_B^*, \mathcal{Z}_B, y\} dF(y) \right] \lambda \exp(-\lambda t) dt.$$

Using (5.6), (5.7) and Lemma 5.2, it follows that[18]

$$\mathcal{Z}_B = \begin{cases} y^* & \text{if } y^* > \delta x_B^* \\ \lambda \left[\delta x_B^* F(\delta x_B^*) + \int_{\delta x_B^*}^1 y dF(y) \right] / (r + \lambda) & \text{if } y^* \leq \delta x_B^*. \end{cases}$$

Equations 5.8 and 5.9 have a unique solution, namely

$$(x_A^*, x_B^*) = \begin{cases} (1/(1+\delta), 1/(1+\delta)) & \text{if } y^* \leq \delta/(1+\delta) \\ (1 - y^*, 1 - \delta(1 - y^*)) & \text{if } y^* > \delta/(1+\delta). \end{cases}$$

It follows that there exists a unique SPE that satisfies Properties 3.1 and 3.2, which is stated below in Proposition 5.4. In fact, I show in the proof to this proposition that there does not exist another subgame perfect equilibrium.

Proposition 5.4. *The unique subgame perfect equilibrium of the bargaining-search game $\mathcal{G}$ is stated in Tables 5.1 and 5.2, depending on whether $y^* \leq \delta/(1+\delta)$ or $y^* > \delta/(1+\delta)$.*

---

[18]The intuition for this is as follows. If $y^* > \delta x_B^*$, then, in equilibrium, player B prefers 'RS' to 'RMC', and 'CS' to 'RNT'. On the other hand, if $y^* \leq \delta x_B^*$, then the reverse is the case: she prefers 'RMC' to 'RS', and 'RNT' to 'CS'. Hence, if $y^* \leq \delta x_B^*$, then, when she receives an outside option, she 'AOO' if its magnitude $y \geq \delta x_B^*$ and 'RNT' if $y < \delta x_B^*$.

Player A	offer	$x_A^* = 1/(1+\delta)$
	accept	$x_B \leq 1/(1+\delta)$
Player B	offer	$x_B^* = 1/(1+\delta)$
	accept	$x_A \leq 1/(1+\delta)$
	'RMC'	$x_A > 1/(1+\delta)$
	'RS'	no
	'AOO'	$y \geq \delta/(1+\delta)$
	'CS'	no
	'RNT'	$y < \delta/(1+\delta)$

Table 5.1: The unique SPE of the bargaining-search game $\mathcal{G}$ if $y^* \leq \delta/(1+\delta)$.

Proof. Using an argument similar to that contained in the proof of Proposition 3.1, it can be shown that if $y^* \leq \delta/(1+\delta)$ (resp., $y^* > \delta/(1+\delta)$), then the pair of strategies stated in Table 5.1 (resp., Table 5.2) is a subgame perfect equilibrium.[19] Through a slight modification of the arguments in Section 3.2.2, it can be shown — which is done in the Appendix — that there does not exist another subgame perfect equilibrium.   □

In the unique SPE there is immediate agreement: player B does not engage in search. In the limit, as $\Delta \to 0$, player B's SPE share $1 - x_A^*$ converges to

$$\begin{cases} 1/2 & \text{if } y^* \leq 1/2 \\ y^* & \text{if } y^* > 1/2. \end{cases}$$

The limiting SPE outcome is identical to the (limiting) SPE in the model studied in Section 5.2 when player B has an outside option $w_B = y^*$ (cf. Remark 5.1). This means that the equilibrium partition in the bargaining-search game $\mathcal{G}$ is identical to the equilibrium partition in the modified version of game $\mathcal{G}$ in which player B does not have the option to return to the negotiating table ('RNT') once she decides to leave it in order to search

---

[19]Notice that this is a *stationary* subgame perfect equilibrium.

	offer	$x_A^* = 1 - y^*$
Player A	accept	$x_B \leq 1 - \delta(1 - y^*)$
	offer	$x_B^* = 1 - \delta(1 - y^*)$
	accept	$x_A \leq 1 - y^*$
	'RMC'	no
Player B	'RS'	$x_A > 1 - y^*$
	'AOO'	$y \geq y^*$
	'CS'	$y < y^*$
	'RNT'	no

Table 5.2: The unique SPE of the bargaining-search game $\mathcal{G}$ if $y^* > \delta/(1 + \delta)$.

for outside options — which suggests that the option to allow player B to 'RNT' is redundant.

5.5.2 Searching while Bargaining

The model studied here, in which player B can search while sitting at the negotiating table, is a simple extension of the basic alternating-offers model studied in Section 3.2. The extension is as follows. At any time $t\Delta$ ($t = 0, 2, 4, \ldots$ and $\Delta > 0$) immediately after player B rejects player A's offer, with probability $\lambda\Delta < 1$ she receives an outside option $y \in [0, 1]$, which she either accepts ('AOO') or rejects ('RMC').[20] With probability $1 - \lambda\Delta$, on the other hand, she does not receive an outside option, and, hence, she makes a counteroffer at time $(t + 1)\Delta$. Denote this bargaining-search game by $\mathcal{W}$. The focus is on arbitrarily small values of Δ.

---

[20]Unlike in the otherwise similar model studied in Section 4.5, the negotiations do not break down in a random manner. Although the opportunity to terminate negotiations is a random event, player B *strategically* decides whether or not to terminate negotiations.

The Unique Subgame Perfect Equilibrium

The analysis involves a minor adaptation of the arguments in Sections 3.2.1 and 3.2.2. In any SPE that satisfies Properties 3.1 and 3.2

$$1 - x_B^* = \delta x_A^* \quad \text{and} \tag{5.10}$$

$$1 - x_A^* = (1 - \lambda\Delta)\delta x_B^* + \lambda\Delta \int_0^1 \max\{\delta x_B^*, y\}dF(y). \tag{5.11}$$

I now show that these equations have a unique solution. After substituting for x_A^* in (5.10) using (5.11), and rearranging, it follows that

$$x_B^* \left[(1 - \delta^2) + \delta^2\lambda\Delta\left[1 - F(\delta x_B^*)\right] \right] - (1 - \delta) - \delta\lambda\Delta \int_{\delta x_B^*}^1 ydF(y) = 0.$$

For each x_B^* and Δ, let $L(x_B^*, \Delta)$ be the LHS of this equation. For any $r > 0$ and $\lambda > 0$, there exists a $\bar{\Delta} > 0$ such that for any $\Delta \in (0, \bar{\Delta})$, $L(1, \Delta) > 0$. Furthermore, $L(0, \Delta) < 0$, the derivative of L w.r.t. x_B^* is strictly positive, and L is continuous in x_B^*. Hence, for any $\Delta > 0$ but sufficiently small, (5.10) and (5.11) have a unique solution in x_A^* and x_B^*. This means that there exists at most a unique SPE that satisfies Properties 3.1 and 3.2, which is stated below in Proposition 5.5. Through a slight modification of the arguments in the proof of Proposition 3.1 and Section 3.2.2, it can be shown that this is the unique SPE. A key modification in the arguments in Section 3.2.2 involves replacing the terms $\delta_B m_B$ and $\delta_B M_B$ respectively with

$$(1 - \lambda\Delta)\delta m_B + \lambda\Delta \int_0^1 \max\{\delta m_B, y\}dF(y) \quad \text{and}$$

$$(1 - \lambda\Delta)\delta M_B + \lambda\Delta \int_0^1 \max\{\delta M_B, y\}dF(y)$$

— which respectively are the infimum and supremum of the set of SPE payoffs to player B if she rejects any offer. It then follows from the uniqueness of the solution to equations 5.10 and 5.11 that $M_A = m_A = x_A^*$ and $M_B = m_B = x_B^*$.

Proposition 5.5. *Assume that $\Delta > 0$ but sufficiently small, and let x_A^* and x_B^* be the unique solution to (5.10) and (5.11). The unique subgame perfect equilibrium of the bargaining-search game $\mathcal{W}$ is as follows:*

- *player A always offers x_A^* and always accepts an offer x_B if and only if $x_B \leq x_B^*$,*
- *player B always offers x_B^*, always accepts an offer x_A if and only if $x_A \leq x_A^*$, and always 'AOO' y if and only if $y \geq \delta x_B^*$.*

In equilibrium agreement is reached immediately, at time 0. In order to provide a relatively transparent comparison between player B's SPE shares in the two bargaining-search games, $\mathcal{G}$ and $\mathcal{W}$, I first characterize player B's limiting SPE share in game $\mathcal{W}$ as $\Delta \to 0$.

Corollary 5.6. *In the limit as $\Delta \to 0$, the share $1 - x_A^*$ to player B in the unique SPE of the bargaining-search game $\mathcal{W}$ converges to $\hat{x}_B$, where $\hat{x}_B$ is the unique solution to*

$$\hat{x}_B = \frac{(r/\lambda) + \int_{\hat{x}_B}^{1} y dF(y)}{(2r/\lambda) + [1 - F(\hat{x}_B)]}.$$

Proof. For any $\Delta > 0$ but sufficiently small, $L(x_B^*(\Delta), \Delta) = 0$. Hence

$$\lim_{\Delta \to 0} \frac{L(x_B^*(\Delta), \Delta)}{\Delta}$$

is derived by applying L'Hopital's Rule. Thus, after differentiating L w.r.t. Δ and then taking the limit, it follows that, as $\Delta \to 0$, x_B^* converges to $\hat{x}_B$, where $\hat{x}_B$ is stated in the corollary. The desired result follows immediately, because in the limit as $\Delta \to 0$, player B's SPE share $1 - x_A^*$ and x_B^* converge to the same number. $\qquad\square$

Unlike in the (limiting) SPE of the bargaining-search game $\mathcal{G}$, the parameters of the search process influence the (limiting) SPE partition of the game $\mathcal{W}$ even when $y^* \leq 1/2$. Indeed, player B's (limiting) SPE share $\hat{x}_B$ may be written as follows: $\hat{x}_B = [\gamma + P(\hat{x}_B)]/(\gamma + 1)$, where P is defined in (5.6) and $\gamma = r/[r + \lambda(1 - F(\hat{x}_B))]$. Since $\gamma > 0$ and $0 < P(\hat{x}_B) < 1$, it follows by Lemma 5.2 that $\hat{x}_B > \max\{y^*, 1/2\}$. Hence, for any values of the parameters, player B obtains a share that strictly exceeds both the expected payoff y^* that she obtains if she searches according to her optimal search strategy and the (limiting) Rubinsteinian SPE share that she obtains in the absence of any outside options — which is equal to one-half, because the players have a common discount rate. Moreover, player B's (limiting) SPE share in the bargaining-search game W is strictly greater than her (limiting) SPE share in the bargaining-search game G.

In contrast to game G, in which player B has to physically leave the negotiating table before any outside options are obtained, in game W outside options arrive during the offer-counteroffer process, and the results above suggest that the latter provides a relatively greater positive effect on player B's bargaining power. The results obtained here may be illustrated with reference to the academic job market. It is typically the case that if you happen to be relatively young and/or not terribly good then you have to apply for professorships and go to interviews in order to receive outside offers, while if you are pretty desirable then you receive outside offers without such efforts. The results derived above thus suggest an explanation for the differences in academics' pay in terms of academic merit.

5.6   The Role of the Communication Technology

In the model studied in Section 5.2 player i can opt out after receiving player j's offer, but not after her offer is rejected by player j. This is plausible if, for example, the players are bargaining face-to-face, because player j can always make an offer when player i is about to opt out, as the channel of communication remains open until player i has physically left the negotiating table. If, on the other hand, the players are bargaining via a telephone (or a computer), then player i may opt out at any point in the negotiation process, since the channel of communication is closed the moment the telephone is hung (or the computer is switched off); in particular, player i can opt out immediately after her offer is rejected.

In this section I study a model with outside options and in which bargaining takes place via a telephone/computer. In order to derive the main consequence of this alternative communication technology in a simple manner, I adopt the following three assumptions: (i) player A cannot opt out, (ii) player B can choose whether or not to opt out only immediately after her offer is rejected, and (iii) player A's payoff when player B opts out is zero.

The model, therefore, that I analyse below involves the following extension of the basic alternating-offers model studied in Section 3.2. Immediately after player A rejects any offer made by player B, player B has to decide whether or not to opt out. If she opts out then negotiations terminate in disagreement, and if she does not opt out then player A makes her counteroffer Δ time units later. If player B opts out at time $t\Delta$ (where t is odd), then the payoffs to players A and B respectively are 0 and $w_B \exp(-r_B t\Delta)$, where $w_B < \pi$.

In order to facilitate the discussion of the role of the communication technology, I refer to the bargaining model with outside options analysed in this section as the telephone game, and the model studied in Section 5.2 as the face-to-face game.[21]

5.6.1 Equilibria in the Telephone Game

I begin by characterizing the subgame perfect equilibria that satisfy Properties 3.1 and 3.2 — the arguments involve a straightforward adaptation of the arguments in Section 3.2.1. In any SPE that satisfies Properties 3.1 and 3.2 player i is indifferent between accepting and rejecting player j's equilibrium offer. That is

$$\pi - x_A^* = \delta_B x_B^* \quad \text{and}$$

$$\pi - x_B^* = \begin{cases} 0 & \text{if } w_B > \delta_B(\pi - x_A^*) \\ \delta_A x_A^* & \text{if } w_B < \delta_B(\pi - x_A^*). \end{cases}$$

Furthermore, since in any SPE that satisfies Properties 3.1 and 3.2 player B either always opts out or always does not opt out, if $w_B = \delta_B(\pi - x_A^*)$, then $\pi - x_B^* = 0$ (resp., $\pi - x_B^* = \delta_A x_A^*$) if player B always opts out (resp., if player B always does not opt out). Solving these equations for x_A^* and x_B^*, it follows that if either $w_B \leq \delta_B^2 \mu_B \pi$ or $w_B \geq \delta_B^2 \pi$ (where μ_B is defined in Proposition 5.1), then these two equations have a unique solution in x_A^* and x_B^* — which means that, for such values of w_B, there exists at most a unique SPE that satisfies Properties 3.1 and 3.2. However, if $\delta_B^2 \mu_B \pi < w_B < \delta_B^2 \pi$, then these two equations do not have a solution in x_A^* and x_B^* — which

---

[21]It may be argued that whatever is the mode of communication (face-to-face or via a telephone/computer), player i can only opt out after rejecting player j's offer — and she cannot opt out after player j rejects her offer — because a 'rejection' can take the form of a counteroffer: that is, after player B makes her offer, player A either accepts it or makes a counteroffer. Although this kind of argument has merit, the players may *perceive* otherwise: they may perceive that offers need to be rejected before counteroffers are made. Hence, the telephone game may have some relevance.

means that, for such values of w_B, there does not exist a SPE that satisfies Properties 3.1 and 3.2.

The following proposition characterizes the unique SPE when either $w_B < \delta_B^2 \mu_B \pi$ or $w_B > \delta_B^2 \pi$.

Proposition 5.6. *If either $w_B < \delta_B^2 \mu_B \pi$ or $w_B > \delta_B^2 \pi$, then the unique subgame perfect equilibrium of the telephone game is as follows:*
- *player A always offers x_A^* and always accepts an offer x_B if and only if $x_B \leq x_B^*$,*
- *player B always offers x_B^*, always accepts an offer x_A if and only if $x_A \leq x_A^*$, and always opts out if $w_B > \delta_B^2 \pi$ and always does not opt out if $w_B < \delta_B^2 \mu_B \pi$, where*

$$(x_A^*, x_B^*) = \begin{cases} (\mu_A \pi, \mu_B \pi) & \text{if } w_B < \delta_B^2 \mu_B \pi \\ ((1 - \delta_B)\pi, \pi) & \text{if } w_B > \delta_B^2 \pi \end{cases}$$

with μ_A and μ_B defined in Proposition 5.1.

Proof. Assume that either $w_B < \delta_B^2 \mu_B \pi$ or $w_B > \delta_B^2 \pi$. It has been shown above that there exists at most a unique SPE that satisfies Properties 3.1 and 3.2, which is stated in the proposition. Through a minor modification of the proof of Proposition 3.1, it can be verified that the pair of strategies stated in the proposition is a subgame perfect equilibrium. I now establish, through a straightforward adaptation of the arguments in Section 3.2.2, that there does not exist another SPE.

First suppose that $w_B < \delta_B n_B$, where n_B is the infimum of the set of SPE payoffs to player B in any subgame beginning with player A's offer. This implies that in any SPE player B always does not opt out. It follows trivially that Lemmas 3.1–3.4 are valid (because it is 'as if' the players are bargaining over the partition of the cake in the absence of any outside options). Hence, the desired result is obtained, because $n_B = \pi - M_B = \delta_B \mu_B \pi$.

Now suppose $w_B > \delta_B N_B$, where N_B is the supremum of the set of SPE payoffs to player B in any subgame beginning with player A's offer. This implies that in any SPE player B always opts out, which, in turn, implies that in any SPE player A always accepts any offer. Hence, $m_B = M_B = \pi$. Since it is trivial to verify that part (i)'s of Lemmas 3.1–3.4 are valid, the desired result is obtained, because $N_B = \pi - m_B = \delta_B \pi$. $\square$

I now show, by construction, that if $\delta_B^2 \mu_B \pi \leq w_B \leq \delta_B^2 \pi$, then there exists many (indeed, a continuum) of subgame perfect equilibria in the telephone game. The key idea involves the construction of two 'extremal' subgame perfect equilibria: these equilibria respectively give players A and B their worst SPE payoffs.

		state s_A	state s_B
Player A	offer	x_A^*	x_A^{**}
	accept	$x_B \leq x_B^*$	$x_B \leq x_B^{**}$
Player B	offer	x_B^*	x_B^{**}
	accept	$x_A \leq x_A^*$	$x_A \leq x_A^{**}$
	opts out	no	yes
	transitions	switch to state s_B if player A makes an offer $x_A > x_A^*$	switch to state s_A if player B does not opt out

Table 5.3: A (non-stationary) SPE in the telephone game when $\delta_B^2 \mu_B \pi \leq w_B \leq \delta_B^2 \pi$, where $x_A^* = \pi - (w_B/\delta_B)$, $x_A^{**} = (1 - \delta_B)\pi$, $x_B^* = \pi - \delta_A x_A^*$ and $x_B^{**} = \pi$.

Table 5.3 describes the two extremal SPE, depending on which of the two *states* is the initial state.[22] If play begins in state s_A, then the SPE payoffs to players A and B (in the limit as $\Delta \to 0$) are $\pi - w_B$ and w_B, respectively — which gives player B her worst SPE payoff.[23] On the other hand, if play begins in state s_B, then the limiting SPE payoffs to players A and B are 0 and π, respectively — which gives player A her worst SPE payoff.

Using the *One-Shot Deviation* property, it can be verified that the strat-

---

[22]It is convenient to describe (simple) non-stationary subgame perfect equilibria using such a table. A player's equilibrium action at any point in the game depends on the *state* that is prevailing at that point. Moreover, a *transition rule* dictates when, and if, the state changes. For further explanation of this kind of table, see Osborne and Rubinstein (1990, Section 3.5).

[23]Since player B can opt out at time Δ after player A rejects her offer, her payoff in any limiting SPE, as $\Delta \to 0$, is greater than or equal to w_B.

egy pair described in Table 5.3 is a subgame perfect equilibrium.[24] I shall show here that in state s_B it is optimal for player B to opt out. Consider a decision node where player B decides whether or not to opt out, and suppose that the state is s_B. If player B plays according to the specified strategy and opts out, then her payoff is w_B. By the *One-Shot Deviation* property, this behaviour is optimal if and only if she does not gain by deviating at that decision node and then conforming to the strategy specified in Table 5.3 thereafter. Suppose she deviates and does not opt out, but thereafter play proceeds according to the strategy pair described in Table 5.3. Since the state immediately switches to s_A (before player A makes her offer), player B's payoff from this one-shot deviation is $\delta_B(\pi - x_A^*) = w_B$, and thus this one-shot deviation is not profitable. I shall also verify that whenever player A has to make an offer and the state is s_A, she does not gain from a one-shot deviation of making an offer $x_A > x_A^*$. By making the proposed equilibrium offer, her payoff is $\pi - (w_B/\delta_B)$. Suppose she makes a one-shot deviation by instead offering $x_A > x_A^*$, and thereafter play proceeds according to the strategy pair described in Table 5.3. This deviation induces the state to switch to s_B. Since the hypothesis $w_B \leq \delta_B^2 \pi$ implies that $\pi - (w_B/\delta_B) \geq (1 - \delta_B)\pi$, player B rejects the offer $x_A > \pi - (w_B/\delta_B)$, and thus, player A's payoff from the proposed one-shot deviation is 0.

It is now straightforward to construct a continuum of subgame perfect equilibria, based on the idea that a path of play is supported as a SPE path of play by the credible threat that play moves to one of the extremal equilibria, depending on which player needs to be 'punished' for having deviated from this path.[25]

For each γ, where $(1 - \delta_B)\pi \leq \gamma \leq \pi - (w_B/\delta_B)$, the pair of strategies stated in Table 5.4 is a SPE, and the SPE payoffs to players A and B are respectively γ and $\pi - \gamma$. The SPE described in Table 5.4 is based on the

---

[24]The *One-Shot Deviation* property, which is also known by other terms, is essentially the principle of optimality for discounted dynamic programming. A pair of strategies is a SPE if and only if each player's strategy is immune to profitable *one-shot* (unilateral) deviations. For a precise statement of this result, see, for example: Fudenberg and Tirole (1991, Theorem 4.2) — who call it the 'one-stage deviation principle'; Osborne and Rubinstein (1994, Exercise 123.1) — who call it the 'one deviation property'; and Hendon, Jacobsen and Sloth (1996) — who call it the 'one-shot-deviation principle'.

[25]This idea also lies at the heart of the theory of infinitely repeated games; for an elegant discussion, see Abreu (1988).

		intial state γ
Player A	offer	$x_A^{***} = \gamma$
	accept	—
Player B	offer	—
	accept	$x_A \leq \gamma$
	opts out	—
	transitions	(i) if player A offers $x_A > \gamma$, then play switches to the SPE stated in Table 5.3 *beginning in state* s_B, and (ii) if player B rejects an offer $x_A \leq \gamma$, then play switches to the SPE stated in Table 5.3 *beginning in state* s_A

Table 5.4: For each γ such that $(1 - \delta_B)\pi \leq \gamma \leq \pi - (w_B/\delta_B)$, I state here a (non-stationary) SPE in the telephone game when $\delta_B^2 \mu_B \pi \leq w_B \leq \delta_B^2 \pi$.

simple idea mentioned above: if player i does not conform to the proposed equilibrium path, then she is immediately punished by moving play to the extremal SPE in which she obtains her worst SPE payoff. I leave it for the reader to verify that neither player has any incentive to conduct a one-shot deviation from any action when play is in the initial state γ. I have thus established the following results.

Proposition 5.7. *If $\delta_B^2 \mu_B \pi \leq w_B \leq \delta_B^2 \pi$, then, for any partition $(\gamma, \pi - \gamma)$, where $(1 - \delta_B)\pi \leq \gamma \leq \pi - (w_B/\delta_B)$, there exists a SPE in the telephone game such that in equilibrium the players reach agreement at time 0 on this partition.*

Corollary 5.7 (Telephone Bargaining). *In the limit, as $\Delta \to 0$, if $0 \leq w_B < \eta_B \pi$ (where η_B is defined in Corollary 3.1) then player B's SPE payoff is uniquely defined and equals $\eta_B \pi$, and if $\eta_B \pi \leq w_B$, then any number in the closed interval $[w_B, \pi]$ can be supported as a SPE payoff to player B.*

A key message that emerges from the above analysis is that the impact of a player's outside option when the players are bargaining via a telephone may be relatively more potent than when they are bargaining face-to-face. The intuition for this insight comes from the observation that, although the credibility of the threat to opt out in the two models is ensured under identical circumstances (i.e., only when the value of the outside option is sufficiently large), the credible threat has a relatively more potent effect in the telephone game, since (by being able to terminate communications instantly) a player can effectively (in equilibrium) make a 'take-it-or-leave-it' offer. Notice the other important insight obtained, which is robust to the specification of the technology of communication, that the outside option is useless if its value is sufficiently small (since the threat to opt out is, under such conditions, not credible).

5.6.2   An Application to Relationship-Specific Investments

I reconsider the problem studied in Section 5.3.1 by modelling the date 1 bargaining situation using the telephone game.

Applying Corollary 5.7, it follows that for each investment level $I \geq 0$ chosen at date 0, if $I/2 > \nu I^2$ then the unique (limiting) SPE payoff to player A is $I/2$, and if $I/2 \leq \nu I^2 < I$ then for every $k \in [\nu I^2, I]$ there exists a (limiting) SPE such that the payoff to player A is k. Furthermore, if $I \leq \nu I^2$ then (since gains to trade do not exist) player A takes up her outside option and her payoff is νI^2.

In characterizing the equilibrium investment, I assume that for any I and ν such that $I/2 \leq \nu I^2 < I$, player A's equilibrium payoff at date 1 bargaining is equal to I. I select this particular SPE payoff because it gives player A the full benefit from her investment, and thus, the equilibrium investment level chosen at date 0 should possess the least amount of inefficiency.

Hence, for each $\nu \in [0, 1]$, the unique equilibrium investment level $I^T(\nu)$ maximizes $P^T(I, \nu) - I^2$, where

$$P^T(I, \nu) = \begin{cases} I/2 & \text{if } \nu I^2 < I/2 \\ I & \text{if } I/2 \leq \nu I^2 < I \\ \nu I^2 & \text{if } \nu I^2 \geq I. \end{cases}$$

It is straightforward to show that, for each $\nu \in [0, 1]$, the unique limiting (as

$\Delta \to 0$) SPE investment level is

$$I^T(\nu) = \begin{cases} 1/4 & \text{if } 0 \le \nu \le 4 - \sqrt{12} \\ 1/(2\nu) & \text{if } 4 - \sqrt{12} < \nu \le 1. \end{cases}$$

I now compare this equilibrium investment level with the first best investment level and with the investment level chosen when the date 1 bargaining takes place according to the face-to-face game — the latter is $I^F(\nu) = 1/4$ for any $\nu \in [0, 1]$ (cf. Section 5.3.1) and the former is $I^* = 1/2$.

If $\nu \le 4 - \sqrt{12}$ then $I^T(\nu) = I^F(\nu) < I^*$ — for such values of ν, in both games there is under-investment relative to the first best. However, if $4 - \sqrt{12} \le \nu < 1$ then $I^T(\nu) > I^* > I^F(\nu)$ — for such values of ν, there is under-investment in the face-to-face game, and over-investment in the telephone game. Finally, if $\nu = 1$ then $I^T(\nu) = I^* > I^F(\nu)$ — investment in the telephone game is at the first best level, while in the face-to-face game there is under-investment.

One main insight thus obtained here is that under some circumstances, investment may be above (rather than below) the efficient level.

5.6.3 Rubinstein Bargaining with Quit Options

Consider the basic alternating-offers model studied in Section 3.2, in which neither player has access to outside options. It is plausible to assume that each player does have the option to quit bargaining at any point in the negotiation process (and, thus, give up any attempt to reach agreement). Of course, in that eventuality each player's payoff is zero. I ignored this issue in Section 3.2 on the implicit assumption that a rational player would never quit bargaining; she would prefer to get some agreement to no agreement. If the players are bargaining face-to-face, and a player can quit only after receiving an offer from her opponent, then this implicit assumption is justified. However, as I now show, if the players are bargaining via a telephone (and a player can quit immediately after her offer is rejected), then the option to quit may have a significant impact on the set of subgame perfect equilibria.

Table 5.5 describes two extremal SPE: if play begins in state s_i, then (in the limit as $\Delta \to 0$) player i obtains the whole cake. Notice that in each of these extremal SPE the first offer (made by player A) is accepted. In equilibrium, neither player actually quits. However, if each player has

		state s_A	state s_B
	offer	$x_A^* = \pi$	$x_A^* = (1 - \delta_B)\pi$
Player A	accept	$x_B \le (1 - \delta_A)\pi$	$x_B \le \pi$
	opts out	yes	no
	offer	$x_B^* = (1 - \delta_A)\pi$	$x_B^* = \pi$
Player B	accept	$x_A \le \pi$	$x_A \le (1 - \delta_B)\pi$
	opts out	no	yes
	transitions	switch to state s_B if player A does not opt out	switch to state s_A if player B does not opt out

Table 5.5: Two extremal SPE in Rubinstein's model with Quit Options.

the option to quit immediately after her offer is rejected, then this pair of strategies is a SPE.[26] Notice that in state s_i player i plans to quit and receive a payoff of zero. She does not find it profitable not to quit, because if she does deviate then the state immediately switches to s_j ($j \ne i$), where player j immediately obtains the whole cake — which is because player j plans to quit in state s_j for exactly the same reason. Thus, in the telephone game, player A plans to quit if and only if player B plans to quit. Of course, since a player plans to quit, she can obtain the whole cake; in equilibrium her offer becomes a 'take-it-or-leave-it' offer. One may interpret these extremal SPE as follows. A player quits because she knows (or correctly expects) that if she does not quit, then next period her opponent gives her no share of the cake as her opponent quits. Her opponent plans to quit for exactly the same reason. Using these extremal SPE it is trivial to construct a continuum of SPE (as I did above).

---

[26]Notice that this pair of strategies is *not* a SPE in the face-to-face game, where each player can only choose whether or not to quit immediately after receiving an offer.

5.7   Appendix: Proofs

Proof of Lemma 5.2

Differentiating P w.r.t. y, it follows that the set of turning points of P is equal to the set of fixed points of P. That is

$$S \equiv \{y : P'(y) = 0\} = \{y : P(y) = y\}. \tag{5.12}$$

Brouwer's fixed point theorem implies that S is non-empty. Since $P(0) > 0$ and P is continuous, $\underline{s} > 0$, where $\underline{s}$ is the infimum of S. I now establish that

$$\forall y \in [0, \underline{s}), P'(y) > 0. \tag{5.13}$$

Suppose, to the contrary, that there exists a $y \in [0, \underline{s})$ such that $P'(y) \leq 0$. If $P'(y) = 0$, then $y \in S$, which contradicts the hypothesis that $y < \underline{s}$. If $P'(y) < 0$, then (since $P'(0) > 0$) there exists an x, where $0 < x < y$, such that $P'(x) = 0$, which is a contradiction, since $x < \underline{s}$. I now establish that

$$\forall y > \underline{s}, y \geq P(y). \tag{5.14}$$

Suppose, to the contrary, that there exists a $y > \underline{s}$ such that $y < P(y)$. This implies that there exists an x where $\underline{s} < x < y$ such that $P(x) = x$ and $P'(x) > 1$, which contradicts (5.12). I now establish that

$$\underline{s} \text{ is a local maximum.} \tag{5.15}$$

Suppose, to the contrary, that $\underline{s}$ is a point of inflexion.[27] Since $P(\underline{s}) > 0$ and $P(1) = 0$, there exists a y, where $y > \underline{s}$, such that y is a local maximum. Hence, using (5.12), there exists an $\epsilon > 0$ such that for any $x \in (y - \epsilon, y)$, $P(x) > x$. This contradicts (5.14) since $y > \underline{s}$. I now establish that

$$\forall y > \underline{s}, P'(y) < 0. \tag{5.16}$$

I argue by contradiction. First, suppose that there exists a $y > \underline{s}$ such that $P'(y) = 0$. From (5.15), it follows that there exists an x, where $\underline{s} < x < y$, such that $P'(x) = 0$ and $P(x) \neq x$, which contradicts (5.12). By a similar argument a contradiction is obtained if there exists a $y > \underline{s}$ such that $P'(y) > 0$. The lemma follows immediately by noting that $P(0) > 0$ and $P(1) = 0$, and by using (5.12), (5.13), (5.15) and (5.16).

---

[27] By (5.13), $\underline{s}$ cannot be a local minimum.

Proof of Proposition 5.4

Let H_B and h_B respectively be the supremum and the infimum of the set of SPE payoffs to player B in any subgame with move-structure $\mathcal{G}_N$. Through a straightforward adaptation of the arguments in Section 3.2.2, it follows that

$$1 - M_B = \delta m_A \tag{5.17}$$

$$1 - m_B = \delta M_A \tag{5.18}$$

$$1 - M_A = \max\{\delta m_B, h_B\} \tag{5.19}$$

$$1 - m_A = \max\{\delta M_B, H_B\} \tag{5.20}$$

$$H_B = \int_0^\infty \left[\exp(-rt) \int_0^1 \max\{\delta M_B, H_B, y\} dF(y) \right] \lambda \exp(-\lambda t) dt \tag{5.21}$$

$$h_B = \int_0^\infty \left[\exp(-rt) \int_0^1 \max\{\delta m_B, h_B, y\} dF(y) \right] \lambda \exp(-\lambda t) dt. \tag{5.22}$$

I now show that these equations have a unique solution, in which $M_A = m_A = x_A^*$, $M_B = m_B = x_B^*$ and $H_B = h_B = \mathcal{Z}_B$.

First suppose that $H_B > \delta M_B$ and $h_B > \delta m_B$. Thus, from (5.21), it follows that

$$H_B = \frac{\int_{H_B}^1 y dF(y)}{(r/\lambda) + 1 - F(H_B)}.$$

Hence, from Lemma 5.2, it follows that $H_B = y^*$. Similarly, $h_B = y^*$, and hence, from (5.19) and (5.20), it follows that $M_A = m_A = 1 - y^*$, and thus, from (5.17) and (5.18), it follows that $M_B = m_B = 1 - \delta(1 - y^*)$. This is the unique solution if the hypothesis holds — that is, if $y^* > \delta/(1 + \delta)$.

Now suppose that $H_B \leq \delta M_B$ and $h_B \leq \delta m_B$. Thus, from (5.17)–(5.20), it follows that $M_A = m_A = M_B = m_B = 1/(1 + \delta)$. From (5.21), I thus obtain that

$$H_B = \frac{\lambda}{r + \lambda} \left[\beta F(\beta) + \int_\beta^1 y dF(y) \right]$$

where $\beta = \delta/(1+\delta)$. Similarly, $h_B = H_B$. This is the unique solution if the hypothesis holds — that is, if $H_B \leq \beta$. Since $H(\beta) \leq \beta$ if and only if $P(\beta) \leq \beta$, it follows from Lemma 5.2 (ii) that $H_B \leq \beta$ if and only if $y^* \leq \beta$.

Finally, it is easy to verify that contradictions are obtained from the remaining possible hypotheses, namely, (i) $H_B > \delta M_B$ and $h_B \leq \delta m_B$, and (ii) $H_B \leq \delta M_B$ and $h_B > \delta m_B$. Having thus established the uniqueness of the SPE payoffs, it is straightforward to show that the SPE stated in the proposition is the unique SPE.

5.8   Notes

The basic ideas and models studied in Sections 5.2 and 5.6 are respectively due to Binmore (1985) and Shaked (1994). The specific observation made in Section 5.6.3 is due to Ponsati and Sakovics (1998).

The application to relationship-specific investments studied in Sections 5.3.1 and 5.6.2 are simplified versions of that studied in Muthoo (1998), while the application to sovereign debt negotiations studied in Section 5.3.2 is a simplified version of the model studied in Bulow and Rogoff (1989). The models studied in Sections 5.5.1 and 5.5.2 are respectively based upon Muthoo (1995c) and Wolinsky (1987).

6   Inside Options

6.1   Introduction

Consider the basic exchange situation in which a seller and a buyer are bargaining over the price at which the seller sells an indivisible object (such as a house) to the buyer. If agreement is reached on price p, then the seller's payoff is p and the buyer's payoff is $\pi - p$. Furthermore, the seller obtains utility at rate g_S while the object is in her possession, where $g_S \geq 0$; thus, for $\Delta > 0$ but small, she obtains a payoff of $g_S\Delta$ if she owns the house for Δ units of time. Given her discount rate $r_S > 0$, this means that if she keeps possession of the house forever, then her payoff is g_S/r_S, which is assumed to be less than π — for otherwise gains from trade do not exist. The payoff that the seller obtains while the parties *temporarily* disagree is her *inside option* — which equals $g_S[1 - \exp(-r_S\Delta)]/r_S$ if they disagree for Δ units of time. In contrast, her *outside option* is the payoff she obtains if she chooses to *permanently* stop bargaining, and chooses not to reach agreement with the buyer; for example, this could be the price p^* (where $p^* > g_S/r_S$) that she obtains by selling the house to some other buyer.

A main objective of this chapter is to explore the role of inside options on the bargaining outcome. In the next section I study a simple extension to Rubinstein's bargaining model in which both players have inside options. It is shown that a player's bargaining power is strictly increasing in her inside option, and strictly decreasing in her opponent's inside option. Furthermore, it is shown that (under some conditions) the equilibrium outcome is identical to an asymmetric Nash bargaining solution of an appropriately defined bargaining problem, with the disagreement point in Nash's framework being identified with the impasse point. It will be shown that the players' inside options influence the impasse point. Section 6.3 contains two applications — one is to takeovers in a duopoly, and the other is to sovereign debt renegotiations.

In Section 6.4 I extend the model studied in Section 6.2 in order to explore the relative impacts of inside options, outside options and a risk of breakdown. If the players' outside options are sufficiently unattractive, then the equilibrium outcome is identical to the equilibrium outcome in the model studied in Section 6.2 when the players do not have outside options — thus, in this case the outside options are irrelevant to the equilibrium outcome. On the other hand, if one player's outside option is sufficiently attractive, then her equilibrium payoff equals her outside option, while her opponent obtains the remaining surplus — thus, in this case the inside options are irrelevant to the bargaining outcome. Section 6.5 contains an application to intrafamily allocation.

In the models of Sections 6.2 and 6.4 the inside options are exogenously given. However, in some bargaining situations the players' inside options between times $t\Delta$ and $(t+1)\Delta$ might be determined strategically after an offer is rejected at time $t\Delta$. In Section 6.6 I study a bargaining model in which the players' inside options are endogenously determined. Section 6.7 contains an application to union-firm wage renegotiations in which, while the parties temporarily disagree, the union decides whether or not to go on strike.

6.2   A Model with Inside Options

Two players, A and B, bargain over the partition of a cake of size π ($\pi > 0$) according to the alternating-offers procedure (described in Section 3.2). The payoffs are as follows. If the players reach agreement at time $t\Delta$ ($t = 0, 1, 2, 3, \ldots$ and $\Delta > 0$) on a partition that gives player i a share x_i ($0 \leq$

$x_i \leq \pi$) of the cake, then her payoff is

$$\int_0^{t\Delta} g_i \exp(-r_i s) ds + x_i \exp(-r_i t\Delta),$$

where $r_i > 0$ and $g_i \geq 0$. The interpretation behind this payoff is as follows: the second term is her (discounted) utility from x_i units of the cake (where r_i is her discount rate), while the first term captures the notion that until agreement is struck player i obtains a flow of utility at rate g_i. After integrating the first term, it follows that this payoff equals

$$\frac{g_i[1 - \exp(-r_i t\Delta)]}{r_i} + x_i \exp(-r_i t\Delta).$$

If an offer is rejected at time $t\Delta$, then in the time interval Δ — before a counteroffer is made at time $(t + 1)\Delta$ — player i obtains a utility of $g_i[1 - \exp(-r_i\Delta)]/r_i$, which is her *inside option*.[1] Notice that for Δ small, her inside option is approximately equal to $g_i\Delta$. The pair (g_A, g_B) is called the *inside option point*.

If the players perpetually disagree (i.e., each player always rejects any offer made to her), then player i's payoff is g_i/r_i. Thus, it follows from Definition 3.1 that the impasse point $(\mathcal{I}_A, \mathcal{I}_B) = (g_A/r_A, g_B/r_B)$. Assume that $g_A/r_A + g_B/r_B < \pi$; for otherwise, gains from co-operation do not exist. The following lemma is an immediate consequence of the observation that player i can guarantee a payoff of g_i/r_i by always asking for the whole cake and always rejecting all offers.

Lemma 6.1. *In any subgame perfect equilibrium of any subgame of the model with inside options and discounting, player i's payoff is greater than or equal to g_i/r_i.*

The following proposition characterizes the unique subgame perfect equilibrium (SPE) of this model. For notational convenience, define $\delta_i \equiv \exp(-r_i\Delta)$.

Proposition 6.1. *The unique subgame perfect equilibrium strategies of the model with inside options and discounting is as follows:*
• *player A always offers x_A^* and always accepts an offer x_B if and only if $x_B \leq x_B^*$,*

---

[1] It is the utility payoff that she obtains while the players *temporarily* disagree.

- *player B always offers x_B^* and always accepts an offer x_A if and only if $x_A \leq x_A^*$, where*

$$x_A^* = \frac{g_A}{r_A} + \frac{1 - \delta_B}{1 - \delta_A \delta_B} \left(\pi - \frac{g_A}{r_A} - \frac{g_B}{r_B} \right) \quad and$$

$$x_B^* = \frac{g_B}{r_B} + \frac{1 - \delta_B}{1 - \delta_A \delta_B} \left(\pi - \frac{g_A}{r_A} - \frac{g_B}{r_B} \right).$$

Proof. The proof involves a straightforward adaptation of the arguments in Sections 3.2.1 and 3.2.2. In particular, in any SPE that satisfies Properties 3.1 and 3.2 player i is indifferent between accepting and rejecting player j's equilibrium offer. That is

$$\pi - x_A^* = \frac{g_B(1 - \delta_B)}{r_B} + \delta_B x_B^* \quad and$$

$$\pi - x_B^* = \frac{g_A(1 - \delta_A)}{r_A} + \delta_A x_A^*.$$

The unique solution to these equations is stated in the proposition. This means that there exists at most a unique SPE that satisfies Properties 3.1 and 3.2, which is described in the proposition. Using an argument similar to that contained in the proof of Proposition 3.1, it can be verified that the pair of strategies described in the proposition is a subgame perfect equilibrium. Through a slight modification of the arguments presented in Section 3.2.2, it can be shown that there does not exist another subgame perfect equilibrium.[2]   □

In the unique SPE, agreement is reached at time 0, and the bargaining outcome is Pareto efficient. Although in equilibrium neither player ever obtains her inside option, the players' inside options have a significant impact on the equilibrium partition of the cake. Since player A makes the first offer, at time 0, the unique SPE share to player A is x_A^* and to player B is $\pi - x_A^*$, where x_A^* is stated in Proposition 6.1. Notice that player i's share is strictly increasing in g_i, and strictly decreasing in g_j. Thus, player i's 'bargaining power' is strictly increasing in her inside option, and strictly decreasing in her opponent's inside option. If $r_A = r_B$ and $g_A = g_B$, then

---

[2]A key modification involves replacing the terms $\delta_i M_i$ and $\delta_i m_i$ respectively with $g_i(1 - \delta_i)/r_i + \delta_i M_i$ and $g_i(1 - \delta_i)/r_i + \delta_i m_i$, which are respectively the maximum and minimum SPE payoffs that player i obtains if she rejects any offer.

$x_A^* > \pi - x_A^*$, which suggests that player A has a first-mover advantage. However, this first-mover advantage disappears in the limit as $\Delta \to 0$: each player obtains one-half of the cake. As I argued in Section 3.2.4, attention should in general be focused upon arbitrarily small values of Δ. I therefore obtain the following corollary to Proposition 6.1.

Corollary 6.1 (Split-The-Difference Rule). *In the limit, as* $\Delta \to 0$, *the unique subgame perfect equilibrium shares of the cake to players A and B respectively converge to*

$$Q_A = \frac{g_A}{r_A} + \eta_A \left(\pi - \frac{g_A}{r_A} - \frac{g_B}{r_B} \right) \quad \text{and}$$

$$Q_B = \frac{g_B}{r_B} + \eta_B \left(\pi - \frac{g_A}{r_A} - \frac{g_B}{r_B} \right),$$

where $\eta_A = r_B/(r_A + r_B)$ and $\eta_B = r_A/(r_A + r_B)$.

The limiting equilibrium partition of the cake, which is independent of who makes the first offer, may be interpreted as follows. The players agree first of all to give each player i a share g_i/r_i of the cake — which gives her a payoff equal to the payoff that she obtains from perpetual disagreement — and then they split the remaining cake.

The limiting SPE payoff pair (Q_A, Q_B) is the unique solution of the following maximization problem:

$$\max_{u_A, u_B} (u_A - d_A)^{\eta_A} (u_B - d_B)^{\eta_B}$$

subject to $(u_A, u_B) \in \Omega$, $u_A \geq d_A$ and $u_B \geq d_B$, where

$$\Omega = \{(u_A, u_B) : 0 \leq u_A \leq \pi \text{ and } u_B = \pi - u_A\} \tag{6.1}$$

$$d = (g_A/r_A, g_B/r_B). \tag{6.2}$$

This observation implies the result — stated in the following corollary — that the limiting SPE payoff pair is identical to the asymmetric Nash bargaining solution of the bargaining problem (Ω, d) with $\tau = \eta_A$, where Ω and d are respectively defined in (6.1) and (6.2).

Corollary 6.2 (Relationship with Nash's Bargaining Solution). *In the limit, as* $\Delta \to 0$, *the unique subgame perfect equilibrium payoff pair in the* *model with inside options and discounting converges to the asymmetric Nash bargaining solution of the bargaining problem* (Ω, d) *with* $\tau = \eta_A$, *where* Ω *and* d *are respectively defined in (6.1) and (6.2), and* $\eta_A = r_B/(r_A + r_B)$.[3]

Corollary 6.2 shows how to incorporate the impact of the inside options — as captured by the flow rates g_A and g_B — in Nash's bargaining solution: they affect the disagreement point in Nash's bargaining solution. This is another illustration of the insight — obtained also in other contexts (such as when bargaining takes place with the possibility of a risk of breakdown (cf. Corollary 4.4)) — that the disagreement point in Nash's framework should be identified with the impasse point.

Remark 6.1 (Two Interpretations of the Model). The model studied above has been motivated by the exchange situation between the seller and the buyer of a house (as described at the beginning of Section 6.1). More generally, the model may be interpreted as capturing the negotiations over some fixed surplus between two players who do not interact with each other after agreement is secured, and who obtain flow payoffs until agreement is secured — where this inside option point may or may not be generated from some kind of interaction between them before agreement is secured. The application studied in Section 6.3.1 fits this interpretation. In contrast, the application studied in Section 6.3.2 fits the following alternative interpretation, in which players A and B interact repeatedly after an agreement is secured. Before an agreement is secured, the players' per period payoffs are captured by the inside option point (g_A, g_B). If the players agree (in some period $t\Delta$) to co-operate with each other in some form, then in each subsequent period they generate a cake of size π' — and they do not obtain their respective inside options. Since $g_A + g_B < \pi'$ (where, assuming that $r_A = r_B = r$, $\pi = \pi'/r$), such co-operation is mutually beneficial. Hence, the players bargain over the partition of the per period cake of size π'. A key assumption is that the players are committed to the agreed partition — that is, they cannot renegotiate in any future period.[4] It should be noted

---

[3]Notice that if $r_A = r_B$, then the asymmetric Nash bargaining solution of this bargaining problem is identical to the Nash bargaining solution of this bargaining problem (cf. Definition 2.1).

[4]In Chapter 10 I study bargaining in long-term relationships without such a commitment assumption — that is, the parties are free to renegotiate in the future an agreement struck in the past.

that the extensions to this model studied in Sections 6.4 and 6.6 may also be interpreted in these two alternative ways.

6.3   Applications

6.3.1   Takeovers in a Duopolistic Market

Consider a market for a homogenous commodity with two firms, A and B. If the market price is $p \geq 0$, then the total quantity demanded per unit time is $\alpha - p$, where $\alpha > 0$. The constant marginal cost of production of firms A and B are respectively c and zero, where $\alpha > 2c > 0$. If q_A and q_B are respectively the quantities produced by firms A and B per unit time, it follows that the profits per unit time to firms A and B are respectively

$$\Pi_A = (\alpha - q_A - q_B)q_A \quad \text{and} \quad \Pi_B = (\alpha - q_A - q_B)q_B - cq_B.$$

Assuming that the firms make their respective quantity decisions simultaneously (and that they do not subsequently change those decisions), the Nash equilibrium quantities of this (Cournot) model — which are derived by first differentiating Π_i w.r.t. q_i, and then solving the two equations for q_A and q_B — are $q_A^C = (\alpha + c)/3$ and $q_B^C = (\alpha - 2c)/3$. This implies that the Nash equilibrium profits per unit time to firms A and B are respectively $\Pi_A^C = (\alpha + c)^2/9$ and $\Pi_B^C = (\alpha - 2c)^2/9$.

Firm B considers an amicable takeover of firm A. If she succeeds in doing so, then she acquires the relatively more efficient production technology of firm A and becomes the monopoly supplier of the commodity. This means that she would then earn a monopoly profit per unit time, which (with zero marginal cost of production) equals $\Pi^m = \alpha^2/4$. Assuming that the two firms discount future profits at a common rate $r > 0$, when the two firms bargain over the price at which firm B buys (or takes over) firm A, their respective payoffs from perpetual disagreement are Π_A^C/r and Π_B^C/r. Applying the bargaining model studied in Section 6.2, note that $g_A = \Pi_A^C$, $g_B = \Pi_B^C$ and $\pi = \Pi^m/r$. Since $\Pi^m > \Pi_A^C + \Pi_B^C$, in this bargaining situation there exist gains from trade: that is, $g_A/r + g_B/r < \pi$. Hence, applying Corollary 6.1, it follows that firm B would buy firm A at time 0 and pay firm A a price

$$p^B = \frac{\Pi_A^C}{r} + \frac{1}{2}\left(\frac{\Pi^m}{r} - \frac{\Pi_A^C}{r} - \frac{\Pi_B^C}{r}\right).$$

Suppose, on the other hand, that firm A takes over firm B — not to buy its relatively less efficient technology but to eliminate its presence from the market. Applying Corollary 6.1 again, it follows that the price firm A would pay firm B in order to buy it is

$$p^A = \frac{\Pi_B^C}{r} + \frac{1}{2}\left(\frac{\Pi^m}{r} - \frac{\Pi_A^C}{r} - \frac{\Pi_B^C}{r}\right).$$

Since $\Pi_B^C < \Pi_A^C$, $p^A < p^B$. However, the equilibrium payoffs to firms A and B do not depend on whether firm B buys firm A, or vice-versa — the payoffs to firms A and B are respectively $\Pi_A^C/r + (\Pi^m/r - \Pi_A^C/r - \Pi_B^C/r)/2$ and $\Pi_B^C/r + (\Pi^m/r - \Pi_A^C/r - \Pi_B^C/r)/2$, whoever ends up being the monopolist.

The initial duopolistic market need not, however, end being a monopoly; although gains to trade exist between the two firms, wealth and borrowing constraints may prevent either firm from buying the other — notice that the prices p^A and p^B are quite large as they embody the present discounted values of all future profits. This argument suggests that since $p^A < p^B$, it is more likely that firm A takes over (or buys) firm B. Thus, one can say that efficient firms will tend to buy inefficient firms.

Since both p^A and p^B are strictly increasing in α, this suggests that as the market size increases, it is less likely that any takeover occurs, and thus, more likely that the market remains a duopoly. Furthermore, since p^A is strictly decreasing in c and p^B is strictly increasing in c, this suggests that as the relative degree of inefficiency between the two firms increases, takeover by the relatively more efficient firm becomes more likely.

6.3.2   Sovereign Debt Renegotiations

Country B, who produces one unit of some domestic commodity β per unit time, owes a large amount of some foreign commodity α to a foreign bank A. By trading on international markets, B obtains P units of commodity α for one unit of commodity β, where $P > 1$. The utility per unit time to B is the sum of the quantities of commodities α and β that it consumes. In the absence of any outside interference, in each unit of time B would trade the unit of commodity β for P units of the foreign commodity α, and obtain a utility of P. However, if A and B fail to reach agreement on some debt repayment scheme, then the bank seizes a fraction ν of the country's traded output.

The players bargain over the payment per unit time x that B makes to A everafter. If agreement is reached on x at time $t\Delta$, then in each future unit of time B trades the unit of its domestic commodity β for P units of the foreign commodity α — and thus, the payoffs to A and B (from time $t\Delta$ onwards) are respectively x/r and $(P-x)/r$, where $r > 0$ is the players' common discount rate. It is assumed that the amount that B owes A exceeds P/r, and furthermore, the parties are committed to the agreed debt repayment scheme. In the framework of the model studied in Section 6.2, the players are bargaining over the partition of a cake of size $\pi = P/r$; and if player A receives a share x_i of this cake, then this means that the per unit time repayment $x = rx_i$.

The inside options to the players are now derived. If any offer is rejected at any time $t\Delta$, then — before a counteroffer is made at time $(t+1)\Delta$ — Δ units of the domestic commodity is produced. Country B either consumes all of it or trades without agreement. In the former case the inside options of B and A are respectively Δ and zero, while in the latter case the inside options of B and A are respectively $(1-\nu)P\Delta$ and $\nu P\Delta - \epsilon$, where ϵ denotes an infinitesimal (small) cost of seizure. Hence, since B makes the decision on whether to consume or trade, it follows (in the notation of Section 6.2) that

$$(g_A, g_B) = \begin{cases} (0, 1) & \text{if } 1 > (1-\nu)P \\ (\nu P - \epsilon, (1-\nu)P) & \text{if } 1 \leq (1-\nu)P. \end{cases}$$

Noting that $g_A/r + g_B/r < \pi$, one may apply Corollary 6.1 and obtain that the players reach agreement immediately (at time 0) with Country B agreeing to pay the foreign bank an amount x per unit time, where, in the limit as $\epsilon \to 0$, x converges to

$$x^* = \begin{cases} (P-1)/2 & \text{if } \nu > 1 - (1/P) \\ \nu P & \text{if } \nu \leq 1 - (1/P). \end{cases}$$

If international trade sanctions (as captured by the value of ν) are sufficiently harsh, then Country B's inside option is derived from consuming the domestic commodity — which implies that the equilibrium debt payment per unit time equals half the gains from trade. On the other hand, if international trade sanctions are not too harsh, then Country B's inside option is derived from trading the domestic commodity — which implies that the equilibrium debt payment per unit time equals the quantity of traded good seized.

A major insight obtained from this analysis is as follows. If ν is sufficiently high, then further international trade sanctions (as captured by an increase in ν) have no effect on debt payments. In contrast, an increase in the terms of Country B's international trade (as captured by an increase in P) always increases debt payments.

It seems reasonable to assume that the value of ν can be (strategically) chosen by the foreign bank. Assuming that ν is chosen before the renegotiations begin, and that the bank is committed to its choice, the bank will set ν to maximize the equilibrium debt payment per unit time x^*. For any P, x^* is strictly increasing in ν over the closed interval $[0, 1 - (1/P)]$, and equals $(P - 1)/2$ for any ν in the interval $(1 - (1/P), 1]$. Hence, since at $\nu = 1 - (1/P)$, $x^* = P - 1$, the optimal value of ν is $\nu^* = 1 - (1/P)$. Thus, since $1 - (1/P) < 1$, the optimal level of ν is strictly less than one; that is, it is not optimal for the foreign bank to seize all the traded output.[5] The optimal level of debt payment per unit time equals $P - 1$, the gains from international trade per unit time. Thus, at the optimum, the bank captures all of the gains from international trade — it cannot, however, extract any greater amount of payment per unit time from Country B.

6.4   The Effect of Outside Options

I now extend the model studied in Section 6.2 by allowing for outside options — in order to explore how they interact with inside options. In particular, I investigate the robustness of the outside option principle (cf. Corollary 5.1) and the generalized split-the-difference rule (cf. Corollary 6.1).

The model analysed here involves the following extension of the model studied in Section 6.2. As in the model studied in Section 5.2, whenever any player has to respond to any offer, she has three choices, namely: (i) accept

---

[5]Notice that this result has been derived on the assumption that it is (virtually) costless for the bank to seize any fraction of the traded output.

the offer, (ii) reject the offer and make a counteroffer Δ time units later and (iii) reject the offer and opt out, in which case negotiations terminate in (permanent) disagreement. As in Section 6.2, between two consecutive offers the players obtain their respective inside options — as embodied in the flow rates g_A and g_B. As in Section 5.2, the *outside option point* is the instantaneous utility pair (w_A, w_B) obtainable if either player opts out. In addition to the assumption that $g_A \geq 0$, $g_B \geq 0$ and $g_A/r_A + g_B/r_B < \pi$, assume, as in Section 5.2, that $w_A < \pi$, $w_B < \pi$ and $w_A + w_B < \pi$; for otherwise gains from co-operation do not exist.

I emphasize that the outside option point is the payoff pair obtainable by the players if a player decides to *permanently* stop bargaining — that is, she decides to *permanently* disagree, while the inside option point — or, more precisely (when Δ is small) the payoff pair $(g_A\Delta, g_B\Delta)$ — is the payoff pair obtainable by the players if a player decides to *temporarily* stop bargaining (for Δ time units) — that is, she decides to *temporarily* disagree.

The following bargaining situation illustrates the distinction between outside options and inside options. When a married couple are bargaining over how to co-operate, their outside options are their respective payoffs from divorce, while their inside options are their respective payoffs from staying married but not co-operating with each other. Notice that it is possible, for example, that the husband's outside option is much smaller than his payoff from perpetual disagreement, because he is quite an unattractive man, while his wife is quite an attractive woman — thus, the utility he obtains from being married to her when they never co-operate is much higher than the utility he obtains from being divorced from her.

As is illustrated above in the bargaining situation faced by the married couple, in general there need not be any relationship between a player's outside option and inside option; thus, w_i can be less than, equal to, or greater than g_i/r_i.[6]

A straightforward adaptation of the arguments in Sections 5.2 and 6.2 (that lead respectively to Propositions 5.1 and 6.1) establishes the existence

---

[6]In some bargaining situations, however, a player's outside option may equal the payoff she obtains from perpetual disagreement. For example, when bargaining over the price of the house, the seller can always stop bargaining and choose not to sell the house. If there are no alternative buyers available, then, indeed, the seller's outside option w_S equals her payoff g_S/r_S obtained from keeping the house for herself.

of a unique SPE. It should be noted that unlike in the model with only inside options studied in Section 6.2, it is no longer true that player i $(i = A, B)$ can guarantee a payoff of g_i/r_i — since player j $(j \neq i)$ can permanently disagree by opting out, in which case player i obtains her outside option w_i. However, since player i can guarantee a payoff of $\delta_i w_i$ by opting out at the first opportunity, the following counterpart to Lemma 6.1 is obtained.

Lemma 6.2. *In any subgame perfect equilibrium of any subgame of the model with inside options, outside options and discounting, player i's payoff is greater than or equal to $\delta_i w_i$.*

In the following proposition I characterize the limit, as $\Delta \to 0$, of the unique SPE of the model described above.

Proposition 6.2. *The unique limiting (as $\Delta \to 0$) subgame perfect equilibrium of the model with inside options, outside options and discounting is as follows:*

- *player A always offers x_A^*, always accepts an offer x_B if and only if $x_B \leq x_B^*$, and always opts out after receiving an offer $x_B > x_B^*$ if and only if $x_A^* \leq w_A$,*
- *player B always offers x_B^*, always accepts an offer x_A if and only if $x_A \leq x_A^*$, and always opts out after receiving an offer $x_A > x_A^*$ if and only if $x_B^* \leq w_B$, where*

$$(x_A^*, x_B^*) = \begin{cases} (Q_A, Q_B) & \text{if } w_A \leq Q_A \text{ and } w_B \leq Q_B \\ (\pi - w_B, w_B) & \text{if } w_A \leq Q_A \text{ and } w_B > Q_B \\ (w_A, \pi - w_A) & \text{if } w_A > Q_A \text{ and } w_B \leq Q_B \end{cases}$$

with Q_A and Q_B defined in Corollary 6.1.

The payoff pair (Q_A, Q_B) is the limiting SPE payoff pair when the players do not have any outside options. Proposition 6.2 may thus be interpreted as a generalization of the outside option principle (cf. Corollary 5.1), in which the reference point is the pair (Q_A, Q_B) rather than the pair $(\eta_A \pi, \eta_B \pi)$, where the latter is the limiting SPE payoff pair in the basic alternating-offers model (cf. Corollary 3.1).

If both players' outside options are sufficiently unattractive (i.e., $w_A \leq Q_A$ and $w_B \leq Q_B$), then the equilibrium partition of the cake is determined by the impasse point (which depends on the players' inside options) — thus, in this case the outside options are irrelevant to the bargaining outcome. On the other hand, if player i's outside option is sufficiently attractive (i.e., $w_i > Q_i$), then the equilibrium partition of the cake is determined solely by her outside option w_i; both players' inside options and player j's outside option have no influence whatsoever on the equilibrium partition, no matter how attractive player j's inside option might be. For example, if $w_i = g_j/r_j = 0.9\pi$ and $w_j = g_i/r_i = 0$, then players i and j respectively obtain 0.9π and 0.1π units of the cake. The message here is that when some player's outside option is sufficiently attractive, then that outside option has the decisive impact on the equilibrium partition of the cake; the inside options are irrelevant to the bargaining outcome. The intuition for this result follows from the fact that player i can opt out immediately (either at $t = 0$ if $i = B$, or at $t = \Delta$ if $i - A$) and obtain her attractive outside option, which thus leaves player j with her unattractive outside option. Player j cannot obtain the attractive payoff of g_j/r_j, because that payoff is obtained if and only if the players perpetually disagree. It is interesting to note that if player i's outside option $w_i > \pi - (g_j/r_j)$ (which implies that $w_j < g_j/r_j$), then player j's limiting SPE payoff $\pi - w_i$ is strictly less than g_j/r_j (but strictly greater than w_j). Thus, as indicated in Lemma 6.2, player j cannot guarantee a payoff of g_j/r_j, because player i would opt out if player j offers $x_j > \pi - w_i$.

6.4.1 And a Risk of Breakdown

I now extend the model with inside options and outside options studied above by allowing for a risk of breakdown. As in Section 4.4, immediately after a player rejects an offer (that is, she chooses neither to opt out nor to accept the offer) with probability $\lambda\Delta$ (where $\lambda\Delta < 1$) the negotiations break down in (permanent) disagreement, and with probability $1 - \lambda\Delta$ the player gets to make her counteroffer Δ time units later, where $\lambda \geq 0$. The breakdown point (b_A, b_B) is the instantaneous payoff pair obtainable in that eventuality, where $b_A \geq 0$, $b_B \geq 0$ and $b_A + b_B < \pi$.

A straightforward adaptation of the arguments used to prove Proposition 6.2 can be used to establish the existence of a unique SPE in this extended model. Proposition 6.3 below characterizes the limit, as $\Delta \to 0$, of this unique SPE.[7] It is useful to first derive the impasse point in this bargaining model with inside options, outside options, discounting and a risk of breakdown.[8] For any $\Delta > 0$ *but small*, player i's payoff from perpetual disagreement (i.e., when each player always rejects any offer made to her, and never opts out) is

$$[\lambda\Delta b_i + (1 - \lambda\Delta)g_i\Delta] \sum_{n=0}^{\infty}(1 - \lambda\Delta)^n\delta_i^n.$$

Since (when $\Delta > 0$ but small) $\delta_i \equiv \exp(-r_i\Delta) = 1 - r_i\Delta$, it follows that (after substituting for δ_i, and then simplifying) the above expression equals

$$\frac{\lambda b_i + (1 - \lambda\Delta)g_i}{r_i + \lambda + r_i\lambda\Delta}.$$

Hence, the (limiting, as $\Delta \to 0$) impasse point

$$(\mathcal{I}_A, \mathcal{I}_B) = \left(\frac{g_A + \lambda b_A}{r_A + \lambda}, \frac{g_B + \lambda b_B}{r_B + \lambda}\right). \tag{6.3}$$

Proposition 6.3. *The unique limiting (as $\Delta \to 0$) subgame perfect equilibrium of the model with inside options, outside options, discounting and a risk of breakdown is as follows:*
• *player A always offers x_A^*, always accepts an offer x_B if and only if $x_B \leq x_B^*$, and always opts out after receiving an offer $x_B > x_B^*$ if and only if $x_A^* \leq w_A$,*
• *player B always offers x_B^*, always accepts an offer x_A if and only if $x_A \leq x_A^*$, and always opts out after receiving an offer $x_A > x_A^*$ if and only if $x_B^* \leq w_B$, where*

$$(x_A^*, x_B^*) = \begin{cases} (Q_A^*, Q_B^*) & \text{if } w_A \leq Q_A^* \text{ and } w_B \leq Q_B^* \\ (\pi - w_B, w_B) & \text{if } w_A \leq Q_A^* \text{ and } w_B > Q_B^* \\ (w_A, \pi - w_A) & \text{if } w_A > Q_A^* \text{ and } w_B \leq Q_B^* \end{cases}$$

with $Q_A^* = \mathcal{I}_A + \sigma_A[\pi - \mathcal{I}_A - \mathcal{I}_B]$ and $Q_B^* = \mathcal{I}_B + \sigma_B[\pi - \mathcal{I}_A - \mathcal{I}_B]$, where $\sigma_A = (r_B + \lambda)/(2\lambda + r_A + r_B)$, $\sigma_B = 1 - \sigma_A$ and $(\mathcal{I}_A, \mathcal{I}_B)$ is defined in (6.3).

---

[7]Notice that Lemma 6.2 is also valid in this extended model.

[8]The impasse point is the payoff pair obtainable when the players perpetually disagree — that is, each player always rejects any offer made to her, and never opts out (cf. Definition 3.1).

Comparing Propositions 6.2 and 6.3, it is evident that the limiting SPE in this extended model is essentially the same as the limiting SPE in the model without a risk of breakdown. The new aspects are: (i) that the impasse point now depends on the breakdown point (b_A, b_B) and on the rate λ at which negotiations break down randomly, and (ii) that player i's 'bargaining power', as reflected in the share σ_i of the remaining cake $\pi - \mathcal{I}_A - \mathcal{I}_B$ that she obtains, depends on λ. A main message here is that when some player's outside option is sufficiently attractive (i.e., $w_i > Q_i^*$), then that outside option has the decisive impact on the equilibrium partition of the cake; the inside options, the breakdown point, the rate at which negotiations break down randomly and the players' discount rates are irrelevant to the bargaining outcome.

6.4.2 Relationship with Nash's Bargaining Solution

It follows from Proposition 6.3 that if $w_B < \pi - \mathcal{I}_A$ and $w_A < \pi - \mathcal{I}_B$, where $(\mathcal{I}_A, \mathcal{I}_B)$ is defined in (6.3), then the limiting SPE payoff pair – which is (x_A^*, x_B^*) as stated in Proposition 6.3 — is the unique solution of the following maximization problem:

$$\max_{u_A, u_B} (u_A - d_A)^{\sigma_A} (u_A - d_B)^{1-\sigma_A}$$

subject to $(u_A, u_B) \in \Omega$, $u_A \geq d_A$ and $u_B \geq d_B$, where

$$\Omega = \{(u_A, u_B) : 0 \leq u_A \leq \pi, u_B = \pi - u_A, u_A \geq w_A \text{ and } u_B \geq w_B\} \quad (6.4)$$

$$d = (\mathcal{I}_A, \mathcal{I}_B) \quad (6.5)$$

$$\sigma_A = (r_B + \lambda)/(2\lambda + r_A + r_B). \quad (6.6)$$

This observation implies the result — stated in Corollary 6.3 below – that if $w_B < \pi - \mathcal{I}_A$ and $w_A < \pi - \mathcal{I}_B$, then the limiting SPE payoff pair is identical to the asymmetric Nash bargaining solution of the bargaining problem (Ω, d) with $\tau = \sigma_A$, where Ω, d and σ_A are defined in (6.4)–(6.6).[9]

On the other hand, if either $w_B \geq \pi - \mathcal{I}_A$ or $w_A \geq \pi - \mathcal{I}_B$, then the bargaining problem (Ω, d), where Ω and d are respectively defined in (6.4) and (6.5), does not satisfy Assumption 2.1 — since there does not exist a utility pair $(u_A, u_B) \in \Omega$ such that $u_A > d_A$ and $u_B > d_B$. Hence, if either

---

[9]It should be noted that if $w_A \geq b_A$ and $w_B \geq b_B$, then $w_A < \pi - \mathcal{I}_B$ and $w_B < \pi - \mathcal{I}_A$.

$w_B \geq \pi - \mathcal{I}_A$ or $w_A \geq \pi - \mathcal{I}_B$, then Nash's bargaining solution is not defined on this bargaining problem.

Corollary 6.3. *If $w_B < \pi - \mathcal{I}_A$ and $w_A < \pi - \mathcal{I}_B$, where $(\mathcal{I}_A, \mathcal{I}_B)$ is defined in (6.3), then the unique SPE payoff pair of the bargaining model with inside options, outside options, discounting and a risk of breakdown converges, as $\Delta \to 0$, to the asymmetric Nash bargaining solution of the bargaining problem (Ω, d) with $\tau = \sigma_A$, where Ω, d and σ_A are defined in (6.4)–(6.6).*

Thus, if for each $i = A, B$, $w_i < \pi - \mathcal{I}_j$ $(j \neq i)$ — which would be satisfied if, for example, $w_i \geq b_i$ $(i = A, B)$ — then Nash's bargaining solution is applicable. The disagreement point in Nash's framework should be identified with the (limiting, as $\Delta \to 0$) impasse point, while the outside option point appropriately constrains the set of possible utility pairs.

Corollary 6.3 is a trivial generalization of Corollary 5.3. It should be noted that in the bargaining situation considered here, there are three possible ways in which the players fail to reach agreement: through perpetual disagreement, when a player opts out and when negotiations break down in a random manner. As such there are three possible payoff pairs associated with a failure to reach agreement, namely, the impasse point $(\mathcal{I}_A, \mathcal{I}_B)$, the outside option point (w_A, w_B) and the breakdown point (b_A, b_B). Corollary 6.3 states that the disagreement point in Nash's set-up should be identified with the impasse point. The outside option point affects the set Ω of possible utility pairs on which the Nash solution should be defined — by requiring that each utility pair $(u_A, u_B) \in \Omega$ be such that u_i is at least as high as player i's outside option. *The breakdown point and the inside option point, on the other hand, affect the disagreement point through their respective impacts on the impasse point.*

6.4.3   A Generalization

I now extend the model studied in Section 6.4.1 by assuming — as in Section 3.4 — that the players are bargaining over a set X of possible agreements, where $U_i : X \to \Re$ is player i's (instantaneous) von Neumann–Morgenstern utility function.

Similar to Assumption 3.1, assume that the Pareto-frontier Ω^e of the set Ω of instantaneous utility pairs obtainable through agreement is the graph of a concave function, denoted by ϕ, whose domain is an interval $I_A \subseteq \Re$ and range an interval $I_B \subseteq \Re$, with $\mathcal{I}_A \in I_A$ and $\mathcal{I}_B \in I_B$ and $\phi(\mathcal{I}_A) > \mathcal{I}_B$, where the impasse point $(\mathcal{I}_A, \mathcal{I}_B)$ is defined in (6.3). Furthermore, assume that there exists an agreement $x \in X$ such that $U_A(x) > w_A$ and $U_B(x) > w_B$.

A minor adaptation of the analysis of Sections 3.4.1 and 3.4.4 characterizes the unique SPE of this model. In particular, it follows that $M_A = m_A = V_A^*$ and $M_B = m_B = V_B^*$, where (V_A^*, V_B^*) is the unique pair that satisfies the following two equations

$$V_A^* = \max\{w_B, \phi^{-1}(\lambda\Delta b_B + (1 - \lambda\Delta)[g_B(1 - \delta_B)/r_B + \delta_B V_B^*]\}$$
$$V_B^* = \max\{w_A, \phi(\lambda\Delta b_A + (1 - \lambda\Delta)[g_A(1 - \delta_A)/r_A + \delta_A V_A^*)]\}.$$

In the following proposition — which can be proven along the lines of Proposition 6.3 — I characterize the limit of the unique SPE payoff pair, as $\Delta \to 0$.

Proposition 6.4. *In the limit, as $\Delta \to 0$, the unique SPE payoff pair of the general model with outside options, inside options, discounting and a risk of breakdown converges to*

$$(u_A^*, u_B^*) = \begin{cases} (\widehat{u}_A, \widehat{u}_B) & \text{if } w_A \le \widehat{u}_A \text{ and } w_B \le \widehat{u}_B \\ (\phi^{-1}(w_B), w_B) & \text{if } w_A \le \widehat{u}_A \text{ and } w_B > \widehat{u}_B \\ (w_A, \phi(w_A)) & \text{if } w_A > \widehat{u}_A \text{ and } w_B \le \widehat{u}_B, \end{cases}$$

where $(\widehat{u}_A, \widehat{u}_B)$ is the unique solution to the maximization problem stated in Corollary 4.5, but with $(\mathcal{I}_A, \mathcal{I}_B)$ as defined in (6.3) and $\lambda_A = \lambda_B = \lambda$.

The following corollary to this proposition parallels the result contained in Corollary 6.3.

Corollary 6.4. *If $w_B < \phi(\mathcal{I}_A)$ and $w_A < \phi^{-1}(\mathcal{I}_B)$, then the unique subgame perfect equilibrium payoff pair in the generalized model with inside options, outside options, discounting and a risk of breakdown converge, as $\Delta \to 0$, to the asymmetric Nash bargaining solution of the bargaining problem (Ω, d) with $\tau = \sigma_A$, where $\Omega = \{(u_A, u_B) : u_A \in I_A, u_B = \phi(u_A), u_A \ge w_A \text{ and } u_B \ge w_B\}$, $d = (\mathcal{I}_A, \mathcal{I}_B)$ — as defined in (6.3) — and σ_A is as defined in (6.6).*[10]

---

[10]It should be noted that if $w_A \ge b_A$ and $w_B \ge b_B$, then $w_A < \phi^{-1}(\mathcal{I}_B)$ and $w_B < \phi(\mathcal{I}_A)$.

6.5   An Application to Intrafamily Allocation

A husband H and a wife W bargain over the quantities of four variables, namely, the per unit time consumption levels of a private good by the husband and the wife (which are respectively denoted by x_H and x_W) and the per unit time quantities of two 'household' public goods (which are denoted by q_1 and q_2). The income per unit time of player i $(i = H, W)$ is $Y_i \geq 0$, where $Y_H + Y_W = Y > 0$. The price of the private good is normalized to one, and the price (or, unit cost) of the public good q_k $(k = 1, 2)$ is p_k. Thus, the set of possible agreements (or, allocations) is

$$X = \{(x_H, x_W, q_1, q_2) : x_H + x_W + p_1 q_1 + p_2 q_2 = Y\}.$$

If and when agreement is struck, the parties are committed to the agreed per unit time allocation; that is, they do not renegotiate it in the future. Thus, if agreement is reached on $x \in X$ at time $t\Delta$, then the payoffs to the husband and the wife (from time $t\Delta$ onwards) are respectively $U_H(x) \equiv V_H(x_H, q_1, q_2)/r$ and $U_W(x) \equiv V_W(x_W, q_1, q_2)/r$, where $r > 0$ is the players' common discount rate and V_i — which is strictly increasing in x_i, q_1 and q_2 — is the utility player i obtains per unit time. Assume that the set Ω of instantaneous utility pairs obtainable from agreement satisfies Assumption 3.1, where $\Omega = \{(u_H, u_W) : \text{ there exists } x \in X \text{ such that } U_H(x) = u_H \text{ and } U_W(x) = u_W\}$.

While bargaining each player has the option to divorce — which entails permanent disagreement. Thus, the instantaneous utility pair associated with divorce is the outside option point. Player i's outside option w_i will depend on Y_i, amongst other parameters. Assume that the outside option point (w_H, w_W) lies below the Pareto frontier of Ω; for, otherwise, there are no gains to being married — the parties would divorce at time 0.

If the players temporarily disagree over the allocation, they continue to function and live as a married couple, but in the absence of co-operation and coordination — which is formally modelled as follows. Based on established gender roles, to which the parties are committed, the husband controls and chooses the quantity of the household public good q_1, and the wife controls and chooses the quantity of the household public good q_2. The players' inside options are the Nash equilibrium payoffs of the following simultaneous-move game. The husband chooses x_H and q_1 subject to his budget constraint

$x_H + p_1q_1 = Y_H$, and simultaneously the wife chooses x_W and q_2 subject to her budget constraint $x_W + p_2q_2 = Y_W$. The payoffs from these strategy choices to the husband and the wife are respectively $V_H(x_H, q_1, q_2)$ and $V_W(x_W, q_1, q_2)$. I assume that the Nash equilibrium payoffs in this game are uniquely defined, and they define the inside option point (g_H, g_W). Each player's inside option depends on Y_H and Y_W, amongst other parameters. Assume that $(g_H/r, g_W/r)$ lies below the Pareto frontier of Ω; for otherwise, there are no gains from co-operation within the marriage — the parties would perpetually disagree (but not divorce, since I have assumed above that the outside option point lies below the Pareto frontier of Ω).

Assuming that there is no risk of breakdown in a random manner (i.e., $\lambda = 0$), and letting the graph of $u_W = \phi(u_H)$ denote the Pareto frontier of Ω, one may apply Proposition 6.4 and obtain that (in the limit as $\Delta \to 0$) the unique SPE payoff pair is[11]

$$(u_H^*, u_W^*) = \begin{cases} (\widehat{u}_H, \widehat{u}_W) & \text{if } w_H \leq \widehat{u}_H \text{ and } w_W \leq \widehat{u}_W \\ (\phi^{-1}(w_W), w_W) & \text{if } w_H \leq \widehat{u}_H \text{ and } w_W > \widehat{u}_W \\ (w_H, \phi(w_H)) & \text{if } w_H > \widehat{u}_H \text{ and } w_W \leq \widehat{u}_W, \end{cases}$$

where $(\widehat{u}_H, \widehat{u}_W)$ is the unique solution to the following maximization problem

$$\max_{u_H, u_W} (u_H - (g_H/r))(u_W - (g_W/r))$$

subject to $(u_H, u_W) \in \Omega, u_H \geq g_H/r$ and $u_W \geq g_W/r$.

The Effects of Family Policies

I now consider the implications on the equilibrium intrafamily distribution (u_H^*, u_W^*) of three family policies aimed at affecting intrafamily distribution of welfare.

First, consider the effect of a government policy that provides an allowance T to the wife which is financed entirely by taxing the husband; thus, $0 < T \leq Y_H$ — assume that $Y_H > 0$. This means that the husband's post-tax income is $Y_H' = Y_H - T$, and the wife's post-allowance income is $Y_W' = Y_W + T$. Since the total family income $Y_H' + Y_W'$ is unaffected by this

---

[11]Notice that in the limiting SPE agreement is reached immediately, at time 0; the bargaining outcome is Pareto efficient.

policy (that is, $Y'_H + Y'_W = Y_H + Y_W$), the set Ω of instantaneous possible utility pairs obtainable from agreement is unaffected. The players' outside options are also unaffected, because this policy is targeted to married couples, not to divorcees. However, the husband's inside option decreases, while the wife's inside option increases — because, although player i's inside option (which is a function of Y_H and Y_W) is increasing in both Y_H and Y_W, the marginal effect of Y_i on player i's inside option is strictly greater than the marginal effect of Y_j on player i's inside option. Hence, it follows (with reference to the pre-policy equilibrium outcome) that the post-policy equilibrium payoff pair is

$$
(u'_H, u'_W) = \begin{cases} (\widehat{u}'_H, \widehat{u}'_W) & \text{if } w_H \leq \widehat{u}'_H \text{ and } w_W \leq \widehat{u}'_W \\ (\phi^{-1}(w_W), w_W) & \text{if } w_H \leq \widehat{u}'_H \text{ and } w_W > \widehat{u}'_W \\ (w_H, \phi(w_H)) & \text{if } w_H > \widehat{u}'_H \text{ and } w_W \leq \widehat{u}'_W, \end{cases}
$$

where $\widehat{u}'_H < \widehat{u}_H$ and $\widehat{u}'_W > \widehat{u}_W$.[12]

If the pre-policy outcome $(u^*_H, u^*_W) = (\widehat{u}_H, \widehat{u}_W)$ (which means that $\widehat{u}_H \geq w_H$ and $\widehat{u}_W \geq w_W$), then for any $T \in (0, Y_H]$ the wife's equilibrium payoff increases and the husband's equilibrium payoff decreases relative to their respective pre-policy equilibrium payoffs. On the other hand, if the pre-policy outcome $(u^*_H, u^*_W) = (w_H, \phi(w_H))$ (which means that $\widehat{u}_H < w_H$ and $\widehat{u}_W \geq w_W$), then the policy has no effect on intrafamily distribution: the players' equilibrium payoffs in the pre-policy and post-policy situations are identical. Finally, if the pre-policy outcome $(u^*_H, u^*_W) = (\phi^{-1}(w_W), w_W)$ (which means that $\widehat{u}_H \geq w_H$ and $\widehat{u}_W < w_W$), then if T is sufficiently small the policy has no effect on intrafamily distribution, but if T is sufficiently large then the policy makes the wife better off and the husband worse off relative to the pre-policy situation. In summary, the key message is that this policy may (but it need not) affect intrafamily distribution of welfare (by making the wife better off and the husband worse off); it depends on the nature of the pre-policy equilibrium outcome, which, in turn, depends in particular on the couples' respective preferences, pre-policy incomes and payoffs following divorce.

---

[12]Since $g'_H < g_H$ and $g'_W > g_W$, and since the set Ω is unaffected by the policy (which means that the function ϕ is unaffected), the solution $(\widehat{u}'_H, \widehat{u}'_W)$ to the maximization problem stated above is such that $\widehat{u}'_H < \widehat{u}_H$ and $\widehat{u}'_W > \widehat{u}_W$.

I now consider the relative effects on intrafamily distribution of two related government child allowance policies (or, schemes). In both schemes, in the event of divorce it is the wife (mother) who gets the child allowance. The two child allowance schemes differ according to which parent receives the child allowance *within* marriage. Suppose that the child allowance is some money C. Since total family income with either of these two child allowance schemes is the same, namely, $Y + C$, it follows that the set Ω of instantaneous possible utility pairs obtainable through agreement is the same under either scheme. Furthermore, the players' outside options are also the same under either scheme — since in both schemes the child allowance is received by the mother when the couple get divorced. It is the inside options which are different under these two schemes. Under the scheme where the husband receives the child allowance within marriage, his inside option increases and the wife's inside option decreases; the reverse is the case under the scheme where the wife receives the allowance within marriage. Thus, the equilibrium distribution when the husband receives the child allowance within marriage is

$$(u_H^H, u_W^H) = \begin{cases} (\widehat{u}_H^H, \widehat{u}_W^H) & \text{if } w_H \leq \widehat{u}_H^H \text{ and } w_W \leq \widehat{u}_W^H \\ (\phi^{-1}(w_W), w_W) & \text{if } w_H \leq \widehat{u}_H^H \text{ and } w_W > \widehat{u}_W^H \\ (w_H, \phi(w_H)) & \text{if } w_H > \widehat{u}_H^H \text{ and } w_W \leq \widehat{u}_W^H, \end{cases}$$

and the equilibrium distribution when the wife receives the child allowance within marriage is

$$(u_H^W, u_W^W) = \begin{cases} (\widehat{u}_H^W, \widehat{u}_W^W) & \text{if } w_H \leq \widehat{u}_H^W \text{ and } w_W \leq \widehat{u}_W^W \\ (\phi^{-1}(w_W), w_W) & \text{if } w_H \leq \widehat{u}_H^W \text{ and } w_W > \widehat{u}_W^W \\ (w_H, \phi(w_H)) & \text{if } w_H > \widehat{u}_H^W \text{ and } w_W \leq \widehat{u}_W^W, \end{cases}$$

where $\widehat{u}_H^H > \widehat{u}_H^W$ and $\widehat{u}_W^H < \widehat{u}_W^W$. The main key message from this analysis — which is self-evident from these two equilibria — is that the two child allowance policies may generate identical equilibrium payoffs. For some values of the parameters (which include the couples' respective preferences and pre-policy incomes, and the level of the child allowance), these two alternative child allowance schemes do not have differing impacts on intrahousehold distribution. When they do (which they will for some parameter values), then the parent who receives the child allowance within marriage is better-off relative to the alternative scheme in which her partner receives the child allowance.

6.6   Endogenously Determined Inside Options

In the models studied in Sections 6.2 and 6.4 the players' inside options are exogenously given. I now study a model in which the players' inside options are endogenously determined.[13]

Two players, A and B, bargain over the partition of a cake of size π ($\pi > 0$) according to a modified version of the basic alternating-offers process. The modification is as follows. At any time $t\Delta$ ($t = 0, 1, 2, \dots$) after any offer is rejected, players A and B simultaneously choose 'actions' from their respective sets of actions S_A and S_B. The players' inside options between times $t\Delta$ and $(t+1)\Delta$ depend on the chosen actions: $g_i(s)$ denotes the rate at which player i obtains utility when the chosen action profile is $s = (s_A, s_B)$, where $g_i(s) \geq 0$. Thus, if at time $t\Delta$ (after an offer is rejected) the players' chosen action profile is s, then player i's inside option between times $t\Delta$ and $(t + 1)\Delta$ is $(1 - \delta_i)g_i(s)/r_i$, where $r_i > 0$ denotes her discount rate and $\delta_i \equiv \exp(-r_i\Delta)$.[14]

If agreement is reached at time $t\Delta$ ($t = 0, 1, 2, 3, \dots$) on a partition that gives player i a share x_i ($0 \leq x_i \leq \pi$) of the cake, and if at time $q\Delta$ ($q = 0, 1, 2, \dots, t - 1$) after the offer is rejected the players' chosen action profile is s^q, then player i's payoff is

$$\sum_{q=0}^{t-1} \frac{(1 - \delta_i)g_i(s^q)}{r_i} \exp(-r_i q\Delta) + x_i \exp(-r_i t\Delta).$$

If, on the other hand, the players perpetually disagree (i.e., each player

---

[13]There is neither a risk of breakdown nor do the players have outside options. The focus in this section is entirely on the role of endogenously determined inside options (and discounting) on the bargaining outcome.

[14]A player's 'inside option' after an offer is rejected at time $t\Delta$ is the utility payoff (discounted to time $t\Delta$) that she obtains during the time interval $[t\Delta, (t + 1)\Delta]$ while the parties temporarily disagree.

always rejects any offer made to her), then player i's payoff is

$$\mathcal{I}_i(\langle s^q \rangle) = \sum_{q=0}^{\infty} \frac{(1 - \delta_i)g_i(s^q)}{r_i} \exp(-r_i q \Delta), \qquad (6.7)$$

where $\langle s^q \rangle$ denotes the infinite sequence of action profiles chosen by the players. Notice, therefore, that the impasse point $(\mathcal{I}_A(\langle s^q \rangle), \mathcal{I}_B(\langle s^q \rangle))$ — which is the payoff pair obtainable from perpetual disagreement — depends on the infinite sequence of chosen action profiles. In order to ensure that there exist gains from co-operation, assume that the sum of the players' payoffs from perpetual disagreement is less than the size of the cake. That is:

Assumption 6.1. For any infinite sequence of action profiles $\langle s^q \rangle$, $\mathcal{I}_A(\langle s^q \rangle) + \mathcal{I}_B(\langle s^q \rangle) < \pi$.

It should be noted that Assumption 6.1 implies that for any $s = (s_A, s_B)$ (where $s_A \in S_A$ and $s_B \in S_B$), $g_i(s)$ is bounded from above. It is helpful to denote the simultaneous-move game with action sets S_A and S_B, and payoff functions $g_A : S \rightarrow \Re$ and $g_B : S \rightarrow \Re$, where $S \equiv S_A \times S_B$, by $\mathcal{G}$. I call this game the 'disagreement' game, as it determines the players' payoffs while they temporarily disagree. It will be assumed that the disagreement game $\mathcal{G}$ has at least one Nash equilibrium (NE).

6.6.1 Stationary Equilibria

In a stationary SPE each player's strategy is independent of history and time: that is, each player always chooses the same action when playing the disagreement game $\mathcal{G}$, always makes the same offer when she has to make an offer and always responds to an offer in the same way when she has to respond to that offer.

Consider an arbitrary stationary SPE, and let s_A and s_B respectively denote the actions that players A and B always take when playing the disagreement game $\mathcal{G}$. It is straightforward to see that the action profile (s_A, s_B) is necessarily a Nash equilibrium of the disagreement game $\mathcal{G}$; for otherwise, some player can benefit from a unilateral deviation to an alternative action when playing $\mathcal{G}$. The set of stationary subgame perfect equilibria are thus characterized in the following proposition.

Proposition 6.5. *If the disagreement game $\mathcal{G}$ has N (where $N \geq 1$) Nash equilibria, then the model with endogenously determined inside options and discounting has N stationary subgame perfect equilibria, which are characterized as follows. For each Nash equilibrium $\widehat{s}$ of the disagreement game $\mathcal{G}$, the unique subgame perfect equilibrium in which player i $(i = A, B)$ always chooses her Nash strategy $\widehat{s}_i$ is as follows:*
- *player A always offers x_A^*, always accepts an offer x_B if and only if $x_B \leq x_B^*$, and always chooses the Nash strategy $\widehat{s}_A$,*
- *player B always offers x_B^*, always accepts an offer x_A if and only if $x_A \leq x_A^*$, and always chooses the Nash strategy $\widehat{s}_B$, where*

$$x_A^* = \frac{\widehat{g}_A}{r_A} + \frac{1 - \delta_B}{1 - \delta_A \delta_B}\left(\pi - \frac{\widehat{g}_A}{r_A} - \frac{\widehat{g}_B}{r_B}\right) \quad and$$

$$x_B^* = \frac{\widehat{g}_B}{r_B} + \frac{1 - \delta_B}{1 - \delta_A \delta_B}\left(\pi - \frac{\widehat{g}_A}{r_A} - \frac{\widehat{g}_B}{r_B}\right),$$

with $\widehat{g}_i \equiv g_i(\widehat{s})$.

Proof. The proposition follows from the argument that precedes it, and Proposition 6.1. $\qquad\square$

If the disagreement game $\mathcal{G}$ has a unique Nash equilibrium, then there exists a unique stationary SPE, which is identical to the unique SPE of the model studied in Section 6.1 in which the inside option point is exogenously specified. In the current model, however, the inside option point is endogenously determined: it is $(g_A(\widehat{s}), g_B(\widehat{s}))$, where $\widehat{s}$ is the unique Nash equilibrium of the disagreement game $\mathcal{G}$.

6.6.2 Markov Equilibria

In a Markov SPE each player's strategy is independent of history (but not necessarily of time): that is, at each time $t\Delta$ $(t = 0, 1, 2, \dots)$ each player chooses the same action when playing the disagreement game $\mathcal{G}$, and (depending on whether she has to make or respond to an offer at time $t\Delta$) she makes the same offer and responds to any offer in the same way, *whatever is the history of play until time $t\Delta$*. Of course, any stationary SPE is a Markov SPE, but the reverse is not true: there can exist a Markov SPE which is not a stationary SPE.

Consider an arbitrary Markov SPE, and let s_A^t and s_B^t respectively denote the actions that players A and B take at time $t\Delta$. It is straightforward to see that the action profile (s_A^t, s_B^t) is necessarily a Nash equilibrium of the disagreement game $\mathcal{G}$; for otherwise, some player can benefit from a unilateral deviation to an alternative action when playing $\mathcal{G}$ at time $t\Delta$. This implies that if $\mathcal{G}$ has a unique Nash equilibrium, then there does not exist a Markov SPE which is not a stationary SPE. However, if $\mathcal{G}$ has two or more Nash equilibria, then there exist many Markov SPE which are not stationary SPE; in such a Markov SPE the players play different Nash equilibria of $\mathcal{G}$ at different times. The following proposition characterizes the set of Markov subgame perfect equilibria that differ from the set of stationary subgame perfect equilibria.

Proposition 6.6. *(i) If the disagreement game $\mathcal{G}$ has a unique Nash equilibrium, then the model with endogenously determined inside options and discounting does not have a Markov SPE that is different from the unique stationary SPE.*

(ii) If the disagreement game $\mathcal{G}$ has N (where $N \geq 2$) Nash equilibria and if $r_A = r_B = r$, then the model with endogenously determined inside options and discounting has an infinite number of Markov SPE (that differ from the N stationary SPE) and are characterized as follows. Let the set of Nash equilibrium action profiles of the disagreement game $\mathcal{G}$ be denoted by $\mathcal{N}$. For any (infinite) sequence of action profiles $\langle s^t \rangle$ such that for each $t = 0, 1, 2, \ldots, s^t \in \mathcal{N}$, and such that for some $t' \neq t''$, $s^{t'} \neq s^{t''}$, the unique subgame perfect equilibrium in which the action profile chosen at time $t\Delta$ $(t = 0, 1, 2, \ldots)$ is s^t is a Markov subgame perfect equilibrium. In this SPE player A's equilibrium offer x_A^0 at time 0 is accepted by player B, where

$$x_A^0 = \frac{\pi}{1+\delta} + \sum_{t=0}^{\infty} \delta^{2t} \left[\frac{\delta(1-\delta)g_A(s^{2t+1})}{r} - \frac{(1-\delta)g_B(s^{2t})}{r} \right].$$

Proof. Proposition 6.6(i) follows from the argument that precedes it, and Proposition 6.6(ii) is proven in the Appendix.[15] $\square$

---

[15]It should be noted that unlike Propositions 6.5 and 6.6(i), Proposition 6.6(ii) requires that the players' discount rates are identical. The reason for this is explained in the proof to Proposition 6.6(ii). It should also be noted that Proposition 6.6(ii) states that the unique subgame perfect equilibrium in which the action profile chosen at time $t\Delta$

Since $N \geq 2$, there exists an infinite number of (infinite) sequences of NE action profiles $\langle s^t \rangle$ as defined in Proposition 6.6(ii); and hence, there exists an infinite number Markov SPE. Any pair of such Markov SPE differ from each other, because there will exist a t' such that the action profiles chosen at time $t'\Delta$ in these two equilibria will differ. However, it should be noted that some of these Markov SPE will be payoff equivalent, because player A's equilibrium offer x_A^0 at time 0 — which is accepted by player B — does not depend on the entire (infinite) sequence of payoff pairs $\langle g(s^t) \rangle$ associated with the infinite sequence of NE action profiles $\langle s^t \rangle$; as is evident from the expression for x_A^0, x_A^0 does not depend on player i's inside option when her offer is rejected (that is, it does not depend on $g_A(s^{2t})$ and $g_B(s^{2t+1})$ for all $t = 0, 1, 2, \ldots$).

In any Markov SPE (when $N \geq 2$) the payoffs to players A and B are respectively x_A^0 and $\pi - x_A^0$. An important thing to notice, as mentioned above, is that x_A^0 does not depend on the entire (infinite) sequence of payoff pairs $\langle g(s^t) \rangle$ associated with the infinite sequence of NE action profiles $\langle s^t \rangle$. This means that player i's 'bargaining power' (as reflected in her share of the cake in any Markov SPE) is: (i) strictly increasing in the inside options that she obtains after she rejects offers made by player j ($j \neq i$), (ii) unaffected by the inside options that she obtains after her offers are rejected by player j ($j \neq i$), (iii) strictly decreasing in the inside options that player j obtains after she rejects the offers made by player i, and (iv) unaffected by the inside options that player j obtains after player i rejects offers made by player j.[16]

Example 6.1. Consider the bargaining situation in which the disagreement

---

($t = 0, 1, 2, \ldots$) is s^t is a Markov subgame perfect equilibrium — although in this section it is only required to characterize the unique Markov SPE in which the action profile chosen at time $t\Delta$ ($t = 0, 1, 2, \ldots$) is s^t. However, this stronger result drops out naturally from the required arguments. It may be noted that this stronger result implies that in any non-Markov SPE (which are the subject of discussion in the next section), it is necessary that at some time (and for some history) the action profile chosen in $\mathcal{G}$ is not a Nash equilibrium.

[16]The intuition for these observations is straightforward, and further illustrates a key insight about bargaining processes (as obtained in other contexts as well), which can be put in the following general manner: a player's 'bargaining power' is independent of what happens to her after her offers are rejected. This is because the decision to accept or reject an offer is made by her opponent, who is only influenced by what happens to her if she rejects an offer (and not by what happens to the proposer if she were to reject the proposer's offer).

game $\mathcal{G}$ is the 'Battle of Sexes' game: Romeo (player R) and Juliet (player J) have two possible actions each, namely, 'Go to the Ballet' (b) and 'Go to the Big Fight at the Colosseum' (f), and Table 6.1 depicts the payoff pairs $(g_R(.,.), g_J(.,.))$ for each possible action profile. Assume that $\pi = 6/r$ and that the players have a common discount rate $r > 0$. Without loss of generality, assume that Romeo makes offers at times $t\Delta$ where t is even (i.e., $t = 0, 2, 4, \dots$) and Juliet makes offers at times $t\Delta$ where t is odd (i.e., $t = 1, 3, 5, \dots$).

Juliet

		b	f
	b	2,3	0,0
Romeo			
	f	0,0	3,2

Table 6.1: The Battle of Sexes game.

This disagreement game has two Nash equilibria in pure strategies: $s(1) = (b, b)$ and $s(2) = (f, f)$. In the former Nash equilibrium $g(1) = (2, 3)$, and in the latter Nash equilibrium $g(2) = (3, 2)$. Hence, applying Proposition 6.5, there are two pure-strategy stationary SPE, and in both of them agreement is reached immediately, at time 0. In the stationary SPE in which the inside option point is $g(1) = (2, 3)$, the limiting (as $\Delta \to 0$) SPE payoffs to R and J are respectively $5/2r$ and $7/2r$, while in the other stationary SPE (in which the inside option point is $g(2) = (3, 2)$), the limiting (as $\Delta \to 0$) SPE payoffs to R and J are respectively $7/2r$ and $5/2r$.

The disagreement game also has a Nash equilibrium in mixed strategies: Romeo chooses b with probability $2/5$, and Juliet chooses b with probability $3/5$. In this mixed NE the inside option point is $(6/5, 6/5)$. Hence, it follows from Proposition 6.5 that there exists a mixed-strategy stationary SPE, in which the limiting (as $\Delta \to 0$) SPE payoff to each player is $3/r$.

I now characterize two pure-strategy Markov SPE, which are not these stationary equilibria. Applying Proposition 6.6(ii), in the SPE in which at times $t\Delta$ where t is even the players play the Nash equilibrium $s(k)$ ($k = 1, 2$) and at times $t\Delta$ where t is odd the players play the Nash equilibrium $s(l)$ ($l \neq k$), agreement is reached immediately at time 0 with player R's equilibrium share being

$$ x_R^0 = \frac{6}{(1+\delta)r} + \frac{\delta g_R(l)}{(1+\delta)r} - \frac{g_J(k)}{(1+\delta)r}. $$

Hence, in the limit, as $\Delta \to 0$, the SPE payoffs to R and J (namely x_R^0 and $\pi - x_R^0$) respectively converge to

$$ \frac{g_R(l)}{r} + \frac{1}{2}\left[\frac{6}{r} - \frac{g_R(l)}{r} - \frac{g_J(k)}{r}\right] \quad \text{and} \quad \frac{g_J(k)}{r} + \frac{1}{2}\left[\frac{6}{r} - \frac{g_R(l)}{r} - \frac{g_J(k)}{r}\right]. $$

Hence, if $k = 1$ and $l = 2$ — which means that after J rejects offers made by R the players' inside options are determined by the pair of flow rates $g(1) = (2, 3)$, while after R rejects offers made by J the players' inside options are determined by the pair of flow rates $g(2) = (3, 2)$ — then the limiting (as $\Delta \to 0$) SPE payoffs to R and J are identical and equal $3/r$. One the other hand, if $k = 2$ and $l = 1$ — which means that after J rejects offers made by R the players' inside options are determined by the pair of flow rates $g(2) = (3, 2)$, while after R rejects offers made by J the players' inside options are determined by the pair of flow rates $g(1) = (2, 3)$ — then the limiting (as $\Delta \to 0$) SPE payoffs to R and J are identical and equal $3/r$. Thus, although the players' limiting payoffs in these two Markov SPE are identical, these two equilibria differ according to the Nash equilibrium played at each time $t\Delta$ ($t = 0, 1, 2, \dots$). Notice that relative to the players' payoffs in each of the pure-strategy stationary SPE described above, these two Markov SPE make one player better off and the other player worse off. On the other hand, the players' payoffs in these two Markov SPE are identical to their payoffs in the mixed-strategy stationary SPE.[17]

---

[17]It should be noted — as indicated in Proposition 6.6(ii) — that there exists infinitely many other Markov SPE.

6.6.3   Uniqueness of SPE and Non-Markov Equilibria

In a non-Markov SPE a player's strategy is not necessarily independent of history and time: that is, at each time $t\Delta$ ($t = 0, 1, 2, \ldots$) each player's action in the disagreement game $\mathcal{G}$, and (depending on whether she has to make or respond to an offer at time $t\Delta$) her offer and response to an offer may depend on the history of play until time $t\Delta$. In this section I investigate the possible existence of non-Markov SPE. As has been noted above, Proposition 6.6(ii) implies that any SPE in which the players' chosen action profile when playing $\mathcal{G}$ is always a Nash equilibrium of $\mathcal{G}$ is necessarily a Markov SPE. Hence, in a non-Markov SPE it is necessary that at some time (and for some history) the action profile chosen in $\mathcal{G}$ is not a Nash equilibrium of $\mathcal{G}$.

In order to investigate the potential existence of such non-Markov SPE, I first derive a useful property of the set of *all* SPE payoffs. This property enables us to state conditions under which there exists an essentially *unique* SPE — under such conditions, non-Markov SPE do not exist.

On the Uniqueness of the SPE

Given the underlying stationarity in the strategic structure of the bargaining model, the sets of subgame perfect equilibria of any two subgames beginning with player i's offer are identical. This implies that the set of SPE payoffs to player i in any subgame beginning with her offer is uniquely defined[18] — which is denoted by G_i.[19] Let m_i and M_i respectively denote the infimum and supremum of G_i. The useful property referred to above, which is stated in Lemma 6.3 below, is a lower bound on m_i and an upper bound on M_i. I shall interpret these bounds after their formal statement in Lemma 6.3. It should be noted that unlike Proposition 6.6(ii), this lemma is valid for any r_A and r_B.

---

[18]That is, this set of SPE payoffs depends neither on the *time* at which such a subgame begins nor on the *history* of play that precedes such a subgame.

[19]Formally, $u_i \in G_i$ if and only if there exists a SPE in a subgame beginning with player i's offer that gives her a payoff of u_i.

Lemma 6.3.

$$m_A \geq \frac{v_A}{r_A} + \frac{1-\delta_B}{1-\delta_A\delta_B}\left(\pi - \frac{v_A}{r_A} - \frac{\bar{v}_B}{r_B}\right)$$

$$M_A \leq \frac{\bar{v}_A}{r_A} + \frac{1-\delta_B}{1-\delta_A\delta_B}\left(\pi - \frac{\bar{v}_A}{r_A} - \frac{v_B}{r_B}\right)$$

$$m_B \geq \frac{v_B}{r_B} + \frac{1-\delta_A}{1-\delta_A\delta_B}\left(\pi - \frac{\bar{v}_A}{r_A} - \frac{v_B}{r_B}\right)$$

$$M_B \leq \frac{\bar{v}_B}{r_B} + \frac{1-\delta_A}{1-\delta_A\delta_B}\left(\pi - \frac{v_A}{r_A} - \frac{\bar{v}_B}{r_B}\right),$$

where $\quad v_A = \inf_{s_B \in S_B}\left(\sup_{s_A \in S_A} g_A(s)\right), \quad v_B = \inf_{s_A \in S_A}\left(\sup_{s_B \in S_B} g_B(s)\right),$

$$\bar{v}_A = \sup_{s \in S}\left(g_A(s) - \gamma_A\left(\sup_{s'_B \in S_B} g_B(s_A, s'_B) - g_B(s)\right)\right) \quad and$$

$$\bar{v}_B = \sup_{s \in S}\left(g_B(s) - \gamma_B\left(\sup_{s'_A \in S_A} g_A(s'_A, s_B) - g_A(s)\right)\right),$$

with $\gamma_A = \delta_A(1-\delta_B)r_A/\delta_B(1-\delta_A)r_B$ and $\gamma_B = \delta_B(1-\delta_A)r_B/\delta_A(1-\delta_B)r_A$.

Proof. In the Appendix.   □

By the definition of v_i, the worst possible payoff that player i can obtain from the disagreement game between two consecutive offers in any SPE is greater than or equal to $(1-\delta_i)v_i/r_i$.[20] In the interpretation to follow of the bounds on m_i and M_j, I assume that $(v_i, \bar{v}_j)$ is a Nash equilibrium payoff pair of the disagreement game — that is, there exists a NE strategy pair $\hat{s}$ in $\mathcal{G}$ such that $g_i(\hat{s}) = v_i$ and $g_j(\hat{s}) = \bar{v}_j$. It follows from Proposition 6.5 that in the unique stationary SPE in which the action profile chosen in $\mathcal{G}$ is always $\hat{s}$, player i's SPE payoff in any subgame beginning with her offer equals the lower bound on m_i, and player j's SPE payoff in any subgame beginning with her offer equals the upper bound on M_j. Hence, for each i ($i = A, B$), the lower bound on m_i (resp., the upper bound on M_i) may

---

[20]That is, in any SPE player j cannot force player i's inside option to be lower than $(1-\delta_i)v_i/r_i$. It should be noted that v_i is player i's minimax payoff in $\mathcal{G}$.

be interpreted as player i's *worst* (resp., *best*) SPE payoff in any subgame beginning with her offer.

Lemma 6.4. *For any Nash equilibrium $\widehat{s}$ of the disagreement game, $\bar{v}_A \geq g_A(\widehat{s}) \geq \underline{v}_A$ and $\bar{v}_B \geq g_B(\widehat{s}) \geq \underline{v}_B$. Furthermore, for each i ($i = A, B$), $\bar{v}_i \geq \underline{v}_i$.*

Proof. For each $s \in S$, let

$$W(s) = g_A(s) - \gamma_A \left(\sup_{s'_B \in S_B} g_B(s_A, s'_B) - g_B(s) \right),$$

where γ_A is defined in Lemma 6.3. Furthermore, let $\widehat{s}$ denote an arbitrary NE of $\mathcal{G}$. Since, by the definition of a Nash equilibrium,

$$g_B(\widehat{s}) = \max_{s'_B \in S_B} g_B(\widehat{s}_A, s'_B)$$

it follows that $W(\widehat{s}) = g_A(\widehat{s})$. Hence, by the definition of $\bar{v}_A$ — as stated in Lemma 6.3 — it follows that $\bar{v}_A \geq g_A(\widehat{s})$. It is a standard result in game theory — and, in fact, trivial to verify — that $g_A(\widehat{s})$ is greater than or equal to player A's minimax payoff, and thus, $g_A(\widehat{s}) \geq \underline{v}_A$. The above results imply — in combination with the assumption that $\mathcal{G}$ has at least one Nash equilibrium — that $\bar{v}_A \geq \underline{v}_A$. A symmetric argument, with the roles of A and B reversed, completes the proof. $\square$

Lemmas 6.3 and 6.4 imply that if for each $i = A, B$, $\underline{v}_i = \bar{v}_i$, then $M_i = m_i - x_i^*$, where

$$x_A^* = \frac{\widehat{g}_A}{r_A} + \frac{1 - \delta_B}{1 - \delta_A \delta_B} \left(\pi - \frac{\widehat{g}_A}{r_A} - \frac{\widehat{g}_B}{r_B} \right) \quad \text{and} \tag{6.8}$$

$$x_B^* = \frac{\widehat{g}_B}{r_B} + \frac{1 - \delta_A}{1 - \delta_A \delta_B} \left(\pi - \frac{\widehat{g}_A}{r_A} - \frac{\widehat{g}_B}{r_B} \right), \tag{6.9}$$

where $(\widehat{g}_A, \widehat{g}_B)$ denotes the uniquely defined Nash equilibrium payoff pair of the disagreement game.[21] Since $M_i = m_i$ ($i = A, B$), it is straightforward to argue that in any SPE of any subgame beginning with player i's offer, player

---

[21]Lemma 6.4 implies that if for each $i = A, B$, $\underline{v}_i = \bar{v}_i$, then all Nash equilibria are payoff-equivalent.

i's equilibrium offer is x_i^*, and it is accepted by player j. This implies that when playing the disagreement game at any time $t\Delta$, the players always choose some Nash equilibrium action profile of $\mathcal{G}$, which, if two or more exist, are payoff equivalent. This, in turn, implies that player j accepts an offer x_i if and only if $\pi - x_i \geq (1 - \delta_j)\widehat{g}_j/r_j + \delta_j x_j^*$ — that is, if and only if $x_i \leq x_i^*$. I have thus established the following proposition.

Proposition 6.7. *If for each $i = A, B$, $\underline{v}_i = \bar{v}_i$, where $\underline{v}_i$ and $\bar{v}_i$ are defined in Lemma 6.3, then the model with endogenously determined inside options and discounting has (essentially) a unique subgame perfect equilibrium. In any SPE player i ($i = A, B$) always offers x_i^* and always accepts an offer x_j ($j \neq i$) if and only if $x_j \leq x_j^*$, where x_A^* and x_B^* are defined in (6.8) and (6.9). Furthermore, when playing the disagreement game, the players' chosen action profile is a Nash equilibrium of $\mathcal{G}$, where all Nash equilibria of $\mathcal{G}$ are payoff-equivalent.*

Proof. The proposition follows from the argument that precedes it.   □

It should be noted that any SPE described in Proposition 6.7 is a Markov SPE; that is, under the hypothesis of Proposition 6.7 there does not exist a non-Markov SPE. Furthermore, since all Markov SPE described in Proposition 6.7 are payoff-equivalent, it is valid for any r_A and r_B — unlike Proposition 6.6(ii), which is valid if $r_A = r_B$. The following example illustrates this proposition.

Example 6.2. Consider the bargaining situation in which the disagreement game $\mathcal{G}$ is the 'Prisoners' Dilemma' game: player A and player B have two possible actions each, namely, c and d, and Table 6.2 depicts the payoff pairs $(g_A(.,.), g_B(.,.))$ for each possible action profile. Assume that $\pi = 4/r$ and that the players have a common discount rate $r > 0$. This disagreement game has a unique Nash equilibrium, namely, $\widehat{s} = (d, d)$. In this unique Nash equilibrium $\widehat{g} = (0, 0)$. Hence, Proposition 6.5 implies that there is a unique stationary SPE, in which the inside option point is $\widehat{g} = (0, 0)$, and the limiting (as $\Delta \to 0$) SPE payoffs to players A and B are respectively $2/r$ and $2/r$. Proposition 6.6(i) implies that there does not exist a Markov SPE that is different from this unique stationary SPE. It is straightforward to show that for each $i = A, B$, $\bar{v}_i = 0$ and $\underline{v}_i = 0$. Hence, it follows from Proposition 6.7, that the unique stationary SPE is the unique SPE of the model — there does not exist a non-Markov SPE.

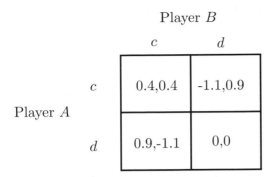

Player B

	c	d
c	0.4,0.4	-1.1,0.9
d	0.9,-1.1	0,0

Player A

Table 6.2: The Prisoners' Dilemma game.

Existence of non-Markov SPE

I now consider disagreement games that fail to satisfy the hypothesis of Proposition 6.7; that is, for some i $(i = A$ or $i = B)$, $\bar{v}_i > \underline{v}_i$. A key result — stated in Lemma 6.5 below — establishes the existence of two ('extremal') SPE: for each $i = A, B$, the lower bound on m_i (as stated in Lemma 6.3) is sustained as a SPE payoff to player i in any subgame beginning with her offer. Thus, the lower bound on m_i is player i's *worst* SPE payoff in any subgame beginning with her offer.

Lemma 6.5. *Assume that* $r_A = r_B = r$. *For each* i $(i = A, B)$ *there exists a* $\Delta_i > 0$ *such that for any* $\Delta < \Delta_i$ *there exists a SPE in any subgame beginning with player* i*'s offer such that player* i*'s equilibrium payoff equals*

$$\underline{u}_i = \frac{v_i}{r} + \frac{1}{1+\delta}\left(\pi - \frac{v_i}{r} - \frac{\bar{v}_j}{r}\right) \quad (j \neq i).$$

Proof. In the Appendix. □

In the limit, as $\Delta \to 0$, player i's worst SPE payoff in any subgame beginning with her offer $\underline{u}_i$ converges to $\underline{y}_i$, where $\underline{y}_i$ is defined in Proposition 6.8 below. It should be noted that if for some i $(i = A$ or $i = B)$ $\bar{v}_i > \underline{v}_i$, then $\underline{y}_A + \underline{y}_B < \pi$. I now provide an informal argument which shows that (in the limit, as $\Delta \to 0$) there exists a multiplicity of SPE. Consider any path of play in which agreement is reached at time $t\Delta$ $(t = 0, 1, 2, 3, \dots)$ on a partition (y_A, y_B) of the cake such that $y_i \geq \underline{y}_i$ $(i = A, B)$, where y_i denotes player i's share.[22] Player i's payoff from this path of play in the limit as $\Delta \to 0$ is y_i. It immediately follows that in the limit as $\Delta \to 0$, the proposed path of play can be supported as a SPE path of play by reverting to one of the two extremal SPE when a player unilaterally deviates from the proposed path of play.[23] This informal argument can be formalized, and shown to be valid for Δ sufficiently small. Hence, I obtain the following result.

Proposition 6.8. *Assume that $r_A = r_B = r$, and that for some i ($i = A$ or $i = B$), $\bar{v}_i > \underline{v}_i$. There exists a $\bar{\Delta}$ such that for any $\Delta < \bar{\Delta}$ there exists a continuum of SPE in the model with endogenously determined inside options and discounting. For any partition (y_A, y_B) of the cake such that $y_i \geq \underline{y}_i$ ($i = A, B$), where y_i denotes player i's share and*

$$\underline{y}_i = \frac{1}{2}\left(\pi + \frac{\bar{v}_i}{r} - \frac{\bar{v}_j}{r}\right) \quad (j \neq i),$$

and any time $t\Delta$ ($t = 0, 1, 2, 3, \dots$), there exists a SPE such that in the limit as $\Delta \to 0$ agreement is reached at time $t\Delta$ on the partition (y_A, y_B).

It should be noted that if the disagreement game satisfies the hypothesis of Proposition 6.8, then (for any Δ sufficiently small) the bargaining model with inside options and discounting has a multiplicity of SPE — notwithstanding the possibility that the disagreement game has a unique Nash equilibrium. Furthermore, there exists a continuum of Pareto-inefficient SPE.

6.7   An Application to Wage Renegotiations

A firm has discovered a new technology that will enable it to produce π^* units of output per worker per unit time, where $\pi^* > 1$. With its existing technology it produces one unit of output per worker per unit time. The current wage per unit time is α, where $0 < \alpha < 1$, and the current profit per

---

[22]Since, as shown above, $\underline{y}_A + \underline{y}_B < \pi$, there exists a continuum of such partitions.

[23]If player i deviates from the proposed path of play, then play proceeds according to the SPE that gives player i her worst SPE payoff in any subgame beginning with her offer. Hence, in the limit as $\Delta \to 0$, player i has no incentive to deviate from the proposed path of play — because her (limiting) payoff from such a unilateral deviation is $\underline{y}_i$, which (by hypothesis) does not exceed her (limiting) payoff from the path of play, namely, y_i.

worker per unit time is $1 - \alpha$. However, before the new technology will be used, the firm F and its union U have to renegotiate the wage rate. Since $\pi^* > 1$, it is mutually beneficial to use the new technology.

While bargaining over the new wage rate w, where $w \in [0, \pi^*]$, the union can decide whether or not to go on strike. The renegotiation process is modelled by the bargaining game described in Section 6.6 in which the players have a common discount rate r, $\pi = \pi^*/r$, and the disagreement game is as follows. The union's set of actions is $\{0, 1\}$, where 0 means that the union goes on strike for Δ units of time, and 1 that it does not go on strike. The firm has no action to take in the disagreement game. If the union goes on strike for Δ units of time, then no output is produced and no wage is paid, and hence, $g_F(0) = g_U(0) = 0$. On the other hand, if the union does not go on strike during the time interval Δ, then Δ units of output is produced, and the payoffs to the firm and the union are respectively $(1 - \delta)g_F(1)/r$ and $(1 - \delta)g_U(1)/r$, where $g_F(1) = 1 - \alpha$ and $g_U(1) = \alpha$.[24] Thus, while the parties temporarily disagree and the union does not go on strike, the old technology is used to produce output, and each worker is employed at the old wage rate.

6.7.1   Multiple Pareto-Efficient Equilibria

The disagreement game — which is a single-person decision problem — has a unique Nash equilibrium, in which the union does not go on strike. Hence, the unique NE payoff pair of the disagreement game is $\hat{g} = (\alpha, 1 - \alpha)$.

It follows from Propositions 6.5 and 6.6(i) that there exists a unique stationary SPE, which is the unique Markov SPE. In the unique (limiting, as $\Delta \to 0$) stationary SPE agreement is reached at time 0 on wage rate w^*, where

$$w^* = \alpha + \frac{1}{2}(\pi^* - 1).$$

The firm's profit per worker per unit time is

$$\pi^* - w^* = (1 - \alpha) + \frac{1}{2}(\pi^* - 1).$$

Notice that this unique (limiting) stationary SPE is Pareto efficient: agreement is reached at time 0, and the union does not go on strike. Furthermore,

---

[24]It is assumed that the union's objective is to maximize the wage rate.

the benefit of the new technology relative to the old technology — as captured by the increase in the output per worker per unit time, namely, $\pi^* - 1$ — is split equally between the firm and a worker.

I now consider the potential existence of Pareto efficient non-Markov SPE. It is straightforward to show that the minimax payoffs to the firm and the union in the disagreement game are respectively zero and α. In the notation of Lemma 6.3, $\underline{v}_F = 0$ and $\underline{v}_U = \alpha$. Furthermore, it is straightforward to show that $\bar{v}_F = 1 - \alpha$ and $\bar{v}_U = \alpha$. Hence, since $\bar{v}_F > \underline{v}_F$, Proposition 6.7 is not applicable. Indeed, it follows from Proposition 6.8 that there exists a $\bar{\Delta}$ such that for any $\Delta < \bar{\Delta}$ there exists a continuum of Pareto-efficient (non-Markov) SPE. In the limit, as $\Delta \to 0$, any partition (y_F, y_U) of the cake agreed to at time 0 such that $y_i \geq \underline{y}_i$ $(i = F, U)$ can be sustained by a SPE, where

$$\underline{y}_F = \frac{1}{2}\left(\frac{\pi^*}{r} - \frac{\alpha}{r}\right) \quad \text{and} \quad \underline{y}_U = \frac{1}{2}\left(\frac{\pi^*}{r} + \frac{\alpha}{r} - \frac{(1-\alpha)}{r}\right).$$

Letting $\underline{w}$ denote the wage rate associated with the (limiting) SPE in which the partition is such that $y_U = \underline{y}_U$, it follows that

$$\underline{w} = \alpha + \frac{1}{2}(\pi^* - 1).$$

Furthermore, letting $\bar{w}$ denote the wage rate associated with the (limiting) SPE in which the partition is such that $y_F = \underline{y}_F$, it follows that

$$\bar{w} = \frac{1}{2}(\pi^* + \alpha).$$

Hence, in the limit as $\Delta \to 0$, any wage rate w such that $\underline{w} \leq w \leq \bar{w}$ agreed to at time 0 can be sustained in a SPE.

Notice that $w^* = \underline{w}$, and, hence, the unique (limiting) stationary SPE — in which the union never goes on strike — sustains (in the limit as $\Delta \to 0$) the worst (limiting) SPE wage (payoff) to the union. The pair of strategies that sustain the worst SPE payoff to the firm are described in Table 6.3, with the initial state being s_F. Notice that in state s_F the union always goes on strike after the firm rejects any offer, and it does not ever go on strike after it rejects any offer made by the firm. The idea is to maximize the 'cost of rejection' to the firm and, at the same time, minimize the 'cost of rejection' to the union. Since striking is costly to the union, it needs to be provided with an incentive to go on strike. As shown in Table 6.3, if the union fails to go on strike, then the state switches to s_U where the union obtains its worst (limiting) SPE wage. Indeed, when Δ is small, the loss from going on strike — which is approximately equal to $\alpha\Delta$ — is outweighed by the gain from going on strike — which equals $(\bar{w} - \underline{w})/r$ (i.e., $(1 - \alpha)/2r$).

		state s_F	state s_U
Firm	offer	$\bar{w}$	$\underline{w}$
	accept	$w \leq \bar{w}$	$w \leq \underline{w}$
Union	offer	$\bar{w}$	$\underline{w}$
	accept	$w \geq \bar{w}$	$w \geq \underline{w}$
	strike?	'yes' after the firm rejects any offer; 'no' after the union rejects any offer	no
	transitions	switch to state s_U if the union does not go on strike after the firm rejects an offer	absorbing

Table 6.3: The two 'extremal' SPE of the wage renegotiations model; if play begins in state s_i ($i - F, U$), then player i obtains her worst SPE payoff.

6.7.2   Equilibria with Strikes

It is easy to construct SPE in which agreement is reached after the union goes on strike for some time. Let w be any wage rate such that $\underline{w} < w < \bar{w}$, and $T = t\Delta$ where $t = \{1, 2, 3, 4, \dots\}$. Consider the following path of play. At any time $t < T$: (i) when a player has to make an offer, she asks for the whole cake (that is, the union offers a wage rate of π^* and the firm offers a wage rate of zero), (ii) when a player has to respond to an offer, she rejects any offer, and (iii) the union always goes on strike. Then at time T the wage rate offered is w and it is accepted. This path of play can be supported (provided Δ is sufficiently small) as a SPE path of play by reverting to one of the two extremal SPE when a player unilaterally deviates from this path of play — and needs to be punished. Thus, if the firm (resp., the union) deviates from this path of play, then immediately play proceeds according to the SPE described in Table 6.3 with the initial state being s_F (resp., s_U). Hence, in this model with perfect information it is possible to rationalize the occurrence of strikes.

6.8   Appendix: Proofs

Proof of Proposition 6.6(ii)

The proof begins by not assuming that $r_A = r_B$, so that I can show exactly why one needs to make this assumption. Fix an arbitrary (infinite) sequence of Nash equilibrium action profiles $\langle s^t \rangle$ as specified in the proposition. The strategy of the proof is as follows. Using an argument similar to that contained in Section 3.2.1, I first establish that there exists a unique Markov SPE in which the action profile chosen at time $t\Delta$ ($t = 0, 1, 2, \dots$) is s^t and in which any equilibrium offer is accepted. I then, using an argument similar to that contained in Section 3.2.2, show that there does not exist any other SPE in which the action profile chosen at time $t\Delta$ ($t = 0, 1, 2, \dots$) is s^t. This would then establish Proposition 6.6(ii).

Consider a Markov SPE in which the action profile chosen at time $t\Delta$ ($t = 0, 1, 2, \dots$) is s^t and in which any equilibrium offer is accepted. Let x_A^{2t} denote the equilibrium offer of player A at time $2t\Delta$ ($t = 0, 1, 2, \dots$) and x_B^{2t+1} the equilibrium offer of player B at time $(2t + 1)\Delta$ ($t = 0, 1, 2, \dots$). Since any equilibrium offer is accepted, it follows that at time $2t\Delta$ ($t = 0, 1, 2, \dots$) player B accepts any offer y_A^{2t} such that $\pi - y_A^{2t} > (1 - \delta_B)g_B(s^{2t})/r_B + \delta_B x_B^{2t+1}$, and rejects any offer y_A^{2t} such that $\pi - y_A^{2t} < (1 - \delta_B)g_B(s^{2t})/r_B + \delta_B x_B^{2t+1}$, where the right-hand side of this inequality is player B's equilibrium payoff from rejecting any offer at time $2t\Delta$. Furthermore, since the equilibrium offer is accepted, $\pi - x_A^{2t} \geq (1 - \delta_B)g_B(s^{2t})/r_B + \delta_B x_B^{2t+1}$. In fact, $\pi - x_A^{2t} = (1 - \delta_B)g_B(s^{2t})/r_B + \delta_B x_B^{2t+1}$; for otherwise player A can profitably deviate by offering $y_A^{2t} > x_A^{2t}$. Since a symmetric argument establishes similar results for player A, it follows that the sequence $\langle x_A^{2t}, x_B^{2t+1} \rangle_{t=0}^{\infty}$ of equilibrium offers must be such that for each $t = 0, 1, 2, \ldots$,

$$\pi - x_A^{2t} = \frac{(1 - \delta_B)g_B(s^{2t})}{r_B} + \delta_B x_B^{2t+1} \quad \text{and} \qquad (6.10)$$

$$\pi - x_B^{2t+1} = \frac{(1 - \delta_A)g_A(s^{2t+1})}{r_A} + \delta_A x_A^{2t+2}. \qquad (6.11)$$

Furthermore, since each player can always adopt the strategy in which she asks for the whole cake and rejects all offers, it follows that for each $k = 0, 1, 2, \ldots$

$$x_A^{2k} \geq I_A^{2k}(\langle s^t \rangle) \qquad (6.12)$$

$$\pi - x_A^{2k} \geq I_B^{2k}(\langle s^t \rangle) \qquad (6.13)$$

$$x_B^{2k+1} \geq I_B^{2k+1}(\langle s^t \rangle) \qquad (6.14)$$

$$\pi - x_B^{2k+1} \geq I_A^{2k+1}(\langle s^t \rangle), \qquad (6.15)$$

where $I_i^k(\langle s^t \rangle)$ is player i's payoff (discounted to time $k\Delta$) from time $k\Delta$ ($k = 0, 1, 2, \ldots$) onwards if the players perpetually disagree. That is

$$I_i^k(\langle s^t \rangle) = \sum_{t=k}^{\infty} \delta_i^{(t-k)} \frac{(1 - \delta_i)g_i(s^t)}{r_i}. \qquad (6.16)$$

Notice that Assumption 6.1 implies that for any k, if inequality 6.12 (resp., 6.14) is satisfied, then inequality 6.13 (resp., 6.15) is also satisfied. Hence, it follows that the Markov SPE being considered here exists only if there exists a sequence $\langle x_A^{2t}, x_B^{2t+1} \rangle_{t=0}^{\infty}$ that satisfies (6.10), (6.11), (6.12) and (6.14).[25]

In Claim 6.1 below I show that there exists a unique sequence $\langle x_A^{2t}, x_B^{2t+1} \rangle_{t=0}^{\infty}$ that satisfies (6.10) and (6.11). This result is valid for any r_A and r_B. Then, in Claim 6.2 I show that if $r_A = r_B$, then this unique sequence also satisfies (6.12) and (6.14). Hence, it is in establishing Claim 6.2 that I require the assumption $r_A = r_B$.

Claims 6.1 and 6.2 thus imply that if $r_A = r_B = r$, then there exists at most a unique Markov SPE in which the action profile chosen at time $t\Delta$ ($t = 0, 1, 2, \ldots$) is s^t and in which any equilibrium offer is accepted. In this

---

[25] It should be noted that any sequence that satisfies (6.10)–(6.15) is 'feasible': that is, for any $t = 0, 1, 2, 3, \ldots$, $x_A^{2t} \in [0, \pi]$ and $x_B^{2t+1} \in [0, \pi]$ — this is implied by (6.12)–(6.15), because for any $k = 0, 1, 2, 3, \ldots$, $I_i^k(\langle s^t \rangle) \geq 0$.

Markov SPE the sequence of equilibrium offers are defined by the sequence $\langle x_A^{2t}, x_B^{2t+1} \rangle_{t=0}^{\infty}$, and when a player has to respond to any offer at any time $t\Delta$ she accepts an offer if and only if it is less than or equal to the equilibrium offer at time $t\Delta$. It follows immediately from the arguments above that this Markov SPE exists — that is, this pair of strategies is a subgame perfect equilibrium.

I now show that there does not exist another SPE in which the action profile chosen at time $t\Delta$ ($t = 0, 1, 2, \dots$) is s^t. The argument is similar to that contained in Section 3.2.2. Let M_A^{2t} and m_A^{2t} ($t = 0, 1, 2, \dots$) respectively denote the supremum and infimum of the set of payoffs to player A obtainable in any SPE *in which the action profile chosen at time $t\Delta$ ($t = 0, 1, 2, \dots$) is s^t of any subgame at time $2t\Delta$*. Similarly, let M_B^{2t+1} and m_B^{2t+1} ($t = 0, 1, 2, \dots$) respectively denote the supremum and infimum of the set of all payoffs to player B obtainable in any SPE *in which the action profile chosen at time $t\Delta$ ($t = 0, 1, 2, \dots$) is s^t of any subgame at time $(2t+1)\Delta$*. Through a slight modification to the arguments in Section 3.2.2, it can be shown that for each $t = 0, 1, 2, \dots$, $(M_A^{2t}, m_B^{2t+1}) = (x_A^{2t}, x_B^{2t+1})$ and $(m_A^{2t}, M_B^{2t+1}) = (x_A^{2t}, x_B^{2t+1})$, where the sequence $\langle x_A^{2t}, x_B^{2t+1} \rangle$ satisfies (6.10) and (6.11).[26] Furthermore, for each $k = 0, 1, 2, \dots$, $m_A^{2k} = x_A^{2k}$ satisfies (6.12) and (6.13), and $m_B^{2k+1} = x_B^{2k+1}$ satisfies (6.14) and (6.15). From Claims 6.1 and 6.2 it follows that for each $t = 0, 1, 2, \dots$, $M_A^{2t} = m_A^{2t}$ and $M_B^{2t+1} = m_B^{2t+1}$. Hence, the payoffs to the players in any SPE in which the action profile chosen at time $t\Delta$ ($t = 0, 1, 2, \dots$) is s^t are uniquely defined. It is then trivial to show, using an argument similar to that used in Section 3.2.2, that in any such SPE the equilibrium offers are accepted and, moreover, that there is only one such SPE — which is the unique Markov SPE characterized above.

Claim 6.1. *There exists a unique sequence $\langle x_A^{2t}, x_B^{2t+1} \rangle_{t=0}^{\infty}$ that satisfies (6.10) and (6.11).*

Proof. After substituting for x_B^{2t+1} in (6.10) by using (6.11), and then rearranging, it follows that $x_A^{2t} = f(2t, 2t+1) + \delta_A \delta_B x_A^{2t+2}$, where $f(2t, 2t+1) \equiv$

---

[26] A key modification involves replacing the terms $\delta_B M_B$ and $\delta_B m_B$ respectively with $g_B(s^{2t})(1-\delta_B)/r_B + \delta_B M_B^{2t+1}$ and $g_B(s^{2t+1})(1-\delta_B)/r_B + \delta_B m_B^{2t+1}$, which are respectively the maximum (supremum, to be precise) and minimum (infimum, to be precise) payoffs that player B obtains in any SPE in which the action profile chosen at time $t\Delta$ ($t = 0, 1, 2, \dots$) is s^t if she rejects any offer at time $2t\Delta$. Similarly, for player A.

$\pi(1 - \delta_B) + \delta_B(1 - \delta_A)g_A(s^{2t+1})/r_A - (1 - \delta_B)g_B(s^{2t})/r_B$. It thus follows that

$$x_A^{2t} = \sum_{z=t}^{\infty} (\delta_A \delta_B)^{(z-t)} f(2z, 2z + 1).$$

After substituting for $f(2z, 2z + 1)$ and simplifying, it follows that for each $t = 0, 1, 2, \ldots$

$$x_A^{2t} = \frac{\pi(1 - \delta_B)}{1 - \delta_A \delta_B} +$$

$$\sum_{z=t}^{\infty} (\delta_A \delta_B)^{(z-t)} \left[\delta_B(1 - \delta_A)g_A(s^{2z+1})/r_A - (1 - \delta_B)g_B(s^{2z})/r_B\right]. \quad (6.17)$$

Finally, x_B^{2t+1} is derived after substituting for x_A^{2t+2} in (6.11). $\qquad \square$

Claim 6.2. *If $r_A = r_B$, then the unique sequence that satisfies (6.10)–(6.11) also satisfies (6.12) and (6.14).*

Proof. Before I provide an example that shows that this claim need not be valid if $r_A \neq r_B$, let us prove it when $r_A = r_B = r$. Since Assumption 6.1 implies that g_i is bounded from above, the supremum of the sum $g_A(s) + g_B(s)$ over all $s = (s_A, s_B) \in S_A \times S_B$ exists, which is denoted by $\bar{g}$. Assumption 6.1 implies that $\pi \geq \bar{g}/r$.[27] Using (6.16) and (6.17), it is straightforward to show that if $r_A = r_B = r$, then for each $k = 0, 1, 2, 3, \ldots$

$$x_A^{2k} = I_A^{2k}(\langle s^t \rangle) + \frac{\pi}{1+\delta} - \frac{1-\delta}{r} \sum_{z=k}^{\infty} \delta^{2(z-k)}[g_A(s^{2z}) + g_B(s^{2z})]. \quad (6.18)$$

By definition

$$\frac{1-\delta}{r} \sum_{z=k}^{\infty} \delta^{2(z-k)} \bar{g} \geq \frac{1-\delta}{r} \sum_{z=k}^{\infty} \delta^{2(z-k)}[g_A(s^{2z}) + g_B(s^{2z})]. \quad (6.19)$$

The left-hand side of inequality 6.19 equals $\bar{g}/r(1+\delta)$. Hence, since $\pi \geq \bar{g}/r$, the right-hand side of inequality 6.19 is less than or equal to $\pi/(1+\delta)$, which thus implies — using (6.18) — that inequality 6.12 is satisfied. Through a symmetric argument it can be shown that inequality 6.14 is satisfied.[28] $\quad \square$

---

[27]Suppose, to the contrary, that $\bar{g} > r\pi$. This implies that there exists an $s \in S_A \times S_B$ such that $\bar{g} \geq g_A(s) + g_B(s) > r\pi$, which contradicts Assumption 6.1.

[28]I now provide an example to show that if $r_A \neq r_B$, then this claim need not be valid.

Proof of Lemma 6.3

I shall establish the lower bound on m_A and the upper bound on M_A; through a symmetric argument, with the roles of A and B reversed, the lower bound on m_B and the upper on M_B can be established.

Let H_B denote the set of all SPE payoffs to player B in any subgame beginning with the play of the disagreement game $\mathcal{G}$, after player B has rejected an offer made by A. Claim 6.3 below establishes that for any $h_B \in H_B$, $h_B \leq \sup_{s \in S} F_B(s)$, where for each $s \in S$

$$F_B(s) = \frac{(1 - \delta_B)g_B(s)}{r_B} + \delta_B\left(\pi - \underline{v}_A(1 - \delta_A)/r_A - \delta_A m_A\right)$$
$$- \frac{\delta_B(1 - \delta_A)}{\delta_A r_A}\left(\sup_{s'_A \in S_A} g_A(s'_A, s_B) - g_A(s)\right), \quad (6.20)$$

with $\underline{v}_A$ as specified in the lemma. Hence, in any SPE of any subgame beginning with player A's offer, player B accepts any offer x_A such that $\pi - x_A > \bar{F}_B$, where

$$\bar{F}_B = \sup_{s \in S} F_B(s) = \delta_B\left(\pi - \underline{v}_A(1 - \delta_A)/r_A - \delta_A m_A\right) + (1 - \delta_B)\bar{v}_B/r_B,$$
$$(6.21)$$

with $\bar{v}_B$ as specified in the lemma. This implies that $m_A \geq \pi - \bar{F}_B$. Thus, after substituting for $\bar{F}_B$ in this latter inequality, using (6.21), and then rearranging, the lower bound for m_A as stated in the lemma is obtained.

I now use this result to establish the upper bound on M_A. I claim that $M_A \leq \pi - (1 - \delta_B)\underline{v}_B/r_B - \delta_B m_B$. Suppose, to the contrary, that this inequality is false. This implies that there exists an SPE in any subgame beginning with player A's offer in which player A's payoff u_A^* is such that $M_A \geq u_A^* > \pi - (1 - \delta_B)\underline{v}_B/r_B - \delta_B m_B$. Since (by Assumption 6.1 and

---

Consider the model with the following disagreement game. The players' strategy sets are as follows: $S_A = \{U, D\}$ and $S_B = \{L, R\}$. The payoffs are as follows: $g_A(U, L) = g_B(U, L) = 1$, $g_A(D, R) = g_B(D, R) = 0$, $g_A(D, L) = g_B(U, R) = 0.2$ and $g_A(U, R) = g_B(D, L) = 0$. Finally, $\pi = 1/r_A + 1/r_B$. This disgreement game has two Nash equilibria, namely: $s(1) = (U, L)$ and $s(2) = (D, R)$. Consider the Markov SPE in which at each time $t\Delta$ the players play $s(1)$ when t is even ($t = 0, 2, 4, \ldots$), and $s(2)$ when t is odd. Applying (6.17), it follows that if such a Markov SPE exists then in equilibrium player A offer's x_A^0 at time 0 which is accepted by player B, where $x_A^0 = (1 - \delta_B)/(1 - \delta_A \delta_B)r_A$, which — if $r_A > r_B$ — is strictly less than $I_A^0(\langle s^t \rangle) = 1/(1 + \delta_A)r_A$.

by the fact that the cake is of size π) $u_A^* + u_B^* \leq \pi$ (where u_B^* denotes player B's payoff in this SPE), it follows that $(1 - \delta_B)\underline{v}_B/r_B + \delta_B m_B > u_B^*$, which is a contradiction, because the left-hand side of this inequality is the worst possible payoff that player B can obtain by rejecting any offer made by player A — since by the definition of $\underline{v}_B$, the worst possible payoff that player B can obtain from the disagreement game between two consecutive offers in any SPE is greater than or equal to $(1 - \delta_B)\underline{v}_B/r_B$. This then establishes the upper bound on M_A.

Claim 6.3. *For any $h_B \in H_B$, $h_B \leq \sup_{s \in S} F_B(s)$, where $F_B(s)$ is stated in (6.20).*

Proof. Suppose, to the contrary, that there exists an $h_B \in H_B$ such that $h_B > \sup_{s \in S} F_B(s)$. Let $s^* \in S$ denote the SPE action profile chosen the first time the disagreement game $\mathcal{G}$ is played in this subgame, and (u_A^*, u_B^*) denotes the SPE payoff pair at the beginning of the subsequent subgame — which begins with player B's turn to make an offer. This means that $h_B = (1 - \delta_B)g_B(s^*)/r_B + \delta_B u_B^*$. I shall show that $h_B \leq F_B(s^*)$, which contradicts my supposition that $h_B > \sup_{s \in S} F_B(s)$.

Since player A should not have an incentive to deviate at the beginning of the subgame under consideration, it must necessarily be the case that

$$\frac{(1 - \delta_A)g_A(s^*)}{r_A} + \delta_A u_A^* \geq \frac{1 - \delta_A}{r_A}\left(\sup_{s'_A \in S_A} g_A(s'_A, s_B^*)\right) + \delta_A n_A,$$

where n_A denotes the infimum of the set of SPE payoffs to player A in any subgame beginning with player B's offer. Since $n_A \geq \underline{v}_A(1 - \delta_A)/r_A + \delta_A m_A$ — because, by the definition of $\underline{v}_A$ as specified in the lemma, the worst possible payoff that player A can obtain from the disagreement game between two consecutive offers in any SPE is greater than or equal to $\underline{v}_A(1 - \delta_A)/r_A$ — it thus follows that

$$\frac{(1 - \delta_A)g_A(s^*)}{r_A} + \delta_A u_A^* \geq \frac{1 - \delta_A}{r_A}\left(\sup_{s'_A \in S_A} g_A(s'_A, s_B^*)\right) + \delta_A\left(\underline{v}_A(1 - \delta_A)/r_A + \delta_A m_A\right). \quad (6.22)$$

Since $u_A^* + u_B^* \leq \pi$ (which implies that $\delta_A u_A^* \leq \delta_A(\pi - u_B^*)$), it follows from

(6.22) that

$$\delta_A(\pi - u_B^*) \geq \frac{1-\delta_A}{r_A}\left(\sup_{s_A'\in S_A} g_A(s_A', s_B^*)\right) +$$

$$\delta_A\Big(\underline{v}_A(1-\delta_A)/r_A + \delta_A m_A\Big) - (1-\delta_A)g_A(s^*)/r_A,$$

which implies that

$$\frac{(1-\delta_B)g_B(s^*)}{r_B} + \delta_B u_B^* \leq \frac{(1-\delta_B)g_B(s^*)}{r_B} + \delta_B\Big(\pi - \underline{v}_A(1-\delta_A)/r_A - \delta_A m_A\Big)$$

$$- \frac{\delta_B(1-\delta_A)}{\delta_A r_A}\left(\sup_{s_A'\in S_A} g_A(s_A', s_B^*) - g_A(s^*)\right),$$

the desired contradiction.   □

The Proof of Lemma 6.5

I shall establish the existence (by construction) of a SPE that supports player A's worst SPE payoff; the existence of a SPE that supports player B's worst SPE payoff follows from a symmetric construction (with the roles of A and B reversed). Let $w = (w_A, w_B)$ and $b = (b_A, b_B)$ denote the strategy pairs of the disagreement game $\mathcal{G}$ such that $\underline{v}_A = g_A(w)$ and[29]

$$\bar{v}_B = g_B(b) - \left(\sup_{s_A'\in S_A} g_A(s_A', b_B) - g_A(b)\right).$$

Letting $\hat{s}$ denote an arbitrary NE of $\mathcal{G}$, I denote by $\hat{\sigma}$ the unique stationary SPE in which the action profile chosen in $\mathcal{G}$ is always $\hat{s}$. Suppose that $(\underline{v}_A, \bar{v}_B) \neq (\hat{g}_A, \hat{g}_B)$, where $\hat{g}_i \equiv g_i(\hat{s})$ $(i = A, B)$.[30] Furthermore, define x_B^*

---

[29]In order to keep the construction relatively straightforward, assume the existence of such strategy pairs.

[30]If $(\underline{v}_A, \bar{v}_B) = (\hat{g}_A, \hat{g}_B)$, then the required result follows immediately from Proposition 6.5.

and x_B^{**} as follows[31]

$$x_B^* = \frac{\pi}{1+\delta} + \frac{\delta \bar{v}_B}{(1+\delta)r} - \frac{\delta \underline{v}_A}{(1+\delta)r}, \quad \text{and}$$

$$x_B^{**} = x_B^* - \frac{(1-\delta)}{\delta r}\left(\sup_{s_A' \in S_A} g_A(s_A', b_B) - g_A(b)\right).$$

It will be shown below (using the *One-Shot Deviation* property) that there exists a $\Delta_A > 0$ such that for any $\Delta < \Delta_A$ the pair of non-Markovian strategies described in Table 6.4 is a SPE.

First consider player A's action in $\mathcal{G}$. If she chooses b_A after player B rejects any offer, then her payoff is $V_A(b_A) = (1-\delta)g_A(b)/r + \delta(\pi - x_B^{**})$. If she instead chooses an alternative action s_A (and thereafter conforms to the strategy specified in Table 6.4), then her payoff is

$$\frac{(1-\delta)}{r}g_A(s_A, b_B) + \delta(\pi - x_B^*) \le$$

$$\frac{(1-\delta)}{r}\left[\sup_{s_A' \in S_A} g_A(s_A', b_B)\right] + \delta(\pi - x_B^*) = V_A(b_A).$$

Hence, a one-shot deviation by player A from b_A after player B rejects any offer is not profitable for player A. If player A chooses w_A after she rejects any offer, then her payoff is $(1-\delta)\underline{v}_A/r + \delta \underline{u}_A$, which — by the definition of $\underline{v}_A$ — is less than or equal to her payoff from a one-shot deviation to an alternative action.

Now consider player A's responses in state 2. If she accepts an offer $x_B \le x_B^*$, then her payoff is $\pi - x_B$. If she instead rejects such an offer, then her payoff is $(1-\delta)\underline{v}_A/r + \delta \underline{u}_A = \pi - x_B^*$. Since $x_B^{**} < x_B^*$, it follows from the above argument that player A's responses in state 1 are also immune to one-shot deviations.

If player A offers $x_A = \underline{u}_A$, then her payoff is $\underline{u}_A$. If player A instead offers $x_A > \underline{u}_A$, then her payoff is $V_A(b_A)$, which (as shown above) equals

$$\frac{(1-\delta)}{r}\left[\sup_{s_A' \in S_A} g_A(s_A', b_B)\right] + \delta(\pi - x_B^*),$$

---

[31]It should be noted that Assumption 6.1 implies that $\underline{u}_A$ (which is defined in the lemma), x_B^* and x_B^{**} are elements of the closed interval $[0, \pi]$ — and, hence, they are feasible offers.

		state 1	state 2
Player A	offer	$x_A = \underline{u}_A$	$x_A = \underline{u}_A$
	accept	$x_B \leq x_B^{**}$	$x_B \leq x_B^{*}$
	action in $\mathcal{G}$	w_A after player A rejects any offer, and b_A after player B rejects any offer	w_A after player A rejects any offer, and b_A after player B rejects any offer
Player B	offer	$x_B = x_B^{**}$	$x_B = x_B^{*}$
	accept	$x_A \leq \underline{u}_A$	$x_A \leq \underline{u}_A$
	action in $\mathcal{G}$	w_B after player A rejects any offer, and b_B after player B rejects any offer	w_B after player A rejects any offer, and b_B after player B rejects any offer
	transitions	(i) switch to the stationary SPE $\hat{\sigma}$ if player B either offers $x_B > x_B^{**}$, or rejects any offer $x_A \leq \underline{u}_A$, or chooses an action in $\mathcal{G}$ different from that specified above, and (ii) switch to state 2 if player A does not choose b_A after player B rejects any offer	(i) switch to the stationary SPE $\hat{\sigma}$ if player B either offers $x_B > x_B^{*}$, or rejects any offer $x_A \leq \underline{u}_A$, or chooses an action in $\mathcal{G}$ different from that specified above, and (ii) switch to state 1 if player A chooses b_A after player B rejects any offer

Table 6.4: The 'extremal' SPE strategies which support player A's worst SPE payoff.

which, after substituting for x_B^*, equals

$$\frac{(1-\delta)}{r}\left[\sup_{s_A' \in S_A} g_A(s_A', b_B)\right] + \delta\left(\frac{(1-\delta)\underline{v}_A}{r} + \delta\underline{u}_A\right),$$

which is strictly less than $\underline{u}_A$ if and only if (after substituting for $\underline{u}_A$ and rearranging)

$$\pi > \frac{\bar{v}_B}{r} + \frac{1}{r}\left[\sup_{s_A' \in S_A} g_A(s_A', b_B)\right] = \frac{g_A(b)}{r} + \frac{g_B(b)}{r},$$

which follows from Assumption 6.1.

Hence, a one-shot deviation from the offer $x_A = \underline{u}_A$ to an offer $x_A > \underline{u}_A$ is not profitable for player A. Since player B accepts any offer such that $x_A \leq \underline{u}_A$, a one-shot deviation from the offer $x_A = \underline{u}_A$ to an offer $x_A < \underline{u}_A$ is also not profitable for player A.

Now consider Player B's action in $\mathcal{G}$. If she chooses the action specified in Table 6.4 — which is either w_B or b_B — then her payoff is *greater than or equal to*

$$\frac{(1-\delta)\underline{g}_B}{r} + \delta\min\{x_B^{**}, \pi - \underline{u}_A\}, \tag{6.23}$$

where $\underline{g}_B$ denotes player B's minimum (infimum, to be precise) payoff in $\mathcal{G}$. If she deviates to an alternative action, then (since play will subsequently switch to the stationary SPE $\hat{\sigma}$) her payoff is *at most* equal to

$$\frac{(1-\delta)\bar{g}_B}{r} + \delta\left[\frac{\hat{g}_B}{r} + \frac{1}{1+\delta}\left(\pi - \frac{\hat{g}_A}{r} - \frac{\hat{g}_B}{r}\right)\right], \tag{6.24}$$

where $\bar{g}_B$ denotes player B's maximum (supremum, to be precise) payoff in $\mathcal{G}$. There exists $\Delta' > 0$ such that for any $\Delta < \Delta'$, (6.23) is *strictly greater than* (6.24).[32] Therefore, for any $\Delta < \Delta'$ a one-shot deviation from either w_B or b_B is not profitable for player B.

---

[32] In the limit as $\Delta \to 0$, both x_B^{**} and $\pi - \underline{u}_A$ converge to $\pi/2 + \bar{v}_B/r - \underline{v}_A/r$, which is *strictly greater* than $\pi/2 + \hat{g}_B/r - \hat{g}_A/r$ — because $(\hat{g}_A, \hat{g}_B) \neq (\underline{v}_A, \bar{v}_B)$ implies (using Lemma 6.4) that either $\bar{v}_B > \hat{g}_B$ or $\hat{g}_A > \underline{v}_A$. Consequently, since (6.23) and (6.24) are continuous in Δ, there exists $\Delta' > 0$ such that for any $\Delta < \Delta'$ (6.23) is strictly greater than (6.24).

Now consider player B's responses. If she accepts the offer $x_A = \underline{u}_A$, then her payoff is $\pi - \underline{u}_A$. If she rejects this offer, then (since play switches to the stationary SPE $\widehat{\sigma}$) her payoff is

$$\widehat{V} = \frac{(1-\delta)\widehat{g}_B}{r} + \delta\left[\frac{\widehat{g}_B}{r} + \frac{1}{1+\delta}\left(\pi - \frac{\widehat{g}_A}{r} - \frac{\widehat{g}_B}{r}\right)\right]. \qquad (6.25)$$

Lemma 6.4 implies that $\pi - \underline{u}_A \geq \widehat{V}$. This, in turn, implies that for any offer $x_A < \underline{u}_A$, $\pi - x_A \geq \widehat{V}$. Hence, it is optimal for player B to accept any offer x_A such that $x_A \leq \underline{u}_A$. If player B rejects an offer $x_A > \underline{u}_A$, then her payoff is $(1-\delta)g_B(b)/r + \delta x_B^{**}$, which equals (after substituting for x_B^{**} and simplifying)

$$V' = \frac{\delta\pi}{1+\delta} + \frac{\bar{v}_B}{(1+\delta)r} - \frac{\delta^2\underline{v}_A}{(1+\delta)r}.$$

If she instead accepts such an offer, then her payoff is $\pi - x_A$, which is strictly less than V', because $V' > \pi - \underline{u}_A$. Hence, it is optimal for player B to reject any offer $x_A > \underline{u}_A$.

Now consider player B's offer in state 2. She does not benefit by instead making an offer $x_B < x_B^*$. If she offers $x_B > x_B^*$, then (since play switches to the stationary SPE $\widehat{\sigma}$) player A rejects the offer because her payoff from rejecting equals

$$\frac{(1-\delta)\widehat{g}_A}{r} + \delta\left[\frac{\widehat{g}_A}{r} + \frac{1}{1+\delta}\left(\pi - \frac{\widehat{g}_A}{r} - \frac{\widehat{g}_B}{r}\right)\right] > \pi - x_B^* > \pi - x_B.$$

Consequently, player B's payoff by offering $x_B > x_B^*$ is stated in (6.25), which is *strictly less* than x_B^* (given Assumption 6.1, and using Lemma 6.4).

Now consider player B's offer in state 1. She does not benefit by instead making an offer $x_B < x_B^{**}$. If she offers $x_B > x_B^{**}$, then play switches to the stationary SPE $\widehat{\sigma}$. Since $x_B^{**} < x_B^*$, it follows from the above argument that player A rejects the offer $x_B > x_B^{**}$. Consequently, player B's payoff by offering $x_B > x_B^{**}$ is stated in (6.25), which is *strictly less* than x_B^*. Hence, there exists $\Delta'' > 0$ such that for any $\Delta < \Delta''$ the payoff in (6.25) is strictly less than x_B^{**}.[33]

The required result follows by setting $\Delta_A = \min\{\Delta', \Delta''\}$.

---

[33]In the limit, as $\Delta \to 0$, $x_B^{**} - x_B^* \to 0$. Hence (since for any $\Delta > 0$, $x_B^* > \widehat{V}$) there exists a $\Delta'' > 0$ such that for any $\Delta < \Delta''$, $x_B^{**} > \widehat{V}$.

6.9   Notes

The application in Section 6.3.2 on soverign debt renegotiations is based
upon Bulow and Rogoff (1989), while the application in Section 6.5 on intrafamily allocation is based upon Lundberg and Pollak (1993). The model
studied in Section 6.6 is due to Busch and Wen (1995) — although the for-
malization and the analysis are slightly different, and some of our results are
valid also when the players have different discount factors. The application
studied in Section 6.7 is related to the work of Haller and Holden (1990) and
Fernandez and Glazer (1991). Holden (1994) shows that a unique SPE is
obtained if the union can *commit* at any time to strike in any future period
— in the limit as $\Delta \to 0$, the unique SPE wage equals $\bar{w}$. Chang (1995)
studies a model in which two countries are bargaining over the gains from
monetary union. Although conceptually the bargaining model is similar
to that of Section 6.6 — with the countries' inside options being determined in the absence of monetary union — the disagreement game is not a
simultaneous-move game.

7   Procedures

7.1   Introduction

The procedure of bargaining is the structure of moves of the bargaining process — it defines the rules of the bargaining game. The alternating-offers procedure — which underlies the models studied in Chapters 3–6 — is an example of a bargaining procedure. In Section 7.2 I describe (and evaluate) several alternative procedures of bargaining that differ from each other on the key procedural matter of 'who makes offers and when'. A main message of this section is that this aspect of procedure — who makes offers and when — can have a significant impact on the bargaining outcome.

After an offer is accepted the proposer of that offer may have the option to retract the offer, in which case the players resume bargaining. This procedural feature is discussed in Section 7.3, where its impact on the bargaining outcome is studied through a modified version of the basic alternating-offers model. It is shown that this procedural feature may have a significant impact on the bargaining outcome. In particular, under some conditions, there exist subgame perfect equilibria that are Pareto inefficient.

While bargaining a player may have the option to temporarily close the channel of communication (and thus, to temporarily stop the bargaining process), which may impose costs on both players. For example, in the context of union-firm negotiations, the union has the option to go on strike.

Such an action may be considered a tactical move, and interpreted as 'burning money'. In Section 7.4 it is shown — through a modified version of the basic alternating-offers model — that this procedural feature may have a significant impact on the bargaining outcome. In particular, under some conditions, there exist subgame perfect equilibria in which a player does burn money.

In this chapter I show that procedures in general, and various specific features of procedures in particular, may have a significant impact on the outcome of bargaining. The question of what or who determines the bargaining procedure, and its various features, is not touched upon. In the language of game theory I show that the rules of the bargaining game matter, but I do not address the issue of what or who determines those rules. In fact, this latter question has hardly been addressed in the economics and game theory literature, because it is a very difficult question. I have nothing substantial to say on this rather thorny issue, but to note that it is an issue that deserves to be investigated in future research. It should also be noted that in many real-life bargaining situations the procedures are, in fact, somewhat ambiguous and/or not precisely well-specified.

7.2   Who Makes Offers and When

A basic characteristic of bargaining is making (and responding to) offers. If neither player ever makes any offers, then agreement (if reached) is struck by some procedure other than bargaining. Indeed, an agreement is determined by bargaining if and only if at least one player makes at least one offer (that is, proposes an agreement).

Rubinstein's model is based upon an alternating-offers procedure: the players make offers alternately at equally spaced points in time, with the responder reacting immediately to any offer. A main objective of this section is to illustrate, by studying several alternative procedures, the insight that the procedure of bargaining is an important determinant of the bargaining outcome. A few of these alternative procedures may prove useful in applications.

Throughout this section I consider the bargaining situation in which two players, A and B, bargain over the partition of a (perfectly divisible) cake of size π (where $\pi > 0$). If agreement is reached that gives player i a share

x_i of the cake, then her instantaneous utility is x_i.

7.2.1 The Ultimatum Game

This is the simplest of bargaining procedures. Player A makes an offer to player B. If player B accepts the offer, then agreement is struck. Otherwise, bargaining terminates in disagreement — and each player obtains a payoff of zero. In the unique SPE — which can be derived by the backward induction process — player A offers $x_A^* = \pi$, and player B accepts any offer $x_A \in [0, \pi]$. It should be noted that there does not exist a SPE in which player B rejects the offer $x_A = \pi$.

In equilibrium, player A obtains the whole cake. This suggests that making offers confers bargaining power, while responding to offers gives no bargaining power. The repeated version of this procedure studied in the next section emphasizes this point. It should be noted that the 'take-it-or-leave-it-offer' procedure implicitly assumes that the players are committed not to continue bargaining if player B rejects player A's offer. In most real-life negotiations making such commitments is rather difficult. As such this procedure is not particularly plausible.

Random Determination of the Proposer

Consider the following extension to the take-it-or-leave-it-offer procedure: with probability q_A player A makes the single offer, and with probability q_B player B makes the single offer, where $q_A + q_B = 1$.

In the unique SPE the expected share of the cake obtained by player i is $q_i \pi$. This means (using Definition 2.3) that if $q_A > 0$ and $q_B > 0$ then the expected SPE payoff pair $(q_A \pi, q_B \pi)$ is identical to the asymmetric Nash bargaining solution of the bargaining problem (Ω, d) with $\tau = q_A$, where $\Omega = \{(u_A, u_B) : 0 \le u_A \le \pi \text{ and } u_B = \pi - u_A\}$ and $d = (0, 0)$.

Notice that the (limiting) SPE payoff pair in Rubinstein's model (cf. Corollary 3.1) is identical to the expected SPE payoff pair in this model if and only if $q_A = r_B/(r_A + r_B)$. This result suggests that this extension of the ultimatum game (with $q_A = r_B/(r_A + r_B)$) may be interpreted as a reduced-form of the more plausible, but more complex, Rubinstein model.

7.2.2 Repeated Offers

Player A makes offers at each time $t\Delta$ ($t = 0, 1, 2, 3, \ldots$ and $\Delta > 0$), while player B immediately responds to each such offer. Assume that player A's discount rate $r_A \geq 0$, and player B's discount rate $r_B > 0$. If the players perpetually disagree, then each player obtains a payoff of zero.

Through a minor adaption of the arguments in Sections 3.2.1 and 3.2.2 it is straightforward to show that in the unique SPE player A always offers $x_A^* = \pi$, and player B always accepts any offer $x_A \in [0, \pi]$.[1] Thus, in the unique SPE player A obtains the whole cake at time 0. Notice that this result holds even if player B is extremely patient relative to player A; that is, it is valid for values of r_A significantly larger than values of r_B.

This result suggests that the procedure can have a far more potent impact on the bargaining outcome than the discount rates. In fact, the discount rates have no influence, whatsoever, in this repeated-offers game — unlike in Rubinstein's alternating-offers game, where their relative magnitude significantly influences the equilibrium partition.[2]

The repeated-offers bargaining game is a useful vehicle to emphasize the point that making offers, rather than responding to them, confers a relatively greater amount of bargaining power. However, it is unlikely that in real-life bargaining situations the procedure of bargaining allows only one of the two players to make offers. Player A has to be committed not to listen to any offers made by player B in order for the repeated-offers procedure to have much practical significance. But, since such a commitment is typically rather difficult to sustain, the repeated-offers type procedure is not particularly plausible.

---

[1]First, one considers a SPE that satisfies Properties 3.1 and 3.2, and shows, in particular, that in such a SPE player B is indifferent between accepting and rejecting player A's offer; i.e., $\pi - x_A^* = \delta_B(\pi - x_A^*)$. Then, one adapts the arguments in Section 3.2.2 and obtains that $m_A = \pi - \delta_B N_B$, $M_A = \pi - \delta_B n_B$, $n_B = \pi - M_A$ and $N_B = \pi - m_A$, where N_B and n_B are respectively the supremum and infimum of the set of SPE payoffs to player B in any subgame beginning with player A's offer.

[2]Furthermore, it is an illustration of the point that the impact of a particular force (discount rates) on the bargaining outcome can depend on the nature of some other force (the procedure).

7.2.3 Simultaneous Offers

It may be quite natural when offers are communicated through certain kinds of media (such as computers and the regular postal system) that the players end up (strategically or otherwise) making 'simultaneous' offers. That is, player A submits an offer to player B, and before that offer reaches her, she also submits an offer to player A. If the two offers are compatible, in a sense made precise below, then a deal is struck. Otherwise, they simultaneously submit fresh offers. This process may continue until a pair of compatible offers are submitted. Below I present a bargaining model that incorporates this repeated, simultaneous-offers, procedure. It is shown that such a model is plagued by a multiplicity of subgame perfect equilibria, and, thus, fails to resolve the fundamental indeterminacy that characterizes the bargaining situation.

This analysis, therefore, further illustrates the potentially powerful impact of the procedure of bargaining. Notice that the simultaneous-offers aspect of the procedure considered here is partly tied in with the underlying mode of communication. For example, if the players bargain face-to-face, it seems unlikely that they would end up making such simultaneous offers.[3]

I consider the following simplest possible bargaining model that captures the notion that the players make simultaneous offers. At each time $t\Delta$ ($t = 0, 1, 2, 3, \ldots$, and $\Delta > 0$), the players simultaneously submit their respective offers, x_A^t and x_B^t, where I adopt the convention that an offer x_i^t submitted by player i at time $t\Delta$ denotes the share that player i would like to have. Furthermore, I interpret the parameter Δ as constituting the time that it takes for an offer submitted by player i to arrive at player j (which is determined, in particular, by the efficiency of the postal system).

A pair of offers x_A and x_B are compatible if and only if the sum $x_A + x_B \leq \pi$. If at time $t\Delta$ the offers submitted are compatible, then the game ends with an agreement that gives player i a share equal to her demand x_i^t. Otherwise the game moves to time $(t+1)\Delta$. The payoffs to the players are as follows. If agreement is reached at time $t\Delta$ with player i's share being

---

[3]The players could, of course, deliberately choose to simultaneously write down their respective offers on pieces of paper, which are then exchanged. But then the procedure would mimic communication via a computer, and thus undermine the spirit of bargaining face-to-face, which is meant to be interpreted as vocal communication (making simultaneous use of player i's mouth and player j's ear).

x_i, then player i's payoff is $x_i \exp(-r_i t)$, where $r_i \geq 0$ denotes her discount rate. If the players perpetually disagree, then each player obtains a payoff of zero.

Fix a pair $x^* = (x_A^*, x_B^*) \in X$, where $X = \{(x_A, x_B) : 0 \leq x_A \leq \pi$ and $x_B = \pi - x_A\}$. It is trivial to verify that the following pair of strategies is a subgame perfect equilibrium of the infinitely repeated simultaneous-offers model: player A always asks for x_A^*, and player B always asks for x_B^*.

This means that this model has a multiplicity (indeed, a continuum) of SPE. In each of the SPE described above, agreement is reached immediately at time 0. However, it is straightforward to construct a continuum of SPE in which agreement is reached after some (considerable) delay.[4] The repeated simultaneous-offers bargaining game thus fails to resolve the basic indeterminacy that characterizes bargaining situations. As is also known from other game-theoretic contexts, it is the 'simultaneity' aspect of this procedure that is responsible for this conclusion.

7.2.4   Random Proposers

Making offers confers relatively greater bargaining power than responding to offers. An interesting bargaining procedure might thus determine the proposer randomly. Although this might not be a descriptively persuasive assumption, it may be a useful modelling assumption, especially because the probabilities with which the players make offers parameterizes the players' relative bargaining powers.

Consider the following bargaining model. At each time $t\Delta$ ($t = 0, 1, 2, 3, \ldots$ and $\Delta > 0$), with probability q_A player A makes the offer to player B and with probability q_B player B makes the offer to player A, where $q_A + q_B = 1$. If agreement is reached at time $t\Delta$ that gives player i a share x_i of the cake, then her payoff is $x_i \exp(-r_i t\Delta)$, where $r_i > 0$ denotes player i's discount rate. On the other hand, if the players perpetually disagree, then each player

---

[4]Fix an arbitrary agreement $x^* = (x_A^*, x_B^*) \in X$, and fix an arbitrary time $T \geq 2\Delta$. Now consider the following path of play: the players make incompatible demands until time $T - 2\Delta$, and then at time $T - \Delta$ the players' demands are defined by x^*. This path of play is sustained as a SPE path of play by the following off-the-equilibrium-path strategies. If player i ever unilaterally deviates from this path of play, then immediately play moves according to that SPE — described above — which gives player i a payoff of zero.

obtains a payoff of zero.

Through a straightforward adaptation of the arguments in Sections 3.2.1 and 3.2.2 it can be shown that this game has a unique SPE,[5] in which player i always offers x_i^* and always accepts an offer x_j if and only if $x_j \leq x_j^*$, where

$$x_i^* = \frac{(1 - \delta_j)(1 - \delta_i q_j)\pi}{1 - \delta_i q_j - \delta_j q_i}.$$

In the limit, as $\Delta \to 0$, the SPE payoffs to players A and B are respectively

$$\frac{r_B q_A \pi}{r_A q_B + r_B q_A} \quad \text{and} \quad \frac{r_A q_B \pi}{r_A q_B + r_B q_A}.$$

Notice that if $q_A = q_B = 1/2$, then the limiting SPE payoff pair is identical to the limiting Rubinsteinian SPE payoff (cf. Corollary 3.1). Furthermore, notice that player i's limiting SPE share is strictly increasing in q_i and strictly decreasing in q_j.

7.2.5   Alternating-Offers with Different Response Times

In the alternating-offers procedure that underlies Rubinstein's model, the time interval between two consecutive offers is $\Delta > 0$. This procedure implicitly assumes that the amount of time it takes player A to make a counteroffer after she rejects player B's offer is identical to the amount of time it takes player B to make a counteroffer after she rejects player A's offer. I now consider the modification to this procedure in which the amount of time it takes player i to make a counteroffer after she rejects player j's offer is $\Delta_i > 0$. I thus allow for the possibility that Δ_A and Δ_B are unequal. To isolate the role of this difference, assume that the players discount future utilities at a common rate $r > 0$. Define $\delta_i \equiv \exp(-r\Delta_i)$, which captures the cost to player i of rejecting an offer.

It is trivial to verify that Theorem 3.1 is applicable, and it characterizes the unique SPE of this model. In particular, when Δ_A and Δ_B are small,

---

[5]First, one considers a SPE that satisfies Properties 3.1 and 3.2, and shows, in particular, that in such a SPE player j is indifferent between accepting and rejecting player i's offer; i.e., $\pi - x_i^* = \delta_j[q_i(\pi - x_i^*) + q_j x_j^*]$. Then, one adapts the arguments in Section 3.2.2 and obtains that $m_i = \pi - \delta_j[q_i(\pi - m_i) + q_j M_j]$ and $M_i = \pi - \delta_j[q_i(\pi - M_i) + q_j m_j]$.

the SPE shares (and payoffs) to players A and B are respectively

$$\frac{\Delta_B \pi}{\Delta_A + \Delta_B} \quad \text{and} \quad \frac{\Delta_A \pi}{\Delta_A + \Delta_B}.$$

The equilibrium partition depends on the ratio Δ_A/Δ_B. If this ratio equals one, then the players split the cake equally. Otherwise, player i obtains a bigger slice of the cake if and only if $\Delta_i < \Delta_j$. For example, if $\Delta_A = 1$ second and $\Delta_B = 2$ seconds, then player A obtains two-thirds of the cake while player B obtains one-third of the cake. This is rather amazing, because a small difference between Δ_A and Δ_B has a significant impact on the SPE partition. It reaffirms the basic message discussed in Section 3.2.3 that the bargaining outcome depends critically upon the relative magnitude of the players' costs of haggling, with the absolute magnitudes being irrelevant to the bargaining outcome. Notice that player A's SPE share is strictly decreasing in the ratio Δ_A/Δ_B, while player B's SPE share is strictly increasing in the ratio Δ_A/Δ_B.

7.3   The Effect of Retractable Offers

I now study a simple extension to the basic alternating-offers model (studied in Section 3.2) in which a proposer has the option to retract her offer after it is accepted. Discussion of this procedural feature — the option to retract accepted offers — is deferred to Section 7.3.4. I first, in Sections 7.3.1–7.3.3, explore the impact of this procedural feature on the bargaining outcome.

Two players, A and B, bargain over the partition of a cake of size π ($\pi > 0$) according to a modified version of the alternating-offers procedure. The modification is as follows. At each time $t\Delta$ ($t = 0, 1, 2, 3, \ldots$ and $\Delta > 0$), immediately after player j accepts an offer made by player i (where $(i, j) = (A, B)$ if t is even, and $(i, j) = (B, A)$ if t is odd), player i has to make a decision: either she retracts her offer, in which case the game proceeds to time $(t + 1)\Delta$ where it is player j's turn to make an offer, or she does not retract her offer, in which case agreement is secured on the accepted offer. The payoffs are as in the basic alternating-offers model (cf. Section 3.2).

7.3.1   A Subgame Perfect Equilibrium

Consider a SPE that satisfies Properties 3.1, 3.2 and the following Property 7.1.

Property 7.1 (No Retraction). A player does not retract her equilibrium offer.

It follows from a minor modification of the arguments in Section 3.2.1 that in equilibrium player i is indifferent between accepting and rejecting player j's equilibrium offer. Hence, the equilibrium offers satisfy equations 3.1 and 3.2. Furthermore, in equilibrium, player i retracts an offer x_i if and only if $x_i < \delta_i(\pi - x_j^*)$.[6] The following lemma thus characterizes the unique SPE that satisfies Properties 3.1, 3.2 and 7.1.

Lemma 7.1. *The following pair of strategies is a subgame perfect equilibrium of the model with retractable offers:*
- *player A always offers x_A^*, always accepts an offer x_B if and only if $x_B \leq x_B^*$, and always retracts an offer x_A if and only if $x_A < \delta_A^2 x_A^*$,*
- *player B always offers x_B^*, always accepts an offer x_A if and only if $x_A \leq x_A^*$, and always retracts an offer x_B if and only if $x_B < \delta_B^2 x_B^*$,*
where $x_A^* = \mu_A \pi$ and $x_B^* = \mu_B \pi$, with $\mu_A = (1 - \delta_B)/(1 - \delta_A \delta_B)$ and $\mu_B = (1 - \delta_A)/(1 - \delta_A \delta_B)$.

Notice that the SPE described in Lemma 7.1 is essentially the unique Rubinsteinian SPE (cf. Theorem 3.1). Furthermore, by assumption, the equilibrium offer is not retracted.

7.3.2   On the Uniqueness of the Equilibrium

I now address the issue of the existence of other SPE — by applying the method of proof used in Section 3.2.2. As I show in Lemma 7.2 below, in order to establish Lemma 3.1 I need to assume that $\delta_A + \delta_B < 1$.[7]

---

[6]Without loss of generality, but in order to simplify the exposition, assume that if player i is indifferent between retracting and not retracting an offer, then she does not retract it.

[7]The proof of Lemma 3.1 is based on the observation that in any SPE of Rubinstein's model, player j accepts any offer x_i such that $\pi - x_i > \delta_j M_j$. This observation is not necessarily valid in Rubinstein's model with retractable offers, because in equilibrium an accepted offer may be retracted.

Lemma 7.2. *If $\delta_A + \delta_B < 1$, then $m_i \geq \pi - \delta_j M_j$ $(i \neq j)$.*

Proof. Suppose, to the contrary, that $m_i < \pi - \delta_j M_j$. This implies that there exists a SPE in the subgame beginning with player i's offer which gives her a payoff u_i such that $m_i \leq u_i < \pi - \delta_j M_j$. Now suppose player i deviates and offers $x_i' = \pi - \delta_j M_j - \epsilon$ for some $\epsilon > 0$ such that $x_i' > u_i$. Notice that there exists $\bar{\epsilon} > 0$ such that for any $\epsilon \in (0, \bar{\epsilon})$, $x_i' > u_i$. Player j accepts this offer provided that player i does not subsequently retract it. The maximum possible payoff to player i from retracting any offer is $\delta_i \pi$. Since $M_j \leq \pi$ and (by assumption) $\delta_A + \delta_B < 1$, it follows that $\pi - \delta_j M_j > \delta_i \pi$. Hence, there exists $\epsilon^* > 0$ such that for any $\epsilon \in (0, \epsilon^*)$, $x_i' > \delta_i \pi$. Thus, for any $\epsilon \in (0, \min\{\bar{\epsilon}, \epsilon^*\})$, $x_i' > \delta_i \pi$ and $x_i' > u_i$; that is, player i does not retract the offer x_i', and (by construction) the deviation is profitable for player i. $\square$

In contrast to Lemma 7.2, which is valid provided $\delta_A + \delta_B < 1$, it is straightforward to verify (through minor modifications to the proofs of Lemmas 3.2–3.4) that Lemmas 3.2–3.4 are valid for any values of the discount factors. Hence, I obtain the following lemma.

Lemma 7.3. *For any δ_A and δ_B, $m_i \leq \pi - \delta_j M_j$ and $M_i = \pi - \delta_j m_j$ $(i \neq j)$.*

Combining Lemmas 7.2 and 7.3, it follows that if $\delta_A + \delta_B < 1$ then $M_A = m_A = x_A^*$ and $M_B = m_B = x_B^*$, and if $\delta_A + \delta_B \geq 1$ then $M_A \geq x_A^* \geq m_A$ and $M_B \geq x_B^* \geq m_B$, where x_A^* and x_B^* are defined in Lemma 7.1. Consequently, the following proposition can be proven (cf. Theorem 3.1).

Proposition 7.1. *If $\delta_A + \delta_B < 1$, then the subgame perfect equilibrium described in Lemma 7.1 is the unique subgame perfect equilibrium of Rubinstein's model with retractable offers.*

It follows from Proposition 7.1 that if $\delta_A + \delta_B < 1$, then the option to retract accepted offers has no influence on the bargaining outcome; the unique Rubinsteinian equilibrium outcome is robust to this procedural feature. Notice that the condition $\delta_A + \delta_B < 1$ implies that Δ is sufficiently large.

7.3.3 Multiple Equilibria and Delay

I now establish (by construction) that if $\delta_A + \delta_B \geq 1$, then there exists a continuum of SPE. The key idea — which is similar to the construction of the multiple equilibria in the telephone game (cf. Section 5.6.1) — involves the construction of two 'extremal' SPE: these equilibria respectively give players A and B their worst SPE payoffs.

Lemma 7.4. *If $\delta_A + \delta_B \geq 1$, then Table 7.1 describes two SPE. If play begins in state s_A, then in equilibrium player A (who makes the first offer) offers $x_A^* = \pi$, which is accepted by player B and subsequently is not retracted by player A. If, on the other hand, play begins in state s_B, then in equilibrium player A offers $x_A^* = 0$, which is accepted by player B and subsequently is not retracted by player A.*

Proof. Using the *One-Shot Deviation* property, it is straightforward to verify that if $\delta_A + \delta_B \geq 1$, then the pair of strategies described in Table 7.1 is a subgame perfect equilibrium. However, in order to elucidate the role of the condition $\delta_A + \delta_B \geq 1$, I now establish the optimality of player A's behaviour, in state s_A, to reject any offer x_B such that $\delta_A \pi < \pi - x_B < \pi$. Suppose that in state s_A player A receives an offer x_B such that $\delta_A \pi < \pi - x_B < \pi$. If she rejects this offer (as she is supposed to according to her strategy described in Table 7.1), then the state does not change (see the transition rule), and hence, her (discounted) payoff is $\delta_A \pi$. Suppose she deviates from the proposed behaviour and instead accepts such an offer (and thereafter play conforms to the pair of strategies described in Table 7.1). Immediately the state switches to s_B (see the transition rule). Since $\delta_A \pi < \pi - x_B$ implies (using the assumption $\delta_A + \delta_B \geq 1$) that $x_B < \delta_B \pi$, it follows from Table 7.1 that, in state s_B, player B retracts such an accepted offer. Thus, player A's payoff from deviating and accepting this offer is zero. Hence, this one-shot deviation is not profitable for player A. $\square$

The next result follows straightforwardly from this lemma.

Proposition 7.2. *If $\delta_A + \delta_B \geq 1$, then for any partition $x \in \{(x_A, x_B) : 0 \leq x_A \leq \pi$ and $x_B = \pi - x_A\}$ and for any $n \in \{0, 1, 2, 3, 4, \ldots\}$ there exists a SPE such that along the equilibrium path the first n offers are rejected and then the $(n + 1)$th offer, which is the offer of the partition x, is accepted*

		state s_A	state s_B
	offer	$x_A^* = \pi$	$x_A^* = 0$
Player A	accept	$x_B = 0$	$0 \leq x_B \leq \pi$
	retracts	$0 \leq x_A < \delta_A \pi$	——
	offer	$x_B^* = 0$	$x_B^* = \pi$
Player B	accept	$0 \leq x_A \leq \pi$	$x_A = 0$
	retracts	——	$0 \leq x_B < \delta_B \pi$
	transitions	switch to state s_B if an offer $x_B > 0$ is accepted by player A	switch to state s_A if an offer $x_A > 0$ is accepted by player B

Table 7.1: Two extremal SPE of the model with retractable offers.

and subsequently is not retracted by the proposer. Hence, in equilibrium, the partition x is implemented at time $n\Delta$.

Proof. I establish the result by construction. Consider the following path of play. At each time $t\Delta \leq (n-1)\Delta$, the proposer demands to receive the whole cake and the responder rejects that demand. Then, at time $n\Delta$, the proposer offers the partition x, which the responder accepts and subsequently is not retracted by the proposer. It is easy to verify (using the *One-Shot Deviation* property) that this path of play can be supported as a SPE path of play by the following off-the-equilibrium-path behaviour. If player i unilaterally deviates from the proposed path of play, then immediately play proceeds according to that extremal SPE described in Table 7.1 which begins in state s_j $(j \neq i)$. □

7.3.4   Discussion and Interpretation

Fix the values of the players' discount rates r_A and r_B, and let Δ^* denote the unique value of Δ such that $\exp(-r_A\Delta) + \exp(-r_B\Delta) = 1$. Note that $\Delta^* > 0$. I have shown (Proposition 7.1) that if $\Delta > \Delta^*$, then the option to retract accepted offers has no influence on the bargaining outcome; the unique Rubinsteinian SPE outcome is robust to this procedural feature. In contrast, if $\Delta \leq \Delta^*$, then I have shown (Proposition 7.2) that this procedural feature can have a significant impact on the bargaining outcome. In particular, the bargaining outcome can be Pareto inefficient. Since, as I argued in Section 3.2.4, interest in Rubinstein-type bargaining models centres on the limiting case, as $\Delta \to 0$, the case of $\Delta \leq \Delta^*$ is most persuasive.

Notice that in each of the continuum of SPE constructed above, along the equilibrium path accepted offers are not retracted — which is consistent with the potential observation that in real-life negotiations accepted offers are not retracted. However, the results obtained above suggest: (i) that this does not necessarily mean that the option to retract offers is unavailable in real-life negotiations, and (ii) that the option to retract accepted offers (even if it is not exercised) may have a potent impact on the bargaining outcome.[8]

If one adopts the 'classical' interpretation of the *game form*,[9] then the bargaining game ought to incorporate the option to retract accepted offers, because it is typically physically feasible to exercise such an option. Making irrevocable commitments not to retract accepted offers may be difficult in real-life bargaining situations — especially because offers are typically made verbally, and there is often a time lag between the acceptance of an offer and its implementation.

If, however, one adopts the 'perceptive' interpretation, then, since the players may perceive that accepted offers are not retractable (or, simply do not even entertain the possibility of such an option), the Rubinstein model *without* retractable offers may be vindicated. On the other hand, if the players perceive that accepted offers are retractable, then the multiplicity of equilibria obtained above becomes relevant.

---

[8]As is well known in game theory, in general the equilibrium path of any game (i.e., the observed behaviour) is very much influenced and determined by what can and cannot happen off the equilibrium path (i.e., by the non-observed behaviours that are admissible and/or feasible). Analogously, the dog that did not bark provided a valuable clue to Sherlock Holmes.

[9]There are two ways of interpreting the *game form* (i.e., the rules of the game). The 'classical' interpretation is that the rules of a game should incorporate all actions which are physically feasible in the situation that the game is meant to represent. In contrast, the 'perceptive' interpretation is that the rules of a game should incorporate only those actions which are perceived by the players to be feasible and relevant. For further, insightful, discussion of these interpretations, see Rubinstein (1991).

7.4   Burning Money: A Tactical Move

While bargaining a player may have the option to take some action after an offer is rejected and before a counteroffer is made that imposes costs on both players. An example of such an action in the context of union-firm negotiations is the union's option to go on strike. I now study a simple extension to the basic alternating-offers model in which a player has the option to take such an action — such an action may be interpreted as 'burning money'. It is shown that this procedural feature may have a significant impact on the bargaining outcome.

Two players, A and B, bargain over the partition of a cake of size π ($\pi > 0$) according to the following modified version of the alternating-offers procedure. At time 0 player A makes an offer to player B, who either accepts or rejects the offer. In the former case agreement is secured and the accepted offer is implemented, while in the latter case the game proceeds to time Δ where it is player B's turn to make an offer. If player A accepts player B's offer then the accepted offer is implemented, but if she rejects the offer then immediately player B has to choose between two actions: either she allows player A to make her counteroffer at the earliest possible point in time, namely at time 2Δ, or she makes player A wait a further Φ units of time, and, thus, player A makes her counteroffer at time $2\Delta + \Phi$. The latter action, to be denoted by 'MB', is interpreted as 'burning money'. The former action is denoted by 'D'. Both Δ and Φ take strictly positive values. The parameter Δ is interpreted as the minimal time required to formulate a counteroffer, while the parameter Φ is the amount of time for which communication between the two players is strategically closed. Following either action ('MB' or 'D'), the structures of the subgames at times 2Δ and $2\Delta + \Phi$ are identical to the game at time 0. Notice, therefore, that the structure of a subgame beginning with player A's offer is independent of whether or not player B burns money.

The payoffs are as in the basic alternating-offers model. If agreement is secured at time $t \geq 0$ with player i obtaining a share $x_i \in [0, \pi]$ of the cake, then her payoff is $x_i \exp(-rt)$, where $r > 0$ denotes her discount rate. If the players perpetually disagree, then each player obtains a payoff of zero. For notational convenience, define $\delta \equiv \exp(-r\Delta)$ and $\alpha \equiv \exp(-r(\Delta + \Phi))$. Notice that $0 < \alpha < \delta < 1$. Furthermore, notice that, as $\Delta \to 0$, $\delta \to 1$ and

$\alpha \to \exp(-r\Phi)$.

7.4.1 A Subgame Perfect Equilibrium

Consider a SPE that satisfies Properties 3.1, 3.2 and the following Property 7.2.

Property 7.2 (No Money Burning). Whenever a player has to decide whether or not to burn money, she chooses not to burn money.

From the arguments in Section 3.2.1, I obtain the following lemma which characterizes the unique SPE that satisfies Properties 3.1, 3.2 and 7.2.

Lemma 7.5. *The following pair of strategies is a subgame perfect equilibrium of the model with money burning:*
- *player A always offers x_A^* and always accepts an offer x_B if and only if $x_B \leq x_B^*$,*
- *player B always offers x_B^*, always accepts an offer x_A if and only if $x_A \leq x_A^*$, and always chooses not to burn money,*
where $x_A^* = x_B^* = \pi/(1 + \delta)$.

Notice that the SPE described in Lemma 7.5 is essentially the unique Rubinsteinian SPE (cf. Theorem 3.1). Furthermore, by construction, in equilibrium player B never burns money.

7.4.2 On the Uniqueness of the Equilibrium

I now address the issue of the existence of other SPE — by applying the method of proof used in Section 3.2.2. Unlike in the model with retractable offers, the arguments underlying the proofs to Lemmas 3.1–3.4 are applicable to the model with money burning. I thus obtain that $m_A = \pi - \delta M_B$, $m_B = \pi - \delta M_A$, $M_A = \pi - \delta m_B$, $M_B \geq \pi - \delta m_A$ and $M_B \leq \pi - \alpha m_A$. Combining these equations and inequalities, it follows that

$$m_B = \frac{\pi}{1 + \delta} \leq M_B \leq \frac{(1 - \alpha)\pi}{1 - \alpha\delta} \quad \text{and} \quad \frac{(1 - \delta)\pi}{1 - \alpha\delta} \leq m_A \leq \frac{\pi}{1 + \delta} = M_A.$$

This means that the SPE described in Lemma 7.5 gives players A and B respectively their best and worst equilibrium payoffs. The following proposition establishes that if $\alpha(1+\delta) < 1$, then the SPE described in Lemma 7.5 is the unique SPE of the model with money burning.[10]

Proposition 7.3. *If $\alpha(1 + \delta) < 1$, then the subgame perfect equilibrium described in Lemma 7.5 is the unique subgame perfect equilibrium of Rubinstein's model with money burning.*

Proof. I first argue that if $\alpha(1 + \delta) < 1$, then there does not exist a SPE in which player B ever chooses to burn money. Let H_B denote the set of all SPE payoffs to player B in any subgame beginning with player A's offer, and let N_B and n_B respectively denote the supremum and infimum of H_B. Since $N_B = \delta M_B$ and $n_B = \delta m_B$, it follows that $N_B \leq \delta(1 - \alpha)\pi/(1 - \alpha\delta)$ and $n_B = \delta\pi/(1 + \delta)$. Now consider any point in the game at which player B has to decide between 'MB' and 'D'. The best possible SPE payoff that player B obtains by burning money is bounded above by αN_B, and the worst possible SPE payoff that player B obtains by not burning money is bounded below by δn_B. Using the hypothesis $\alpha(1 + \delta) < 1$, it follows that $\delta n_B > \alpha N_B$. Hence, if $\alpha(1 + \delta) < 1$ then there does not exist a SPE in which player B ever chooses to burn money; that is, in any SPE player B always chooses the action 'D'. The proposition follows trivially from this result.   □

It follows from Proposition 7.3 that if $\alpha(1 + \delta) < 1$, then the option to burn money has no influence on the bargaining outcome; the unique Rubinsteinian equilibrium outcome is robust to this procedural feature. Notice that the condition $\alpha(1 + \delta) < 1$ means that Φ is sufficiently large. In the limit, as $\Delta \to 0$, $\alpha(1 + \delta) < 1$ if and only if $\Phi > \ln 2/r$.

7.4.3   Multiple Equilibria

I now establish (by construction) that if $\alpha(1 + \delta) \geq 1$, then there exists a continuum of SPE. As in Section 7.3.3, I first characterize the 'extremal' SPE that gives player A her worst equilibrium payoff.[11]

---

[10]The intuition for this result is as follows. If α is sufficiently small relative to δ (i.e., Φ is sufficiently large), then it is not optimal for player B to burn money in any SPE. To see this in a rather stark form, just consider the limiting case of $\Phi \to \infty$, given a finite value of Δ.

[11]Lemma 7.5 characterizes the 'extremal' SPE that gives player B her worst equilibrium payoff.

Lemma 7.6. *If and only if* $\alpha(1 + \delta) \geq 1$, *the pair of strategies described in Table 7.2 is a subgame perfect equilibrium. In equilibrium the game begins in state* $\hat{s}$ *and player A offers* $\hat{x}_A = (1 - \delta)\pi/(1 - \alpha\delta)$, *which is accepted by player B. Furthermore, if and only if* $\alpha(1 + \delta) \geq 1$, $m_A = (1 - \delta)\pi/(1 - \alpha\delta)$ *and* $M_B = (1 - \alpha)\pi/(1 - \alpha\delta)$.

Proof. It is easy to verify (using the *One-Shot Deviation* property) that the pair of strategies described in Table 7.2 is a subgame perfect equilibrium. However, in order to demonstrate the role played by the condition $\alpha(1+\delta) \geq 1$, I show that it is optimal for player B to burn money when play is in state $\hat{s}$. Consider any point in the game where player B has to decide between 'MB' and 'D', and suppose play is in state $\hat{s}$. According to her strategy described in Table 7.2 she is supposed to burn money. Her payoff from conforming to this behaviour is $\alpha(\pi - \hat{x}_A)$. Suppose she instead deviates and does not burn money (and thereafter she conforms to her strategy described in Table 7.2). Since the state immediately switches to s^*, her payoff from this one-shot deviation is $\delta(\pi - x_A^*)$. The latter payoff from the one-shot deviation is less than or equal to her former payoff from conforming if and only if $\alpha(1 + \delta) \geq 1$. $\square$

		state $\hat{s}$	state s^*
Player A	offer	$\hat{x}_A$	x_A^*
	accept	$x_B \leq \hat{x}_B$	$x_B \leq x_B^*$
Player B	offer	$\hat{x}_B$	x_B^*
	accept	$x_A \leq \hat{x}_A$	$x_A \leq x_A^*$
	'MB' or 'D'	'MB'	'D'
	transitions	switch to state s^* if player B ever chooses 'D'	absorbing

Table 7.2: A SPE of the model with money burning, where $x_A^* = x_B^* = \pi/(1 + \delta)$, $\hat{x}_A = (1 - \delta)\pi/(1 - \alpha\delta)$ and $\hat{x}_B = (1 - \alpha)\pi/(1 - \alpha\delta)$.

The intuition behind the SPE described in Table 7.2 is as follows. Player B's plan (or, threat) to burn money is credible, because if she fails to take that action then play immediately moves to the 'extremal' SPE that gives player B her worst possible equilibrium payoff. Thus, in equilibrium, players A and B have to wait respectively for $\Delta + \Phi$ and Δ time units before being able to make their respective counteroffers. Therefore, it is 'as if' the players are playing Rubinstein's game (in which player B does not have the option to burn money), where player B's discount factor is δ and player A's discount factor is α.

Using the results contained in Lemmas 7.5 and 7.6 — which characterize the two 'extremal' equilibria — it is now straightforward to construct a continuum of SPE.

Proposition 7.4. *If $\alpha(1 + \delta) \geq 1$, then for any partition $x \in \{(x_A, x_B) : 0 \leq x_A \leq \pi \text{ and } x_B = \pi - x_A\}$ of the cake such that*

$$\frac{(1 - \delta)\pi}{1 - \alpha\delta} \leq x_A \leq \frac{\pi}{1 + \delta} \tag{7.1}$$

there exists a SPE in which agreement is reached at time 0 on the partition x.

Proof. Fix an arbitrary partition x satisfying (7.1), and consider the following pair of strategies. At time 0 player A offers x_A and player B accepts that offer. If player A deviates and instead offers $x'_A \neq x_A$, then immediately (before player B decides whether to accept or reject the offer) play proceeds according to the SPE described in Lemma 7.6. Furthermore, if player B rejects the offer x_A, then immediately play proceeds according to the SPE described in Lemma 7.5. It is straightforward to verify, using the *One-Shot Deviation* property (and given that x_A satisfies inequality 7.1), that neither player can benefit from a unilateral deviation at time 0.   □

Notice that each SPE described in Proposition 7.4 is Pareto efficient, in that (in equilibrium) agreement is reached immediately without any delay.

7.4.4 Equilibrium Delay

I now construct a set of equilibria such that in each such SPE agreement is reached on some partition of the cake at some time T; and moreover, along the equilibrium path, player B burns money whenever she has to decide whether or not to do so. Of course, assume that $\alpha(1 + \delta) \geq 1$.

Fix an arbitrary non-negative integer k (i.e., $k = 0, 1, 2, 3, \ldots$) and define $T = k(\Delta + \Phi)$. Furthermore, let $x = (x_A, x_B)$ denote an arbitrary partition of the cake such that x_A satisfies (7.1).

It is convenient to specify the proposed SPE by first describing the proposed SPE *path of play*, and then specifying how play proceeds if a player deviates from this path. Consider the following path of play. At any time $t < T$, whenever player i has to make an offer, she offers $x_i = \pi$ and player j ($j \neq i$) rejects that offer. Furthermore, at any time $t < T$, whenever player B has to decide between 'MB' and 'D', she chooses 'MB'. Given this behaviour at any time $t < T$ it follows (by the definition of T) that at time T it is player A's turn to make an offer. Assume that she offers the partition specified above, namely x, which player B accepts. Now I describe how play proceeds if at any time $t \leq T$ a player deviates from this path of play. If player A (resp., player B) ever deviates from this path of play, then immediately play proceeds according to the SPE described in Lemma 7.6 (resp., Lemma 7.5).

I now proceed to characterize the values (if any) of k and x for which the pair of strategies thus described is a SPE. Letting V_i denote the payoff to player i in this proposed SPE, I note that $V_i = x_i \exp(-rT)$. Since, by construction, unilateral deviations from the proposed path of play moves play to a SPE, I need to only address the issue of whether or not a player has an incentive to deviate from the path of play. That neither player has an incentive to unilaterally deviate at time T follows from Proposition 7.4. Now I consider any point of time $t < T$ at which some player has to make a decision.

First consider any point along the path of play at which a player, say player j, has to reject the offer $x_i = \pi$. Since $V_j \geq 0$, it follows that player j does not benefit by instead accepting that offer.

Now consider any point of time $t < T$ at which player A has to make an offer. If she conforms to the proposed behaviour and offers $x_A = \pi$, then her payoff is V_A. Suppose she considers a one-shot deviation and instead offers $x'_A < \pi$. Then, immediately play moves to the SPE described in Lemma 7.6. If $x'_A \leq \hat{x}_A$, where $\hat{x}_A$ is defined in Lemma 7.6, then (as can be seen from Table 7.2) player B accepts that offer, and, thus, the payoff $V'_A(x'_A, t)$ to player A from this one-shot deviation is $x'_A \exp(-rt)$. For any $0 \leq t < T$ and any $0 \leq x'_A \leq \hat{x}_A$, such a one-shot deviation is not beneficial (i.e.,

$V_A \geq V'_A(x'_A, t))$ if and only if

$$x_A \exp(-rT) \geq \frac{(1-\delta)\pi}{1-\alpha\delta}. \tag{7.2}$$

On the other hand, if $\hat{x}_A < x'_A < 1$, then (as can be seen from Table 7.2) player B rejects that offer, and, thus, the payoff to player A from such a one-shot deviation is $\alpha\hat{x}_A \exp(-r(t+\Delta))$ which is less than V_A if x_A satisfies (7.2). In summary, (7.2) is a necessary and sufficient condition to ensure that player A never has any incentive to unilaterally deviate from the path of play at any point in time $t < T$.

Now consider any point of time $t < T$ at which player B has to make an offer. If she conforms to the proposed behaviour and offers $x_B = \pi$, then her payoff is V_B. Suppose she considers a one-shot deviation and instead offers $x'_B < \pi$. Then, immediately play moves according to the SPE described in Lemma 7.5. By a similar argument to that provided above, it follows that such a one-shot deviation is not beneficial if and only if

$$x_B \exp(-rT) \geq \frac{\delta\pi}{1+\delta}. \tag{7.3}$$

Now consider any point of time $t < T$ at which player B has to decide between 'MB' and 'D'. It is easy to verify that (7.3) is a sufficient condition to ensure that she does not benefit from a one-shot deviation. In summary, (7.3) is a necessary and sufficient condition to ensure that player B never has any incentive to unilaterally deviate from the path of play at point in time $t < T$.

Since $x_B = \pi - x_A$, (7.3) is equivalent to

$$x_A \exp(-rT) \leq \pi \exp(-rT) - \frac{\delta\pi}{1+\delta}. \tag{7.4}$$

Notice that if x_A satisfies (7.2) and (7.4), then x_A satisfies (7.1). Hence, the pair of strategies described above is a subgame perfect equilibrium if and only if k and x_A satisfy

$$\frac{(1-\delta)\pi}{(1-\alpha\delta)\exp(-rT)} \leq x_A \leq \pi - \frac{\delta\pi}{(1+\delta)\exp(-rT)}. \tag{7.5}$$

Define the set $W = \{(k, x_A) : k \text{ is a non-negative integer, } x_A \in [0, \pi] \text{ and } (k, x_A) \text{ satisfy (7.5)}\}$. It is easy to verify that W is non-empty, and that it is illustrated in Figure 7.1, where k^* denotes the real number at which point the two curves intersect and $\bar{k}$ denotes the largest integer smaller than k^*. Hence, I summarize the main insight thus derived in Proposition 7.5.

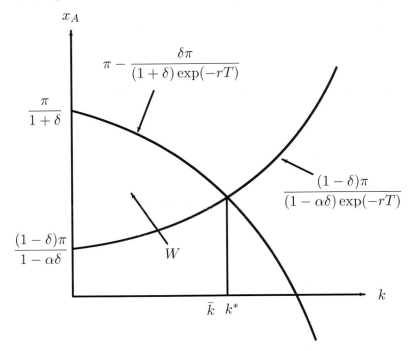

Figure 7.1: An illustration of the set W, which characterizes the set of SPE with delay in the model with money burning — as stated in Proposition 7.5.

Proposition 7.5. *If $\alpha(1+\delta) \geq 1$, then for any $(k, x_A) \in W$ there exists a SPE of the model with money burning such that in equilibrium agreement is reached at time $T = k(\Delta + \Phi)$ on the partition that gives player A a share x_A (and player B a share $\pi - x_A$), and in equilibrium player B burns money k times.*

Notice (from Figure 7.1, for example) that in any such SPE, agreement is reached at some time $T \leq \bar{T}$, where $\bar{T} = \bar{k}(\Delta + \Phi)$. Thus, $\bar{T}$ denotes the maximal possible delay consistent with equilibrium behaviour. Assuming for simplicity that k^* is an integer — in which case $\bar{k}$ is that value of k where the two curves intersect — in the limit, as $\Delta \to 0$, $\bar{k} \to \ln 2/r\Phi$ and $\bar{T} \to \ln 2/r$. Notice that, in this limit, the maximal possible equilibrium delay is unaffected by the value of Φ.

7.4.5   Discussion

The basic insight (on the effect that money burning can have on the bargaining outcome) established above can be generalized in many ways, and can be applied to a variety of contexts. For example, one could also allow player A the option to burn money immediately after her offer is rejected. Notice, however, that I precluded player B from taking such 'money burning' action immediately after she rejects player A's offers. The reason for doing so comes from the result (which is straightforward to verify) that player B would never, in any SPE, burn money after rejecting offers made by player A. The intuition behind this result is as follows. By burning money at such points in the game would, by increasing player B's cost of rejecting offers, decrease the share that player A would need to offer her. Thus, player B would certainly not burn money after rejecting any offer made by player A. On the contrary, she would wish to make her counteroffer as soon as possible. In contrast, by burning money after player A rejects player B's offers, player B increases the cost to player A of rejecting her offers, and, thus, she is able to offer player A a relatively smaller share. Indeed, the reason for why 'money burning' by player i, after player j $(j \neq i)$ rejects offers made by player i, increases player i's 'bargaining power' is precisely because such an action increases the cost to player j of rejecting player i's offers.

7.4.6   An Application to Surplus Destruction

Consider a bargaining situation in which a player can take an action (immediately after her offer is rejected and before her opponent gets to make a counteroffer) that results in the immediate and literal destruction of some fraction of the (remaining) cake. This action, which does not affect the times at which offers are made, is different from the particular 'money burning' action modelled in the preceding section. However, since the strategic structures are identical, the analysis of the preceding section is applicable.

   At each time $t\Delta$ (where $t = 1, 3, 5, \ldots$), immediately after player A rejects an offer made by player B, player B decides between 'MB' and 'D'. The former action involves the destruction of a fraction $1 - \gamma$ of the (remaining) cake available at time $t\Delta$. Thus, if π_t denotes the size of the cake at time $t\Delta$ and if player B chooses 'MB', then the size of the cake at time $(t + 1)\Delta$ is $\pi_{t+1} = \gamma\pi_t$. On the other hand, if she chooses 'D', then

$\pi_{t+1} = \pi_t$. Note that $\gamma \in [0,1]$ and $\pi_0 = \pi$. As before, $r > 0$ denotes the common discount rate. For notational convenience and for comparability sake, let $\delta \equiv \exp(-r\Delta)$ and $\alpha \equiv \gamma\delta$.[12] For simplicity, I do not give player A the option to 'burn money'. Thus, at each time $t\Delta$ ($t = 0, 2, 4, \dots$), immediately after player A makes her offer, player B either accepts the offer (in which case the game ends) or she rejects the offer (in which case bargaining continues with player B making her offer at time $(t+1)\Delta$).

Propositions 7.3–7.5 are applicable.[13] This means that if $\gamma < 1/\delta(1+\delta)$, then there exists a unique SPE in which the cake is never destroyed, and the equilibrium partition agreed to at time 0 is the Rubinsteinian equilibrium partition. On the other hand, if $\gamma \geq 1/\delta(1 + \delta)$, then there exists a multiplicity of equilibria. Let us focus on the set of equilibria in the limit as $\Delta \to 0$. In this limit, if $\gamma < 1/2$, then in the unique SPE the cake is never destroyed. Thus, if the 'MB' action involves destroying more than $1/2$ of the (remaining) cake, then player B never takes this action. On the other hand, if $\gamma \geq 1/2$, then there exists a continuum of SPE. In particular, in any SPE the cake is destroyed at most $\bar{k}$ times, where (assuming for simplicity that k^* is an integer) $\gamma^{\bar{k}} = \pi/2$. Hence, the maximal amount of cake destroyed consistent with equilibrium is $\pi/2$.

7.5 Notes

For further analysis of the infinitely repeated simultaneous-offers model see Binmore (1987) and Chatterjee and Samuelson (1990). Perry and Reny (1993) study a fairly complex continuous time bargaining model in which a player can make an offer at almost any point in time. They show that under some conditions the subgame perfect equilibria of such a model approximates the unique SPE of Rubinstein's (alternating-offers) model. Thus, their analysis provides some further support for Rubinstein's model.

The model with retractable offers discussed in Section 7.3 is based upon Muthoo (1990). Similar results hold in several other kinds of bargaining

---

[12]Indeed, γ is 'equivalent' to $\exp(-r\Phi)$

[13]It may be convenient — when verifying that these results are applicable — to interpret an offer x_i^t at time $t\Delta$ by player i as constituting the fraction of the cake of size π_t (available at time $t\Delta$) that player i obtains; thus, players i and j respectively obtain $\pi_t x_i^t$ and $\pi_t(1 - x_i^t)$ amounts of the cake.

models which allow for retractable offers (see, for example, Chaudhuri (1992, Chapter 6) and Muthoo (1995a)). Furthermore, it is easy to establish similar results to those established in Section 7.3, if, for example, a responder has the option to retract her acceptance of an offer after the proposer decides not to retract her offer. Chaudhuri (1994) contains an application of the model with retractable offers that relates a firm's pricing policy to its size.

Avery and Zemsky (1994) coin the term 'money burning'. Their paper generalizes the results described in Section 7.4 in some useful ways, and, furthermore, contains examples of this type of action. The application discussed in Section 7.4.6 is motivated by the work of Busch, Shi and Wen (1998) and Manzini (1999), who derive some further results about this model.

In some bargaining situations the set of possible agreements is finite. For example, the set of agreements is finite when bargaining over the partition of one dollar, because of the existence of a smallest unit of money, namely, one cent. Since this feature affects the set of actions (offers) available to a proposer, it affects the rules of the bargaining game. van Damme, Selten and Winter (1990) and Muthoo (1991) show that (under some conditions) Rubinstein's model with a finite number of agreements possesses a multiplicity of subgame perfect equilibria.

8 Commitment Tactics

8.1 Introduction

In many bargaining situations the players often take actions prior to and/or during the negotiation process that *partially* commit them to some strategically chosen bargaining positions. Such commitments are partial in that they are revocable, but revoking a partial commitment can be costly. The following two extracts from Schelling (1960) illustrate this 'commitment' tactic.

> it has not been uncommon for union officials to stir up excitement and determination on the part of the membership during or prior to a wage negotiation. If the union is going to insist on $2 and expects the management to counter with $1.60, an effort is made to persuade the membership not only that the management could pay $2 but even perhaps that the negotiators themselves are incompetent if they fail to obtain close to $2. The purpose ... is to make clear to the management that the negotiators could not accept less than $2 *even if they wished to* because they no longer control the members or because they would lose their own positions if they tried. In other words, the negotiators reduce the scope of their own authority and confront the management with the threat of a strike that the union itself cannot avert, even

though it was the union's own action that eliminated its power to prevent strike. Schelling (1960, p. 27)

When national representatives go to international negotiations knowing that there is a wide range of potential agreement within which the outcome will depend on bargaining, they seem often to create a bargaining position by public statements, statements calculated to arouse a public opinion that permits no concessions to be made. Schelling (1960, p. 28)

The main objective of this chapter is to investigate the role of such commitment tactics on the outcome of bargaining. I conduct this investigation by studying models based on the following ideas:

• Before embarking on some negotiation process (such as an offer-counteroffer process), each player takes actions that partially commit her to some bargaining position.

• Revoking such partial commitments can be costly.

• After such partial commitments have been made the players engage in some negotiation process in order to strike a deal. Each player will wish to minimize the extent to which she revokes her partial commitment.

In many bargaining situations there often exist a variety of 'mechanisms' through which a player can achieve partial commitment to some bargaining position. The two extracts from Schelling (1960) cited above suggest some such mechanisms. It seems intuitive that the higher is the player's cost of revoking a partial commitment, the greater is the degree to which she is committed to her chosen bargaining position. For example, if this cost of revoking is zero, then it is 'as if' she is not committed at all. At the other extreme, if this cost of revoking is sufficiently high (perhaps infinite), then it is 'as if' the bargainer is irrevocably committed to her chosen bargaining position. Of course, different mechanisms induce different costs of revoking, and, hence, different degrees to which commitment is achieved.

The models studied in this chapter do not formalize the mechanism (or mechanisms) through which a bargainer may achieve partial commitment — I assume that some such mechanism exists. The models, however, formalize the key features of such mechanisms, which are the induced costs of revoking such partial commitments. Much insight on the role of commitment tactics is obtained from the analyses of such abstract (reduced-form) models. This is especially the case since, by parameterizing the costs of revoking, the models encompass a wide variety of mechanisms that may be used to achieve partial commitment, from those which induce small costs of revoking to those that induce large costs of revoking.

In addition to exploring the effect that such commitment tactics may have on the players' 'bargaining powers', I also explore the idea that the deployment of such tactics may increase the likelihood of disagreements in bargaining. Since it is possible that the players end up locking themselves into incompatible bargaining positions, they may fail to reach agreement if each player's cost of revoking is sufficiently high.

The models that I study are two-stage games (or, can be interpreted as such). At the first stage the two players choose their respective partial commitments. This stage can be interpreted as taking place outside the formal negotiating process. After such partial commitments become known, at the second stage the players enter the formal negotiating process, where they attempt to reach agreement. This second stage could, for example, be either a Rubinstein-type alternating-offers game or a concession-type game (that may resemble a war of attrition). Broadly put, then, such bargaining models can be interpreted as models of 'claims' and 'concessions'.

A main focus of interest is the nature of the equilibrium at the first stage of such models, as it is at that stage that partial commitments are strategically chosen. For example, as mentioned above, an important issue from a welfare point of view is to study the circumstances under which, in equilibrium, the players make incompatible partial commitments. Hence, although the equilibrium at the first stage is influenced by the second stage game, it is the first stage equilibrium actions that are the focus of interest in this chapter.

The chapter is organized as follows. In the next section I formulate, interpret and analyse the basic model designed to explore the role of commitment tactics. A detailed discussion of the results obtained from this model are contained in Section 8.3, where I also explore the robustness of the main result to two extensions of this model. Section 8.4 contains an application of this model to the role of delegation in bargaining. A crucial assumption underlying Sections 8.2–8.4 is that the players' costs of revoking their respective partial commitments are known to both players. Partly as a result of this assumption, the unique equilibrium is always Pareto efficient.

In particular, in equilibrium the players do not make incompatible partial commitments. In Sections 8.5 and 8.6 I analyse two models in which this assumption is dropped. More precisely, when taking actions that partially commit the players to strategically chosen bargaining positions, both players do not know either player's costs of revoking. Each player's costs become known *only* to her after the 'claims' stage but before the second 'concessions' stage. A main objective of these two sections is to explore whether or not (as a result of the symmetric uncertainty at the first stage and asymmetric information at the second stage) the players, in equilibrium, make incompatible partial commitments.

8.2   The Basic Model

Although it will become evident that the model described here can be interpreted as a two-stage game (in which at the second stage the players are engaged in Rubinstein's alternating-offers game), the formal structure of the model constitutes a one-shot, static, game. That is, I will not formally model the second ('concessions') stage. Instead, I use the Nash bargaining solution to characterize the outcome of the second ('concessions') stage.[1] This modelling assumption simplifies the analysis, and allows attention to be focused on the first ('claims') stage.

8.2.1   The Formal Structure

Two players, A and B, bargain over the partition of a cake of size π (where $\pi > 0$) according to the following static game. They simultaneously and independently choose numbers from the closed interval $[0, \pi]$. Let z_i denote the number chosen by player i ($i = A, B$). The interpretation is that player i takes 'actions' which *partially* commit her not to accept a share strictly less than z_i. A partial commitment can later be revoked at some cost to the player.

The utility $U_i(x_i, z_i)$ to player i from obtaining a share $x_i \in [0, \pi]$ of the

---

[1]This can be justified by appealing to the result that the unique subgame perfect equilibrium payoff pair in Rubinstein's model converges (as the time interval between two consecutive offers converges to zero) to Nash's bargaining solution (cf. Corollary 3.4).

cake, given that she partially committed herself to $z_i \in [0, \pi]$, is

$$U_i(x_i, z_i) = x_i - C_i(x_i, z_i), \tag{8.1}$$

where $C_i(x_i, z_i)$ denotes the cost to player i of revoking her partial commitment z_i and obtaining a share x_i. It is assumed that $C_i(x_i, z_i) = 0$ if $x_i \geq z_i$, and that $C_i(x_i, z_i) > 0$ if $x_i < z_i$.

More specifically

$$C_i(x_i, z_i) = \begin{cases} 0 & \text{if } x_i \geq z_i \\ k_i(z_i - x_i) & \text{if } x_i < z_i, \end{cases} \tag{8.2}$$

where $k_i > 0$. Notice that this cost of revoking function captures the notion that the cost of revoking a partial commitment is strictly increasing in the extent to which it is actually revoked.[2]

I now turn to a description of the players' payoffs, where I denote player i's payoff from a strategy pair $z = (z_A, z_B)$ by $P_i(z)$.

First I describe the payoffs when the chosen partial commitments z_A and z_B are such that $z_A + z_B \leq \pi$. In this case, neither player revokes her partial commitment: the share x_i of the cake obtained by player i is such that $x_i \geq z_i$. Specifically, the share obtained by player i is given by $\lambda_i(z)$, where λ_A and λ_B are any functions such that $\lambda_A(z) \geq z_A$ and $\lambda_B(z) = \pi - \lambda_A(z) \geq z_B$. For example, it may be assumed that $\lambda_i(z) = z_i + (\pi - z_A - z_B)/2$. Hence, if $z_A + z_B < \pi$, then player i's payoff $P_i(z) = \lambda_i(z)$.

If, when $z_A + z_B > \pi$, agreement over the partition of the cake is struck, then at least one of the players must have revoked her partial commitment. The set $\Omega(z)$ of possible utility pairs that can be the outcome of bargaining is constructed using the set X of possible partitions of the cake and the utility functions U_A and U_B, where $X = \{(x_A, x_B) : 0 \leq x_A \leq \pi \text{ and } x_B = \pi - x_A\}$. That is, the set $\Omega(z)$ is the union of all pairs $(U_A(x_A, z_A), U_B(x_B, z_B))$ for $(x_A, x_B) \in X$. Indeed, for each pair $z \in [0, \pi]^2$ such that $z_A + z_B > \pi$, the set $\Omega(z)$ is the graph of the function $g(.; z)$ defined by

$$g(u_A; z) = U_B(\pi - U_A^{-1}(u_A; z_A); z_B),$$

---

[2] In Section 8.3.5 I study a more general version of the model studied here in which (i) I do not impose any specific functional form on the cost of revoking functions, but I instead restrict the class of such functions by a set of assumptions, and (ii) I assume that the utility to player i from obtaining x_i units of the cake is given by a strictly increasing and concave function.

where the domain and range of $g(.;z)$ are the closed intervals $[-k_A z_A, \pi]$ and $[-k_B z_B, \pi]$, respectively (cf. Section 2.2). Notice that $g(.;z)$ is concave and strictly decreasing in u_A (cf. Lemma 2.1).

If the players do not reach agreement, then each player obtains a payoff of zero.

It is possible (but not necessary) that there exists values of z_A and z_B such that $g(0;z) \leq 0$; in this case, $P_A(z) = P_B(z) = 0$. However, if $g(0;z) > 0$, then the payoff pair $(P_A(z), P_B(z))$ is defined as the Nash bargaining solution of the bargaining problem $(\Omega(z), d)$, where the disagreement point $d = (0,0)$ (cf. Definition 2.1). That is, $(P_A(z), P_B(z))$ is the unique solution to the following maximization problem

$$\max_{u_A, u_B} u_A u_B \text{ subject to } u_B = g(u_A; z), u_A \geq 0 \text{ and } u_B \geq 0.$$

This completes the formal description of the simultaneous-move game.

Figure 8.1 illustrates the utility possibility set $\Omega(z)$ for an arbitrary pair $z = (z_A, z_B)$ such that $z_A + z_B > \pi$. The line segment RS depicts the set X of possible partitions of the cake, while the graph $TNQM$ depicts the utility possibility set $\Omega(z)$. If the agreed partition lies on the line segment RV (resp., WS), then it is only player A (resp., B) who is revoking her partial commitment. But, if the agreed partition lies in the interior of the line segment VW, then both players are revoking their respective partial commitments. Consider, for example, the partition (x_A, x_B) depicted by the point a. The utility $x_A - k_A(z_A - x_A)$ to player A is the 'x-coordinate' of point c, while the utility $x_B - k_B(z_B - x_B)$ to player B is the 'y-coordinate' of point b. Hence, this defines the utility pair (point d) associated with such a partition.

It is straightforward to verify that the line segments TW, VM and NQ are defined by equations 8.3, 8.4 and 8.5, respectively:[3]

$$u_A + (1 + k_A)u_B = \pi + k_A(\pi - z_A) \tag{8.3}$$

$$u_B + (1 + k_B)u_A = \pi + k_B(\pi - z_B) \tag{8.4}$$

---

[3]Let (u_A, u_B) be a utility pair on the line segment NQ. This means that the partition (x_A, x_B) of the cake associated with this utility pair is such that $x_A < z_A$ and $x_B < z_B$. Hence, $u_A = x_A - k_A(z_A - x_A)$ and $u_B = x_B - k_B(z_B - x_B)$. That is, $u_A/(1 + k_A) = x_A - k_A z_A/(1 + k_A)$ $u_B/(1 + k_B) = x_B - k_B z_B/(1 + k_B)$. Equation 8.5 follows from adding the latter two equations, and then noting that $x_A + x_B = \pi$.

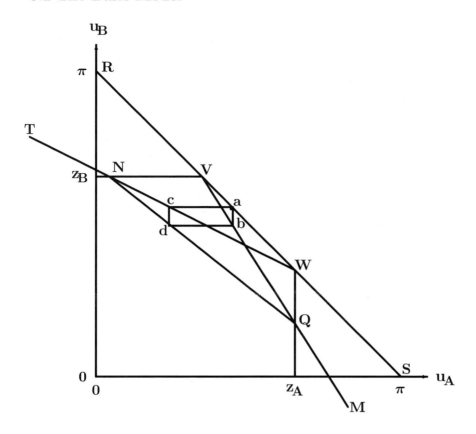

Figure 8.1: $TNQM$ is an illustration of the graph of the function $g(.; z)$ — which is the set $\Omega(z)$ of possible utility pairs.

$$(1 + k_A)u_B + (1 + k_B)u_A = \pi + k_A(\pi - z_A) +$$
$$k_B(\pi - z_B) + k_A k_B(\pi - z_A - z_B) \quad (8.5)$$

I note here that the slopes of these equations (and, in particular, the fact that they are independent of z_A and z_B) play an important role in my geometric analysis of the Nash equilibria of this model.

8.2.2 Interpretation

The model described above is designed to explore the role of commitment tactics on the outcome of bargaining. It is a fairly simple and abstract model. As I argue below, the model captures (in that it explicitly formalizes) some salient aspects of such tactics, but omits (from its formal structure) a significant amount of the richness that characterizes the deployment of such tactics. As is the case in the construction of any theoretical model, what is included in the formal structure is chosen deliberately so that the analysis is tractable and, at the same time, provides some insights on the impact of such tactics on the bargaining outcome. Once this model is understood, it may then become clear as to how it could fruitfully be enriched.

The mechanism through which a bargainer achieves partial commitment to her chosen bargaining position is not specified in the formal structure of the model. Moreover, the events that follow if the agreement involves the bargainer revoking her chosen partial commitment are also not incorporated in the formal structure of the model. Both of these crucial features of the commitment tactic are represented in the model by her cost-of-revoking function. It seems intuitive that the impact, if any, on the outcome of bargaining is due to the costs of revoking partial commitments. Hence, it seems reasonable to adopt this 'reduced-form' modelling approach.

In the model described above, I have imposed a particular structure (functional form) on these cost-of-revoking functions, because the analysis of the Nash equilibria is relatively straightforward, and it can be conducted geometrically — which provides a relatively more intuitive understanding of the arguments. However, in Section 8.3.5, I show that the unique Nash equilibrium is robust to alternative forms of the costs of revoking functions. Notice that the cost-of-revoking function stated in equation 8.2 captures some rather intuitive features (such as the notion that the cost is increasing in the extent to which a bargainer revokes her partial commitment).

8.2.3   The Equilibrium

I now derive the unique Nash equilibrium (NE) of the model described above. The first result below establishes that any pair of *more-than-compatible* partial commitments is not a NE.

Lemma 8.1. *If $z_A + z_B < \pi$, then the pair $z = (z_A, z_B)$ is not a Nash equilibrium.*

Proof. The proof is straightforward, because there exists an i ($i = A$ or $i = B$) such that $\pi - z_j > \lambda_i(z)$ ($j \neq i$); for otherwise, $\lambda_A(z) \geq \pi - z_B$ and $\lambda_B(z) \geq \pi - z_A$ imply that $z_A + z_B \geq \pi$. Hence, player i can benefit from a unilateral deviation to $z_i' = \pi - z_j$.   □

The next result establishes that any pair of *incompatible* partial commitments is not a NE.

Lemma 8.2. *If* $z_A + z_B > \pi$, *then the pair* $z = (z_A, z_B)$ *is not a Nash equilibrium.*

For notational convenience, define $\gamma \equiv (1 + k_B)/(1 + k_A)$.

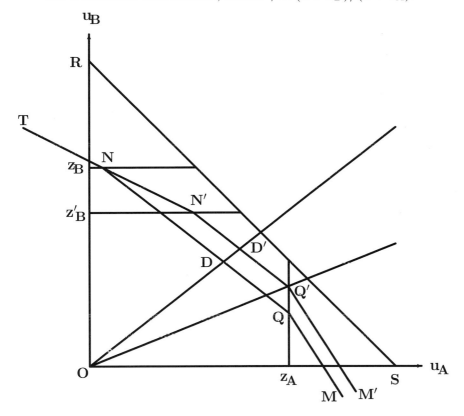

Figure 8.2: The geometry behind the proof of Lemma 8.2.

Proof. First, assume that $g(0; z) > 0$. The argument, by contradiction, is as follows (allowing for the roles of A and B to be reversed).[4] Suppose $P_B(z) < z_B$ (i.e., in Figure 8.1, the payoff pair $(P_A(z), P_B(z))$ lies either in the interior of the line segment NQ or on the line segment QM). I now

---

[4]A central part of my argument is based on the geometric characterization of the Nash bargaining solution, that it is the unique point (u_A, u_B) on the graph of the function $g(.; z)$ where some tangent has slope $-u_B/u_A$ (cf. Figures 2.2 and 2.3).

argue that player B can benefit from a decrease in her partial commitment to $z'_B = z_B - \epsilon$ for some ϵ such that $0 < \epsilon < z_B$. Consider Figure 8.2 in which the graphs $TNQM$ and $TN'Q'M'$ respectively illustrate the utility possibility sets $\Omega(z)$ and $\Omega(z')$, where $z' = (z_A, z'_B)$. Note that the line segment $N'Q'$ has the same slope (namely, $-\gamma$) as the line segment NQ (cf. equation 8.5). Hence, if the pair $(P_A(z), P_B(z))$ lies in the interior of the line segment NQ, such as at point D, then there exists an $\epsilon \in (0, z_B)$ such that the payoff pair $(P_A(z'), P_B(z'))$ is at the point D' that lies on the ray OD. By a similar argument, if the payoff pair $(P_A(z), P_B(z))$ lies in the interior of the line segment QM, then player B can (also) benefit from a decrease in her partial commitment.

Now suppose that the payoff pair $(P_A(z), P_B(z))$ is at point Q, where there is a kink in the graph $TNQM$. If the ratio $-P_B(z)/P_A(z)$ is equal to the slope of the line segment QM (namely, $-(1 + k_B)$), then (by a similar argument to that given above) it follows that player B can benefit from a decrease in her partial commitment. Now consider $-P_B(z)/P_A(z) > -(1 + k_B)$. Since the slope of the line segment $Q'M'$ is (also) equal to $-(1 + k_B)$, it follows by continuity that there exists an $\epsilon \in (0, z_B)$ such that the slope of the ray OQ' is (also) strictly less than $1 + k_B$. Consequently, the payoff pair $(P_A(z'), P_B(z'))$ lies either at point Q' or to the left of point Q'; thus, $P_B(z') > P_B(z)$.

Now assume that $g(0; z) \leq 0$, in which case $P_A(z) = P_B(z) = 0$. If $z_A + z_B < 2\pi$, then there exists an i ($i = A$ or $i = B$) such that $\pi - z_i > 0$. And, hence, player j ($j \neq i$) can benefit by unilaterally deviating to $z'_j = \pi - z_i$. Finally, consider the case $z = (\pi, \pi)$. Let $z'(\epsilon) = (\pi, \epsilon)$ where $0 \leq \epsilon < \pi$. Since $g(0; z'(0)) > 0$ and since $g(0; z'(\epsilon))$ is continuous in ϵ, there exists an $\epsilon' \in (0, \pi)$ such that $g(0; z'(\epsilon')) > 0$. And, hence, player B can benefit by unilaterally deviating to $z'_B = \epsilon'$. $\square$

The following result establishes that any pair of *exactly-compatible* partial commitments that does not satisfy a particular condition is not a NE.

Lemma 8.3. *If $z_A + z_B = \pi$ and $z_B/z_A \neq \gamma$, where $\gamma \equiv (1 + k_B)/(1 + k_A)$, then the pair $z = (z_A, z_B)$ is not a Nash equilibrium.*

Proof. By contradiction. First suppose that there exists a pair (z_A, z_B) such that $z_A + z_B = \pi$ and $z_B/z_A > \gamma$ which is a Nash equilibrium. I now show that player A can benefit from an increase in her partial commitment to $z'_A = z_A + \epsilon$ for some ϵ such that $0 < \epsilon < \pi - z_A$. Consider Figure 8.3. The graph $TNQM$ illustrates the utility possibility set $\Omega(z')$, where $z' = (z'_A, z_B)$. Since (by hypothesis) the slope of the ray OV (which equals z_B/z_A) strictly exceeds γ, it follows (by continuity) that there exists an $\epsilon \in (0, \pi - z_A)$ such that the slope of the ray OQ is (also) strictly greater than γ. Hence, since the slope of the line segment NQ is equal to $-\gamma$ (cf. equation 8.5), the Nash bargaining solution of the bargaining problem $(\Omega(z'), d)$ — where $d = (0,0)$ — lies on the line segment QM. Consequently, $P_A(z') \geq z'_A$, which implies that $P_A(z') > z_A$ (a contradiction). A symmetric argument establishes a contradiction when $z_B/z_A < \gamma$. $\qquad\square$

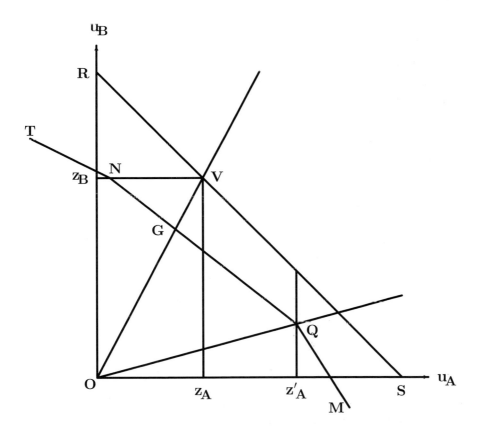

Figure 8.3: The geometry behind the proofs of Lemma 8.3 and Proposition 8.1.

I now use Lemmas 8.1–8.3 to characterize the unique NE.

Proposition 8.1. *The basic model with commitment tactics has a unique Nash equilibrium, namely*

$$z_A^* = \frac{\pi}{1+\gamma} \quad and \quad z_B^* = \frac{\gamma\pi}{1+\gamma},$$

where $\gamma \equiv (1 + k_B)/(1 + k_A)$.

Proof. Lemmas 8.1–8.3 imply that if a pair $z = (z_A, z_B)$ is a NE, then $z_A + z_B = \pi$ and $z_B/z_A = \gamma$; that is, the pair is as defined in the proposition. I now establish that this pair is a NE. First, suppose player A unilaterally deviates to $z_A' = z_A^* + \epsilon$, where ϵ is such that $0 < \epsilon \leq \pi - z_A^*$. The graph $TNQM$ in Figure 8.3 illustrates the utility possibility set $\Omega(z')$, where $z' = (z_A', z_B^*)$. Since the slope of the line segment NQ is equal to $-\gamma$, it follows that the payoff pair $(P_A(z'), P_B(z'))$ is at the point G that lies on the ray OV. Hence, the deviation is not profitable. Second, it is straightforward to show that player A does not benefit from a unilateral deviation to any z_A' such that $0 \leq z_A' < z_A^*$. Finally, by a symmetric argument it follows that player B does not benefit from a unilateral deviation to a partial commitment $z_B' \neq z_B^*$.   □

8.3   Discussion

The model formulated above is explicitly built upon Nash's bargaining solution. However, it can also be interpreted as an extension to Rubinstein's model, in which the bargainers make partial commitments before engaging in the offer-counteroffer process. It should be noted that this model is one example of the framework of two-stage games of 'claims' and 'concessions'. One could, for example, formulate second-stage 'concession' games that are not based on Nash's bargaining solution or Rubinstein's model — as is done in Sections 8.5 and 8.6.

8.3.1   Properties of the Equilibrium

I now turn to a discussion of some key properties of the equilibrium of the model analysed above. I begin by emphasizing the conclusion that the model has a *unique* Nash equilibrium. This is a remarkable property of the model; it demonstrates that commitment tactics can be a decisive force in resolving the fundamental indeterminacy that characterizes the bargaining situation.

In the unique Nash equilibrium, neither player revokes her partial commitment; the unique NE is Pareto efficient. In particular, the model does not predict any disagreement in equilibrium.

Player i's equilibrium partial commitment — which is identical to the equilibrium share of the cake she obtains — is strictly increasing in k_i, and strictly decreasing in k_j $(j \neq i)$. Thus, if a high k_i is interpreted as a weak bargaining position for player i (as one's intuition may suggest), then this model supports the viewpoint that, in bargaining, weakness can often be a source of strength.[5]

The result that player i's 'bargaining power' increases as her marginal cost k_i of revoking a partial commitment increases seems counterintuitive.[6] As player i's marginal cost of revoking increases *ceteris paribus* (that is, relative to player j's marginal cost of revoking), it is relatively less costly, at the margin, for player j to revoke her partial commitment. It is 'as if' player i's hands are tied behind her back in a relatively tighter manner. Thus, if, for example, the players make incompatible commitments, then it is player j who is more 'able' (and thus, more likely) to revoke her partial commitment — and, hence, player i's payoff increases as her marginal cost of revoking increases.[7]

8.3.2   Relationship with Nash's Bargaining Solution

Since the unique NE partial commitments are exactly compatible, it means that the equilibrium payoff pair $(P_A(z^*), P_B(z^*)) = (z_A^*, z_B^*)$. I now show that the equilibrium payoff pair (z_A^*, z_B^*) is identical to the asymmetric Nash bargaining solution of an appropriately defined bargaining problem (Ω, d) with an appropriate value for the parameter τ.[8]

---

[5]This basic insight about bargaining situations is informally, but persuasively, articulated — and discussed at some great length with many examples — by Thomas Schelling in his classic essay on bargaining (cf. Schelling (1960)).

[6]In the context of non-strategic decision making environments, the higher the cost the lower typically is the decision maker's payoff. However, as is often the case, what is valid in such non-interactive decision situations is invalid in strategic settings, such as bargaining situations.

[7]The insight is most transparent when, for example, k_i is arbitrarily close to infinity and k_j is arbitrarily close to zero.

[8]It should be noted that this is quite a remarkable result, notwithstanding the fact that Nash's bargaining solution is used to determine the players' payoffs when they make

It is natural to define Ω as the set of possible utility pairs available to the players before they make their partial commitments, which, since player i's utility from a partition of the cake equals the share that she obtains, means that $\Omega = \{(u_A, u_B) : 0 \leq u_A \leq \pi \text{ and } u_B = \pi - u_A\}$. Furthermore, since if the players fail to reach agreement then each player obtains a payoff of zero, it is appropriate to define the disagreement point $d = (0,0)$. Applying Corollary 2.3, it follows that the unique NE utility pair (z_A^*, z_B^*) is identical to the asymmetric Nash bargaining solution of the bargaining problem (Ω, d) with $\tau = (1 + k_A)/(2 + k_A + k_B)$. Notice that τ (resp., $1 - \tau$) is strictly increasing (resp., decreasing) in k_A and strictly decreasing (resp., increasing) in k_B — which makes sense since τ and $1 - \tau$ respectively reflect the bargaining powers of players A and B. If $k_A = k_B$, then $\tau = 1 - \tau = 1/2$, and the players split the cake equally. Indeed, if $k_A = k_B$, then the payoff pair (z_A^*, z_B^*) is identical to the Nash bargaining solution of (Ω, d) — which makes sense since the Nash bargaining solution (cf. Definition 2.1) embodies a symmetry axiom that would not be satisfied by the model with commitment tactics unless $k_A = k_B$.

8.3.3   Comparison with the Nash Demand Game

In the *Nash demand game*, two players A and B simultaneously and independently choose numbers from the closed interval $[0, \pi]$. Let z_i denote the number chosen by player i. If the players' demands are incompatible (i.e., $z_A + z_B > \pi$), then the players fail to reach agreement over the partition of the cake, and each player obtains a payoff of zero. The interpretation is that player i has taken actions which *irrevocably* commit her not to accept a share strictly less than z_i. If, on the other hand, the players' demands are compatible (i.e., $z_A + z_B \leq \pi$), then player i obtains a payoff equal to z_i. It is straightforward to verify that the Nash demand game possesses a continuum of Nash equilibria. In particular, any pair of exactly compatible demands is a Nash equilibrium.

At the heart of the Nash demand game lies the assumption that the

---

incompatible partial commitments. In fact, letting $\Pi_i(x_i)$ denote the utility that player i obtains from x_i units of the cake — where Π_i is linear (i.e, $\Pi_i(x_i) = x_i$) in the basic model studied here (cf. Equation 8.1) — I shall show in Section 8.3.5 that this result does not hold if for some i ($i = A$ or $i = B$), Π_i is strictly concave (and, of course, strictly increasing).

bargainers can make *irrevocable* commitments. The model studied in Section 8.2 can be interpreted as a perturbation to the 'commitment' structure of the Nash demand game, where this perturbation becomes arbitrarily small in the limit as both k_A and k_B diverge to plus infinity. It follows from Proposition 8.1 that in the limit as $k_A \to \infty$ and $k_B \to \infty$, keeping the ratio k_A/k_B constant at some positive value γ^*, the unique NE equilibrium partial commitments z_A^* and z_B^* converge respectively to $\pi\gamma^*/(1+\gamma^*)$ and $\pi/(1+\gamma^*)$. This result, besides selecting a unique equilibrium in the Nash demand game, provides an interpretation of the indeterminacy (multiplicity of equilibria) in the Nash demand game: the ratio k_A/k_B is an important determinant of the equilibrium demands, but is undetermined in the Nash demand game because, in this game, it is 'as if' $k_A = +\infty$ and $k_B = +\infty$.

It is interesting to note that these results are somewhat analogous to the results obtained in Rubinstein's bargaining model (cf. Chapter 3). If the players' discount rates, r_A and r_B, are such that $r_A = r_B = 0$, then Rubinstein's model has a continuum of subgame perfect equilibria. But if $r_A > 0$ and $r_B > 0$ then there exists a unique subgame perfect equilibrium, and moreover, even in the limit as $r_A \to 0$ and $r_B \to 0$ the unique equilibrium partition depends on the ratio r_A/r_B (cf. Corollary 3.1). By studying the limiting model ($k_A \to \infty$ and $k_B \to \infty$) rather than the model at the limit ($k_A = k_B = +\infty$), one discovers the significant role played by the ratio k_A/k_B. In fact, it is rather intuitive that in order to generate a unique equilibrium partition, one needs to know how 'strong' player A is *relative* to player B. Since this question cannot be addressed when $k_A = k_B = +\infty$, it is not surprising therefore that every partition can be supported as an equilibrium in the Nash demand game. The metaphor of a boxing match — used in the context of Rubinstein's model (cf. The discussion at the end of Section 2.2.1) — is once again useful: who wins the match depends crucially on which player is *relatively* stronger. The absolute magnitudes of the players' strengths are relevant to the final outcome only in so far as they determine the relative magnitude of their strengths.

8.3.4   Robustness

I now show that the unique NE is robust to two extensions of the model.

Sequential Moves

How would the results obtained here change if one of the players, say player A, were to choose her partial commitment z_A *after observing* the partial commitment z_B chosen by player B. Would player B benefit from being the 'first-mover'? I now sketch an argument which establishes that the outcome is unaffected: that is, the unique subgame perfect equilibrium partial commitments in the sequential-move game are identical to the unique Nash equilibrium partial commitments in the simultaneous-move game. The argument exploits the property of the unique Nash equilibrium that the ratio $z_B^*/z_A^* = \gamma$ (cf. Proposition 8.1).

If $z_B < z_B^*$, then $z_B/(\pi - z_B) < \gamma$. Using geometric arguments similar to those contained in the proofs of Lemmas 8.2 and 8.3, it follows that player A's unique best response is to set $z_A = \pi - z_B$. Now suppose that player B chooses $z_B > z_B^*$. This implies that $z_B/(\pi - z_B) > \gamma$. It can be verified, again using such geometric arguments, that player A's unique best response is to set z_A equal to the unique solution of the following equation: $g(z_A; z)/z_A = \gamma$, where $g(z_A; z) = (1 + k_B)(\pi - z_A) - k_B z_B$. Hence, player A's unique best response to a $z_B > z_B^*$ is: $z_A = [\pi + k_B(\pi - z_B)]/\gamma(2 + k_A)$. For each $z_B > z_B^*$, player B's payoff equals $g(z_A; z)$ *with* z_A being player A's unique best response to z_B. Straightforward computation, therefore, establishes that player B's optimal choice is z_B^*.[9]

On the Payoff Rule

I have assumed that if the players' partial commitments are compatible (i.e., $z_A + z_B \leq \pi$), then neither player revokes their respective partial commitment. It may, however, be reasonable (in some contexts) not to make this assumption. In that case one can define the players' payoffs using Nash's bargaining solution, as I did if $z_A + z_B > \pi$. With such a change in the rule that defines the payoffs, the results are unaffected: Proposition 8.1 continues to describe the unique Nash equilibrium.

---

[9]The intuition for this result, that the sequential-move game and the simultaneous-move game have the same equilibrium outcome, comes partly from the observation that each player's indifference curves are kinked at certain key points. For example, player B's indifference curve through (z_A^*, z_B^*) is kinked at that point. This observation can be obtained, at least informally, through the geometric arguments.

8.3.5   A Generalization

In the model studied in Section 8.2 each player's cost of revoking function is defined in equation 8.2; the cost to player i of revoking a partial commitment z_i and obtaining a share $x_i < z_i$ is proportional to the difference $z_i - x_i$. I now study a generalized version of the model in which player i's cost of revoking function satisfies the conditions stated below in Assumption 8.1 — which allow it to be non-linear.

Assumption 8.1. For each i, the cost of revoking function $C_i : [0,1] \times [0,1] \to \Re$ is continuous. Furthermore, (i) for any pair (x_i, z_i) such that $x_i \geq z_i$, $C_i(x_i, z_i) = 0$; (ii) for each $z_i \in (0,1]$, C_i is strictly decreasing, convex and twice continuously differentiable in x_i on the interval $(0, z_i)$; (iii) for each $x_i \in [0,1)$, C_i is strictly increasing, convex and twice continuously differentiable in z_i on the interval $(x_i, 1)$; and (iv) for each $z_i \in (0,1]$, the left-hand derivative of C_i w.r.t. x_i, evaluated at $x_i = z_i$, is strictly negative and is independent of the value of z_i (that is, there exists a constant $k_i > 0$ such that for any $z_i \in (0,1]$, $C_i^1(z_i-; z_i) = -k_i$).

The continuity and monotonicity assumptions on C_i capture the notion that the cost to player i of revoking her partial commitment z_i and obtaining a share $x_i < z_i$ depends on the amount by which she revokes (deviates from) her partial commitment. The assumption that the marginal cost $-C_i^1(z_i-; z_i)$ of revoking a partial commitment is strictly positive is quite reasonable. However, the assumption that this marginal cost is a constant and independent of z_i is made for simplicity. Having said this, it is not clear whether it is reasonable to assume that it is relatively easier (less costly) to revoke, at the margin, moderate (or extreme) partial commitments. Below I shall briefly discuss whether and how the results obtained here would be affected by any alternative assumption describing the dependence of the marginal cost $-C_i^1(z_i-; z_i)$ on z_i. An example of a cost of revoking function that satisfies Assumption 8.1 is: $C_i = 0$ if $x_i \geq z_i$ and $C_i = k_i(z_i - x_i) + (q_i/2)(z_i - x_i)^2$ if $x_i < z_i$, where $k_i > 0$ and $q_i \geq 0$.

I also generalize the model studied in Section 8.2 by assuming that the utility $U_i(x_i, z_i)$ to player i from obtaining a share $x_i \in [0, \pi]$ of the cake, given that she partially committed herself to $z_i \in [0, \pi]$, is

$$U_i(x_i, z_i) = \Pi_i(x_i) - C_i(x_i, z_i),$$

where I now allow the utility from consuming a share x_i to be $\Pi_i(x_i)$. It is assumed that Π_i satisfies the conditions stated below in Assumption 8.2.

Assumption 8.2. For each i, the function Π_i is twice continuously differentiable, strictly increasing and concave. Furthermore, without loss of generality, I normalize and set $\Pi_i(0) = 0$ and $\Pi_i(\pi) = 1$.

The result stated below establishes the uniqueness of the Nash equilibrium, and provides a characterization of this equilibrium.

Proposition 8.2. *The generalized model with commitment tactics described here in which Assumptions 8.1 and 8.2 are satisfied has at most a unique Nash equilibrium. In this equilibrium the players' partial commitments z_A^* and z_B^* are the unique solution to $z_A + z_B = \pi$ and*

$$\frac{\Pi_B(z_B)}{\Pi_A(z_A)} = \frac{\Pi_B'(z_B) + k_B}{\Pi_A'(z_A) + k_A}. \tag{8.6}$$

Proof. See Muthoo (1996, Proposition 2). □

This unique NE is similar to that derived in the basic model studied in Section 8.2 (cf. Proposition 8.1). In fact, if Π_i is linear (that is, $\Pi_i(x_i) = x_i$ for $i = A, B$) and C_i ($i = A, B$) satisfies Assumption 8.1, then the equilibrium is exactly the same. Indeed, a key (and rather interesting) feature of the equilibrium partial commitments is that they depend only upon the players' *marginal* costs, k_A and k_B, of revoking their respective partial commitments. The equilibrium partial commitments are independent of other features of the cost of revoking functions, including, for example, the degrees of convexity of these functions.

Before I turn to the issue of the existence of this unique Nash equilibrium, I briefly discuss the properties of this unique NE when for some i ($i = A$ or $i = B$), Π_i is non-linear — which, given Assumption 8.2, means that Π_i is strictly concave — and C_i ($i = A, B$) satisfies Assumption 8.1. As in the linear case (i.e., when for $i = A, B$, $\Pi_i(x_i) = x_i$ and C_i satisfies Assumption 8.1), the unique equilibrium partial commitments are exactly compatible, and, hence, the equilibrium is Pareto efficient. Furthermore, as in the linear case, player i's equilibrium partial commitment z_i^* — which is identical to the share of the cake she obtains — is strictly increasing in k_i and strictly decreasing in k_j ($j \neq i$). However, unlike in the linear case, the equilibrium payoff pair $(\Pi_A(z_A^*), \Pi_B(z_B^*))$ is not identical to *any* asymmetric Nash bargaining solution defined on the appropriate bargaining problem (Ω, d), where Ω is the set of possible utility pairs available to the players before any partial commitments are made,[10] and $d = (0,0)$.[11]

I now turn to the issue of the existence of this unique Nash equilibrium. Since, given Assumptions 8.1 and 8.2, the payoff function P_i need not be quasi-concave in z_i (although it is continuous in z and although the strategy sets are compact), it is not possible to appeal to the standard theorems on the existence of (pure-strategy) NE. Indeed, it turns out that the degree of convexity of C_i is important to establish the existence of the unique NE.[12] The next result, stated below, establishes the existence of this unique NE under some additional set of conditions (stated below in Assumption 8.3) and under the assumption that the degree of convexity of C_i is sufficiently small.

Assumption 8.3. For each i and for any pair (x_i, z_i) such that $x_i < z_i$: (i) $-C_i^1(x_i, z_i) = C_i^2(x_i, z_i)$ and (ii) $C_i^{11}(x_i, z_i) \geq -C_i^{12}(x_i, z_i)$.

This set of assumptions embodies the notion that x_i and z_i are to be treated symmetrically in the cost of revoking function C_i. For example, if the cost of revoking z_i and obtaining $x_i < z_i$ is a (possibly non-linear) function of the difference $z_i - x_i$, then Assumption 8.3 is satisfied.

Proposition 8.3. *If Assumptions 8.1–8.3 are satisfied, and if for each i and any pair (x_i, z_i) such that $x_i < z_i$, $C_i^{11}(x_i, z_i) < k_i^2/\Pi_i(z_i^*)$, then the unique Nash equilibrium described in Proposition 8.2 does exist.*

Proof. Muthoo (1996, Proposition 3). $\qquad\qquad\qquad\qquad\qquad\qquad$ □

Therefore, if the 'degree of convexity' C_i^{11} of the function C_i is strictly less than $k_i^2/\Pi_i(z_i^*)$, then the unique NE exists. Consider, for example, the

---

[10] That is, $\Omega = \{(u_A, u_B) :$ there exists a partition of the cake (x_A, x_B) such that $\Pi_A(x_A) = u_A$ and $\Pi_B(x_B) = u_B\}$.

[11] It follows from Definition 2.3 that the partition (x_A^N, x_B^N) of the cake associated with the asymmetric Nash bargaining solution defined on the bargaining problem (Ω, d) with parameter τ is the unique solution to: $x_A + x_B = \pi$ and $\Pi_B(x_B)/\Pi_A(x_A) = (1 - \tau)\Pi_B'(x_B)/\tau\Pi_A'(x_A)$. The desired conclusion follows because there does *not* exist a τ such that for any exactly compatible partition, $(1 - \tau)\Pi_B'(x_B)/\tau\Pi_A'(x_A) = (\Pi_B'(x_B) + k_B)/(\Pi_A'(x_A) + k_A)$.

[12] In Muthoo (1996), an example is constructed to show that this unique NE fails to exist if the degree of convexity of C_i is sufficiently large.

following function, which satisfies Assumptions 8.1 and 8.3: $C_i = 0$ if $x_i \geq z_i$, and if $x_i < z_i$ then $C_i = k_i(z_i - x_i) + (q_i/2)(z_i - x_i)^2$, where $k_i > 0$ and $q_i \geq 0$. Furthermore, assume that $\Pi_i(x_i) = x_i$. Thus, if $q_i < k_i^2(2 + k_A + k_B)/(1 + k_i)$, then the unique NE exists. Notice that this bound on q_i is strictly increasing in k_A (and in k_B), and it converges to plus infinity as either k_A or k_B or both k_A and k_B tend to plus infinity. Clearly, therefore, for a large class of convex cost of revoking functions satisfying Assumptions 8.1 and 8.3, the unique NE exists.

I now briefly discuss whether and how the results contained in Propositions 8.2 and 8.3 are affected by any alternative assumption describing the dependence of the marginal cost $-C_i^1(z_i-; z_i)$ on z_i. The characterization of an equilibrium is essentially unaffected: $z_A + z_B = \pi$ and (8.6) are to be satisfied, but with k_i replaced by $-C_i^1(z_i-; z_i)$. Continuity of the marginal cost in z_i ensures that the model possesses at most an odd number of Nash equilibria. If in addition, for example, the marginal cost $-C_i^1(z_i-; z_i)$ is non-increasing in z_i, then uniqueness is (re)obtained. The necessary and sufficient conditions for the existence of an equilibrium — stated in Muthoo (1996, Lemma 4A) — are unaffected; however, whether they would be satisfied depends on how the marginal cost varies with z_i.

8.4 An Application to Delegation

A simple extension of the model studied in Section 8.2 can provide some insight on why players in a bargaining situation often delegate to some other persons the job of negotiating on their behalfs. The extension involves endogenously determining the values of the marginal costs k_A and k_B.

Formally, before the game described in Section 8.2 is played, the two players, A and B, simultaneously and independently choose numbers $k_A \geq 0$ and $k_B \geq 0$, respectively.

The interpretation is as follows. There is a large number of heterogeneous professional negotiators who are up for hire. Each negotiator is characterized by a number $k > 0$. If player i chooses $k_i = 0$, then this means that she does not hire a professional negotiator, but instead plays the bargaining game herself. If, on the other hand, she chooses $k_i > 0$, then she hires a professional negotiator with characteristic k_i to play the bargaining game on her behalf. The point is that for each player revoking a partial commitment is not costly. But for a professional negotiator with characteristic k_i the cost of revoking a partial commitment is described by equation 8.2. The wage of a professional negotiator with characteristic k is fixed and is denoted by $W(k)$, where W is a differentiable, strictly increasing and convex function, with $W(0) = 0$.

From Proposition 8.1, it follows that the payoff to player i if she chooses k_i and player j $(j \neq i)$ chooses k_j is[13]

$$Z_i = \frac{(1+k_i)\pi}{2+k_i+k_j} - W(k_i).$$

Differentiating Z_i with respect to k_i, it follows that

$$\frac{\partial Z_i}{\partial k_i} = \frac{(1+k_j)\pi}{(2+k_i+k_j)^2} \quad W'(k_i).$$

Hence, since Z_i is strictly concave in k_i, it follows that if k_j is such that $W'(0) \geq \pi(1+k_j)/(2+k_j)^2$ then player i's unique best response is $k_i = 0$; and if k_j is such that $W'(0) < \pi(1+k_j)/(2+k_j)^2$ then player i's unique best response is the unique solution to

$$\frac{(1+k_j)\pi}{(2+k_i+k_j)^2} - W'(k_i) = 0.$$

Since $\pi(1+k_j)/(2+k_j)^2$ is strictly decreasing in k_j, it follows that if $W'(0) \geq \pi/4$, then for any $k_j \geq 0$, player i's unique best response is $k_i = 0$. Hence, if $W'(0) \geq \pi/4$, then the unique Nash equilibrium is $k_A = k_B = 0$.

If $W'(0) < \pi/4$, on the other hand, then in any Nash equilibrium $k_A > 0$ and $k_B > 0$. In particular, any solution to the following first-order conditions is a Nash equilibrium

$$\frac{(1+k_B)\pi}{(2+k_A+k_B)^2} - W'(k_A) = 0$$

$$\frac{(1+k_A)\pi}{(2+k_A+k_B)^2} - W'(k_B) = 0.$$

---

[13] Although Proposition 8.1 is valid for $k_A > 0$ and $k_B > 0$ (cf. equation 8.2), it is trivial to show that if for some i, $k_i = 0$ then (although there may exist multiple Nash equilibria) in any Nash equilibrium the payoffs to players A and B are respectively z_A^* and z_B^* — as stated in Proposition 8.1.

This system of equations has a unique solution in which $k_A = k_B = k^*$, where $k^* > 0$ is such that $\pi/4 = W'(k^*)$.[14] Thus if $W'(0) < \pi/4$, then in the unique Nash equilibrium both players hire *identical* negotiators, which implies that each player ends up receiving one-half of the cake; and, since each player has to also pay a wage of $W(k^*)$, each player's equilibrium payoff is strictly less than $\pi/2$ — which is the payoff to each player if both players do not hire any negotiators, but instead bargain themselves. This means that the unique Nash equilibrium is Pareto inefficient. Although equilibrium delegation is thus Pareto inefficient, for each player hiring a costly negotiator strictly dominates bargaining by herself. Delegation occurs not because the players are made better off, but because it is consistent with Nash equilibrium behaviour.[15]

8.5   Uncertainty and Simultaneous Concessions

The model studied in Section 8.2 has shown that the deployment of commitment tactics influences the equilibrium distribution of the 'gains from trade' in a bargaining situation. The unique equilibrium outcome, however, is Pareto efficient: the equilibrium partial commitments are not incompatible. As such the deployment of such tactics do not generate disagreement in a bargaining situation.

In this section I inject some uncertainty into the commitment process: when a player chooses the bargaining position to which she partially commits herself, she is uncertain about the costs of revoking such partial commitments. The key message of this section is that with uncertainty in the commitment process the equilibrium partial commitments are incompatible, and with strictly positive probability the players fail to reach agreement.

---

[14]Suppose there exists a solution to the first-order conditions in which $k_A > k_B$. This implies that $(1 + k_B)\pi/(2 + k_A + k_B)^2 < (1 + k_A)\pi/(2 + k_A + k_B)^2$. Hence, using the first-order conditions, this in turn implies that $W'(k_A) < W'(k_B)$, which is a contradiction.

[15]This result may be interpreted in terms of a Prisoners' Dilemma type game. Assume that each player has to choose between two values of k: $k = k^*$ (hire a particular type of professional negotiator) and $k = 0$ (do not hire the professional negotiator). It thus follows from the analysis above that for each player delegation is a strictly dominant strategy, which leads to a Pareto inefficient outcome: as in the classic Prisoners' Dilemma game, individual rationality conflicts with collective rationality.

8.5.1   A Model with Simultaneous Concessions

I study a model of bargaining based on commitment tactics with the feature that when the players simultaneously and independently choose their respective partial commitments, both players do not know *either* players' costs of revoking such partial commitments. This is a plausible feature of many bargaining situations, because the costs to a player of revoking a partial commitment may only become known to her as/after she actually takes actions that partially commit her to some bargaining position.

In order to bring out the main insight in as transparent and simple a way as possible, I assume that the cost to each player of revoking any partial commitment is either zero or infinite. I model this assumption as follows. Player i's cost of revoking function is defined in equation 8.2. But, at the first stage, both players are uncertain about the exact values of both k_A and k_B; with probability p_i, $k_i = 0$, and with probability $1 - p_i$, $k_i = +\infty$, where $0 < p_i < 1$.

At the first stage, given the players' uncertainty about the values of k_A and k_B, the players simultaneously and independently choose their respective partial commitments z_A and z_B. Immediately after the partial commitments have been made, they become known to both players. Furthermore, the values of k_A and k_B are then drawn (randomly and independently), and player i learns the value of k_i but does not learn the value of k_j.

If the partial commitments z_A and z_B are compatible (i.e., $z_A + z_B \leq \pi$), then — as in the model studied in Section 8.2 — neither player revokes her partial commitment: the share x_i of the cake obtained by player i is such that $x_i \geq z_i$. Specifically, the share obtained by player i is given by $\lambda_i(z)$, where λ_A and λ_B are any functions such that $\lambda_A(z) \geq z_A$ and $\lambda_B(z) = \pi - \lambda_A(z) \geq z_B$. For example, it may be assumed that $\lambda_i(z) = z_i + (\pi - z_A - z_B)/2$. Hence, if $z_A + z_B \leq \pi$, then player i's payoff is $\lambda_i(z)$.

If, on the other hand, the partial commitments z_A and z_B are incompatible (i.e., $z_A + z_B > \pi$), then play moves to the second stage of the game: the players simultaneously and independently decide whether or not to back down from their respective partial commitments. If both players choose to back down, then each player obtains one-half of the cake. If player i only backs down, then her share $x_i = \pi - z_j$ and player j's share $x_j = z_j$. And if neither player backs down, then the players fail to reach agreement (and each player obtains no share of the cake).

The utility payoff to player i if she obtains a share x_i of the cake, given that she chose z_i, is defined by equation 8.1. This completes the description of the two-stage game. Notice that — unlike the model studied in Section 8.2 — the second stage is not based on Nash's bargaining solution or Rubinstein's model: it is a simultaneous, one-shot, concession game.

8.5.2   An Example: Two Bargaining Positions

In this section I analyse the above model with the assumption that for each i, z_i can take only two values, namely, 0 and $2\pi/3$. This additional assumption considerably simplifies the analysis of the model. In particular, it proves straightforward to derive the main result that for a large class of values of the probabilities p_A and p_B, in the *unique* Perfect Bayesian Equilibrium (PBE) $z_A = z_B = 2\pi/3$, and with probability $(1 - p_A)(1 - p_B)$ the players fail to reach agreement.[16]

Suppose that at the first stage player A chooses $z_A = 2\pi/3$ and player B chooses $z_B = 2\pi/3$. This means that the game proceeds to the second stage, where player i knows the value of k_i but does not know the value of k_j. In any Bayesian Nash Equilibrium (BNE) of the second stage game, if $k_i = +\infty$ then player i does not back down. Letting q_i denote the probability with which player i backs down if $k_i = 0$, the (conditional) expected payoff to player i if $k_i = 0$ from backing down, $E_i(BD)$, and from not backing down, $E_i(D)$, are respectively

$$E_i(BD) = p_j[q_j(\pi/2) + (1 - q_j)(\pi/3)] + (1 - p_j)(\pi/3) \quad \text{and}$$
$$E_i(D) = p_j q_j(2\pi/3).$$

It is trivial to verify that if $p_j < 2/3$, then for any $q_j \in [0, 1]$, $E_i(BD) > E_i(D)$. That is, if $p_j < 2/3$, then backing down is a strictly dominant action for player i if $k_i = 0$.[17] Hence, if $p_A < 2/3$ and $p_B < 2/3$, then the second stage subgame (after the players choose $z_A = 2\pi/3$ and $z_B = 2\pi/3$) has a unique BNE: each player i backs down if $k_i = 0$ and does not back down if

---

[16] In the next section I extend this kind of result to the general case when for each i, z_i can take any value in the interval $[0, \pi]$.

[17] This result is fairly intuitive. If the maximum (unconditional) probability with which player j backs down — which equals p_j — is not too large, then it is optimal for player i to back down if $k_i = 0$.

$k_i = +\infty$. In this unique BNE the (conditional) expected payoffs to player i if $k_i = 0$ and if $k_i = +\infty$ are respectively

$$E_i(k_i = 0) = p_j(\pi/2) + (1 - p_j)(\pi/3) \quad \text{and} \quad E_i(k_i = +\infty) = p_j(2\pi/3).$$

I now proceed backwards to characterize the Nash equilibria of the first stage of the game. First, notice that $(z_A, z_B) = (0, 0)$ is not a Nash equilibrium, because player i can benefit from unilaterally deviating to $z_i = 2\pi/3$ — since $\lambda_i(\nu_i) \geq 2\pi/3$, where $\nu_A = (2\pi/3, 0)$ and $\nu_B = (0, 2\pi/3)$. Given the unique BNE of the second stage game, the (unconditional) expected payoff to player i at the first stage if $z_A = 2\pi/3$ and $z_B = 2\pi/3$ is

$$E_i(2\pi/3, 2\pi/3) = p_i E_i(k_i = 0) + (1 - p_i) E_i(k_i = +\infty),$$

where $E_i(k_i = 0)$ and $E_i(k_i = +\infty)$ are defined above. Hence, $(z_A, z_B) = (2\pi/3, 2\pi/3)$ is the unique Nash equilibrium if and only if

$$E_A(2\pi/3, 2\pi/3) \geq \lambda_A(\nu_B) \quad \text{and} \quad E_B(2\pi/3, 2\pi/3) \geq \lambda_B(\nu_A).$$

Since $\lambda_i(\nu_i) \geq 2\pi/3$ implies that $\lambda_j(\nu_i) \leq \pi/3$, $(z_A, z_B) = (2\pi/3, 2\pi/3)$ is the unique Nash equilibrium if and only if $E_A(2\pi/3, 2\pi/3) \geq \pi/3$ and $E_B(2\pi/3, 2\pi/3) \geq \pi/3$. That is, $(z_A, z_B) = (2\pi/3, 2\pi/3)$ is the unique Nash equilibrium if and only if the following two inequalities hold

$$2p_A + 4p_B - 3p_A p_B \geq 2 \tag{8.7}$$

$$2p_B + 4p_A - 3p_A p_B \geq 2. \tag{8.8}$$

It is straightforward to show that there exists a large set of values of p_A and p_B that satisfy inequalities 8.7 and 8.8 — which I denote by $\mathcal{J}$, and which is shown in Figure 8.4. Proposition 8.4 summarizes the main result obtained here.

Proposition 8.4. *If p_A and p_B satisfy inequalities 8.7 and 8.8 — that is, the pair (p_A, p_B) belongs to the set $\mathcal{J}$ shown in Figure 8.4 — then in the unique perfect Bayesian equilibrium of the example studied here, $z_A = z_B = 2\pi/3$, and with probability $(1 - p_A)(1 - p_B)$ the players fail to reach agreement.*

This proposition illustrates the main message of this section: if the values of p_A and p_B are neither too high nor too low, then the uncertainty in

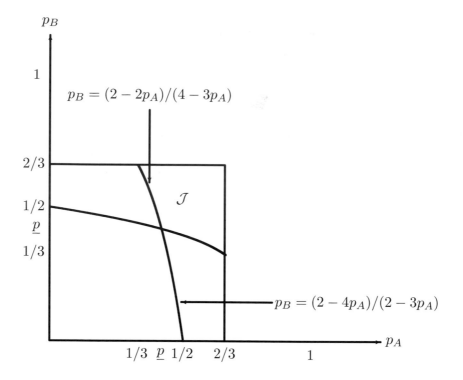

Figure 8.4: The area between $p_A = 2/3$, $p_B = 2/3$, $p_B = (2 - 2p_A)/(4 - 3p_A)$ and $p_B = (2 - 4p_A)/(2 - 3p_A)$ — where the latter two functions are strictly decreasing and concave — is the set $\mathcal{J}$: that is, the set of all pairs (p_A, p_B) which satisfy inequalities 8.7 and 8.8. The point where the latter two functions intersect is $(\underline{p}, \underline{p})$, where $\underline{p} = 1 - 1/\sqrt{3} \approx 0.42$.

the commitment process necessarily implies that players' equilibrium partial commitments are incompatible, and with strictly positive probability the players fail to reach agreement. The intuition behind this result is straightforward. If p_j is not too high, then in the second stage subgame it is optimal for player i to back down if $k_i = 0$. Consequently, if p_j is not too small, then it is optimal for player i to choose $z_i = 2\pi/3$, because with a sufficiently large probability player j backs down when $k_i = 0$.

8.5.3 A Generalization

I now generalize the result derived above to the case when, for each i, $z_i \in [0, \pi]$. In particular, I show that there exists a large class of values of p_A and

p_B such that in *any* PBE, the players' partial commitments are incompatible, and with strictly positive probability the players fail to reach agreement.

Suppose that at the first stage the players' partial commitments z_A and z_B are incompatible (i.e., $z_A + z_B > \pi$). This means that the game proceeds to the second stage, where player i knows the value of k_i but does not know the value of k_j. In any BNE of the second stage game, if $k_i = +\infty$ then player i does not back down. Letting q_i denote the probability with which player i backs down if $k_i = 0$, the (conditional) expected payoff to player i if $k_i = 0$ from backing down, $E_i(BD)$, and from not backing down, $E_i(D)$, are respectively

$$E_i(BD) = p_j q_j (\pi/2) + (1 - p_j q_j)(\pi - z_j) \quad \text{and} \tag{8.9}$$
$$E_i(D) = p_j q_j z_i. \tag{8.10}$$

I now derive the following proposition.

Proposition 8.5. *If* $1/2 < p_A < 2/3$, $1/2 < p_B < 2/3$ *and*

$$\frac{p_A p_B}{2[1 - (1 - p_A)p_B - (1 - p_B)p_A]} > \max\{1 - p_A, 1 - p_B\} \tag{8.11}$$

then in any PBE the equilibrium partial commitments z_A^* *and* z_B^* *are incompatible (that is,* $z_A^* + z_B^* > \pi$*), and with strictly positive probability the players fail to reach agreement.*

Since inequality 8.11 is satisfied when $p_A = p_B = 2/3$, and since the left-hand side and the right-hand side of this inequality are continuous in p_A and p_B, there exists $\bar{p}_A < 2/3$ and $\bar{p}_B < 2/3$ such that the inequality is satisfied for any pair $(p_A, p_B) \in (\bar{p}_A, 2/3) \times (\bar{p}_B, 2/3)$. This establishes that there exists a set of values of p_A and p_B under which the conclusion contained in this proposition is valid.

Proof. Suppose, to the contrary, that there exists a PBE in which the equilibrium partial commitments z_A^* and z_B^* are exactly compatible (i.e., $z_A^* + z_B^* = \pi$).[18] This implies that there exists an i (where $i = A$ or $i = B$) such that $z_i^* \leq \pi/2$ — and, thus, $z_j^* \geq \pi/2$ ($j \neq i$).

First, suppose that $z_j^* < \pi p_i$ — which is possible since $p_i > 1/2$. I show that player j can benefit from a unilateral deviation to a partial commitment

---

[18]Since Lemma 8.1 is valid in this model as well, there does not exist a PBE in which the equilibrium partial commitments z_A^* and z_B^* are more than compatible (i.e., $z_A^* + z_B^* < \pi$).

z_j' such that $z_j^* < z_j' < \pi$ and $p_i z_j' > z_j^*$. Consider the second stage subgame following this unilateral deviation. Since $z_i^* \leq \pi/2$ and $z_j' < \pi$, it follows from (8.9) and (8.10) that for any $q_j \in [0, 1]$, $E_i(BD) > E_i(D)$ — which implies that in the BNE of this subgame $q_i^*(z') = 1$, where $z' = (z_i^*, z_j')$; that is, in equilibrium player i backs down with probability one if $k_i = 0$. Hence, the (unconditional) expected payoff to player j from this unilateral deviation equals

$$E_j(z') = p_j \max\{p_i(\pi/2) + (1 - p_i)(\pi - z_i^*), p_i z_j'\} + (1 - p_j)p_i z_j'.$$

Hence, $E_j(z') \geq p_i z_j'$, which implies that $E_j(z') > z_j^*$, which is a contradiction (since the equilibrium expected payoff to player j, $E_j(z_A^*, z_B^*) = z_j^*$).

Now suppose that $z_j^* \geq \pi p_i$, which implies that $z_i^* \leq \pi(1 - p_i)$ — and which in turn implies, since $p_i > 1/2$, that $z_i^* < \pi/2$. I show that player i can benefit from a unilateral deviation to a partial commitment $z_i' = z_i^* + \epsilon$ for some $\epsilon \in (0, \pi/2 - z_i^*)$ — which implies that $z_i' < \pi/2$. Consider the second stage subgame following this unilateral deviation. From (8.9) and (8.10), it follows that $E_j(BD) = p_i q_i(\pi/2) + (1 - p_i q_i)(\pi - z_i')$ and $E_j(D) = p_i q_i z_j^*$. It is trivial to show that for any $q_i \in [0, 1]$, $E_j(BD)$ is minimized at $q_i = 1$ and $E_j(D)$ is maximized at $q_i = 1$. The assumption $1/2 < p_i < 2/3$ implies that the minimized value of $E_j(BD)$ — which equals $p_i(\pi/2) + (1 - p_i)(\pi - z_i')$ — strictly exceeds the maximized value of $E_j(D)$ — which equals $p_i z_j^*$. This implies that in the BNE of this subgame, $q_j^*(z') = 1$ — that is, in equilibrium player j backs down with probability one if $k_j = 0$. Given this result, it follows that there exists an $\epsilon_1 > 0$ such that for any $\epsilon \in (0, \epsilon_1)$, the (conditional) expected payoff to player i from backing down if $k_i = 0$ — which (using 8.9) equals $p_j(\pi/2) + (1 - p_j)z_i^*$ — is strictly greater than her (conditional) expected payoff from not backing down — which equals $p_j(z_i^* + \epsilon)$. This means that in the unique BNE at this second stage subgame $q_i^*(z') = 1$ as well. Hence, the (unconditional) expected payoff to player i from this unilateral deviation equals

$$E_i(z') = p_i[p_j(\pi/2) + (1 - p_j)z_i^*] + (1 - p_i)p_j(z_i^* + \epsilon). \qquad (8.12)$$

Since $z_i^* \leq \pi(1 - p_i)$, (8.11) ensures that there exists an $\epsilon \in (0, \pi/2 - z_i^*)$ such that (8.12) is strictly greater than z_i^*, which constitutes a contradiction. □

It follows from Proposition 8.5 that provided p_A and p_B are neither too large nor too small, uncertainty in the commitment process necessarily implies that the players' equilibrium partial commitments are incompatible, and with strictly positive probability the players fail to reach agreement.

Proposition 8.5 provides a characterization of *any* PBE. In the following proposition I establish the *existence* of such a PBE.[19]

Proposition 8.6. *If $p_A > 1/2$ and $p_B > 1/2$, then there exists a perfect Bayesian equilibrium in which the partial commitments of players A and B are respectively*

$$z_A^* = \frac{2\beta_A(1 - \beta_B) + 1 - \beta_A}{2(1 - \beta_A\beta_B)} \quad and \quad z_B^* = \frac{2\beta_B(1 - \beta_A) + 1 - \beta_B}{2(1 - \beta_A\beta_B)},$$

where $\beta_i = (1 - p_i)/p_i$.[20]

Proof. Unless otherwise specified below, fix an arbitrary BNE in each second stage subgame that follows a pair of incompatible partial commitments.[21] By construction, the pair (z_A^*, z_B^*) is the unique solution to the following pair of equations

$$p_A(\pi/2) + (1 - p_A)(\pi - z_A) = p_A z_B$$
$$p_B(\pi/2) + (1 - p_B)(\pi - z_B) = p_B z_A.$$

Hence, in the second stage subgame following the (proposed) equilibrium partial commitments, if $k_i = 0$ then player i is indifferent between backing down and not backing down, given that player j backs down with probability one if $k_j = 0$ (cf. (8.9) and (8.10)). This implies that in this second stage subgame there exists a BNE in which each player i backs down with probability one if $k_i = 0$. Given this BNE, the (unconditional) payoff to player i in the proposed PBE is $p_j z_i^*$.

I now show that the pair $z^* = (z_A^*, z_B^*)$ is a Nash equilibrium of the first stage game. First, observe that since $p_j z_i^* > \pi - z_j^*$, player i does not profit from a unilateral deviation to a partial commitment $z_i' = \pi - z_j^*$. Hence,

---

[19]The proof is by construction for the following reason. Although there exists a BNE in each second stage subgame (because such a subgame is finite), since the first stage game is not finite and since the (unconditional) expected payoffs need not be continuous, it is not possible to appeal to one of the standard theorems on the existence of Nash equilibria.

[20]Notice that since $p_A > 1/2$ and $p_B > 1/2$, $\pi/2 < z_i^* < \pi$ — hence, these equilibrium partial commitments are incompatible.

[21]Notice that since each such subgame is finite, existence of BNE is ensured.

it follows that she does not benefit from a unilateral deviation to a partial commitment $z_i' < \pi - z_j^*$.

Now consider a unilateral deviation by player i to z_i' such that $\pi - z_j^* < z_i < z_i^*$. This implies that in the second stage subgame that follows the choice of the pair $z' = (z_i', z_j^*)$ there exists a BNE in which each player i backs down with probability one if $k_i = 0$. Therefore, given this BNE, the unconditional expected payoff to player i from this deviation is strictly less than $p_j z_i^*$.

Finally, consider a unilateral deviation by player i to z_i such that $z_i^* < z_i'$, and consider the second stage subgame that follows the choice of the pair z'. Define, for each $i = A, B$

$$q_i^*(z') = \frac{1 - z_j^*}{p_j(z_i' - z_j^* + 1/2)}.$$

Notice that since $p_A > 1/2$, $p_B > 1/2$ and $z_i' > z_i^*$, $0 < q_i^*(z') < 1$. This probability is constructed to ensure that player i is indifferent between not backing down and backing down if $k_i = 0$. Hence, the pair $(q_A^*(z'), q_B^*(z'))$ constitutes a BNE of this subgame. It follows that player i's unconditional expected payoff from this deviation is $p_j q_j^*(z') z_i'$ — which is strictly decreasing in z_i' on the interval $(z_i^*, \pi]$. Since this payoff $p_j q_j^*(z') z_i'$ converges to $p_j z_i^*$ as z_i' tends to z_i^* from above, it follows that deviating to $z_i' > z_i^*$ is not profitable. $\square$

8.6 Uncertainty and Wars of Attrition

In the preceding section I have shown that with uncertainty in the commitment process the players' equilibrium partial commitments are necessarily incompatible, and with strictly positive probability the players fail to reach agreement. As is shown in the current section, a crucial feature of the model studied above that contributes to this result is that at the second stage the players engage in a one-shot, simultaneous, concession game. In particular, if, when $z_A + z_B > \pi$, both players do not back down, then the game ends in disagreement. This seems unpersuasive; it seems more reasonable to allow (in that eventuality) the bargainers the option to play the one-shot, simultaneous, concession game one more time. The criticism levelled here, however, would continue to have force. Indeed, it seems much more plausible to allow the players to engage in a so-called 'war of attrition' game, where each player decides at any point in time whether or not to back down, and in which the game ends if and only if some player backs down. This type of infinite concession game captures the notion that the bargainers keep on exploring the possibility of reaching agreement. A finite concession game, on the other hand, embodies the implausible feature that the bargainers are somewhat forced to terminate bargaining if neither player backs down before the end of the exogenously specified finite horizon.

In this section I show that if, unlike in the model specified in Section 8.5, the second stage subgames constitute such wars of attrition, then in any PBE of the two-stage game the players' partial commitments are exactly compatible. Thus, from this analysis one may conclude that uncertainty in the commitment process need not generate disagreement in a bargaining situation.

8.6.1 A Model with Wars of Attrition

Although the model studied here differs from that studied in Section 8.5 mainly in the specification of the second stage game, I shall provide a full description of the model to be analysed here. Player i's cost of revoking function is defined in equation 8.2. But, at the first stage, both players are uncertain about the exact values of both k_A and k_B; with probability p_i, $k_i = 0$, and with probability $1 - p_i$, $k_i = +\infty$, where $0 < p_i < 1$.

At the first stage, given the players' uncertainty about the values of k_A and k_B, the players simultaneously and independently choose their respective partial commitments z_A and z_B, where $0 \leq z_i < \pi$.[22] Immediately after the partial commitments have been made, they become known to both players. Furthermore, the values of k_A and k_B are then drawn (randomly and independently), and player i learns the value of k_i but does not learn the value of k_j.

If the partial commitments z_A and z_B are compatible (i.e., $z_A + z_B \leq \pi$), then — as in the models studied in Sections 8.2 and 8.5 — neither player revokes her partial commitment: the share x_i of the cake obtained by player

---

[22]In this model I do not allow each player i to set $z_i = \pi$, because the analysis of the war of attrition subgames presented in the next section applies only if $z_i < \pi$.

i is such that $x_i \geq z_i$. Specifically, the share obtained by player i is given by $\lambda_i(z)$, where λ_A and λ_B are any functions such that $\lambda_A(z) \geq z_A$ and $\lambda_B(z) = \pi - \lambda_A(z) \geq z_B$. For example, it may be assumed that $\lambda_i(z) = z_i + (\pi - z_A - z_B)/2$. Hence, if $z_A + z_B \leq \pi$, then player i's payoff is $\lambda_i(z)$.

If, on the other hand, the partial commitments z_A and z_B are incompatible (i.e., $z_A + z_B > \pi$), then play moves to the second stage of the game, which is the following 'war of attrition' game. At any time $t \geq 0$, each player decides whether or not to back down. The game ends at time t if and only if at least one player backs down at time t. If the game ends with only player i having backed down, then her share $x_i = \pi - z_j$ and player j's share $x_j = z_j$. On the other hand, if the game ends with both players simultaneously having backed down, then each player obtains one-half of the cake. Finally, if neither player ever backs down, then the players fail to reach agreement (and each player obtains no share of the cake).

The utility payoff to player i if she obtains a share x_i of the cake at time t, given that she chose z_i, is $U_i(x_i, z_i) \exp(-r_i t)$, where the utility function U_i is defined in (8.1) and $r_i > 0$ denotes player i's discount rate. This completes the description of the model.

8.6.2 Equilibrium in the War of Attrition Subgames

Fix an arbitrary pair of partial commitments z_A and z_B which are incompatible (that is, $z_A + z_B > \pi$). A pure strategy for each player i in the war of attrition game involves deciding whether or not to back down at each time $t \geq 0$, conditional on the game not having ended before time t and conditional on whether $k_i = 0$ or $k_i = +\infty$. Define a mixed strategy for each player i by a probability distribution function F_i, which is defined on the closed interval $[0, +\infty]$, where for each $t \geq 0$, $F_i(t)$ denotes the (unconditional) probability that player i has backed down by time t (inclusive). Notice that, since player i never backs down if $k_i = +\infty$, for any finite $t \geq 0$, $F_i(t) \leq p_i$. Without loss of generality, define $F_i(+\infty) = 1$.

The first lemma establishes that in any PBE of this war of attrition game player i does not back down with probability one at time 0 if $k_i = 0$.

Lemma 8.4. *In any perfect Bayesian equilibrium of the war of attrition game, $F_A(0) < p_A$ and $F_B(0) < p_B$.*

Proof. Suppose, to the contrary, that there exists a PBE and an i such that $F_i(0) = p_i$; that is, player i backs down with probability one at time 0 if $k_i = 0$. Therefore, the (conditional) equilibrium expected payoffs to player j if $k_j = 0$ from backing down at $t = 0$ and from not backing down at $t = 0$ are respectively[23]

$$p_i(\pi/2) + (1 - p_i)(\pi - z_i) \quad \text{and} \tag{8.13}$$

$$p_i z_j + (1 - p_i)(\pi - z_i)\exp(-r_j\epsilon), \tag{8.14}$$

where $\epsilon > 0$ but arbitrarily small. By comparing (8.13) and (8.14) — and noting that $\epsilon > 0$ but arbitrarily small — it follows that in equilibrium, $F_j(0) = p_j$ if $z_j \leq \pi/2$ and $F_j(0) = 0$ if $z_j > \pi/2$. Therefore, the (conditional) equilibrium expected payoff to player i if $k_i = 0$ is

$$\begin{cases} p_j(\pi/2) + (1 - p_j)(\pi - z_j) & \text{if } z_j \leq \pi/2 \\ \pi - z_j & \text{if } z_j > \pi/2. \end{cases}$$

Now suppose player i unilaterally deviates to an alternative strategy $\widehat{F}_i$ in which $\widehat{F}_i(0) = 0$ and $\widehat{F}_i(\epsilon) = p_i$ for some $\epsilon > 0$ but small. Player i's (conditional) expected payoff from this unilateral deviation if $k_i = 0$ is greater than or equal to $[p_j z_i + (1 - p_j)(\pi - z_j)]\exp(-r_i\epsilon)$.[24] A contradiction follows immediately, because this payoff is strictly greater than player i's (conditional) equilibrium expected payoff if $k_i = 0$. □

The next lemma establishes some key properties of any PBE in the war of attrition game. In particular, if $k_i = 0$ then player i backs down 'continuously' before some time T^*: that is, in any positive interval of time within the interval $(0, T^*)$, she backs down with strictly positive probability.

Lemma 8.5. *In any perfect Bayesian equilibrium of the war of attrition game there exists a T^* such that for each i $(i = A, B)$, $F_i(T^*) = p_i$, F_i is*

---

[23]In deriving (8.14) I employ the following argument. With probability $1 - p_i$, $k_i = +\infty$. Hence, given player i's equilibrium strategy, if she does not back down at time 0, then player j's equilibrium posterior probabilistic belief that $k_i = +\infty$ equals one. Therefore, if $k_j = 0$ then (in equilibrium) player j back downs 'immediately after' $t = 0$, at $t = \epsilon$.

[24]This is because, given player i's equilibrium strategy, with probability p_j: if $z_j \leq \pi/2$ then player j backs down at $t = 0$, and if $z_j > \pi/2$ then player j backs down immediately after $t = 0$. And with probability $1 - p_j$, she never backs down.

differentiable on the interval $(0, T^*)$ and for each $t \in (0, T^*)$,

$$\lim_{\Delta \to 0} \frac{F_i(t + \Delta) - F_i(t)}{\Delta[1 - F_i(t)]} = \alpha_i > 0.$$

Proof. See Abreu and Gul (1999, Proposition 2).[25]   □

An immediate consequence of Lemma 8.5 is that for any $t \leq T^*$, $F_i(t) = 1 - c_i \exp(-\alpha_i t)$, where c_i is the constant of integration. Since for all $t \in [0, +\infty)$, $F_i(t) \leq p_i$, this implies that T^* is finite. The condition $F_i(T^*) = p_i$ implies that the constant

$$c_i = (1 - p_i) \exp(\alpha_i T^*). \tag{8.15}$$

Lemma 8.4 implies that $T^* > 0$, and, hence, since F_i is strictly increasing on the open interval $(0, T^*)$, if $k_i = 0$ then at any time $t \in (0, T^*)$, player i is indifferent between backing down and not backing down. If $k_i = 0$, then player i's equilibrium expected payoffs at any time $t \in (0, T^*)$ from backing down and from not backing down are respectively $\pi - z_j$ and $[\alpha_j \Delta z_i + (1 - \alpha_j \Delta)(\pi - z_j)] \exp(-r_i \Delta)$ — because, if she does not back down at time t, then after an infinitesimal time interval Δ player j backs down with probability $\alpha_j \Delta$. Equating these two expressions, and solving for α_j, it follows that[26]

$$\alpha_j = \frac{r_i(\pi - z_j)}{z_i + z_j - \pi}. \tag{8.16}$$

The following result establishes that for at least some i $(i = A$ or $i = B)$, $F_i(0) = 0$ (which implies that $c_i = 1$).

Lemma 8.6. *In any perfect Bayesian equilibrium of the war of attrition game there exists an i $(i = A$ or $i = B)$ such that $F_i(0) = 0$.*

---

[25]Lemma 8.5 implies that at any time $t \in (0, T^*)$, player i's (unconditional) instantaneous rate of backing down, α_i, is strictly positive and independent of t. Notice that, since player i never backs down if $k_i = +\infty$, in order to maintain this (unconditional) constant and strictly positive instantaneous rate of backing down, player i backs down at an *increasing* rate if $k_i = 0$.

[26]As is standard in a mixed strategy equilibrium, player j's equilibrium instantaneous rate of backing down ensures that player i is indifferent between backing down and not backing down if $k_i = 0$. Notice that, since $z_A < \pi$, $z_B < \pi$ and $z_A + z_B > \pi$, $\alpha_A > 0$ and $\alpha_B > 0$.

Proof. Suppose, to the contrary, that $F_A(0) > 0$ and $F_B(0) > 0$. Therefore, the conditional equilibrium expected payoff to each player i if $k_i = 0$ is $F_j(0)[F_i(0)(\pi/2)+(1-F_i(0))z_i]+(1-F_j(0))(\pi-z_j)$, because her conditional equilibrium expected payoff at any time $t \in (0, T^*)$ is $\pi - z_j$. On the other hand, the conditional equilibrium expected payoff to each player i if $k_i = 0$ from a unilateral deviation to an alternative strategy $\widehat{F}_i$ in which $\widehat{F}_i(0) = 0$ and $\widehat{F}_i(\epsilon) = p_i$ for some $\epsilon > 0$ but small is greater than or equal to $F_j(0)z_i + (1 - F_j(0))(\pi - z_j)\exp(-r_i\epsilon)$. Since there exists an i ($i = A$ or $i = B$) such that $z_i > \pi/2$, and since $\epsilon > 0$ can be chosen to be arbitrarily small, player i benefits from such a unilateral deviation — which is a contradiction. $\quad\square$

Now define, for each $i = A, B$

$$T_i = \frac{1}{\alpha_i} \ln\left(\frac{1}{1 - p_i}\right). \tag{8.17}$$

By construction, $1 - \exp(-\alpha_i T_i) = p_i$. That is, T_i denotes the time by which player i will have backed down with probability p_i, given that she backs down at time 0 with probability zero. Therefore, if $T_A > T_B$, then $c_A < 1$ (because if $c_A = 1$ then $T^* = T_A > T_B$, which is a contradiction). Hence, by Lemma 8.6 it follows that $c_B = 1$. Moreover, if $T_A > T_B$, then $T^* = T_B$ and the value of c_A is determined by (8.15). Hence

$$T^* = \min\{T_A, T_B\} \tag{8.18}$$

and c_i ($i = A, B$) is determined by (8.15). I have thus established the following result.

Proposition 8.7. *For each pair of partial commitments z_A and z_B such that $z_A + z_B > \pi$, $z_A < \pi$ and $z_B < \pi$, the war of attrition game has a unique PBE in which*

$$F_i(t) = \begin{cases} 1 - c_i \exp(-\alpha_i t) & \text{if } t \leq T^* \\ p_i & \text{if } T^* \leq t < +\infty \\ 1 & \text{if } t = +\infty, \end{cases}$$

where α_i is defined in (8.16), T^* in (8.18) — with T_i defined in (8.17) — and c_i in (8.15).

The unique PBE has the following properties. If $T_i > T_j$, then player i backs down at time 0 with probability $1-c_i$ and player j backs down at time 0 with probability zero. Furthermore, if $T_A = T_B$, then each player backs down at time 0 with probability zero. Thereafter, on the open interval $(0, T^*)$, each player i backs down at a constant, strictly positive, rate α_i. At time T^* it becomes common knowledge that with probability one, $k_A = k_B = +\infty$, and, thus, neither player ever backs down after this time.

8.6.3　Equilibrium Partial Commitments

Given the characterization of the unique PBE of each war of attrition subgame derived above, I now show in the following proposition that in *any* Nash equilibrium at the first ('claims') stage of the game, the players' partial commitments are exactly compatible, and, thus, in equilibrium, the players reach immediate agreement without playing a war of attrition game.

Proposition 8.8. *In any PBE of the entire two-stage game described in Section 8.6.1, the players' equilibrium partial commitments z_A and z_B are exactly compatible (that is, $z_A + z_B = \pi$).*

Proof. Using Proposition 8.7, I first compute the expected payoffs to the players if the chosen partial commitments are incompatible. Fix an arbitrary pair of partial commitments z_A and z_B which are incompatible (i.e., $z_A + z_B > \pi$), and consider the war of attrition subgame. There exists an i ($i = A$ or $i = B$) such that $T_i \geq T_j$ ($j \neq i$). Note that $c_i < 1$ if $T_i > T_j$ and $c_i = 1$ if $T_i = T_j$. Moreover, note that $c_j = 1$ and that $T^* = T_j$.

I first derive player j's conditional equilibrium expected payoff if $k_j = 0$. With probability $1 - c_i$, player i backs down at time 0 and (since player j backs down at time 0 with probability zero) she obtains z_j. With probability c_i, therefore, her expected payoff equals $\pi - z_j$. This is because at each time $t \in (0, T^*)$, she is indifferent between backing down and not backing down. Hence, player j's conditional equilibrium expected payoff if $k_j = 0$ is $(1 - c_i)z_j + c_i(\pi - z_i)$.

By definition, player j's conditional equilibrium expected payoff if $k_j = +\infty$ is

$$(1 - c_i)z_j + \int_0^{T^*} z_j \exp(-r_j t)dF_i(t),$$

which equals $(1 - c_i)z_j + c_i(\pi - z_i) - (1 - p_i)(\pi - z_i)\exp(-r_jT^*)$.[27]

By similar arguments, but noting that player j backs down at time 0 with probability zero, it follows that player i's conditional equilibrium expected payoffs if $k_i = 0$ and if $k_i = +\infty$ are respectively $\pi - z_j$ and $(\pi - z_j) - (1 - p_j)(\pi - z_j)\exp(-r_iT^*)$.

Hence, if the pair of partial commitments z_A and z_B are incompatible and such that $T_i \geq T_j$ ($i \neq j$, $i, j = A, B$), then player j's (unconditional) expected payoff is

$$(1 - c_i)z_j + c_i(\pi - z_i) - (1 - p_j)(1 - p_i)(\pi - z_i)\exp(-r_jT^*), \qquad (8.19)$$

and player i's (unconditional) expected payoff is

$$(\pi - z_j) - (1 - p_i)(1 - p_j)(\pi - z_j)\exp(-r_iT^*), \qquad (8.20)$$

where $T^* = T_j$ and c_i is defined by (8.15).

I am now ready to establish the proposition. Suppose, to the contrary, that $z_A + z_B > \pi$.[28] There exists an i such that $T_i \geq T_j$, and, hence, player i's expected payoff is given by (8.20). But, since $z_j < \pi$ and since $T^*(= T_j)$ is finite, she can benefit from a unilateral deviation to the partial commitment $z_i' = \pi - z_j$, which is a contradiction. $\qquad \square$

Thus, in contrast to the model studied in Section 8.5, in the current model — where the bargainers engage in a war of attrition if their chosen partial commitments are incompatible — the equilibrium partial commitments are never incompatible. Thus, in any PBE agreement is reached with probability one, without the players ever having to engage in any war of attrition. Indeed, this model establishes that uncertainty in the commitment process need not generate disagreement in a bargaining situation.

Proposition 8.8 characterizes *any* Nash equilibrium of the first stage game. In the following proposition I establish the existence (by construction) of such an equilibrium.

Proposition 8.9. *There exists a perfect Bayesian equilibrium in the entire two-stage game described in Section 8.6.1 in which the equilibrium partial*

---

[27]Notice that this payoff is strictly less than j's conditional equilibrium expected payoff if $k_j = 0$.

[28]Notice that since Lemma 8.1 applies here as well, the equilibrium partial commitments are not more-than-compatible.

commitments are

$$z_A^* = \frac{r_B \ln(1 - p_B)}{r_A \ln(1 - p_A) + r_B \ln(1 - p_B)} \quad and$$

$$z_B^* = \frac{r_A \ln(1 - p_A)}{r_A \ln(1 - p_A) + r_B \ln(1 - p_B)}.$$

Proof. It should be noted that the pair of partial commitments z_A^* and z_B^* defined in the proposition is the unique pair of exactly compatible partial commitments such that $T_A = T_B$. Since $z_A^* + z_B^* = \pi$, the payoff to player i in the (proposed) equilibrium is z_i^*. Suppose player i unilaterally deviates to a partial commitment $z_i' > z_i^*$.[29] In the war of attrition subgame that follows the pair (z_i', z_j^*) of partial commitments, $T_i > T_j$, and, hence, player i's expected payoff from this unilateral deviation is given by (8.20) with $z_j = z_j^*$. Since that payoff is strictly less than z_i^*, the desired conclusion follows immediately.   □

In general, there may exist other pairs of exactly compatible partial commitments that form part of a PBE. However, Kambe (1999) has shown that in the limit as both p_A and p_B converge to one with the ratio $r_A \ln(1 - p_A)/r_B \ln(1 - p_B)$ kept constant at some positive level η, the model has a unique PBE in which $z_A = 1/1 + \eta$ and $z_B = \eta/1 + \eta$. Notice that these partial commitments constitute the limiting values of z_A^* and z_B^* defined in Proposition 8.9.

8.7   Notes

Thomas Schelling (in Schelling (1960)) was the first to informally explore the role, feasibility and persuasiveness of commitment tactics in bargaining situations. His paper contains brilliant discussions about the many issues involved. In particular, he discusses at great length the details of several mechanisms through which a bargainer may achieve partial commitment to some bargaining position. The interested reader is urged to combine their study of the models in this chapter with a reading of his classic essay.

The model studied in Section 8.2 is due to Muthoo (1996), while the model studied in Section 8.5 is a simplified (and slightly different) version of

---

[29]It is trivial to note that player i does not benefit from a unilateral deviation to a partial commitment $z_i' < z_i^*$.

the model studied in Crawford (1982). The analysis and results in Section
8.5 are based upon Crawford (1982) — the latter paper contains thought-
provoking discussions of some of the issues involved in studying the role of
commitment tactics on the bargaining outcome. Section 8.6 is inspired by
the work of Kambe (1999). The analysis of the war of attrition subgames,
however, is based on the work by Abreu and Gul (1999). The analysis and
results of Section 8.6.3 is based on Kambe (1999).

In this chapter I have focused on the notion that a player makes a partial
commitment to the share of the cake (or, utility) that she would like to
have. The partial commitments affect the utility possiblity set, but do not
affect the players' payoffs if they fail to reach agreement. However, in some
bargaining situations the players make partial commitments to actions that
affect the 'disagreement' outcome. The Nash *variable threat* model (cf. Nash
(1953); alternatively, see Osborne and Rubinstein (1990)) is a model of a
situation in which the bargainers make *irrevocable* commitments to actions
that affect the payoffs from disagreement — thus, in this model, it is 'as if'
the costs of revoking are infinite. Bolt and Houba (1997) also study a model
in which the bargainers take actions that affect the disagreement outcome,
but — in extreme contrast to Nash's variable threat model — their main
analysis assumes that the bargainers cannot make any partial commitments
— thus, in this model, it is 'as if' the costs of revoking are zero.

In Section 8.3.3 I argued that the model studied in Section 8.2 can be
interpreted as a perturbation to the 'commitment' structure of the Nash
demand game. An alternative way to perturb the Nash demand game is
by introducing some shared (or, symmetric) uncertainty about the size of
the cake (or, more generally, about the Pareto frontier of the set of possible
utility pairs obtainable through agreement) — which implies that there is
some uncertainty as to whether a pair of demands are compatible or incompatible. This is a perturbation to the 'information' structure of the demand
game; it retains the assumption that the players are *irrevocably* committed
to their respective demands. This interesting idea is due to Nash (1953),
where he in fact introduced (what is now called) the Nash demand game.
John Nash showed, in Nash (1953), that in the limit, as the uncertainty
becomes arbitrarily small, there is a unique equilibrium. For detailed analyses of this idea, see Binmore (1987), Osborne and Rubinstein (1990) and
van Damme (1991). Although the specific type of uncertainty introduced

in Nash (1953) is interesting and generates a powerful result — in that it selects a unique equilibrium — the plausibility of this type of perturbation is questionable. Carlsson (1991) studies an alternative type of perturbation to the information structure of the Nash demand game that is relatively more plausible.

9   Asymmetric Information

9.1   Introduction

In some bargaining situations at least one of the players knows something of relevance that the other player does not. For example, when bargaining over the price of her second-hand car the seller knows its quality but the buyer does not. In such a bargaining situation, the seller has private information; and there exists an asymmetry in information between the players. In this chapter I study the role of asymmetric information on the bargaining outcome.

A player may in general have private information about a variety of things that may be relevant for the bargaining outcome, such as her preferences, outside option and inside option. However, in order to develop the main fundamental insights in a simple manner attention is focused on the following archetypal bargaining situation. A seller and a buyer are bargaining over the price at which to trade an indivisible object (such as a second-hand car, or a unit of labour). The payoff to each player (from trading) depends on the agreed price and on her reservation value.[1] A key assumption is that at least one player's reservation value is her private information.

I begin the study of this bargaining situation by addressing the *normative*

---

[1] The buyer's reservation value is the maximum price at which she is willing to buy. Symmetrically, the seller's reservation value is the minimum price at which she is willing to sell.

question of whether or not the bargaining outcome can be *ex-post* efficient.[2] Let me make this question a bit more precise. A bargaining procedure combined with the players' information and preferences in the bargaining situation under consideration defines a bargaining game with imperfect information. I shall say that a procedure *induces* a bargaining game. If there exists a bargaining procedure — no matter how implausible or plausible it may be — such that the induced bargaining game has a Bayesian Nash Equilibrium (BNE) that generates an *ex-post* efficient outcome, then the bargaining outcome can be *ex-post* efficient. On the other hand, if for *any* bargaining procedure *all* of the BNE of the induced bargaining game generate *ex-post* inefficient outcomes, then the bargaining outcome cannot be *ex-post* efficient.

The following argument illustrates the possibility that the bargaining outcome cannot be *ex-post* efficient. A buyer and a seller are bargaining over the price of a second-hand car, whose quality is the seller's private information. If she owns a low quality car, then she has an incentive to pretend to own a high quality car in order to obtain a relatively high price. Since the buyer is aware of this 'incentive to lie', the maximum price that she might be willing to pay may be strictly less than the high reservation value of a seller owning a high quality car. Thus, if the seller actually owns a high quality car, then mutually beneficial trade between the two parties may fail to occur.[3]

Section 9.2 addresses the normative question stated above when exactly one player's reservation value is her private information. The answer to the normative question depends on whether or not the players' reservation values are independent of each other. When the players' reservation values are independent of each other, I say that the values are *private*; otherwise, they are *correlated*. If the players' reservation values are private, then the bargaining outcome can be *ex-post* efficient. But if the reservation values are correlated, then (under a fairly general condition) the bargaining outcome cannot be *ex-post* efficient. Two applications are studied in Section 9.3.

---

[2]The bargaining outcome is *ex-post* efficient if and only if after all of the information is revealed the players' payoffs associated with the bargaining outcome are Pareto-efficient. The concept of *ex-post* efficiency is also known as full-information efficiency.

[3]In his classic paper, Akerlof (1970), George Akerlof put forward this type of argument, but in the context of competitive markets (with asymmetric information).

One application concerns the normative question of whether or not it is possible for a firm and its unionized workforce to reach an agreement (over the wage rate) without any costly delay. The other application concerns the normative question of whether or not it is possible for a plantiff and a defendant to settle their dispute out-of-court.

Section 9.4 addresses the normative question when each player's reservation is her private information. A main result obtained here is that (under some fairly general conditions) the bargaining outcome cannot be *ex-post* efficient, whether or not the players' reservation values are independent of each other. Section 9.5 extends the two applications studied in Section 9.3.

Section 9.6 addresses some *positive* questions in the context of a bargaining model in which exactly one player has private information, and the other player makes repeated offers. The two main questions that motivate the study of this model are as follows. Firstly, to what extent is the equilibrium payoff of the player who makes all the offers adversely affected when her opponent has private information? And secondly, under what conditions (if any) is the privately held information revealed through time via the sequence of equilibrium offers? It will be shown that the answers to these questions depend, in particular, on (i) whether or not offers are retractable, (ii) whether or not the costs to the players of haggling are small, and (iii) whether or not gains from trade are strictly positive with probability one. An application to bargaining over a *menu* of wage-quality contracts is studied in Section 9.7.

9.2 Efficiency under One-Sided Uncertainty

I study a bargaining situation in which player S owns (or, can produce) an indivisible object that player B wants to buy. If agreement is reached to trade at price p ($p \geq 0$), then the payoffs to the seller (player S) and the buyer (player B) are respectively $p - c$ and $v - p$, where c denotes the seller's reservation value (or, cost of production) and v denotes the buyer's reservation value (or, the maximum price at which she is willing to buy). If the players do not reach an agreement to trade, then each player's payoff is zero.

A key assumption is that exactly one player's reservation value is her private information. Section 9.2.1 studies the case in which the players' reservation values are independent of each other, while Section 9.2.2 studies the case in which the players' reservation values are correlated.

The outcome of this bargaining situation is *ex-post* efficient if and only if when $v \geq c$ the players reach an agreement to trade, and when $v < c$ the players do not reach an agreement to trade.

My objective is to address the normative question of whether or not the outcome of the bargaining situation described above can be *ex-post* efficient. As mentioned in Section 9.1, if there exists a bargaining procedure such that the induced bargaining game has a BNE that generates an *ex-post* efficient outcome, then the bargaining outcome can be *ex-post* efficient. On the other hand, if for *any* bargaining procedure *all* of the BNE of the induced bargaining game generate *ex-post* inefficient outcomes, then the bargaining outcome cannot be *ex-post* efficient.

9.2.1   The Case of Private Values

In this section it is assumed that the players' reservation values are independent of each other, and exactly one player has private information about her reservation value. The other player's reservation value is known to both players.

I begin by studying the case in which the buyer's reservation value is her private information. This asymmetry in information is modelled as follows. The buyer's reservation value is a random draw from the following (binary) probability distribution: with probability α (where $0 < \alpha < 1$) the buyer's reservation value is H, and with probability $1 - \alpha$ the buyer's reservation value is L, where $H > L$. The buyer knows the realization of the random draw, but the seller does not. The seller only knows that the buyer's reservation value is a random draw from this probability distribution. The following lemma establishes that the bargaining outcome can be *ex-post* efficient.[4]

Lemma 9.1. *There exists a bargaining procedure such that the induced bargaining game has an ex-post efficient BNE.*

---

[4] The lemma is valid whatever is the magnitude of c relative to H and L. It should be noted that if $c > H$ then gains from trade do not exist, but if $L \geq c$ then gains from trade exist with probability one. And if $H \geq c > L$ then with probability α they exist, but with probability $1 - \alpha$ they do not.

Proof. Consider the following bargaining procedure. The buyer makes an offer to the seller. If she accepts the offer, then agreement is struck and the game ends. But if she rejects the offer, then the game ends with no agreement. Letting p_H^* and p_L^* respectively denote the buyer's price offers when $v = H$ and $v = L$, the following pair of strategies is a BNE: $p_H^* = \min\{H, c\}$, $p_L^* = \min\{L, c\}$, and the seller accepts a price offer p if and only if $p \geq c$. The lemma follows immediately, because this BNE is *ex-post* efficient. $\square$

It is now shown that Lemma 9.1 is also valid when the buyer's reservation value can take more than two possible numbers. Let F_B denote the cumulative probability distribution from which the buyer's reservation value is randomly drawn, where the support of F_B contains two or more numbers. The proof of Lemma 9.1 is still valid, but with the following modification to the buyer's equilibrium strategy: $p^*(v) = \min\{v, c\}$ for all v, where $p^*(v)$ denotes the buyer's price offer when her reservation value is v.

I now study the case in which the seller's reservation value is her private information, and the buyer's reservation value is known to both players. As above, I model this asymmetry in information by considering the seller's reservation value to be a random draw from a probability distribution F_S — whose support contains two or more numbers — the realisation of which is only revealed to the seller. Consider the following bargaining procedure. The seller makes an offer to the buyer. If she accepts the offer, then agreement is struck and the game ends. But if she rejects the offer, then the game ends with no agreement. The following pair of strategies is a BNE of the induced bargaining game: $p^*(c) = \max\{v, c\}$ for all c, where $p^*(c)$ denotes the seller's price offer when her reservation value is c, and the buyer accepts a price offer p if and only if $p \leq v$. Lemma 9.1 follows immediately, because this BNE is *ex-post* efficient.

The following proposition summarizes the results obtained above.

Proposition 9.1 (One-Sided Uncertainty with Private Values). *If the players' reservation values are independent of each other, and exactly one player's reservation value is her private information, then the bargaining outcome can be ex-post efficient.*

9.2.2 The Case of Correlated Values

In this section I assume that the player's reservation values are correlated, and exactly one player has private information about her reservation value. This assumption is modelled as follows. There is a parameter θ — which is a real number — that determines both players' reservation values, and furthermore, the value of θ is the private information of exactly one player. It is assumed that each player's reservation value is strictly increasing in θ. Furthermore, for any θ, the buyer's reservation value — which is denoted by $v(\theta)$ — is greater than or equal to the seller's reservation value — which is denoted by $c(\theta)$.[5]

I begin by considering the case in which it is the seller who has private information about θ. This asymmetry in information is modelled as follows. The value of θ is a random draw from the following (binary) probability distribution: with probability α (where $0 < \alpha < 1$) the value of θ is H, and with probability $1 - \alpha$ the value of θ is L, where $H > L$. The seller knows the realization of the random draw, but the buyer does not. The buyer only knows that the value of θ is a random draw from this probability distribution. The following lemma establishes that the bargaining outcome can be *ex-post* efficient if and only if $v^e \geq c(H)$, where $v^e = \alpha v(H) + (1 - \alpha)v(L)$ is the buyer's expected reservation value.

Lemma 9.2. *(a) If $v^e \geq c(H)$, where $v^e = \alpha v(H) + (1-\alpha)v(L)$, then there exists a bargaining procedure such that the induced bargaining game has an ex-post efficient BNE.*
(b) If $v^e < c(H)$, then for any bargaining procedure the induced bargaining game does not have an ex-post efficient BNE.

Proof. I first establish Lemma 9.2(a). Consider the following bargaining procedure. The seller makes an offer to the buyer. If she accepts the offer, then agreement is struck and the game ends. But if she rejects the offer, then the game ends with no agreement. Since $v^e \geq c(H)$, the following pair of strategies is a BNE: $p^*(H) = p^*(L) = c(H)$ (where $p^*(H)$ and $p^*(L)$ are respectively the seller's price offers when $\theta = H$ and $\theta = L$), the buyer accepts the price $p = c(H)$ and rejects any price $p \neq c(H)$. The desired conclusion follows immediately, because this BNE is *ex-post* efficient. □

---

[5]This implies that the outcome of this bargaining situation is *ex-post* efficient if and only if the players reach an agreement to trade whatever value θ takes.

I now proceed to prove Lemma 9.2(b). In order to do so I need to consider the set of *all* possible bargaining procedures. However, I begin by considering a particular subset of the set of all bargaining procedures, which is called the set of all *direct revelation* procedures. In the context of the bargaining situation under consideration, a direct revelation procedure (DRP) is characterized by four numbers: λ_L, λ_H, p_L and p_H, where $\lambda_s \in [0, 1]$ and $p_s \geq 0$ ($s = L, H$). In a DRP the seller announces a possible value of θ. If s denotes the announced value (where $s \in \{L, H\}$), then with probability λ_s trade occurs at price p_s, and with probability $1 - \lambda_s$ trade does not occur.

Fix an arbitrary DRP, and consider the induced bargaining game (which is a single-person decision problem). Let $s(\theta) \in \{L, H\}$ denote the seller's announcement if the true (realized) value is θ ($\theta = L, H$). The DRP is *incentive-compatible* if and only if in the induced bargaining game the seller announces the truth — that is, $s^*(L) = L$ and $s^*(H) = H$. Thus, the DRP is incentive-compatible if and only if the following two inequalities are satisfied

$$\lambda_L(p_L - c(L)) \geq \lambda_H(p_H - c(L)) \tag{9.1}$$

$$\lambda_H(p_H - c(H)) \geq \lambda_L(p_L - c(H)). \tag{9.2}$$

Inequalities 9.1 and 9.2 are respectively known as the incentive-compatibility constraints for the *low-type* seller and *high-type* seller.[6] Inequality 9.1 states that the expected payoff to the low-type seller by announcing the truth is greater than or equal to her expected payoff by telling a lie. Similarly, inequality 9.2 states that the expected payoff to the high-type seller by announcing the truth is greater than or equal to her expected payoff by telling a lie.

An incentive-compatible DRP is *individually-rational* if and only if in the incentive-compatible DRP each type of seller and the buyer obtain an expected payoff that is not less than their respective payoff from disagreement (which equals zero). That is, if and only if the following three inequalities

---

[6]The seller is said to be of 'low-type' (respectively, 'high-type') if the true (realized) value of θ is L (respectively, H).

are satisfied

$$\lambda_L(p_L - c(L)) \geq 0 \qquad (9.3)$$

$$\lambda_H(p_H - c(H)) \geq 0 \qquad (9.4)$$

$$\alpha\lambda_H(v(H) - p_H) + (1 - \alpha)\lambda_L(v(L) - p_L) \geq 0. \qquad (9.5)$$

Since (by assumption) $v(H) \geq c(H)$ and $v(L) \geq c(L)$, a DRP is *ex-post efficient* if and only if the buyer trades with the seller of either type with probability one. That is, if and only if

$$\lambda_L = \lambda_H = 1. \qquad (9.6)$$

I now state a rather powerful result — which is known as the Revelation Principle — that allows me to establish Lemma 9.2(b) by considering only the set of all incentive-compatible and individually-rational direct revelation procedures.

Theorem 9.1 (The Revelation Principle). *Fix an arbitrary bargaining situation with asymmetric information and an arbitrary bargaining procedure. For any BNE outcome of the induced bargaining game there exists an incentive-compatible and individually-rational DRP that implements the BNE outcome.*

Proof. This result is proven and discussed in the context of bargaining situations in Myerson (1979). The proof can also be found in most advanced microeconomics and game theory texts — see, for example, Kreps (1990a), Fudenberg and Tirole (1991), Gibbons (1992) and Mas-Colell, Whinston and Green (1995). □

It follows from the Revelation Principle that if there does not exist an incentive-compatible and individually-rational DRP that is *ex-post* efficient, then there does not exist a bargaining procedure whose induced bargaining game has an *ex-post* efficient BNE. Lemma 9.2(b) is therefore an immediate consequence of the following claim.

Claim 9.1. *If $v^e < c(H)$, where v^e is defined in Lemma 9.2, then there does not exist an incentive-compatible and individually-rational DRP that is ex-post efficient.*

Proof. Suppose, to the contrary, that there exists a DRP that satisfies (9.1)–(9.6). Substituting (9.6) into (9.1) and (9.2), it follows that $p_L = p_H$. Hence, after substituting (9.6) into (9.3)–(9.5), it follows from (9.3)–(9.5) that $v^e \geq c(H)$, thus contradicting the hypothesis. $\qquad\square$

A Generalization to More Than Two Types

The results obtained above may be generalized quite easily to the case when θ takes more than two possible values. Assume that θ is a random draw from a probability distribution G — whose support J contains two or more numbers — the realization of which is only revealed to the seller. Let $\underline{\theta}$ and $\bar{\theta}$ respectively denote the minimum and maximum values of J.

A DRP is characterized by a pair of functions (λ, p), where for each $s \in J$, $\lambda(s)$ and $p(s)$ are respectively the probability with which trade occurs and the price at which it occurs if the seller announces that the value of θ is s. A DRP is incentive-compatible if and only if

$$\forall \theta \in J, \quad \lambda(\theta)[p(\theta) - c(\theta)] \geq \lambda(s)[p(s) - c(\theta)], \quad \forall s \in J. \qquad (9.7)$$

Inequality 9.7 states that for any possible true (realized) value of θ, the expected payoff to the θ-type seller by announcing the truth is greater than or equal to her expected payoff by telling a lie.[7]

An incentive-compatible DRP is individually-rational if and only if

$$\forall \theta \in J, \quad \lambda(\theta)[p(\theta) - c(\theta)] \geq 0, \quad \text{and} \qquad (9.8)$$

$$E_\theta \Big[\lambda(\theta)[v(\theta) - p(\theta)] \Big] \geq 0. \qquad (9.9)$$

Inequalities 9.8 and 9.9 respectively state that the expected payoffs to the θ-type seller and the buyer in an incentive-compatible DRP are greater than or equal to their respective payoffs from disagreement (which equal zero). Since (by assumption) $v(\theta) \geq c(\theta)$ for all θ, a DRP is *ex-post* efficient if and only if

$$\forall \theta \in J, \quad \lambda(\theta) = 1. \qquad (9.10)$$

The following claim is a generalization of Claim 9.1.

---

[7]The seller is said to be of 'θ-type' if the realization of the random draw from G is θ.

Claim 9.2. *If $v^e < c(\bar{\theta})$, where v^e is the buyer's expected reservation value — that is, $v^e = E_\theta[v(\theta)]$ — then there does not exist an incentive-compatible and individually-rational DRP that is ex-post efficient.*

Proof. Suppose, to the contrary, that there exists a DRP that satisfies (9.7)–(9.10). Substituting (9.10) into (9.7) implies that $p(\theta)$ is constant for all $\theta \in J$. Letting $p = p(\theta)$ for all $\theta \in J$, it follows using (9.8) that $p \geq c(\bar{\theta})$. Hence, using (9.9) it follows that $v^e \geq c(\bar{\theta})$, which contradicts the hypothesis. □

It follows from the Revelation Principle that if $v^e < c(\bar{\theta})$, then for any bargaining procedure the induced bargaining game does not have an *ex-post* efficient BNE. Therefore, if $v^e < c(\bar{\theta})$, then the bargaining outcome cannot be *ex-post* efficient. On the other hand, if $v^e \geq c(\bar{\theta})$, then there exists a bargaining procedure such that the induced bargaining game has an *ex-post* efficient BNE.[8]

Remark 9.1 (The Buyer has Private Information). Now consider the case in which it is the buyer (and not the seller) who has private information about θ. Thus, the realization of the random draw from the probability distribution G is only revealed to the buyer. It is straightforward to appropriately modify the above analysis and show that the bargaining outcome can be *ex-post* efficient if and only if $c^e \leq v(\underline{\theta})$, where c^e is the seller's expected reservation value — that is, $c^e = E_\theta[c(\theta)]$.

Hence, I have established the following proposition.

Proposition 9.2 (One-Sided Uncertainty with Correlated Values).
(a) When the seller has private information about θ the bargaining outcome can be ex-post efficient if and only if the buyer's expected reservation value $v^e \geq c(\bar{\theta})$, the seller's maximum possible reservation value.
(b) When the buyer has private information about θ the bargaining outcome can be ex-post efficient if and only if the seller's expected reservation value $c^e \leq v(\underline{\theta})$, the buyer's minimum possible reservation value.

---

[8]Consider the following bargaining procedure. The seller makes an offer to the buyer. If she accepts the offer, then agreement is struck and the game ends. But if she rejects the offer, then the game ends with no agreement. If $v^e \geq c(\bar{\theta})$, then the following pair of strategies is a BNE: $p^*(\theta) = c(\bar{\theta})$ (where $p^*(\theta)$ is the seller's price offer when the realization of the random draw from G is θ), the buyer accepts the price $p = c(\bar{\theta})$ and rejects any price $p \neq c(\bar{\theta})$.

An Example in which Trade Never Occurs

Suppose that J is equal to the closed interval $[0, 1]$, G is a uniform distribution (i.e., $G(\theta) = \theta$), $v(\theta) = 3\theta$ and $c(\theta) = 2\theta$. Assume that the seller has private information about θ. Since $v^e = 1.5$ and $c(1) = 2$, it follows from Proposition 9.2(a) that the bargaining outcome cannot be *ex-post* efficient. In fact, it is shown below that in any incentive-compatible and individually-rational DRP, $\lambda(\theta) = 0$ for all $\theta \in [0, 1]$. This striking result implies (by appealing to the Revelation Principle) that for any bargaining procedure and any BNE of the induced bargaining game trade occurs with probability zero.

Fix an arbitrary incentive-compatible and individually-rational DRP. Let U_B and $U_S(\theta)$ respectively denote the expected payoffs (in the induced bargaining game) to the buyer and the θ-type seller. Inequality 9.7 implies that for each $\theta \in [0, 1]$

$$U_S(\theta) \equiv \lambda(\theta)[p(\theta) - 2\theta] = \max_{s \in [0,1]} \lambda(s)[p(s) - 2\theta].$$

From the *Envelope Theorem*, it follows that $U_S(.)$ is differentiable almost everywhere with derivative $U_S'(\theta) = -2\lambda(\theta)$. This implies that

$$\int_0^1 \theta dU_S(\theta) = -2 \int_0^1 \theta\lambda(\theta)d\theta. \qquad (9.11)$$

After integrating by parts the LHS of equation 9.11, and then simplifying, it follows that

$$\int_0^1 U_S(\theta)d\theta = U_S(1) + 2 \int_0^1 \theta\lambda(\theta)d\theta. \qquad (9.12)$$

Now consider the expected payoff U_B to the buyer, which is the LHS of inequality 9.9. After substituting for $\lambda(\theta)p(\theta)$ using the expression for $U_S(\theta)$, it follows that

$$U_B = \int_0^1 [\theta\lambda(\theta) - U_S(\theta)]d\theta,$$

which (using (9.12)) implies that

$$U_B = -U_S(1) - \int_0^1 \theta\lambda(\theta)d\theta.$$

Hence, it follows from inequalities 9.8 and 9.9 that

$$\int_0^1 \theta \lambda(\theta) d\theta \le 0,$$

which implies that $\lambda(\theta) = 0$ for all $\theta \in [0, 1]$.

9.3   Applications

9.3.1   Efficient Wage Agreements

Consider a firm whose workforce is represented by a union. The firm and the union are bargaining over the wage rate on the assumption that there will be no firing and hiring. In order to simplify the notation, normalize the mass of workers employed at this firm to unity. Assuming that the union's payoff is the same as a worker's payoff, if agreement is reached on wage rate w, then the (average) payoffs to the firm and the union are respectively $R - w$ and w, where R ($R > 0$) is the value of the (average) output generated by the firm's workforce. If the players do not reach agreement on a wage rate, then the entire workforce goes on indefinite strike. In this eventuality the firm shuts down and obtains a payoff of zero, while each worker has recourse to the union's strike fund and obtains an average payoff of α, where $\alpha > 0$. The bargaining outcome is *ex-post* efficient if and only if when $R \ge \alpha$ the players reach a wage agreement, and when $R < \alpha$ the union goes on indefinite strike and the firm shuts down.

It is helpful to normalize the union's payoffs so that its average payoff from disagreement is zero. This implies that its (normalized) average payoff from agreement on wage rate w is $w - \alpha$. Indeed, the firm and the union are bargaining over the price at which the union will sell a fixed amount of labour to the firm, where the firm's and the union's reservation values are respectively R and α.

It follows from Proposition 9.1 that if either the firm has private information about R, or the union has private information about α (but not both), then the bargaining outcome can be *ex-post* efficient. That is, there exists a bargaining procedure whose induced bargaining game has a Bayesian Nash equilibrium with the following property: when $R \ge \alpha$ a wage agreement is reached, and when $R < \alpha$ the union goes on indefinite strike. It should be noted that it is not unreasonable that the value of the (average) output generated by the entire workforce is the firm's private information, and that the magnitude of the union's strike fund is its private information.[9]

9.3.2   Litigation or Out-of-Court Settlement

Individual D has injured individual P, and they are bargaining over the amount of monetary compensation that D will give P. The individuals can either reach an agreement (and thus settle out-of-court), or litigate. If they agree to settle out-of-court with individual D — the defendant — paying individual P — the plantiff — an amount p $(p \geq 0)$, then the payoffs to the defendant and the plantiff are respectively $-p$ and p. If, on the other hand, they litigate, then with probability γ $(0 < \gamma < 1)$ the court will find the defendant guilty of the crime, in which case she will be required to pay an amount x $(x > 0)$ to the plantiff. However, with probability $1 - \gamma$ the defendant will not be found guilty, in which case she pays nothing to the plantiff. Litigation will cost each individual an amount f $(f > 0)$.[10] Hence, the (expected) payoffs from litigation to the defendant and the plantiff are respectively $-\gamma x - f$ and $\gamma x - f$.

It is helpful to normalize the players' payoffs so that each player's payoff from litigation is zero. This implies that the defendant's and the plantiff's (normalized) payoffs from an out-of-court settlement on price p are respectively $v - p$ and $p - c$, where $v = \gamma x + f$ and $c = \gamma x - f$. Furthermore, each player's payoff from disagreement — that is, from litigation — is zero. Indeed, the defendant and the plantiff are bargaining over the price at which the plantiff will sell her claim to the lawsuit, where the defendant's and the plantiff's reservation values are respectively v and c. Notice that their reservation values are correlated.

I apply Proposition 9.2. First, consider the case in which the plantiff (the seller) has private information about x — which is not an unreasonable assumption, because it is possible that the plantiff only knows the exact extent of her injury. In the current bargaining situation the condition $v^e \geq c(\bar{x})$ can be written as $f \geq \gamma(\bar{x} - x^e)/2$, where x^e is the expected value of x. Hence, the bargaining outcome can be *ex-post* efficient if and only

---

[9]In Section 9.5.1 it is shown that if the firm has private information about R *and* the union has private information about α, then the bargaining outcome cannot be *ex-post* efficient.

[10]This is partly because litigation involves hiring a lawyer.

if the cost of litigation to each player $f \geq \gamma(\bar{x} - x^e)/2$. In particular, if $f < \gamma(\bar{x} - x^e)/2$, then for any bargaining procedure and any BNE of the induced (pre-trial) bargaining game with a strictly positive probability the plantiff and the defendant will proceed to litigation.

Now consider the case in which the value of x is known to both players, but the defendant (the buyer) has private information about γ — which is not an unreasonable assumption, because it is possible that the defendant only knows the exact extent to which her crime is provable in a court of law.[11] In the current bargaining situation the condition $c^e \leq v(\underline{\gamma})$ can be written as $f \geq x(\gamma^e - \underline{\gamma})/2$, where γ^e is the expected value of γ. Hence, the bargaining outcome can be *ex-post* efficient if and only if the cost of litigation to each player $f \geq x(\gamma^e - \underline{\gamma})/2$. In particular, if $f < x(\gamma^e - \underline{\gamma})/2$, then for any bargaining procedure and any BNE of the induced (pre-trial) bargaining game with a strictly positive probability the plantiff and the defendant will proceed to litigation.

The Effect of a Fee-Shifting Rule

In the analysis above it is (implicitly) assumed that each player bears her cost of litigation. This is known as the American rule, because it is typical in the USA. In England, on the other hand, it is typically the case that the loser bears the winner's cost of litigation — hence, this is called the English rule. I now consider the normative question in the context of the English rule.

If the players proceed to litigation, then with probability γ the court will find the defendant guilty of the crime. Hence, with probability γ the plantiff wins the lawsuit, while with probability $1 - \gamma$ the defendant is the winner. This implies that the (expected) payoffs from litigation to the defendant and the plantiff are respectively $-\gamma x - 2\gamma f$ and $\gamma x - 2(1-\gamma)f$. Notice that these disagreement payoffs differ from those under the American rule. As above, normalize the players' payoffs so that each player's payoff from litigation is zero. This implies that the defendant's and the plantiff's (normalized) payoffs from an out-of-court settlement on price p are respectively $v - p$ and $p - c$, where $v = \gamma x + 2\gamma f$ and $c = \gamma x - 2(1 - \gamma)f$.

---

[11]In Section 9.5.1, I analyse the (pre-trial) bargaining situation under the assumption that the plantiff has private information about x *and* the defendant has private information about γ.

I apply Proposition 9.2. First, consider the case in which the plantiff has private information about x. It is straightforward to show that the conclusion is the same as under the American rule. Now consider the case in which the value of x is known to both players, but the defendant (the buyer) has private information about γ. In this case it follows that the bargaining outcome can be *ex-post* efficient if and only if the cost of litigation to each player $f \geq x(\gamma^e - \underline{\gamma})/2(1 - \gamma^e + \underline{\gamma})$. Since $\gamma^e > \underline{\gamma}$, it follows that if

$$\frac{x(\gamma^e - \underline{\gamma})}{2} < f < \frac{x(\gamma^e - \underline{\gamma})}{2(1 - \gamma^e + \underline{\gamma})},$$

then under the American rule the bargaining outcome can be *ex-post* efficient, while under the English rule it cannot be *ex-post* efficient.

A main message contained in the results obtained above is as follows. If and only if the probability with which the plantiff wins at trial is the defendant's private information, then the disputants are more likely to proceed to litigation under the English rule than under the American Rule.

9.4 Efficiency under Two-Sided Uncertainty

This section extends the analysis of Section 9.2 to the case when each player has some private information. As in Section 9.2, I study the bargaining situation in which player S owns (or, can produce) an indivisible object that player B wants to buy. If agreement is reached to trade at price p ($p \geq 0$), then the payoffs to the seller (player S) and the buyer (player B) are respectively $p - c$ and $v - p$, where c denotes the seller's reservation value (or, cost of production) and v denotes the buyer's reservation value (or, the maximum price at which she is willing to buy). If the players do not reach an agreement to trade, then each player's payoff is zero.

Section 9.4.1 studies the case in which the players' reservation values are independent of each other, and each player's reservation value is her private information. Section 9.4.2 studies the case in which the players' reservation values are correlated, and each player has some relevant private information.

As in Section 9.2, my objective is to address the normative question of whether or not the bargaining outcome can be *ex-post* efficient.[12] As in

---

[12]The outcome of this bargaining situation is *ex-post* efficient if and only if when $v \geq c$

Section 9.2.2, the analysis involves studying the set of incentive-compatible and individually-rational direct revelation procedures.

9.4.1 The Case of Private Values

In this section the players' reservation values are independent of each other, the seller's reservation value is her private information, and the buyer's reservation value is her private information. This asymmetry in information is modelled as follows. The buyer's reservation value is a random draw from a probability distribution F_B, and the seller's reservation value is an independent and random draw from a probability distribution F_S. The buyer knows the realization of the draw from F_B, but the seller does not: she only knows that the buyer's reservation value is an independent and random draw from F_B. Symmetrically, the seller knows the realization of the draw from F_S, but the buyer does not: she only knows that the seller's reservation value is an independent and random draw from F_S.

Letting I_i $(i = B, S)$ denote the support of F_i, denote the minimum and maximum values of I_B respectively by $\underline{v}$ and $\bar{v}$, and the minimum and maximum values of I_S respectively by $\underline{c}$ and $\bar{c}$.

In the context of the bargaining situation under consideration, a direct revelation procedure (DRP) is characterized by a pair of functions (λ, p). In a DRP the seller and the buyer simultaneously announce their respective reservation values. If the seller's announced value is c $(c \in I_S)$ and the buyer's announced value is v $(v \in I_B)$, then with probability $\lambda(c, v)$ trade occurs at price $p(c, v)$, and with probability $1 - \lambda(c, v)$ trade does not occur.

A DRP is *incentive-compatible* if and only if the following inequalities are satisfied

$$\forall c, c' \in I_S, \quad U_S(c) \equiv E_v\Big[\lambda(c, v)[p(c, v) - c]\Big] \geq$$
$$E_v\Big[\lambda(c', v)[p(c', v) - c]\Big] \quad (9.13)$$

$$\forall v, v' \in I_B, \quad U_B(v) \equiv E_c\Big[\lambda(c, v)[v - p(c, v)]\Big] \geq$$
$$E_c\Big[\lambda(c, v')[v - p(c, v')]\Big]. \quad (9.14)$$

---

the players reach an agreement to trade, and when $v < c$ the players do not reach an agreement to trade.

An incentive-compatible DRP is *individually-rational* if and only if

$$\forall c \in I_S, \quad U_S(c) \geq 0 \quad \text{and} \tag{9.15}$$

$$\forall v \in I_B, \quad U_B(v) \geq 0. \tag{9.16}$$

A DRP is *ex-post efficient* if and only if the buyer and the seller trade when it is mutually beneficial to do so, but not otherwise. That is, if and only if for each $c \in I_S$ and $v \in I_B$

$$\lambda(c, v) = \begin{cases} 1 & \text{if } v \geq c \\ 0 & \text{if } v < c. \end{cases} \tag{9.17}$$

In Proposition 9.3(a) below it is shown that if $\underline{v} \geq \bar{c}$ — which implies that gains from trade exist with probability one — then the bargaining outcome can be *ex-post* efficient. In contrast, in Proposition 9.3(b) it is shown that under some conditions on the distributions — which imply that there is uncertainty over whether or not gains from trade exist — the bargaining outcome cannot be *ex-post* efficient.

Proposition 9.3 (Two-Sided Uncertainty with Private Values). *(a) If $\underline{v} \geq \bar{c}$, then the bargaining outcome can be ex-post efficient.*
(b) If $I_B = [\underline{v}, \bar{v}]$, $I_S = [\underline{c}, \bar{c}]$, F_i $(i = B, S)$ has a continuous and strictly positive density, and the interiors of the intervals I_B and I_S have a non-empty intersection, then the bargaining outcome cannot be ex-post efficient.

Proof. I first prove of part (a). Consider the following bargaining procedure. The seller makes an offer to the buyer. If she accepts the offer, then agreement is struck and the game ends. But if she rejects the offer, then the game ends with no agreement. Since $\underline{v} \geq \bar{c}$, the following pair of strategies is a BNE: $p^*(c) = \bar{c}$ (where $p^*(c)$ is the seller's price offer when her reservation value is c), the buyer accepts the price $p = \bar{c}$ and rejects any price $p \neq \bar{c}$ whatever is her reservation value. The desired conclusion follows immediately, because this BNE is *ex-post* efficient.

Since the proof of part (b) is a bit technical, I omit it, and instead refer the interested reader to Myerson and Satterthwaite (1983) — the authors of this result. However, as I now show, it is straightforward to establish part (b) under the following specific assumptions: $I_B = I_S = [0, 1]$ and

F_i $(i = B, S)$ is uniform (i.e., $F_i(x) = x$ for $x \in [0, 1]$).[13] By the Revelation Principle it suffices to show that there does not exist an incentive-compatible and individually-rational DRP that is *ex-post* efficient. Suppose, to the contrary, that there exists a DRP that satisfies (9.13)–(9.17). Inequality 9.13 implies (using the *Envelope Theorem*) that $U_S(c)$ is differentiable almost everywhere with derivative $U'_S(c) = -E_v[\lambda(c, v)]$. Since (9.17) implies that $E_v[\lambda(c, v)] = 1 - c$, it follows that the seller's (unconditional) expected payoff $U^e_S = U_S(1) + 1/6$. By a symmetric argument it follows that the buyer's (unconditional) expected payoff $U^e_B = U_B(0) + 1/6$. However, by definition, the sum of the players' (unconditional) expected payoffs is $E_{v,c}[(v - c)\lambda(c, v)]$. Substituting (9.17) into this expression, and integrating, it follows that $E_{v,c}[(v - c)\lambda(c, v)] = 1/6$. This therefore implies that $U_S(1) + U_B(0) = -1/6$, which contradicts (9.15)–(9.16).   □

9.4.2 The Case of Correlated Values

In this section the player's reservation values are correlated, and each player has some relevant private information. This assumption is modelled as follows. There are two parameters θ and ρ — both of which are real numbers — that determine both players' reservation values, and, furthermore, the value of θ is the private information of the seller and the value of ρ is the private information of the buyer. The asymmetry in information is modelled as follows. The values of θ and ρ are independent and random draws from the probability distributions G and H, respectively. The seller knows the realization of the draw from G, but the buyer does not: she only knows that the value of θ is an independent and random draw from G. Symmetrically, the buyer knows the realization of the draw from H, but the seller does not: she only knows that the value of ρ is an independent and random draw from H.

Letting J and K respectively denote the supports of G and H, denote the minimum and maximum values of J respectively by $\underline{\theta}$ and $\bar{\theta}$, and the minimum and maximum values of K respectively by $\underline{\rho}$ and $\bar{\rho}$.

Both the seller's reservation value — denoted by $c(\theta, \rho)$ — and the buyer's reservation value — denoted by $v(\theta, \rho)$ — are strictly increasing

---

[13]The conceptual argument in the proof of the general case in Myerson and Satterthwaite (1983) is similar to that in the proof to follow in this special case.

in θ and in ρ. Furthermore, assume that for any θ and ρ, $v(\theta, \rho) \geq c(\theta, \rho)$.

In the context of the bargaining situation under consideration, a direct revelation procedure (DRP) is characterized by a pair of functions (λ, p). In a DRP the seller announces the value of θ and simultaneously the buyer announces the value of ρ. If the seller's announced value is θ' ($\theta' \in J$) and the buyer's announced value is ρ' ($\rho' \in K$), then with probability $\lambda(\theta', \rho')$ trade occurs at price $p(\theta', \rho')$, and with probability $1 - \lambda(\theta', \rho')$ trade does not occur.

A DRP is *incentive-compatible* if and only if the following inequalities are satisfied

$$\forall \theta, \theta' \in J, \quad U_S(\theta) \equiv E_\rho\Big[\lambda(\theta, \rho)[p(\theta, \rho) - c(\theta, \rho)]\Big] \geq$$
$$E_\rho\Big[\lambda(\theta', \rho)[p(\theta', \rho) - c(\theta, \rho)]\Big] \quad (9.18)$$

$$\forall \rho, \rho' \in K, \quad U_B(\rho) \equiv E_\theta\Big[\lambda(\theta, \rho)[v(\theta, \rho) - p(\theta, \rho)]\Big] \geq$$
$$E_\theta\Big[\lambda(\theta, \rho')[v(\theta, \rho) - p(\theta, \rho')]\Big]. \quad (9.19)$$

An incentive-compatible DRP is *individually-rational* if and only if

$$\forall \theta \in J, \quad U_S(\theta) \geq 0 \quad \text{and} \quad (9.20)$$
$$\forall \rho \in K, \quad U_B(\rho) \geq 0. \quad (9.21)$$

A DRP is *ex-post efficient* if and only if

$$\forall \theta \in J \text{ and } \forall \rho \in K, \quad \lambda(\theta, \rho) = 1. \quad (9.22)$$

The following proposition addresses the normative question of whether or not the bargaining outcome can be *ex-post* efficient.

Proposition 9.4 (Two-Sided Uncertainty with Correlated Values).
The bargaining outcome can be ex-post efficient if and only if $v^e(\underline{\rho}) \geq c^e(\bar{\theta})$, where $v^e(\underline{\rho}) = E_\theta[v(\theta, \underline{\rho})]$ and $c^e(\bar{\theta}) = E_\rho[c(\bar{\theta}, \rho)]$.

Proof. I first establish *sufficiency*. Consider the following bargaining procedure. The buyer makes a price offer to the seller. If she accepts the offer, then agreement is struck and the game ends. But if she rejects the offer, then the game ends with no agreement. If $v^e(\underline{\rho}) \geq c^e(\bar{\theta})$, then the following pair of strategies is a BNE: for any value of ρ the buyer offers the price $p = c^e(\bar{\theta})$, and for any value of θ the seller accepts the price $p = c^e(\bar{\theta})$ and rejects any price $p \neq c^e(\bar{\theta})$. The desired conclusion follows immediately, because this BNE is *ex-post* efficient. I now establish *necessity*. By the Revelation Principle it suffices to show that if $v^e(\underline{\rho}) < c^e(\bar{\theta})$, then there does not exist a DRP that satisfies (9.18)–(9.22). Suppose, to the contrary, that there exists such a DRP. After substituting the *ex-post* efficiency condition (9.22) into the seller's incentive-compatibility condition (9.18), it follows that the expectation of $p(\theta, \rho)$ with respect to ρ is independent of θ. Let it be denoted by p_S^e. Similarly, after substituting the *ex-post* efficiency condition (9.22) into the buyer's incentive-compatibility condition (9.19), it follows that the expectation of $p(\theta, \rho)$ with respect to θ is independent of ρ. Let it be denoted by p_B^e. After substituting (9.22) into (9.20) it thus follows from the seller's individual-rationality condition (9.20) that for any $\theta \in J$, $p_S^e \geq E_\rho[c(\theta, \rho)]$. Symmetrically, after substituting (9.22) into (9.21) it follows from the buyer's individual-rationality condition (9.21) that for any $\rho \in K$, $E_\theta[v(\theta, \rho)] \geq p_B^e$. This implies that $p^e \geq c^e(\bar{\theta})$ and $v^e(\underline{\rho}) \geq p^e$, where p^e is the expectation of $p(\theta, \rho)$ with respect to θ and ρ. Consequently, $v^e(\underline{\rho}) \geq c^e(\bar{\theta})$, which contradicts the hypothesis. $\square$

9.5   Applications

9.5.1   Indefinite Strikes

Consider the bargaining situation between the firm and its union as laid out in Section 9.3.1, but with the assumption that the firm has private information about R *and* the union has private information about α. Assume that R and α are independent and random draws from two continuous probability distributions with strictly positive densities, where R and α respectively take values from the closed intervals $[\underline{R}, \bar{R}]$ and $[\underline{\alpha}, \bar{\alpha}]$.

It follows from Proposition 9.3(a) that if $\underline{R} \geq \bar{\alpha}$, then the bargaining outcome can be *ex-post* efficient. Thus, if with probability one it is mutually beneficial for the union to sell its labour to the firm, then there exists a bargaining procedure whose induced bargaining game has a BNE with the following property: with probability one a wage agreement is reached.

On the other hand, if $\underline{\alpha} < \underline{R} < \bar{\alpha} < \bar{R}$, then Proposition 9.3(b) implies that the bargaining outcome cannot be *ex-post* efficient. Thus, if there is uncertainty as to whether or not it is mutually beneficial for the union to sell its labour to the firm, then any BNE of the bargaining game induced by any bargaining procedure has the following property: when $R \geq \alpha$ with a strictly positive probability the union goes on indefinite strike.

9.5.2 Litigation or Out-of-Court Settlement Revisited

Consider the bargaining situation between the defendant and the plantiff as laid out in Section 9.3.2, but with the assumption that the defendant has private information about γ *and* the plantiff has private information about x. Assume that x is a random draw from a probability distribution G, and γ is an independent random draw from a probability distribution H.

It follows from Proposition 9.4 that the bargaining outcome can be *ex-post* efficient if and only if $v^e(\gamma) \geq c^e(\bar{x})$. Under the American rule — in which each party bears her cost of litigation — this implies that if $f < (\gamma^e \bar{x} - \underline{\gamma} x^e)/2$, then the bargaining outcome cannot be *ex-post* efficient. On the other hand, under the English rule — in which the loser at trial bears the winner's cost of litigation — it follows that if $f < (\gamma^e \bar{x} - \underline{\gamma} x^e)/2(1 - \gamma^e + \underline{\gamma})$, then the bargaining outcome cannot be *ex-post* efficient. Hence, since $\gamma^e > \underline{\gamma}$, the players are more likely to proceed to litigation under the English rule than under the American rule.

Since $\gamma^e \bar{x} - \underline{\gamma} x^e$ is strictly greater than both $\gamma(\bar{x} - x^e)$ and $x(\gamma^e - \underline{\gamma})$, it follows by comparing the results obtained here with those obtained in Section 9.3.2 that the players are more likely to proceed to litigation under two-sided uncertainty than under one-sided uncertainty, whether they operate under the American rule or under the English rule.

9.6 Bargaining Power and Uncertainty

This section studies a bargaining model in which exactly one player has private information about her reservation value, while her opponent makes all the offers. In Section 7.2.2 I studied the repeated-offers game with perfect information, and established that (in the unique subgame perfect equilibrium) the player who makes all the offers obtains all of the gains from trade.

This section explores the extent to which the equilibrium payoff of the player who makes all the offers is adversely affected when her opponent has private information. Another motivation for the model studied in this section is to explore whether or not the uninformed player *screens* her opponent's private information through time via the sequence of equilibrium price offers. The existence of such a *screening equilibrium* would illustrate the notion that in the presence of asymmetric information the bargaining procedure can be a mechanism through which private information is revealed over time.

Two players, B and S, bargain over the price at which to trade an indivisible object — that is owned (or, can be produced) by player S — according to the following procedure. At each time $t = 0, \Delta, 2\Delta, \ldots$, where $\Delta > 0$, the buyer (player B) makes a price offer p ($p \geq 0$) to the seller (player S). If the seller accepts the price offer, then agreement is struck and trade occurs. On the other hand, if the seller rejects the price offer, then bargaining continues (and the game proceeds to time $t + \Delta$). If agreement is reached at time t on price p, then the payoffs to the seller and the buyer are respectively $(p - c) \exp(-rt)$ and $(v - p) \exp(-rt)$, where c is the seller's reservation value (or, cost of production), v the buyer's reservation value and r ($r > 0$) the players' common discount rate. If the players perpetually disagree (i.e., the seller rejects all the offers), then trade does not occur and each player's payoff is zero. For notational convenience, define $\delta \equiv \exp(-r\Delta)$. Notice that the discount factor $\delta \in (0, 1)$.

The players' reservation values are independent of each other, and the seller's reservation value is her private information. This asymmetry in information is modelled as follows. The seller's reservation value is a random draw from a probability distribution G. The seller knows the realization of the random draw, but the buyer does not. The buyer only knows that the seller's reservation value is a random draw from G. Hence, she believes that the probability that the seller's reservation value is less than or equal to c is $G(c)$. Thus, G defines the buyer's *prior* beliefs, as they are her beliefs about the seller's reservation value before bargaining begins. For short, I say that G is the buyer's prior. The minimum value (or, infimum) and the maximum value (or, supremum) of the support of G are respectively denoted by $\underline{c}$ and $\bar{c}$, where $\bar{c} > \underline{c} \geq 0$. That is, $G(\bar{c}) = 1$, $G(c) = 0$ if $c < \underline{c}$ and $G(c) > 0$ if $c > \underline{c}$. When the seller's reservation value is c, it is convenient to call her the c-type seller.

An important feature of this bargaining game is that the buyer may acquire some information about the seller's reservation value after any offer is rejected. Thus, at each time $t \geq \Delta$, before making her offer she will update her beliefs about the seller's reservation value, and base her price offer on her updated (or, *posterior*) beliefs.[14] I employ the perfect Bayesian equilibrium (PBE) concept to characterize the outcome of this bargaining model, which ensures, in particular, that (in equilibrium) the buyer does not update her beliefs in an arbitrary manner, but (whenever possible) she updates her beliefs in accordance with Bayes' rule.

It is helpful to introduce the following notation to describe the buyer's posterior beliefs about the seller's reservation value. Fix an arbitrary subgame beginning at time $n\Delta$ $(n \geq 1)$. Denote by G_n the probability distribution that defines the buyer's (posterior) beliefs at the beginning of this subgame. Thus, she believes that with probability $G_n(c)$ the seller's reservation value is less than or equal to c. Furthermore, denote by λ_n the minimum value (or, infimum) of the support of G_n — that is, $G_n(c) = 0$ if $c < \lambda_n$ and $G_n(c) > 0$ if $c > \lambda_n$. Thus, λ_n denotes the lowest possible reservation value that the buyer believes the seller could have.

9.6.1 An Example of a Screening Equilibrium

In this section I derive some of the main insights in a simple manner. In order to do so, however, it is convenient to assume that the buyer's prior G is uniformly distributed on the closed interval $[0, 1]$ — that is, $\bar{c} = 1$, $\underline{c} = 0$ and $G(c) = c$ (when $c \in [0, 1]$) — and that the buyer's reservation value $v = \bar{c}$.

Fix an arbitrary PBE in which the players use the following pair of strategies.

• (*Seller's strategy*). Fix an arbitrary $c \in [0, 1]$. At time 0 the c-type seller accepts price p if and only if $p \geq \alpha + (1 - \alpha)c$, where $\alpha > 0$. Fix any time t $(t \geq \Delta)$, and any history of price offers $(p_0, p_1, \ldots, p_{t-\Delta})$. If the c-type

---

[14] Although the buyer may also acquire some information about the seller's reservation value after any offer is *accepted*, in this game that is irrelevant, since once a price offer is accepted the game ends with trade taking place at the accepted price. In Section 9.6.3 I shall, however, study the effect on the equilibria of this game of allowing the buyer the option to retract her offer after it is accepted. The role of such an option on the bargaining outcome in bargaining situations with perfect information has been studied in Section 7.3.

seller rejected all these price offers, then at time t she accepts price p if and only if $p \geq \alpha + (1 - \alpha)c$.[15]

- (*Buyer's strategy*). If the buyer believes that the lowest possible reservation value the seller could have is λ (where $\lambda \in [0,1]$), then she offers price $p(\lambda) = \beta + (1 - \beta)\lambda$, where $1 > \beta > \alpha$.

Notice that the seller's strategy is *stationary*, in the sense that her decision to accept or reject a price offer p at any time t (when she is still around, which means that she did not accept any of the prices offered until time $t - \Delta$) depends only upon her reservation value c and the price offered p — it does not depend upon the history of prices offered until time $t - \Delta$. Furthermore, notice that the buyer's strategy is *Markovian*, in the sense that her price offer p at any time t depends only upon the lowest possible reservation value that she believes at time t the seller could have — it does not depend upon the history of prices offered until time $t - \Delta$.[16] It may also be noted that both strategies are 'linear', in the obvious sense.

This (stationary, linear) PBE is parameterized by two numbers: α and β such that $1 > \beta > \alpha > 0$. Since there are many such values of α and β, there may exist many such equilibria.[17] The strategy of my analysis is as follows. I first derive for an arbitrary such (stationary, linear) PBE the buyer's equilibrium posterior beliefs at the beginning of any subgame. Then, I show that there exists a unique pair (α^*, β^*), where $1 > \beta^* > \alpha^* > 0$, such that the strategies described above is a PBE if and only if $(\alpha, \beta) = (\alpha^*, \beta^*)$. I conclude with a discussion of the main features of this unique (stationary, linear) PBE.

Equilibrium Posterior Beliefs

Fix an arbitrary subgame beginning at time $t = n\Delta$ ($n \geq 1$). The buyer's equilibrium posterior beliefs G_n at the beginning of this subgame will depend on the seller's equilibrium strategy and the history of price offers. Let $\bar{p}_n$

---

[15]Notice that I do not specify the c-type seller's behaviour — whether or not to accept a price offer p — after any history of price offers $(p_0, p_1, \ldots, p_{t-\Delta})$ such that she accepted one of these price offers. Another way to express the c-type seller's strategy is as follows. She has a 'reservation' price — which equals $\alpha + (1 - \alpha)c$ — and the instant a price greater than or equal to it is offered, she accepts to trade at that price.

[16]In general, and this will be the case in equilibrium, the history of prices determines the buyer's beliefs at time t.

[17]It should be noted that I have yet to establish the existence of such an equilibrium.

denote the maximum price offered thus far — that is, $\bar{p}_n$ is the maximum of $\{p_0, p_1, \ldots, p_{t-\Delta}\}$. And let λ_n denote the minimum value (or, infimum) of the support of G_n — it is the lowest possible reservation value the buyer believes at time t the seller could have.

It follows from the seller's equilibrium strategy and Bayes' rule that $\lambda_n = 0$ if $\bar{p}_n < \alpha$ and $\lambda_n = c^*(\bar{p}_n)$ if $\alpha \leq \bar{p}_n < 1$, where

$$c^*(p) = \frac{p - \alpha}{1 - \alpha}$$

and, moreover, $G_n(c) = (c - \lambda_n)/(1 - \lambda_n)$ if $\lambda_n \leq c \leq 1$, and $G_n(c) = 0$ if $0 \leq c < \lambda_n$.[18]

Notice that G_n is a truncation of the (uniformly distributed) prior at λ_n. Hence, the buyer's equilibrium posterior beliefs at the beginning of any subgame can be characterized by a unique number, namely, the lowest possible reservation value that the buyer believes the seller could have.

Existence and Uniqueness

At time 0 the equilibrium price offered $p_0 = \beta$, which the seller accepts if and only if her reservation value $c \leq c^*(\beta)$. Hence, at time 1 the equilibrium price offered $p_1 = \beta + (1 - \beta)c^*(\beta)$, since the lowest possible reservation value that the buyer believes (at time 1) the seller could have is $c^*(\beta)$. The seller accepts p_1 if her reservation value c is such that $c^*(\beta) < c \leq c^*(p_1)$. It thus follows that $p_0 - c^*(\beta) = \delta[p_1 - c^*(\beta)]$.[19] After substituting for p_0, p_1 and $c^*(\beta)$, and then simplifying, it follows that

$$\alpha = \beta\delta. \tag{9.23}$$

Hence, the pair of strategies stated above is a PBE only if α and β satisfy equation 9.23. I now show that the seller's strategy is immune to profitable one-shot (unilateral) deviations if and only if α and β satisfy equation 9.23.

---

[18] Given the seller's and the buyer's equilibrium strategies, the buyer's posterior beliefs G_n when $\bar{p}_n \geq 1$ are irrelevant — since the buyer never offers a price strictly greater than one, and all types of sellers always accept any price that is greater than or equal to one.

[19] Suppose, to the contrary, that $p_0 - c^*(\beta) > \delta[p_1 - c^*(\beta)]$. This implies that there exists a $c \in (c^*(\beta), c^*(p_1))$ such that $p_0 - c > \delta(p_1 - c)$, which contradicts the result (stated above) that such a c-type seller rejects p_0, and then accepts p_1. Now suppose, to the contrary, that $p_0 - c^*(\beta) < \delta[p_1 - c^*(\beta)]$. This implies that there exists a $c \in (0, c^*(\beta))$ such that $p_0 - c < \delta(p_1 - c)$, which contradicts the result that such a c-type seller accepts p_0.

Fix an arbitrary $c \in [0,1]$, a subgame in which the c-type seller is still around, and a price offer $p' \geq 0$. First suppose that $p' \geq \alpha + (1-\alpha)c$, which implies that in equilibrium she accepts p'. Thus, her equilibrium payoff is $p' - c$. Now suppose she considers a one-shot deviation: that is, she rejects p', and then plays according to her equilibrium strategy. Her payoff from this one-shot deviation is $\delta[p(c^*(p')) - c]$, where $p(c^*(p')) = \beta + (1 - \beta)c^*(p')$.[20] If α and β satisfy equation 9.23, then $p' - c \geq \delta[p(c^*(p')) - c]$, as required. Now suppose that $p' < \alpha + (1 - \alpha)c$, which means that in equilibrium the c-type seller rejects this price offer. Since (after rejecting p') she can accept the equilibrium price offered Δ time units later — which I denote by p'' — it follows that her equilibrium payoff $U_S(c) \geq \delta(p'' - c)$. It is straightforward to show, as required, that if α and β satisfy equation 9.23, then $\delta(p'' - c) \geq p' - c$, where $p' - c$ denotes her payoff from the one-shot deviation in which she instead accepts p'.[21]

Let $U_B(\lambda)$ denote the buyer's equilibrium payoff at the beginning of any subgame when the lowest possible reservation value the buyer believes the seller could have is λ. Fix any such subgame, and let $W_B(p, \lambda)$ denote the buyer's payoff if she offers price p at the beginning of this subgame and then (if the price is rejected) she plays according to her equilibrium strategy. The buyer's equilibrium strategy is immune to profitable one-shot (unilateral) deviations if and only if

$$\text{for all } \lambda \in [0, 1], \quad W_B(p(\lambda), \lambda) \geq W_B(p, \lambda) \quad \text{for all } p \geq 0,$$

where $p(\lambda) = \beta + (1 - \beta)\lambda$.

It is trivial to note that if $\lambda = 1$, then $W_B(1, 1) = 0 \geq W_B(p, \lambda)$ for all $p \geq 0$. Now suppose that $\lambda < 1$. If $p \geq 1$ then $W_B(p, \lambda) = 1 - p$, and if $p \leq \alpha + (1-\alpha)\lambda$ then $W_B(p, \lambda) = \delta U_B(\lambda)$. Furthermore, if $1 > p > \alpha + (1-\alpha)\lambda$,

---

[20]Since the c-type seller is still around, the lowest possible reservation value that the buyer believes (when making the price offer p') the seller could have is less than or equal to c. This implies, since $p' \geq \alpha + (1-\alpha)c$, that if p' is rejected, then the lowest possible reservation value that the buyer believes the seller could have is $c^*(p')$. Hence, she offers the equilibrium price $p(c^*(p'))$. Since $p \geq \alpha + (1-\alpha)c$, this equilibrium price offer would be accepted by the c-type seller if she rejects the price p'.

[21]If $p' < \alpha + (1-\alpha)\lambda'$, where λ' $(\lambda' < c)$ denotes the lowest possible reservation value that the buyer believes (when making the price offer p') the seller could have, then $p'' = p(\lambda') = \beta + (1 - \beta)\lambda'$. And if $p' > \alpha + (1-\alpha)\lambda'$, then $p'' = p(c^*(p'))$.

then

$$W_B(p, \lambda) = \left[\frac{c^*(p) - \lambda}{1 - \lambda} \right] (1 - p) + \left[\frac{1 - c^*(p)}{1 - \lambda} \right] \delta U_B(c^*(p)).$$

Since for any $\lambda < 1$ and $p \notin (\alpha + (1 - \alpha)\lambda, 1)$, $W_B(p, \lambda) \leq 0$, it follows that for all $\lambda < 1$

$$U_B(\lambda) = \max_{1 > p > \alpha + (1-\alpha)\lambda} \left[\frac{c^*(p) - \lambda}{1 - \lambda} \right] (1 - p) + \left[\frac{1 - c^*(p)}{1 - \lambda} \right] \delta U_B(c^*(p)).$$

$$(9.24)$$

Furthermore, it follows that the buyer's equilibrium strategy is immune to one-shot deviations if and only if for all $\lambda < 1$, a solution to the maximization problem defined in 9.24 is $p = p(\lambda)$.

It is convenient to define $V_B(\lambda) = (1 - \lambda)U_B(\lambda)$, and rewrite the statement in (9.24) as follows

$$V_B(\lambda) = \max_{1 > p > \alpha + (1-\alpha)\lambda} (c^*(p) - \lambda)(1 - p) + \delta V_B(c^*(p)). \qquad (9.25)$$

Let p^* denote an *arbitrary* solution to the maximization problem defined in (9.25). Applying the *Envelope Theorem* to (9.25), it follows that

$$V_B'(\lambda) = -(1 - p^*). \qquad (9.26)$$

The first-order condition, which p^* must satisfy, is

$$\frac{1 - p^*}{1 - \alpha} - \frac{p^* - \alpha}{1 - \alpha} + \lambda + \frac{\delta}{1 - \alpha} V_B'\left(\frac{p^* - \alpha}{1 - \alpha} \right) = 0. \qquad (9.27)$$

Substituting $p^* = p(\lambda)$ into (9.27), it follows that $p(\lambda)$ satisfies the first-order condition if and only if

$$(1 - \lambda)(1 - 2\beta + \alpha) + \delta V_B'\left(\frac{\beta + (1 - \beta)\lambda - \alpha}{1 - \alpha} \right) = 0. \qquad (9.28)$$

After substituting $p^* = p(\lambda)$ into (9.26), it follows that $V_B'(\lambda) = -(1-\beta)(1-\lambda)$. This implies that

$$V_B'\left(\frac{\beta + (1 - \beta)\lambda - \alpha}{1 - \alpha} \right) = -\frac{(1 - \beta)^2(1 - \lambda)}{1 - \alpha}. \qquad (9.29)$$

Using (9.29) to substitute for $V'_B(.)$ in (9.28), it follows that for all $\lambda < 1$, $p(\lambda)$ satisfies the first-order condition if and only if

$$(1 - \alpha)(1 - 2\beta + \alpha) - \delta(1 - \beta)^2 = 0. \tag{9.30}$$

If α and β satisfy equation 9.23, then the second-order condition is satisfied.[22] Hence, since (9.26) implies that the first-order condition (9.27) has at most a unique solution, it follows that for all $\lambda < 1$, the unique solution to the maximization problem defined in (9.24) is $p = p(\lambda)$ if and only if α and β satisfy equations 9.23 and 9.30. This thus establishes that the buyer's equilibrium strategy is immune to profitable one-shot (unilateral) deviations if and only if α and β satisfy equations 9.23 and 9.30.

There exists a *unique* pair (α, β) such that $1 > \beta > \alpha > 0$ which satisfies equations 9.23 and 9.30, namely

$$\alpha = 1 - \sqrt{1 - \delta} \quad \text{and} \quad \beta = \frac{1 - \sqrt{1 - \delta}}{\delta}. \tag{9.31}$$

Consequently, there exists a unique (stationary, linear) PBE in which the players use the pair of strategies described above with α and β taking the values stated in (9.31).

Main Insights

The sequence of prices $\langle p_n \rangle$ and the sequence of the buyer's posteriors $\langle \lambda_n \rangle$ *along the equilibrium path* of the unique (stationary, linear) PBE are defined by the following two difference equations: $p_n = \beta + (1 - \beta)\lambda_n$ and $\lambda_{n+1} = c^*(p_n)$, given that $\lambda_0 = 0$, where α and β are defined in (9.31). Solving these equations, it follows that

$$p_n = 1 - (1 - \beta)\beta^n \quad \text{and} \quad \lambda_n = 1 - \beta^n \quad (n = 0, 1, 2, \dots).$$

Notice that $1 > p_{n+1} > p_n > 0$ and $1 > \lambda_{n+1} > \lambda_n \geq 0$ (for all $n = 0, 1, 2, \dots$).

---

[22] An arbitrary solution p^* to the maximization problem defined in (9.25) satisfies the second-order condition if and only if $-2(1 - \alpha) + \delta V''_B((p^* - \alpha)/(1 - \alpha)) < 0$. It follows from (9.26) that $V''_B(\lambda) = dp^*/d\lambda$. Hence, at $p^* = p(\lambda)$, $V''_B(\lambda) = 1 - \beta$. Therefore, $p^* = p(\lambda)$ satisfies the second-order condition if and only if $-2(1 - \alpha) + \delta(1 - \beta) < 0$. The latter inequality is satisfied if α and β satisfy equation 9.23.

Along the equilibrium path of this unique (stationary, linear) PBE, the prices are strictly increasing, and trade occurs at each time with a strictly positive probability. The time at which trade occurs is increasing in the seller's cost of production (or, reservation value). A low cost seller trades at an earlier time and at a lower price, since she is more eager to trade and does not want to wait to trade at a higher price that is offered in the future. Indeed, the buyer screens the seller's private information through the equilibrium price path — the seller's privately held information is (partly) revealed through time. It is 'as if' the buyer engages in *intertemporal* price discrimination.

The equilibrium is inefficient, since trade occurs with positive probability after time 0 — which is costly, since both players discount future payoffs. Furthermore, trade does not occur with probability one in finite time. However, since $p_n \to 1$ (and $\lambda_n \to 1$) as $n \to \infty$, it follows that trade occurs with probability one in infinite time.

I now discuss the properties of the PBE in the limit as $\Delta \to 0$. In this limit, $\delta \to 1$, which implies that the first price offered $p_0 \to 1$. Hence, as the time interval between two consecutive offers becomes arbitrarily small, the buyer's equilibrium price offer at time 0 becomes arbitrarily close to the 'reservation' price of the highest cost-type seller — which means that (in this limit) *all* types of the seller accept the first price offered. Hence, in this limit there is no screening of the seller's private information, and trade occurs with probability one at time 0. Furthermore, in this limit, the buyer's equilibrium payoff converges to zero. The intuition behind these limiting properties is straightforward. In the limit as Δ becomes arbitrarily small, the cost of rejecting any offer to a c-type seller (for any $c \in [0, 1]$) becomes arbitrarily small. Hence, she is willing to wait to obtain a high price that might be offered in the future. Thus, the buyer effectively gives up any attempt to screen (and engage in intertemporal price discrimination), and consequently, she offers the price $p = 1$ at time 0.

It follows from the above discussion that the screening equilibrium satisfies the following two properties — which are related to those of the equilibrium pricing strategy of a durable-good monopolist (cf. Coase (1972)).

Property 9.1 (Coasian Dynamics). Prices are monotonic across time, and the more eager a player the earlier she trades.

Property 9.2 (Coase Conjecture). In the limit, as $\Delta \to 0$, (i) all potential gains from trade are realized without any costly delay, and (ii) the profit of the uninformed player (who makes all the offers) is arbitrarily close to zero — that is, she loses almost all the bargaining power that making offers confers.

There are two main messages contained in the screening equilibrium derived above. Firstly, the bargaining process may reveal none of the privately held information if and only if the cost of haggling is arbitrarily small. And secondly, the player who makes all the offers loses all her bargaining power when her opponent has private information if and only if the cost of haggling is arbitrarily small.[23]

9.6.2   General Results

I now analyse the set of all PBE of the model. Unless otherwise stated, the formal results in this section impose no restrictions on the buyer's prior G. However, for ease of interpretation, it is helpful to assume that G is continuously distributed on the closed interval $[\underline{c}, \bar{c}]$. The first preliminary result is Lemma 9.3 below, which implies that in any PBE if a high cost seller accepts to trade at price p with a positive probability, then any lower cost seller accepts to trade at this price for sure (with probability one). The intuition for this result comes from the observation that a low cost seller is more eager to trade than a high cost seller.

Lemma 9.3 (The Skimming Property). *Fix an arbitrary PBE, a reservation value c, a price p, and a subgame beginning with the buyer's offer. If at the beginning of this subgame the c-type seller accepts the price p with a strictly positive probability, then, for any $c' < c$, at the beginning of this subgame the c'-type seller accepts the price p with probability one.*

Proof. The hypothesis implies that $p - c \geq U_S(c)$, where $U_S(c)$ is the PBE payoff to the c-type seller if she rejects the price p at the beginning of this subgame. I now show that for any $c' < c$, $p - c' > U_S(c')$. After rejecting the price p, the c'-type seller will accept with positive probability the equilibrium price $p_{t+n\Delta}$ offered by the buyer at time $t + n\Delta$ for some

---

[23]Notice therefore that the buyer's bargaining power is intimately connected with her ability to screen the seller's private information across time.

$n \geq 1$, where t denotes the time at which the subgame under consideration begins. Hence, $U_S(c') = \delta^n(p_{t+n\Delta} - c')$. Since the c-type seller can mimic the c'-type seller's strategy, it follows that $U_S(c) \geq \delta^n(p_{t+n\Delta} - c)$. Hence, $U_S(c) \geq U_S(c') + \delta^n(c' - c)$. Since $p - c \geq U_S(c)$, it follows that $p - c' \geq U_S(c') + (1 - \delta^n)(c - c')$. The desired result follows immediately, since $\delta < 1$ and $n \geq 1$. $\qquad\square$

As is the case in the screening equilibrium derived in the previous section, it is now shown that in any PBE the buyer's posterior belief at the beginning of any subgame is a truncation of her prior G. Fix an arbitrary PBE and a price $p \geq 0$. Suppose that at time 0 the buyer offers the price p. Either it is rejected with probability one, or it is accepted with positive probability. In the latter case, it follows from Lemma 9.3 that there exists a $\lambda_1 \in [\underline{c}, \bar{c}]$ — where λ_1 in general depends on p — such that the price p is accepted if and only if the seller's reservation value $c \leq \lambda_1$. Letting G_1 denote the buyer's posterior at time Δ after the rejection of the price p, it follows from Bayes' rule that $G_1(c) = [G(c) - G(\lambda_1)]/[1 - G(\lambda_1)]$ if $\lambda_1 \leq c \leq \bar{c}$ and $G_1(c) = 0$ if $\underline{c} \leq c \leq \lambda_1$. The following corollary, which generalizes this relationship, follows immediately from the above argument.

Corollary 9.1. *Fix an arbitrary PBE and a time $n\Delta$ (where $n \geq 1$). In any subgame beginning at time $n\Delta$ there exists a $\lambda_n \in [\underline{c}, \bar{c}]$ such that the buyer's posterior G_n at the beginning of this subgame is a truncation of the prior G at λ_n. That is, $G_n(c) = [G(c) - G(\lambda_n)]/[1 - G(\lambda_n)]$ if $\lambda_n \leq c \leq \bar{c}$ and $G_n(c) = 0$ if $\underline{c} \leq c \leq \lambda_n$.*

Corollary 9.1 implies that (given the prior G) in any PBE the buyer's posterior at any time $n\Delta$ can be characterized by a unique number, namely, λ_n (which is the lowest possible reservation value the buyer believes that the seller could have). Lemma 9.4 below implies that in any PBE the buyer never offers a price strictly greater than $\bar{c}$, which, in turn, implies that for any $c \in [\underline{c}, \bar{c}]$ the c-type seller always accepts the price $p = \bar{c}$.

Lemma 9.4. *Fix an arbitrary PBE and time t. In any subgame beginning at time t, the equilibrium price offered p_t at time t is such that $p_t \leq \min\{\bar{c}, v\}$.*

Proof. By contradiction. Suppose that there exists a PBE in which the maximum price ever offered by the buyer is $\bar{p} > \min\{\bar{c}, v\}$.[24] Fix a subgame in which at the beginning of this subgame the buyer's equilibrium price offer is $p = \bar{p}$. Since this is the maximum price ever to be offered, trade occurs with probability one, and hence, the buyer's PBE payoff in this subgame is $v - \bar{p}$. If $\min\{\bar{c}, v\} = v$, then a contradiction is obtained, since the buyer's equilibrium payoff is strictly negative. Now suppose that $\min\{\bar{c}, v\} = \bar{c}$, and suppose the buyer considers the following one-shot deviation: she offers the price $p' = \bar{p} - \epsilon$ where $\epsilon > 0$ and satisfies $p' - c > \delta(\bar{p} - c)$ for all $c \in [\underline{c}, \bar{c}]$. Since $\bar{p} > \bar{c}$, such a price exists, and, hence, it is accepted with probability one. This implies that the buyer's payoff in this subgame from this one-shot deviation strictly exceeds $v - \bar{p}$, which is a contradiction. $\square$

Lemmas 9.3–9.4 and Corollary 9.1 are valid whatever the magnitude of the buyer's reservation value v relative to $\bar{c}$. It is now shown that if $v = \bar{c}$ then there exists a continuum of PBE, but if $v > \bar{c}$ then there exists a unique PBE. When $v > \bar{c}$, gains from trade exist with probability one *and* they are bounded away from zero. However, when $v = \bar{c}$, gains from trade need not exist. It may be recalled that the screening equilibrium described in Section 9.6.1 is based on the assumption that $v = \bar{c}$.

The Gap Case

Here it is assumed that $v > \bar{c}$, which is called the *gap* case. It is instructive to first of all understand why the (stationary, linear) strategies described in Section 9.6.1 is not a PBE. Assume, as is done in Section 9.6.1, that the buyer's prior G is uniformly distributed on the closed interval $[0, 1]$. But, in contrast to the assumption made in Section 9.6.1, assume that $v > 1$. It follows from the buyer's strategy that for any $\lambda < 1$, $p(\lambda) < 1$. Thus, even if the lowest possible reservation value the buyer believes the seller could have is arbitrarily close to one, the buyer does not offer the price equal to one. This is not optimal when $v > 1$. The intuition for this result is straightforward, and runs as follows. When the buyer is sufficiently 'pessimistic' — that is, she believes λ is sufficiently close to one — then

---

[24]It should be noted that $\bar{p}$ cannot be infinite. For otherwise, the buyer would obtain a negative payoff, which is impossible, since the buyer can guarantee a payoff of zero by always offering the price $p = 0$.

(since $v > 1$ and $\delta < 1$) her payoff from offering the price equal to one strictly exceeds the maximum possible payoff she can obtain from offering a price strictly less than one.[25]

The above intuitive argument is, in fact, valid for any prior G and any PBE. Indeed, in any PBE and at the beginning of any subgame in which the buyer is sufficiently pessimistic — that is, the lowest possible reservation value the buyer believes the seller could have is sufficiently close to $\bar{c}$ — the buyer offers the price equal to $\bar{c}$. It then follows that in any PBE trade occurs with probability one in *finite* time, since (by Corollary 9.1) at some finite point in time the buyer will become sufficiently pessimistic. Hence, unlike the screening equilibrium derived in Section 9.6.1, when $v > \bar{c}$ bargaining terminates in finite time. However, just like the screening equilibrium derived in Section 9.6.1, when $v > \bar{c}$ in the unique PBE — which is formally stated below in Proposition 9.5 — the equilibrium path prices are strictly increasing, and the buyer screens (some of) the seller's privately held information. Furthermore, the unique PBE satisfies the Coase conjecture — which, as mentioned above, is also satisfied by the screening equilibrium derived in Section 9.6.1.

Proposition 9.5 (Gap Case). *If $v > \bar{c}$, and either $G(\bar{c}) > 0$ or G has a strictly positive and continuous density at $\bar{c}$, then there exists a (essentially) unique PBE. In particular, the unique PBE path of play is characterized as follows. There exists an N such that the price offered at time 0 is $p_0 \geq \underline{c}$, and the price offered at time $N\Delta$ is $p_{N\Delta} = \bar{c}$. Furthermore, the equilibrium path prices are strictly increasing: $p_{t+\Delta} > p_t$ for $t = 0, \Delta, 2\Delta, \ldots, (N-1)\Delta$. The seller accepts each of these $N + 1$ price offers with a probability that is strictly positive but strictly less than one. In the limit, as $\Delta \to 0$, $p^*(0) \to \bar{c}$ and trade occurs with probability one at time 0.*

Proof. The proof is based on a backward induction argument, since in any PBE bargaining ends in finite time. However, the proof is rather complex. Hence, I omit it and refer the reader to Fudenberg, Levine and Tirole (1985) and Gul, Sonnenschein and Wilson (1986). □

---

[25]Her payoff from offering the price equal to one is $v - 1$, since (by Lemma 9.4) all types of sellers will accept this price offer. On the other hand, her maximum possible payoff from offering a price strictly less than one is arbitrarily close to $\delta(v - 1)$ as λ becomes arbitrarily close to one. Indeed, since $\delta < 1$ and $v > 1$, there exists a $\lambda^* < 1$ such that if $\lambda > \lambda^*$ then it is optimal to offer the price equal to one.

Notice that the unique PBE possesses most of the key properties of the screening equilibrium derived in Section 9.6.1. Indeed, this unique PBE is also a *screening equilibrium*. The only main difference is that trade occurs in finite time with probability one. Hence, with probability zero the players will perpetually disagree and fail to reach a price agreement. The equilibrium is nevertheless inefficient, because with a strictly positive probability trade occurs after some costly delay. However, the delay to agreement vanishes in the limit as the time interval between two consecutive offers tends to zero. Furthermore, in this limit, the buyer's payoff converges to $v - \bar{c}$, and the lowest cost seller earns a payoff of $\bar{c} - \underline{c}$. It can be said that, in this limit, a player looses much of the bargaining power that making offers confers when her opponent (the responder) has private information.

The No Gap Case

Now assume that $v = \bar{c}$, which is called the *no gap* case. In any PBE of the no gap case, trade does not occur with probability one in finite time — as is shown in the screening equilibrium derived in Section 9.6.1. This is because in any PBE there is no incentive for the buyer to offer a price greater than or equal to v at any finite point in time. This implies that, unlike in the gap case, one cannot use a backward induction argument to characterize the set of PBE. It turns out that there exists a multiplicity of PBE. In particular, there exists a large number of PBE that do satisfy the Coase conjecture, but there also exists a large number of PBE that do not satisfy the Coase conjecture. Hence, even when the costs of haggling are arbitrarily small, it is possible (in the no gap case) for the buyer to retain the bargaining power that making offers confers even when the seller has private information.

Let $\widehat{u}_B$ denote the buyer's unique PBE payoff if she could make a take-it-or-leave-it-offer to the seller. Thus, $\widehat{u}_B \geq (v - p)G(p)$ for all $p \geq 0$. In any PBE of the repeated-offers model, the buyer's equilibrium payoff is less than or equal to $\widehat{u}_B$. The buyer would obtain a payoff equal to $\widehat{u}_B$ (in the repeated-offers model) if she could *commit* to always offering the price p^*, where $(v - p^*)G(p^*) \geq (v - p)G(p)$ for all $p \geq 0$. However, making such a commitment stick is rather difficult. Suppose she offers price p^* at time 0. Any c-type seller such that $c > p^*$ will not accept this price offer. Hence, if this price offer is rejected, then at time 1 the buyer will update her beliefs, and consequently, she has an incentive to offer a higher price (and thus break her commitment). I call $\widehat{u}_B$ the buyer's *commitment* payoff.

The following proposition provides a characterization of the set of buyer payoffs sustainable as a PBE.

Proposition 9.6 (No Gap Case). *Assume that $v = \bar{c}$, and that G is continuously distributed on the closed interval $[\underline{c}, \bar{c}]$. Let $\widehat{u}_B$ be such that $\widehat{u}_B \geq (v - p)G(p)$ for all $p \geq 0$. For any $\epsilon > 0$ there exists a $\Delta' > 0$ such that for any $\Delta \leq \Delta'$ and any $u_B \in [\epsilon, \widehat{u}_B - \epsilon]$ there exists a PBE such that the buyer's payoff equals u_B.*

Proof. The basic idea of the proof involves the construction of *reputational equilibria*. In such PBE almost any path of play is supported as a PBE path by the threat of reverting play to a PBE that satisfies the Coase conjecture if the buyer deviates from any given path of play.[26] However, the details of the proof are complex. Hence, I omit the proof and refer the interested reader to Ausubel and Deneckere (1989) — the authors of this result. □

Thus, when the time interval between two consecutive offers is arbitrarily small, there exists a PBE in which the uninformed buyer's payoff is arbitrarily close to her *commitment* payoff $\widehat{u}_B$. As such this result overturns the Coase conjecture that characterizes the unique PBE in the gap case (cf. Proposition 9.5).

9.6.3   The Effect of Retractable Offers

This section extends the model studied above by allowing the buyer the option to retract her offer after it is accepted (and then to make a new offer). In Section 7.3 I have studied the role of such an option, but in the context of the alternating-offers model with perfect information. The pros and cons of this option are discussed in Section 7.3.4. In the context of the current setting of asymmetric information, this option may have a significant effect on the nature of the equilibria, since accepting an offer may reveal some of the seller's privately held information. Indeed, it is shown below that provided Δ is sufficiently small, a result similar to Proposition 9.6 is valid in both the gap case and the no gap case.

---

[26]In a PBE that satisfies the Coase conjecture, the buyer's payoff is arbitrarily close to zero.

Let me first clarify the nature of the extension. Whenever the seller accepts a price offer p, the buyer then has to decide whether or not to retract it. If she does not retract it, then trade occurs at price p. But if she retracts the price offer, then (Δ time units later) she makes a new price offer to the seller.

The following lemma contains the key result behind the analysis of the set of PBE of this extended model. It describes a PBE — for values of $\delta \geq 1/2$ (i.e., for values of Δ sufficiently small) — in which trade occurs with probability one at time 0 on price v, and the buyer's equilibrium payoff equals zero.[27]

		state s^*	state s'
	offer	$p = v$	$p = \underline{c}$
buyer	retracts	$p > v$	$p > v(1 - \delta) + \delta \underline{c}$
	beliefs	G	D
c-type seller	accepts	$p = v$	$p \geq c$
	transitions	switch to state s' if a price offer $p < v$ is accepted by the seller	absorbing

Table 9.1: A PBE in the repeated-offers model with asymmetric information and retractable offers, where G is the buyer's prior beliefs and D is the (degenerate) distribution function whose mass is concentrated at $c = \underline{c}$ (i.e., $D(\underline{c}) = 1$ and $D(c) = 0$ for $c < \underline{c}$).

Lemma 9.5. *If $v \geq \bar{c}$ and $\delta \geq 1/2$, then the pair of strategies and buyer beliefs described in Table 9.1 is a PBE of the repeated-offers model with asymmetric information and retractable offers. In equilibrium trade occurs with probability one at time 0 on price v, and the buyer's equilibrium payoff equals zero.*

---

[27]It should be noted that in the model studied above — when the buyer does not have the option to retract offers — such a PBE does not exist. Furthermore, in the gap case, when $v > \bar{c}$, such a PBE does not exist even in the limit as $\Delta \to 0$.

Proof. First, note that in state s' the buyer believes that with probability one the seller's reservation value $c = \underline{c}$. Hence, since this is an absorbing state, the actions of the players in this state is the unique SPE of the repeated-offers model with perfect information. Now consider the initial state s^*. It is easy to verify using the *One-Shot Deviation* property that no player can benefit from a one-shot (unilateral) deviation. For example, suppose a price $p' \leq v(1 - \delta) + \delta\underline{c}$ is offered. In the proposed equilibrium the c-type seller (for any $c \in [\underline{c}, \bar{c}]$) rejects this price offer, and obtains a payoff of $\delta(v - c)$. Suppose she considers a one-shot deviation, and instead accepts the offer. In that case the state switches to s', and the buyer does not retract this offer, which implies that the c-type seller's payoff from this one-shot deviation is $p' - c$. Since $\delta \geq 1/2$ — and I note that this is the only point in the proof at which this condition is required — it follows that $\delta v + (1-\delta)c \geq v(1-\delta)+\delta\underline{c}$. This inequality implies that $p' \leq \delta v + (1 - \delta)c$. That is, $p' - c \leq \delta(v - c)$. Hence, the one-shot deviation is not profitable. $\qquad\square$

Along the equilibrium path of the PBE described in Table 9.1, the buyer offers price v, which is accepted by all seller types, and the buyer does not retract this price offer. In equilibrium, therefore, trade occurs with probability one at time 0 on price v. The buyer's equilibrium payoff equals zero.

Remark 9.2. In the PBE described in Lemma 9.5, if a price $p < v$ is accepted by the seller in the initial state s^*, then a 'zero-probability' event has occurred, since (given the seller's strategy) no seller type accepts such a price in the initial state. Thus, the buyer cannot use Bayes' rule to update her beliefs about the seller's reservation value. In the PBE described above, it is assumed that the buyer conjectures that the deviation (i.e., the acceptance of the price $p < v$ in the initial state) was made by the lowest cost-type seller. This *optimistic* conjecture is not unreasonable, since the type who has the strongest incentive to deviate is the seller with the lowest cost. Thus, many refinements of the PBE concept — including, for example, those proposed and used in Rubinstein (1985a), and Grossman and Perry (1986) — would not eliminate this PBE. Having said this, in Muthoo (1994), I construct an alternative PBE which also supports the outcome of the PBE described in Lemma 9.5, but has the feature that the buyer makes only reasonable *pessimistic* conjectures. I therefore suspect that the 'zero buyer profit' PBE outcome is robust to any refinement of the PBE concept that only acts to constrain the buyer's off-the-equilibrium-path beliefs.

I call the PBE stated in Lemma 9.5 the zero buyer-profit equilibrium. Given this 'extremal' equilibrium, it is straightforward to construct a continuum of other PBE (when $v \geq \bar{c}$ and $\delta \geq 1/2$). In particular, any price path $\langle p_t \rangle$ is supported as a PBE path as follows. If at any time t the buyer does not offer p_t, or retracts the price p_t, then immediately play proceeds according to the zero buyer-profit equilibrium. The seller's strategy is a best response to the buyer's strategy. I omit the details of the construction of such reputational equilibria, and simply state the main result in the following proposition.

Proposition 9.7. *If $v \geq \bar{c}$ and $\delta \geq 1/2$, then any buyer payoff between zero and $\widehat{u}_B$ can be supported by a PBE of the repeated-offers model with asymmetric information and retractable offers, where $\widehat{u}_B$ is defined in Proposition 9.6.*

By comparing Propositions 9.5–9.7, it is clear that the impact of the option to retract offers is non-trivial. When offers are retractable there is no relevant distinction between the gap case and the no gap case: the set of equilibria does not depend on the relative magnitude of v and $\bar{c}$. This seems like a more plausible conclusion, since the sharp 'discontinuity' in the equilibrium set at $v = \bar{c}$ in the model without retractable offers is somewhat problematic. Furthermore, with retractable offers the Coase conjecture does not hold when $v > \bar{c}$. This result is also more plausible, since it is unlikely that the player who makes all the offers will lose all her bargaining power when her opponent has private information. It should also be noted that Proposition 9.7 is a much stronger result than Proposition 9.6 in the sense that it is valid for any $\Delta \in (0, \Delta')$, where Δ' is the unique solution to $\exp(-r\Delta) = 1/2$, while the full force of Proposition 9.6 comes only in the limit as $\Delta \to 0$. As such with retractable offers there exists a PBE in which the buyer obtains her *commitment* payoff $\widehat{u}_B$ even when $\Delta > 0$. In contrast, the same is true in the model without retractable offers if and only if $v = \bar{c}$ and Δ is arbitrarily close to zero.

9.7   An Application to Wage-Quality Contracts

Consider a firm and a worker who are bargaining over the wage w and the quality q of a unit of output, where $w \geq 0$ and $q \geq 0$. If agreement is reached at time t $(t = 0, \Delta, 2\Delta, \ldots)$ on a wage-quality contract (w, q), then the payoffs to the firm and the worker are respectively

$$\sqrt{q} - w \quad \text{and} \quad w - \theta q,$$

where θ is the worker's private information. This asymmetry in information is modelled in the usual way by considering the value of θ to be a random draw from some distribution, with its realization only revealed to the worker. Assume that the distribution from which θ is randomly drawn is as follows: $\theta = 2$ with probability α, and $\theta = 1$ with probability $1 - \alpha$, where $0 < \alpha < 1$. I call the worker 'good-type' if $\theta = 1$, and 'bad-type' if $\theta = 2$.

At each point in time t the firm offers a *menu* of wage-quality contracts. More precisely, an offer is a pair $\{m_b, m_g\}$, where $m_i = (w_i, q_i)$ $(i = b, g)$. The worker then decides whether to accept one of the two contracts on offer, or to reject both of them (in which case bargaining continues with the firm proposing a new menu of contracts at time $t + \Delta$). If the players perpetually disagree, then each player obtains a payoff of zero. Thus, this bargaining model is an extension to the one studied in Section 9.6. The key difference is that the uninformed player now has two devices through which she can attempt to screen the informed player's private information: through time (as in the model above) and through the menu of contracts (at a single point in time).

As I show below, since the players are bargaining over two variables (or, two 'dimensions'), this additional screening device turns out to significantly affect the nature of the PBE. However, it may be noted that when bargaining over a single dimension (such as price), the set of PBE is independent of whether or not the uninformed player — who makes all the offers — may offer a menu of (price) contracts.

It will be shown below that for *any* $\Delta > 0$, in the unique PBE agreement is reached at time 0 with probability one, and, furthermore, the firm retains all of its bargaining power. This striking result sharply contrasts with the PBE derived in the model studied in the previous section in which the players bargain over a single dimension. Before proceeding further, it may be noted that with *perfect* information about the value of θ, the quality that maximizes the 'surplus' (or, gains from trade) $\sqrt{q} - \theta q$ is $q^* = 1/4\theta^2$, which is called the *first best* quality level.

9.7.1   The Commitment Equilibrium

As a preliminary exercise, I derive the menu of contracts that maximizes the firm's expected profit subject to appropriate incentive-compatibility and individual-rationality constraints. That is

$$\max_{m_b, m_g} \alpha(\sqrt{q_b} - w_b) + (1 - \alpha)(\sqrt{q_g} - w_g)$$

subject to $w_b - 2q_b \geq w_g - 2q_g$, $w_g - q_g \geq w_b - q_b$, $w_b - 2q_b \geq 0$ and $w_g - q_g \geq 0$. The former two inequalities respectively are the incentive-compatibility constraints for the bad-type worker and the good-type worker, while the latter two inequalities are their respective individual-rationality constraints. The solution to this maximization problem characterizes the equilibrium of the model in which the firm makes a take-it-or-leave-it-offer. As such I call it the *commitment equilibrium*, since it involves the firm being able to commit itself to making a single offer. It may be noted that the firm's payoff in any PBE of the repeated-offers model is less than or equal to her payoff in the commitment equilibrium.[28]

Let us now solve this maximization problem. It is straightforward to show that the single-crossing property of the worker's payoff function implies that at the optimum only the bad-type worker's individual-rationality constraint and the good-type worker's incentive-compatible constraint bind. Thus, at the optimum, $w_b = 2q_b$ and $w_g = w_b + q_g - q_b$. Using these expressions to substitute for w_b and w_g in the maximand, it follows that I need to now solve the following unconstrained maximization problem

$$\max_{q_b, q_g} \alpha(\sqrt{q_b} - 2q_b) + (1 - \alpha)(\sqrt{q_g} - q_g - q_b).$$

---

[28]One may, alternatively, provide the following (normative) interpretation of the maximization problem stated above. Its solution characterizes the maximum expected profit to the firm in any incentive-compatible and individually-rational direct revelation procedure. Hence, the Revelation Principle (which is stated in Section 9.2.2) implies that its solution characterizes the maximum expected profit to the firm in any BNE of any bargaining game.

The first-order conditions imply that the solution is

$$\widehat{q}_b = \frac{\alpha^2}{4(1+\alpha)^2} \quad \text{and} \quad \widehat{q}_g = \frac{1}{4}.$$

Hence, it follows that

$$\widehat{w}_b = \frac{\alpha^2}{2(1+\alpha)^2} \quad \text{and} \quad \widehat{w}_g = \frac{2\alpha^2 + 2\alpha + 1}{4(1+\alpha)^2}.$$

Therefore, the commitment equilibrium — i.e., the solution to the constrained maximization problem stated above — is the following menu of contracts: $\{\widehat{m}_b, \widehat{m}_g\}$, where $\widehat{m}_i = (\widehat{w}_i, \widehat{q}_i)$. It may be noted that in the commitment equilibrium the good-type worker produces her first-best quality, while the bad-type worker a suboptimal quality. Furthermore, the good-type worker's payoff is strictly positive, while the bad-type worker's payoff is zero.

9.7.2 The Unique Perfect Bayesian Equilibrium

In the following proposition I characterize the unique PBE of the repeated-offers model described above (in which the firm cannot commit to making a single offer).

Proposition 9.8. *For any $\Delta > 0$ there exists a unique PBE. In equilibrium agreement is reached at time 0 with probability one. The firm's equilibrium offer at time 0 is the menu of contracts $\{\widehat{m}_b, \widehat{m}_g\}$ that is offered in the commitment equilibrium stated above. The bad-type worker accepts the contract $\widehat{m}_b$ and the good-type worker accepts the contract $\widehat{m}_g$.*

Proof. Since the proof is rather lengthy, I omit it, and instead refer the reader to Wang (1998) — the author of this result. However, I now sketch an argument which shows that there *exists* a PBE that supports the outcome stated in the proposition. If the proposed equilibrium offer at time 0 — namely, $\{\widehat{m}_b, \widehat{m}_g\}$ — is rejected, then (since in the proposed equilibrium both types accept one of the two contracts in the equilibrium menu) a 'zero-probability' event has occurred. In the PBE the firm conjectures (following this zero-probability event) that the worker is good-type with probability one. Hence, in the subgame that begins at time 1, the players' strategies are the unique SPE strategies of the repeated-offers model with perfect information (that the worker is good-type). In this equilibrium the firm always offers a single contract, namely, $(w, q) = (1/4, 1/4)$. Such a contract gives the bad-type worker a negative payoff and the good-type worker a payoff of zero. Hence, both worker types will accept the appropriate contract from the equilibrium menu offered at time 0. The existence of the desired PBE follows immediately, since the firm has no incentive to offer at time 0 a menu that differs from $\{\widehat{m}_b, \widehat{m}_g\}$ — because, by definition, this equilibrium menu generates the maximum possible payoff that she can obtain in any PBE.[29]   □

This is a striking result, for many reasons. It shows that (in multi-dimensional bargaining situations) the *commitment equilibrium* is supported in the unique PBE of the repeated-offers model in which commitment to a single offer is not assumed possible. Furthermore, the unique PBE does not satisfy the Coase conjecture, since the firm retains all its bargaining power. In particular, the firm obtains her commitment equilibrium payoff. Moreover, agreement is reached without any costly delay. Of course, the PBE outcome is not *ex-post* efficient, since the bad-type worker does not produce the first best quality.

9.8   Notes

The normative question studied in Sections 9.2 and 9.4 was first studied by Myerson and Satterthwaite (1983) in the context of private values, and by Samuelson (1984) in the context of correlated values. Indeed, Proposition 9.3(b) is due to Myerson and Satterthwaite (1983). The focus of attention in these two sections is on whether or not the bargaining outcome can be *ex-post* efficient. When the bargaining outcome cannot be *ex-post* efficient, it might be interesting to derive the maximum expected gains from trade consummated in any BNE of any bargaining game. By the Revelation Principle this involves characterizing the incentive-compatible and individually-rational DRP with maximal consummated expected gains from

---

[29]The proof of *uniqueness* involves two key results. First, one shows that in *any* PBE the bad-type worker earns a payoff of zero. And then, using this result, one shows that in any PBE the firm's payoff equals her commitment equilibrium payoff.

trade. Myerson and Satterthwaite (1983) have addressed this normative issue in the context of private values, while Samuelson (1984) does the same with correlated values.

The application to litigation (in Sections 9.3.2 and 9.5.2) is inspired by Spier (1994) and Hay and Spier (1998). Spier (1994) studies the effect on the likelihood of an out-of-court settlement of various legal rules that allocate the private costs of litigation between the plantiff and the defendant — see also Bebchuk (1984) and Reinganum and Wilde (1986). Hay and Spier (1998) provide a nice discussion of the many fascinating issues involved on this topic, and a guide to the literature on litigation and (pre-trial) bargaining.

The repeated-offers bargaining model with asymmetric information studied in Section 9.6 was first studied by Fudenberg, Levine and Tirole (1985) and Gul, Sonnenschein and Wilson (1986) — in the context of private values and without retractable offers. Proposition 9.5 is due to them. However, Proposition 9.6 is due to Ausubel and Deneckere (1989). For an alternative exposition of the model, see Fudenberg and Tirole (1991) — who also show how this model may be reinterpreted as a model of the pricing behaviour of a durable-good monopolist. As such the model underlies the large literature on the Coase conjecture (put forward by Coase (1972)). The effect of retractable offers was studied in Muthoo (1994). The repeated-offers model with correlated values (but without retractable offers) has been studied in Evans (1989) and Vincent (1989). Not surprisingly (given Lemma 9.2), they show that (under some conditions) the (generically) unique PBE of the model is not *ex-post* efficient. In particular, the Coase conjecture is not satisfied by this equilibrium. The application studied in Section 9.7 is a special case of the model in Wang (1998).

I have not discussed the kinds of positive questions addressed in Section 9.6 in the context of models in which a player with private information can make offers. The reasons for this omission are two-fold: (i) such models are plagued by a great multiplicity of perfect Bayesian equilibria, since in such models an informed player has the opportunity to *signal* her private information when making a price offer, and (ii) the analysis of the PBE in such a model is quite complex. It is well known that *signalling* models — such as Spence's classic job market model (cf. Spence (1974)) — are characterized by a great multiplicity of perfect Bayesian equilibria. The root cause of such multiplicity of equilibria are the 'zero-probability' events that pervade signalling models. Following such an event, Bayes' rule cannot be used to update a player's beliefs. As such the player has to form *new* beliefs, which are called *conjectures*. Rubinstein (1985b) contains a discussion and analysis of several types of conjectures. For an overview of the literature on bargaining models in which a player with private information can make offers, see Fudenberg and Tirole (1991, Section 10.4).

10   Repeated Bargaining Situations

10.1   Introduction

In this chapter I study situations in which two players have the opportunity
to be involved in a sequence of (possibly different and/or interdependent)
bargaining situations. Such a situation will be called a 'repeated' bargaining
situation (RBS). Examples of repeated bargaining situations abound. For
instance: (i) in any marriage the wife and the husband are in a RBS, and (ii)
in most bilateral monopoly markets the seller and the buyer are in a RBS. To
illustrate the potential for interdependence amongst the bargaining situations in a RBS, consider a bilateral monopoly market for some input in which
the seller and the buyer have the opportunity to be involved in a sequence of
'one-shot' transactions, and suppose that the buyer's reservation value for
the input depends on the level of her capital stock. Since the price at which
trade occurs determines the buyer's profit — which, in turn, determines her
investment in capital stock — it follows that the buyer's reservation value
in any one transaction is determined by the outcomes of past transactions.
Hence, any pair of one-shot transactions are interdependent.

In Sections 10.2–10.4 I study repeated bargaining models, in which the
outcomes of any pair of bargaining situations are negotiated separately, and
moreover, the outcome of each bargaining situation is negotiated when (and
if) it materializes. Although in the formal structure of these repeated bar-

gaining models there is no reference to contracts, it is possible to provide the following contractual interpretation: the repeated bargaining models embody the notion that the RBS is governed by a sequence of short-term (or, limited-term) contracts.

Section 10.2 studies a model of a simple RBS in which two players sequentially bargain over the partition of an infinite number of cakes. Subject to two important qualifications, the repeated bargaining model studied here is an infinite repetition of Rubinstein's bargaining game (that is studied in Section 3.2). The reasons for studying this simple model are two-fold: (i) to lay down the basic structure of the models of relatively more complex repeated bargaining situations that are studied in later sections, and (ii) to focus attention on the role of the players' discount rates in repeated bargaining situations.

It will be shown that the impact of the players' discount rates on the outcome of the RBS depends on the *frequency* of the bargaining situations. For example, if this frequency is large, then it is possible that a player's share of each and every cake is increasing in her discount rate. In contrast, the opposite is the case in Rubinstein's bargaining model — when the players bargain over the partition of the single available cake.[1] Indeed, this result (and the other results derived in Section 10.2) imply that a RBS is fundamentally different from a single ('one-shot') bargaining situation.

Section 10.3 considers a RBS in which two players bargain in each period over the amount of the current output to save and invest in the creation of new capital, and over the partition of the remaining output for current consumption. The sequence of bargaining situations in this RBS are interdependent.

A key assumption of the repeated bargaining situations studied in Sections 10.2 and 10.3 is that the players do not have any outside options. This means, in particular, that they are *committed* to the RBS, in the sense that they will attempt to reach agreement in each and every bargaining situation. As such the players are in a *long-term relationship*. Section 10.4 explores the role of outside options in a simple RBS. An application to firm-provided general training is contained in Section 10.4.1.

---

[1]It will be shown that the repeated play of the unique subgame perfect equilibrium (SPE) of Rubinstein's model (cf. Theorem 3.1) is *not* an SPE of the repeated bargaining model studied in Section 10.2.

Section 10.5 studies the role of long-term contracts in repeated bargaining situations. Such a contract specifies the outcome of each and every bargaining situation to be encountered. A main message obtained is that long-term contracts can have a beneficial role in those repeated bargaining situations in which the parties have the opportunity to engage in relationship-specific investments that enhance the value of the RBS — notwithstanding the possibility that such contracts may be highly incomplete.

Section 10.6 explores the notion that in a RBS a player has an incentive to acquire a *reputation* for being a particular *type* of bargainer.

10.2   A Basic Repeated Bargaining Model

Consider a RBS in which two players have the opportunity to sequentially produce an infinite number of 'cakes'. Subject to two important qualifications, the model of this RBS described below is an infinite repetition of Rubinstein's bargaining game studied in Section 3.2. The first qualification is that the players start bargaining over the partition of the $(n+1)$th cake (where $n = 1, 2, \ldots$) if and only if they reach agreement on the partition of the nth cake. Thus, if the players perpetually disagree over the partition of the nth cake, then their relationship is terminated. The second qualification is that the time at which the players start bargaining over the partition of the $(n+1)$th cake is determined by the time at which agreement is struck over the partition of the nth cake. A description of the model now follows.

Two players, A and B, bargain over the partition of a cake of size π ($\pi >$ 0) according to the alternating-offers procedure (as described in Section 3.2). If agreement is reached at time t_1, where $t_1 = 0, \Delta, 2\Delta, \ldots$, and Δ ($\Delta > 0$) is the time interval between two consecutive offers, then immediately the players consume their respective (agreed) shares. Then τ ($\tau > 0$) time units later, at time $t_1 + \tau$, the players bargain over the partition of a second cake of size π according to the alternating-offers procedure. Agreement at time t_2, where $t_2 = t_1 + \tau, t_1 + \tau + \Delta, t_1 + \tau + 2\Delta, \ldots$, is followed immediately with the players consuming their respective (agreed) shares. Then τ time units later, at time $t_2 + \tau$, the players bargain over the partition of a third cake of size π according to the alternating-offers procedure. This process continues indefinitely, provided that the players always reach agreement. However, if the players perpetually disagree over the partition of some cake, then there is no further bargaining over new cakes; the players have terminated their relationship.[2] Without loss of generality, I assume that player i makes the first offer when bargaining begins over the partition of the $(n + 1)$th cake $(n = 1, 2, \dots)$ if it was player j $(j \neq i)$ whose offer over the partition of the nth cake was accepted by player i. Furthermore, player A makes the offer at time 0.

The payoffs to the players depend on the number N (where $N = 0, 1, 2, \dots$) of cakes that they partition. If $N = 0$ — that is, they perpetually disagree over the partition of the first cake — then each player's payoff is zero. If $1 \leq N < \infty$ — that is, they partition N cakes and perpetually disagree over the partition of the $(N + 1)$th cake — then player i's $(i = A, B)$ payoff is

$$\sum_{n=1}^{N} x_i^n \exp(-r_i t_n),$$

where x_i^n $(0 \leq x_i^n \leq \pi)$ is player i's share of the nth cake, t_n is the time at which agreement over the partition of the nth cake is struck, and r_i $(r_i > 0)$ is player i's discount rate. Finally, if $N = \infty$ — that is, they partition all the cakes — then player i's payoff is

$$\sum_{n=1}^{\infty} x_i^n \exp(-r_i t_n).$$

Define for each $i = A, B$, $\delta_i \equiv \exp(-r_i \Delta)$ and $\alpha_i \equiv \exp(-r_i \tau)$. The parameters δ_A and δ_B capture the bargaining frictions: they respectively represent the costs to players A and B of haggling over the partition of a cake. In contrast, the parameters α_A and α_B respectively represent the values to players A and B of future bargaining situations.

One main result obtained below (in Section 10.2.1) is that if $\tau > \Delta$, then in the unique stationary subgame perfect equilibrium player i's share of each and every cake is strictly increasing in δ_i, but strictly decreasing in α_i. This result implies that a decrease in r_i has two opposite effects on player i's equilibrium share of each and every cake — because a decrease in r_i increases both δ_i and α_i. It will be shown that under some plausible

---

[2]It may be noted that, therefore, this dynamic game is not a standard infinitely repeated game. For an analysis of such games, see any game theory text (such as Fudenberg and Tirole (1991), Gibbons (1992) and Osborne and Rubinstein (1994)).

conditions the effect through α_i dominates that through δ_i, thus implying that as player i becomes more patient her equilibrium share of each and every cake decreases. Before I turn to a derivation of these (and other) results, the following remarks are in order.

Remark 10.1 (On the notion of long-term relationships). Loosely stated, the players in a RBS are in a *long-term relationship* if they are somewhat committed to the RBS — that is, they expect to exploit most of the bargaining situations in the RBS, since the cost to each player of refusing to do so is sufficiently high. For example: (i) if the cost of divorce to either partner is sufficiently high, then the married couple are in a long-term relationship, and (ii) if the players have no outside options (such as in the RBS modelled above), then the players are in a long-term relationship. On the other hand, for example, if at least one player's outside option is sufficiently attractive, then the players need not be in a long-term relationship — since the player concerned could choose (with negligible cost) to exercise her attractive outside option at any point during the RBS.

Remark 10.2 (Finite versus infinite number of bargaining situations). In the repeated bargaining model described above it is assumed that the players have the opportunity to sequentially produce an *infinite* number of cakes — that is, there exists an *infinite* sequence of bargaining situations. This is not an unreasonable assumption. Many repeated bargaining situations — such as those in a marriage (which can potentially last forever) — are literally consistent with this assumption. Furthermore, an alternative model in which it is assumed that there is a *finite* number of bargaining situations is not particularly plausible, since such a model (implicitly) assumes that the players know (from the start of their relationship) the exact number of cakes that they can partition. In most repeated bargaining situations in which the players know that they will encounter a *finite* number of bargaining situations, it is typically the case that the players are *uncertain* about the exact number of bargaining situations that they will encounter. A simple extension and/or re-interpretation of the repeated bargaining model described above is the appropriate model of such a RBS.[3]

---

[3]For example, α_i may be interpreted as player i's probabilistic belief that they can partition another cake after consuming the current cake.

Remark 10.3 (Simplifying assumptions). The RBS modelled above is very simple. For example, it is assumed that the bargaining situations in the RBS are identical. This assumption has been deliberately chosen so as to develop some of the *fundamental* insights (especially about the role of the players' discount rates) in a simple manner. It is, however, conceptually straightforward to extend the model to more complex (and more realistic) repeated bargaining situations. In Section 10.3, for example, I consider a RBS in which the size of the $(n+1)$th cake is determined by the outcome of the nth cake.

Remark 10.4 (Two interpretations). One interpretation of the repeated bargaining model described above is as follows. Two players have the opportunity to engage in an infinite sequence of 'one-shot' transactions, where π denotes the size of the *surplus* generated from each one-shot transaction and τ the *frequency* of such one-shot transactions. The outcomes of any pair of one-shot transactions are negotiated separately, and, moreover, the outcome of each one-shot transaction is negotiated when (and if) it materializes. Letting a *one-shot* contract denote a contract that specifies the outcome of a single one-shot transaction, the model embodies the notion that the long-term relationship is governed by a sequence of one-shot contracts. An alternative interpretation of the model is as follows. Two players have the opportunity to generate (through some form of co-operation) a *flow* of money at rate $\widehat{\pi}$. They bargain over a contract that specifies the partition of the money over the duration of the contract, where τ is the *duration* of the contract. Thus, the present discounted value of the total amount of money generated over the duration of any single contract is $\pi = \widehat{\pi}[1 - \exp(-r_m\tau)]/r_m$, where r_m $(r_m > 0)$ is the market interest rate. The model embodies the notion that the long-term relationship is governed by a sequence of *limited-term* contracts (of duration τ).

10.2.1 The Unique Stationary Subgame Perfect Equilibrium

Fix an arbitrary subgame perfect equilibrium (SPE) that satisfies Properties 3.1 and 3.2 (which are stated in Section 3.2.1). Property 3.1 states that whenever a player has to make an offer, her equilibrium offer is accepted by the other player, while Property 3.2 states that in equilibrium a player makes the same offer whenever she has to make an offer.

Given Property 3.2, let x_i^* ($i = A, B$) denote the equilibrium offer that player i makes whenever she has to make an offer. I adopt the convention that an offer is the share to the proposer. Furthermore, letting V_i^* denote player i's equilibrium payoff in any subgame beginning with her offer, it follows from Properties 3.1 and 3.2 that $V_i^* = x_i^* + \alpha_i(\pi - x_j^*) + \alpha_i^2 V_i^*$ ($j \neq i$). Hence, it follows that

$$V_A^* = \frac{x_A^* + \alpha_A(\pi - x_B^*)}{1 - \alpha_A^2} \quad \text{and} \quad V_B^* = \frac{x_B^* + \alpha_B(\pi - x_A^*)}{1 - \alpha_B^2}. \tag{10.1}$$

Consider an arbitrary point in time at which player i has to make an offer to player j. By definition, player j's equilibrium payoff from rejecting any offer is $\delta_j V_j^*$. Therefore, perfection requires that player j accept any offer x_i (where $0 \leq x_i \leq \pi$) such that $\pi - x_i + \alpha_j V_j^* > \delta_j V_j^*$, and reject any offer x_i such that $\pi - x_i + \alpha_j V_j^* < \delta_j V_j^*$. Hence, if $\Delta \geq \tau$, then optimality implies that $x_A^* = x_B^* = \pi$.

On the other hand, if $\Delta < \tau$ then player i is indifferent between accepting and rejecting player j's equilibrium offer.[4] That is

$$\pi - x_B^* + \alpha_A V_A^* = \delta_A V_A^* \quad \text{and} \quad \pi - x_A^* + \alpha_B V_B^* = \delta_B V_B^*. \tag{10.2}$$

After substituting for V_A^* and V_B^* in (10.2) using (10.1), and then solving for x_A^* and x_B^*, it follows that

$$x_A^* = \frac{(1 - \delta_A \alpha_A)(1 - \delta_B)(1 + \alpha_B)\pi}{(1 - \delta_A \alpha_A)(1 - \delta_B \alpha_B) - (\delta_A - \alpha_A)(\delta_B \quad \alpha_B)} \quad \text{and} \tag{10.3}$$

$$x_B^* = \frac{(1 - \delta_B \alpha_B)(1 - \delta_A)(1 + \alpha_A)\pi}{(1 - \delta_A \alpha_A)(1 - \delta_B \alpha_B) - (\delta_A - \alpha_A)(\delta_B - \alpha_B)}. \tag{10.4}$$

Hence, I have characterized the unique SPE that satisfies Properties 3.1 and 3.2, which is described in the following proposition.

Proposition 10.1. *The unique subgame perfect equilibrium that satisfies Properties 3.1 and 3.2 is as follows:*
- *player A always offers x_A^* and always accepts an offer x_B if and only if $x_B \leq x_B^*$,*
- *player B always offers x_B^* and always accepts an offer x_A if and only if $x_A \leq x_A^*$,*

---

[4]It should be noted that $\Delta < \tau$ implies that $\pi + \alpha_j V_j^* > \delta_j V_j^*$, because by definition $V_j^* \leq \pi/(1 - \alpha_j)$.

where if $\Delta \geq \tau$ then $x_A^* = x_B^* = \pi$, and if $\Delta < \tau$ then x_A^* and x_B^* are respectively stated in equations 10.3 and 10.4. In equilibrium agreement is reached immediately over the partition of each and every cake. The equilibrium partition of the nth cake is $(x_A^*, \pi - x_A^*)$ if n is odd (i.e., $n = 1, 3, 5, \ldots$), and $(\pi - x_B^*, x_B^*)$ if n is even (i.e., $n = 2, 4, 6, \ldots$).

Remark 10.5 (Stationary SPE). A *stationary* SPE is a subgame perfect equilibrium that satisfies Property 3.2 and the following property: in equilibrium, for any offer $x_i \in [0, \pi]$ made by player i, player j always either accepts it or rejects it.[5] Proposition 10.1 characterizes the unique stationary SPE, because — as I now show — any stationary SPE must satisfy Property 3.1. Suppose, to the contrary, that there exists a stationary SPE that does not satisfy Property 3.1. This means that there exists an i ($i = A$ or $i = B$) such that player i's equilibrium offer x_i^* is always rejected by player j. Let V_j and W_i respectively denote player j's and player i's equilibrium payoffs in any subgame beginning with player j's offer. It must be the case that $\pi - x_i^* + \alpha_j V_j \leq \delta_j V_j$. If $\Delta > \tau$, then a contradiction is obtained. Hence, in what follows, assume that $\Delta \leq \tau$. In this stationary SPE player j accepts any offer x_i such that $\pi - x_i + \alpha_j V_j > \delta_j V_j$. Fix an arbitrary subgame beginning with player i's offer, and suppose player i considers the following one-shot deviation: she offers x_i' such that $x_i' < \pi + (\alpha_j - \delta_j)V_j$. Any such offer is accepted by player j. Hence, if there exists such an x_i' that makes the one-shot deviation profitable for player i, then a contradiction is obtained. This will be the case if there exists an $x_i' < \pi + (\alpha_j - \delta_j)V_j$ such that $x_i' + \alpha_i W_i > \delta_i W_i$, which is implied if the following inequality holds: $\pi + (\alpha_j - \delta_j)V_j > (\delta_i - \alpha_i)W_i$ — that is, $\pi > (\delta_j - \alpha_j)V_j + (\delta_i - \alpha_i)W_i$. If player j's equilibrium offer is also always rejected by player i, then $V_j = W_i = 0$. On the other hand, if player j's equilibrium offer x_j^* is always accepted by player i, then $V_j = x_j^*/(1 - \alpha_j^2)$ and $W_i = (1 - x_j^*)/(1 - \alpha_i^2)$. In either case, the desired inequality holds.

Hence, if $\Delta \geq \tau$, then in the unique stationary subgame perfect equilibrium (SSPE) player A obtains the whole of the nth cake when n is odd and player B obtains the whole of the nth cake when n is even. The intuition behind this result is that if $\Delta \geq \tau$, then (in a SSPE) the proposer effectively

---

[5]This property and Property 3.2 imply that each player's strategy is history-independent.

makes a 'take-it-or-leave-it-offer'. Although this result is rather provocative, it is not plausible that $\Delta \geq \tau$. It is more likely that $\tau > \Delta$ — the time interval between two consecutive offers during bargaining over the partition of any cake is smaller than the time taken for the 'arrival' of a new cake. Indeed, in terms of either interpretation described above in Remark 10.4, it is implausible that $\Delta \geq \tau$. Hence, from now on I assume that $\tau > \Delta$.

Before proceeding further, however, I note that (in general) the unique SSPE partition of each and every cake is different from the unique SPE partition of the *single* available cake in Rubinstein's bargaining model (cf. Theorem 3.1). The intuition for this difference — which is further developed below — is based on the following observation. In Rubinstein's model the cost to player i of rejecting an offer is captured by δ_i; rejecting an offer shrinks, from player i's perspective, the single available cake by a factor of δ_i. In contrast, in the model studied here the rejection of an offer not only shrinks the current cake, but it also shrinks *all* the future cakes, thus inducing a relatively higher cost of rejecting an offer.

As is evident from the expressions for x_A^* and x_B^* in (10.3) and (10.4), when $\tau > \Delta$ the equilibrium partition of each and every cake depends on the parameters r_A, r_B, Δ and τ in a rather complex manner. However, one of the main insights of the model can be obtained in a simple manner by examining the impact of the *derived* parameters α_A, α_B, δ_A and δ_B on the unique SSPE partitions. Notice that if $\tau > \Delta$, then $\delta_i > \alpha_i$ ($i = A, B$).

Corollary 10.1. *For each $i = A, B$, x_i^* is (i) strictly increasing in δ_i on the set Z, (ii) strictly decreasing in α_i on the set Z, (iii) strictly decreasing in δ_j ($j \neq i$) on the set Z and (iv) strictly increasing in α_j on the set Z, where*

$$Z = \{(\alpha_A, \alpha_B, \delta_A, \delta_B) : \delta_A > \alpha_A \text{ and } \delta_B > \alpha_B\}.$$

Proof. The corollary follows in a straightforward manner from the four derivatives of x_i^* (which is stated in (10.3)–(10.4)) — with respect to δ_i, α_i, δ_j and α_j. $\qquad\square$

It follows immediately from Corollary 10.1 and Proposition 10.1 that if $\tau > \Delta$, then player i's share of *each and every cake* in the unique SSPE is strictly increasing in δ_i, but strictly decreasing in α_i. The former effect is consistent with the insight obtained in the context of Rubinstein's bargaining model when the players bargain over the partition of the *single* available cake (cf. Theorem 3.1; for intuition, see Section 3.2.3). The latter effect, however, is novel, but the intuition behind it is straightforward. As α_i increases, the value to player i of future bargaining situations increases. Thus, when bargaining over the partition of any cake, her desire to proceed to bargain over the partition of the next cake has increased, which works to player j's advantage.

Notice that Corollary 10.1 implies that a decrease in r_i has two opposite effects on player i's equilibrium share of each and every cake — because a decrease in r_i increases both δ_i and α_i. It will be shown below that if Δ is arbitrarily small and (for each $i = A, B$) $r_i\tau > 0$ but small, then the effect through α_i dominates that through δ_i, thus implying that as player i becomes more patient her equilibrium share of each and every cake decreases.

10.2.2   Small Time Intervals Between Consecutive Offers

In Corollary 10.2 below I characterize the unique SSPE in the limit, as $\Delta \to 0$. I focus attention on this limit because it is the most persuasive case (cf. the discussion in Section 3.2.4). Besides, the expressions for x_A^* and x_B^* in this limit are relatively more transparent compared to those in (10.3) and (10.4).

Corollary 10.2. *Fix any* $r_A > 0$, $r_B > 0$ *and* $\tau > 0$. *In the limit, as* $\Delta \to 0$, x_A^* *and* x_B^* *(as defined in Proposition 10.1) respectively converge to*

$$z_A^* = \frac{r_B\pi}{r_B + \phi_A r_A} \quad and \quad z_B^* = \frac{r_A\pi}{r_A + \phi_B r_B}, \quad where$$

$$\phi_A = \frac{(1+\alpha_A)(1-\alpha_B)}{(1-\alpha_A)(1+\alpha_B)} \quad and \quad \phi_B = \frac{(1+\alpha_B)(1-\alpha_A)}{(1-\alpha_B)(1+\alpha_A)}.$$

Furthermore, the payoffs to players A *and* B *in the limiting (as* $\Delta \to 0$*) unique SSPE are respectively*

$$V_A^{**} = \frac{z_A^*}{1-\alpha_A} \quad and \quad V_B^{**} = \frac{z_B^*}{1-\alpha_B}.$$

Proof. Fix $\tau > \Delta$. When $\Delta > 0$ but small, $\delta_i = 1 - r_i\Delta$. Using this to substitute for δ_A and δ_B in (10.3) and (10.4), it follows (after simplifying) that when $\Delta > 0$ but small

$$x_A^* = \frac{(1 - \alpha_A + r_A \alpha_A \Delta)(1 + \alpha_B) r_B \Delta \pi}{(1 - \alpha_A \alpha_B)(r_A + r_B - r_A r_B \Delta)\Delta + (\alpha_B - \alpha_A)(r_B - r_A)\Delta} \quad \text{and}$$

$$x_B^* = \frac{(1 - \alpha_B + r_B \alpha_B \Delta)(1 + \alpha_A) r_A \Delta \pi}{(1 - \alpha_A \alpha_B)(r_A + r_B - r_A r_B \Delta)\Delta + (\alpha_A - \alpha_B)(r_A - r_B)\Delta}.$$

After dividing the numerator and the denominator of each of these expressions by Δ, and then letting Δ tend to zero, it follows that $x_i^* \to z_i^*$. Since $z_A^* + z_B^* = \pi$, it follows from Proposition 10.1 that the equilibrium payoffs in this limit are as stated in the corollary. $\qquad \square$

It follows from Corollaries 10.2 and 3.1 that unless $\phi_A = \phi_B = 1$, the limiting (as $\Delta \to 0$) unique SSPE partition of each and every cake in the repeated bargaining model is different from the limiting (as $\Delta \to 0$) unique SPE partition of the single available cake in Rubinstein's bargaining model. Notice that for any $r_A > 0$, $r_B > 0$ and $\tau > 0$, $\phi_i = 1$ if and only if $r_A = r_B$. Furthermore, since $\phi_i \to 1$ as $r_i \tau \to \infty$, it follows that when $r_A \neq r_B$, the limiting (as $\Delta \to 0$) unique SSPE partition of each and every cake will have similar properties to the limiting (as $\Delta \to 0$) unique SPE partition of the single available cake in Rubinstein's model if and only if the value to each player of future bargaining situations is arbitrarily small.

The following corollary characterizes the properties of the limiting (as $\Delta \to 0$) unique SSPE when $r_A \neq r_B$ and (for each $i = A, B$) $r_i \tau$ is small (which means that the value to player i of future bargaining situations is large).

Corollary 10.3. *Assume that $r_A \neq r_B$, $r_A \tau > 0$ but small and $r_B \tau > 0$ but small.*
(i) *z_i^* ($i = A, B$) is strictly increasing in r_i, and strictly decreasing in r_j ($j \neq i$).*
(ii) *If $r_i > r_j$ ($i \neq j$), then $z_i^* > z_j^*$.*
(iii) *If $r_i > r_j$ ($i \neq j$), then $V_i^{**} < V_j^{**}$.*
(iv) *V_i^{**} ($i = A, B$) is strictly decreasing in r_i, and strictly decreasing in r_j ($j \neq i$).*
(v) *If $r_i > r_j$ ($i \neq j$) then z_i^* is strictly increasing in τ, and if $r_i < r_j$ then z_i^* is strictly decreasing in τ.*
(vi) *In the limit as $r_A \tau \to 0$ and $r_B \tau \to 0$, $z_A^* \to \pi/2$ and $z_B^* \to \pi/2$.*

Proof. When $r_i\tau > 0$ but small, $\alpha_i = 1 - r_i\tau$. Using this to substitute for α_A and α_B in the expressions for ϕ_A and ϕ_B (stated in Corollary 10.2), it follows that when (for each $i = A, B$) $r_i\tau > 0$ but small

$$\phi_A = \frac{(2 - r_A\tau)r_B}{r_A(2 - r_B\tau)} \quad \text{and} \quad \phi_B = \frac{(2 - r_B\tau)r_A}{r_B(2 - r_A\tau)}.$$

This implies that when (for each $i = A, B$) $r_i\tau > 0$ but small

$$z_A^* = \frac{(2 - r_B\tau)\pi}{4 - (r_A + r_B)\tau} \quad \text{and} \quad z_B^* = \frac{(2 - r_A\tau)\pi}{4 - (r_A + r_B)\tau}.$$

The results in the corollary are now straightforward to derive, given these simple expressions for z_A^* and z_B^*. □

Corollary 10.3(i) states that when $r_A \neq r_B$ and the value to each player of future bargaining situations is large, player i's ($i = A, B$) share of each and every cake in the limiting (as $\Delta \to 0$) unique SSPE decreases as she becomes more patient and/or her opponent becomes less patient. In contrast, in Rubinstein's bargaining model a player's share of the single available cake in the limiting (as $\Delta \to 0$) unique SPE increases as she becomes more patient and/or her opponent becomes less patient (cf. Corollary 3.1). Thus, this fundamental insight of Rubinstein's model does not carry over to long-term relationships when the players have the opportunity to bargain (sequentially) over the partition of an infinite number of cakes and the value to each player of future bargaining situations is large. The intuition behind this conclusion is as follows.

In the repeated bargaining model studied here a player's discount rate determines not only her cost of rejecting an offer, but also her value of future bargaining situations. Suppose that one of the players — say, player i — becomes more patient. This means that her cost of rejecting an offer decreases. However, it also means that her value of future bargaining situations increases. When bargaining over the partition of a cake, the former effect increases her bargaining power (as she is more willing to reject offers), but the latter effect decreases her bargaining power — because she is more willing to accept offers so that the players can proceed to bargain over the partition of the next cake (cf. Corollary 10.1). When Δ is arbitrarily small the former effect is negligible, and when $r_i\tau > 0$ (but small) the latter effect is non-negligible. Thus, the latter effect dominates the former effect.

The above argument also provides intuition for the result stated in Corollary 10.3(ii) that the less patient of the two players receives a greater share of each and every cake. Not surprisingly, however, the limiting (as $\Delta \rightarrow 0$) unique SSPE *payoff* of the less patient of the two players is smaller than her opponent's limiting unique SSPE payoff (Corollary 10.3(iii)). This means that the more patient player's *overall* bargaining power *in the long-term relationship* is relatively higher. And Corollary 10.3(iv) shows that overall bargaining power increases as she becomes even more patient, but decreases as her opponent becomes less patient.

Corollary 10.3(v) implies that the more patient player's limiting (as $\Delta \rightarrow 0$) SSPE share of each and every cake decreases as τ increases. The intuition behind this conclusion runs as follows. As τ increases, the decrease in the more patient player's value of future bargaining situations is smaller than the decrease in her opponent's value of future bargaining situations, which works to her opponent's advantage.

Notice that if $r_A\tau > 0$ and $r_B\tau > 0$, then the players' shares of each and every cake (and payoffs) in the limiting (as $\Delta \rightarrow 0$) unique SSPE depend on the *relative* magnitude of the players' discount rates. However, Corollary 10.3(vi) shows that in the limit as $r_A\tau \rightarrow 0$ and $r_B\tau \rightarrow 0$, this is no longer true. This implies that (under these limiting conditions) the players' bargaining powers are identical no matter how patient or impatient player A is *relative* to player B. Hence, the insight of Rubinstein's bargaining model — that the *relative* magnitude of the players' discount rates critically determine the players' bargaining powers even when the time interval between two consecutive offers is arbitrarily small — does not carry over to long-term relationships when the players have the opportunity to bargain (sequentially) over an infinite number of cakes and the value to each player of future bargaining situations is arbitrarily large.

10.2.3 Comparison with a Long-Term Contract

For any $r_A > 0$, $r_B > 0$ and $\tau > 0$, the payoffs to players A and B in the limiting (as $\Delta \rightarrow 0$) unique SSPE are respectively V_A^{**} and V_B^{**} as stated in Corollary 10.2. With reference to the interpretations described above in Remark 10.4, these are the players' (equilibrium) payoffs from their long-term relationship when that relationship is governed by a sequence of short-term contracts. It is instructive to compare these payoffs with those the players obtain if, instead, their relationship is governed by a long-term contract, which is the unique SPE outcome of the following non-repeated bargaining model.

The players bargain (according to the alternating-offers procedure) over long-term contracts, where such a contract specifies the same partition of each and every cake. Thus, a long-term contract is characterized by a single number $x \in [0, \pi]$, which denotes player A's share of each and every cake. If agreement is reached at time $t = 0, \Delta, 2\Delta, \ldots$ on a long-term contract $x \in [0, \pi]$, then bargaining ends and the payoffs to players A and B are respectively

$$\frac{x \exp(-r_A t)}{1 - \alpha_A} \quad \text{and} \quad \frac{(\pi - x) \exp(-r_B t)}{1 - \alpha_B}.$$

If the players perpetually disagree, then each player's payoff is zero. This model is very similar to Rubinstein's bargaining model studied in Section 3.2. Indeed, the unique SPE of this model is similar to the unique SPE of Rubinstein's bargaining model. In particular, in the limiting (as $\Delta \to 0$) unique SPE player i ($i = A, B$) receives a share $r_j \pi / (r_A + r_B)$ ($j \neq i$) of each and every cake. Hence, it follows that for any $r_A > 0$, $r_B > 0$ and $\tau > 0$, the payoffs to players A and B in the limiting (as $\Delta \to 0$) unique SPE of this alternative model are respectively

$$V_A^{LT} = \frac{r_B \pi}{(1 - \alpha_A)(r_A + r_B)} \quad \text{and} \quad V_B^{LT} = \frac{r_A \pi}{(1 - \alpha_B)(r_A + r_B)}.$$

It is straightforward to establish the following corollary, which provides the desired comparison.

Corollary 10.4. *For any $r_A > 0$, $r_B > 0$ and $\tau > 0$*

$$V_i^{**} \gtreqless V_i^{LT} \quad \text{if and only if} \quad r_i \gtreqless r_j \quad (i, j = A, B \text{ and } j \neq i).$$

Thus, if the players are equally patient/impatient ($r_A = r_B$), then each player is indifferent between the equilibrium sequence of short-term contracts and the equilibrium long-term contract. If, on the other hand, player i is more impatient than player j ($r_i > r_j$), then player i prefers the equilibrium sequence of short-term contracts over the equilibrium long-term contract, while player j has the opposite preference. The intuition for this conclusion is based on the intuition provided for Corollary 10.3(i). In the repeated bargaining model the more patient player is more keen to secure agreement over a short-term contract — so as to consummate it, and then proceed to the next set of negotiations over another short-term contract. This works to the advantage of the less patient player. However, when bargaining over long-term contracts, this advantage (to the less patient player) is not present. That is why the more patient player prefers the equilibrium long-term contract, while the less patient player prefers the equilibrium sequence of short-term contracts.

10.2.4   Non-Stationary Subgame Perfect Equilibria

In this section I explore the potential existence of *non-stationary* SPE.[6] The following lemma establishes the existence (for some values of the parameters) of two non-stationary SPE, which are described in Table 10.1. In one SPE play begins in state s_A, while in the other SPE play begins in state s_B. In both of these equilibria agreement is reached immediately on the partition of each and every cake. In the SPE in which play begins in state s_i $(i = A, B)$, player i obtains, for all n $(n = 1, 2, 3, \dots)$, the whole of the nth cake. Thus, in this SPE players i and j $(j \neq i)$ respectively obtain their best and worst possible SPE payoffs.

Lemma 10.1. *The pair of strategies described in Table 10.1 is a SPE if and only if $\alpha_A + \delta_A \geq 1$ and $\alpha_B + \delta_B \geq 1$. If play begins in state s_i $(i = A, B)$, then in equilibrium for all n $(n = 1, 2, 3, \dots)$ agreement over the partition of the nth cake is reached immdiately with player i obtaining the whole of the nth cake.*

Proof. Using the *One-Shot Deviation* property it is straightforward to verify that the pair of strategies described in Table 10.1 is a SPE if and only if $\alpha_A + \delta_A \geq 1$ and $\alpha_B + \delta_B \geq 1$. Note that if and only if $\alpha_i + \delta_i \geq 1$ is it optimal for player i in state s_i to reject any offer x_j such that $0 < x_j \leq \pi$.   □

Given the existence of these two ('extremal') SPE, it is straightforward to show that if $\alpha_A + \delta_A \geq 1$ and $\alpha_B + \delta_B \geq 1$, then there exists a large number (indeed, a continuum) of other non-stationary SPE. Indeed, any sequence of

---

[6]In such a SPE a player's strategy is history-dependent.

		state s_A	state s_B
	offer	$x_A^* = \pi$	$x_A^* = 0$
Player A	accept	$x_B = 0$	$0 \le x_B \le \pi$
	rejects	$0 < x_B \le \pi$	——
	offer	$x_B^* = 0$	$x_B^* = \pi$
Player B	accept	$0 \le x_A \le \pi$	$x_A = 0$
	rejects	——	$0 < x_A \le \pi$
	transitions	switch to state s_B if an offer x_B such that $0 < x_B \le \pi$ is accepted by player A	switch to state s_A if an offer x_A such that $0 < x_A \le \pi$ is accepted by player B

Table 10.1: Two non-stationary SPE in the repeated bargaining model.

bargaining outcomes can be supported by a non-stationary SPE.[7] The basic idea is as follows. Fix an arbitrary sequence of bargaining outcomes. Consider the path of play that generates this sequence, and in which each player otherwise always demands the whole cake. This path of play is supported as a SPE path by the threat of reverting to an appropriate extremal SPE: if player i deviates from the path of play, then the appropriate extremal SPE is the one which gives player i her worst possible SPE payoff (which is a payoff of zero). I state this result in the following proposition.

Proposition 10.2. *If $\alpha_A + \delta_A \ge 1$ and $\alpha_B + \delta_B \ge 1$, then there exists a large number (continuum) of non-stationary SPE. In particular, any sequence of bargaining outcomes can be supported by a non-stationary SPE.*

In the limit, as $\Delta \to 0$, the hypothesis (namely, the two inequalities) of Proposition 10.2 are valid, and thus, in this limit there exists a large number of (non-stationary) SPE. It should be noted that this result is valid for any

---

[7]In an arbitrary sequence of bargaining outcomes agreement is reached over the partition of N cakes (where $0 \le N \le \infty$), and the players perpetually disagree over the partition of the $(N+1)$th cake. The sequence also specifies the times at which agreements are struck, and the agreed partitions.

$r_A > 0$, $r_B > 0$ and $\tau > 0$ (i.e., for any $\alpha_A \in (0,1)$ and $\alpha_B \in (0,1)$).[8] The case of $\tau \to \infty$, in particular, has the following striking interpretation. The uniqueness property of Rubinstein's bargaining model (cf. Theorem 3.1) is not robust to small 'external effects', in the sense that the basic indeterminacy of a bargaining situation is re-obtained if the players expect to bargain, *with an arbitrarily small probability*, over the partition of another cake each time they reach agreement over the partition of an existing cake.[9]

Remark 10.6 (Static versus dynamic efficiency). The unique stationary SPE is efficient in the following 'static' sense: agreement over the partition of each and every cake is reached without any costly delay. However, as I now show, when $r_A \neq r_B$ it is not efficient in the following 'dynamic' sense: there exists an alternative sequence of partitions of the cakes that makes both players strictly better-off (in terms of their payoffs). Suppose that $r_B > r_A$, and consider the following alternative sequence of partitions of the cakes: player B receives the whole of the first N cakes, and player A the whole of the remaining (infinite number of) cakes. The payoffs to players A and B respectively from this alternative sequence are $\alpha_A^N \pi / (1 - \alpha_A)$ and $(1 - \alpha_B^N)\pi / (1 - \alpha_B)$, where $\alpha_i^N = \exp(-r_i \tau N)$ $(i = A, B)$. It is straightforward to verify that since $r_B > r_A$, there exists an N such that each player's payoff from this alternative sequence is strictly greater than her payoff in the unique SSPE (which is stated in Corollary 10.2). In contrast, there exist non-stationary SPE which satisfy neither notions of efficiency, and there also exist non-stationary SPE that do satisfy both notions of efficiency.[10]

---

[8]In contrast, in a standard infinitely repeated game it is typically the case that a multiplicity of SPE is obtainable if and only if the discount factors (α_A and α_B) are sufficiently large — see any game theory text (such as Fudenberg and Tirole (1991), Gibbons (1992) and Osborne and Rubinstein (1994)).

[9]This interpretation makes sense since α, where $\alpha = \alpha_A = \alpha_B$, may be interpreted as the *probability* that the players (expect to) bargain over the partition of *another* cake after reaching agreement over the partition of the currently available cake.

[10]A sequence of bargaining outcomes is dynamically efficient when $r_B > r_A$ — that is, maximizes one player's payoff subject to her opponent receiving some fixed payoff level u — only if there exists an $N \geq 1$ (which depends on u) such that the more patient player A receives the whole of the nth cake for all $n > N$, and if $N > 1$ then the less patient player receives the whole of the nth cake for all $n < N$. It should be noted that a sequence of bargaining outcomes satisfies dynamic efficiency only if it satisfies static efficiency, but not vice-versa.

10.3 An Application to Dynamic Capital Investment

Two players, A and B, have access to a technology of production which allows them to generate output by using capital as input. The output per period is $F(K)$ if the capital stock is K, where the production function F is continuously differentiable, strictly increasing and strictly concave. Furthermore

$$F(0) = 0, \quad \lim_{K \to \infty} F'(K) = 0 \quad \text{and} \quad \lim_{K \to 0} F'(K) = \infty.$$

The initial capital stock is $K_1 > 0$. Capital depreciates during the production process at a constant rate γ per period, where $0 < \gamma < 1$. It does not, however, depreciate when it is not in use (such as during the bargaining process).

At the beginning of each period the players bargain over the amount of output to be saved and invested in the creation of new capital, and over the partition of the remaining output for their current consumption. Letting I_n denote the quantity of output saved and invested in period n (where $n = 1, 2, 3, \dots$), it follows that the capital stock in period $n + 1$ is

$$K_{n+1} = (1 - \gamma)K_n + I_n.$$

The model of the repeated bargaining situation faced by the two players is an extension of the repeated bargaining model studied in Section 10.2. In particular, at time 0 the players bargain (according to the alternating-offers procedure) over how much of the output $F(K_1)$ to save and invest, and how to partition the remaining output for their current consumption. Thus, an offer may be described by a pair of numbers (x, I) where $0 \le x, I \le F(K_1)$ and $x + I \le F(K_1)$, with the following interpretation: I denotes the quantity of output saved for investment, while x and $F(K_1) - I - x$ respectively denote the shares to the proposer and the responder of the remaining output for their current consumption. If agreement is reached at time t_1, then immediately they produce the output, save and invest the agreed quantity I_1, and consume their respective (agreed) shares of the remaining output.[11]

---

[11]If the players perpetually disagree, then no output is produced — and furthermore, the players' relationship is terminated and each player's payoff is zero.

Then, τ time units later — that is, next period — the process starts again with capital stock $K_2 = (1 - \gamma)K_1 + I_1$, and so on.

Notice that the output level in period $n + 1$ is $F(K_{n+1})$. Hence, since (for any $n \geq 1$) K_{n+1} depends on the investment level I_n agreed to in the previous period, the output level in period $n + 1$ depends on the outcome of bargaining in the previous period. As such the sequence of bargaining situations in this RBS are interdependent.

One could now proceed to study the set of *Markov* subgame perfect equilibria of this dynamic model, in which each player adopts a Markov strategy. In such a strategy a player's offer is conditioned only upon the current capital stock, and her response to any offer is conditioned only upon that offer and the current capital stock.[12] Thus, a Markov strategy for player i can be defined by three functions x_i^*, I_i^* and R_i^*, with the following interpretation. Whenever player i has to make an offer, she offers $(x_i^*(K), I_i^*(K))$ if the current capital stock is K, and whenever she has to respond to any offer (x_j, I_j) made by player j $(j \neq i)$, her response is $R_i^*(x_j, I_j, K) \in \{\text{Accept}, \text{Reject}\}$.

Although the analysis of the set of Markov SPE of this dynamic model is conceptually straightforward, it is technically demanding, and hence I leave it for future research. Instead, in the following section I characterize the unique steady state SSPE of the model under the assumption that the players do not bargain in any period over the investment level, which allows for a straightforward application of Proposition 10.1.

Bargaining Equilibrium with an Exogenous Savings Rate

Assume that the players do not bargain (in any period) over the investment level. The amount of output that will be invested in period n $(n = 1, 2, 3, \ldots)$ is $sF(K_n)$, where s $(0 < s < 1)$ is an exogenously given savings rate. This assumption implies that the sequence of bargaining situations are not interdependent. Furthermore, the output level $F(K_{n+1})$ in period $n + 1$ (for any $n \geq 1$) is exogenously given, since the capital stock K_{n+1} in period $n + 1$ is uniquely determined by the following recursive equation

$$K_{n+1} = (1 - \gamma)K_n + sF(K_n),$$

---

[12]History matters only to the extent that it determines the current capital stock and the current offer.

where $K_1 > 0$ is exogenously given.

Given our assumptions on F, the equation $sF(K) = \gamma K$ has a unique (strictly positive) solution, which is denoted by K^* — it is the unique (strictly positive) *steady state* capital stock. If, for some N ($N \geq 1$), $K_N = K^*$, then, for all $n > N$, $K_n = K^*$. The intuition behind this observation is straightforward. Suppose that in period N the capital stock is K^*. By the definition of K^*, it follows that in period N the amount of output saved and invested in new capital $sF(K^*)$ is equal to the amount of capital lost through depreciation γK^*. Hence, the capital stock in the next period stays at K^*.

Thus, if $K_1 = K^*$, then $K_n = K^*$ (for all n). But if $K_1 < K^*$, then the infinite sequence of capital stocks $\langle K_n \rangle$ — defined by the above recursive equation — is strictly increasing and converges to K^* (as n tends to infinity). On the other hand, if $K_1 > K^*$, then the infinite sequence of capital stocks is strictly decreasing and also converges to K^*.

The size of the cake in period n available for current consumption — over which the two players will bargain — is $\pi_n = (1 - s)F(K_n)$. It follows from the above properties of the infinite sequence of capital stocks that if $K_1 = K^*$, then $\pi_n = (1 - s)F(K^*)$ for all $n \geq 1$. But if, $K_1 < K^*$, then the sequence of cakes is strictly increasing and converges to $(1 - s)F(K^*)$. On the other hand, if $K_1 > K^*$ then the sequence of the cakes is strictly decreasing and also converges to $(1 - \pi)F(K^*)$.

The Unique Steady State SSPE

It thus follows that if $K_1 = K^*$, then Proposition 10.1 — with $\pi = (1 - s)F(K^*)$ — characterizes the unique SSPE of this repeated bargaining model. This is the unique *steady state* SSPE, since $K_n = K^*$ for all $n \geq 1$. The role of the players' discount rates r_A and r_B in the limiting (as $\Delta \to 0$) unique steady state SSPE is as discussed in Section 10.2.2. Furthermore, it follows from Corollary 10.2 that the payoff to player i ($i = A, B$) in the limiting (as $\Delta \to 0$) unique steady state SSPE is $V_i^* = \varphi_i \pi$, where $\pi = (1 - s)F(K^*)$ and $\varphi_i = r_j/(1 - \alpha_i)(r_j + \phi_i r_i)$ ($j \neq i$).

The Optimal Unique Steady State SSPE

Consider any pair (s', s'') of exogenously given savings rates, where $0 < s' < s'' < 1$. Since $K^*(s') < K^*(s'')$, it follows that $\pi' = (1 - s')F(K^*(s'))$ is less than, equal to, or greater than $\pi'' = (1 - s'')F(K^*(s''))$. This implies that $V_A^*(s') + V_B(s')$ is less than, equal to, or greater than $V_A^*(s'') + V_B^*(s'')$, where $V_A^*(s) + V_B^*(s)$ is the sum of the players' payoffs in the limiting (as $\Delta \to 0$) unique steady state SSPE when the exogenously given savings rate is s. I now derive the value of $s \in (0, 1)$ that maximizes the sum $V_A^*(s) + V_B^*(s)$. It follows from the expression above for V_i^* that this value is identical to the value of $s \in (0, 1)$ that maximizes $\pi = (1 - s)F(K^*(s))$.

Differentiating π w.r.t. s, it follows that $d\pi/ds = (1-s)F'(K^*)[dK^*/ds] - F(K^*)$. Since $sF(K^*) = \gamma K^*$, it follows that $dK^*/ds = -F(K^*)/[sF'(K^*) - \gamma]$. Therefore, $d\pi/ds = -F(K^*)[F'(K^*) - \gamma]/[sF'(K^*) - \gamma]$.

Now, given my assumptions on F, there exists a unique solution to $F'(K) = \gamma$, which is denoted K^g. Furthermore, define $s^g = \gamma K^g/F(K^g)$. It thus follows that π is strictly increasing in s on the open interval $(0, s^g)$, achieves a maximum at $s = s^g$, and is strictly decreasing on the open interval $(s^g, 1)$. Indeed, the 'optimal' unique steady state SSPE — which maximizes the sum of the players' equilibrium payoffs — is the one in which the exogenously given savings rate is s^g. Notice that when $s = s^g$, the steady state capital stock K^g has the property that $F'(K^g) = \gamma$. That is, the marginal product of capital equals the rate of capital depreciation.[13]

Bargaining over the Set of Unique Steady State SSPE

It follows from the properties (derived above) about the relationship between π and s that for any $s \in (0, 1)$ such that $s \neq s^g$, $V_A^*(s^g) > V_A^*(s)$ and $V_B^*(s^g) > V_B^*(s)$. Hence, if the players were to bargain at the beginning of their relationship over the set of all unique steady state SSPE, and if the bargaining outcome is Pareto efficient, then the players would agree to implement the optimal unique steady state SSPE derived above in which the savings rate is set at s^g.

---

[13]It may be noted that in the context of the one-sector Solow-Swan growth model, s^g is known as the *golden rule* savings rate, and K^g the golden rule steady state capital stock (cf. Phelps (1961)).

10.4   The Role of Outside Options

The role of outside options in one-shot bargaining situations has been studied in Chapter 5. In this section I explore their role in repeated bargaining situations. In Section 10.2 it has been shown that the impact of the players' discount rates in repeated bargaining situations can differ fundamentally to that in one-shot bargaining situations. In contrast, it is shown below that the impact of outside options in repeated bargaining situations is identical to that in one-shot bargaining situations. In particular, the *outside option principle* (which is stated in Corollary 5.1) carries over to repeated bargaining situations.

A player's outside option in a RBS is defined as the payoff she obtains when (and if) either player terminates the relationship that underlies the RBS. For example, the payoffs from divorce are the players' outside options in a marriage. Let E_i (where $E_i \geq 0$) denote player i's ($i = A, B$) outside option. Thus, if some player terminates the relationship at time t ($t \geq 0$), then player i's payoff is $E_i \exp(-r_i t)$. Assume that

$$(1 - \alpha_A)E_A + (1 - \alpha_B)E_B < \pi,$$

which ensures that it is mutually beneficial for the players never to exercise their outside options. Notice that $(1 - \alpha_i)E_i$ is player i's 'average' outside option.

I explore the role of outside options in the context of a simple extension to the repeated bargaining model studied in Section 10.2. The extension is as follows. Whenever player j has to respond to an offer of a partition of some cake made by player i ($i \neq j$), she has three options: (i) she can accept the offer, (ii) she can reject the offer and (iii) she can 'opt out', in which case the relationship between the players is terminated.

It is straightforward to adapt the arguments in Section 10.2.1 to characterize the unique SSPE in this extended repeated bargaining model. In the following proposition I characterize the unique SSPE in the limit as $\Delta \to 0$.

Proposition 10.3 (Outside Option Principle in a RBS). *The extended repeated bargaining model with outside options has a unique SSPE. In equilibrium, agreement is reached immediately on the partition of each and every cake. In the limit, as $\Delta \to 0$, the equilibrium shares of each and every cake* to players A and B are respectively z_A^{**} and z_B^{**}, where $z_B^{**} = \pi - z_A^{**}$ and

$$
z_A^{**} = \begin{cases} z_A^* & \text{if } z_A^* \geq w_A \text{ and } z_B^* \geq w_B \\ \pi - w_B & \text{if } z_A^* \geq w_A \text{ and } z_B^* < w_B \\ w_A & \text{if } z_A^* < w_A \text{ and } z_B^* \geq w_B, \end{cases}
$$

with z_A^* and z_B^* defined in Corollary 10.2, $w_A = (1 - \alpha_A)E_A$ and $w_B = (1 - \alpha_B)E_B$. Furthermore, in this limit, the equilibrium payoffs to players A and B are respectively V_A^{**} and V_B^{**}, where, for each $i, j = A, B$ and $i \neq j$

$$
V_i^{**} = \begin{cases} V_i^* & \text{if } z_A^* \geq w_A \text{ and } z_B^* \geq w_B \\ (\pi - w_j)/(1 - \alpha_i) & \text{if } z_i^* \geq w_i \text{ and } z_j^* < w_j \\ E_i & \text{if } z_i^* < w_i \text{ and } z_j^* \geq w_j, \end{cases}
$$

with V_A^* and V_B^* defined in Corollary 10.2.

Proof. Since the proof is a straightforward adaptation of the argument leading to Proposition 10.1, I only sketch out the main amendments to that argument. The critical difference is that in a SSPE player j's payoff from not accepting any offer is now $\max\{E_j, \delta_j V_j^*\}$. It follows immediately that if $E_A \leq \delta_A V_A^*$ and $E_B \leq \delta_B V_B^*$, then the unique SSPE is as stated in Proposition 10.1. This means that in the limit, as $\Delta \to 0$, the unique SSPE is as stated in Corollary 10.2 provided that $w_A \leq z_A^*$ and $w_B \leq z_B^*$.

Now suppose that $E_A \leq \delta_A V_A^*$ and $E_B > \delta_B V_B^*$. Assuming that $\Delta > 0$ but small and in particular $\tau > \Delta$ — since I am going to focus on the limiting case when Δ is arbitrarily small — it follows that the first equation in (10.2) continues to be valid, while the second equation in (10.2) needs to be slightly amended: the right-hand side is to be replaced by E_B. These two equations combined with the two equations in (10.1) — which continue to be valid — have a unique solution, namely

$$
\widehat{V}_A = \frac{\pi(1 + \alpha_B) - (1 - \alpha_B^2)E_B}{1 - \alpha_A \delta_A + \alpha_B(\delta_A - \alpha_A)}
$$
$$
\widehat{V}_B = \pi + \alpha_B E_B - (\delta_A - \alpha_A)\widehat{V}_A
$$
$$
\widehat{x}_A = \pi - E_B + \alpha_B \widehat{V}_B
$$
$$
\widehat{x}_B = \pi - (\delta_A - \alpha_A)\widehat{V}_A.
$$

Hence, this solution characterizes the unique SSPE provided that $E_A \leq \delta_A \widehat{V}_A$ and $E_B > \delta_B \widehat{V}_B$ — that is, provided that

$$(1 - \alpha_A)E_A + \delta_A(1 - \alpha_B)E_B \leq \delta_A \pi \quad \text{and} \quad E_B > \frac{x_B^*}{1 - \alpha_B \delta_B},$$

where x_B^* is stated in equation 10.4. In the limit, as $\Delta \to 0$, $\widehat{x}_A \to \pi - w_B$, $\widehat{x}_B \to w_B$, $\widehat{V}_A \to (\pi - w_B)/(1 - \alpha_A)$ and $\widehat{V}_B \to E_B$. Hence, since (from Corollary 10.2) $x_B^* \to z_B^*$ as $\Delta \to 0$, it follows that in the limiting (as $\Delta \to 0$) unique SSPE, the shares of each and every cake to players A and B are respectively $\pi - w_B$ and w_B, provided that $w_B > z_B^*$.[14] By a symmetric argument, with the roles of A and B reversed, one may characterize the limiting (as $\Delta \to 0$) unique SSPE when $w_A > z_A^*$ and $w_B \leq z_B^*$.[15] $\qquad \square$

In Proposition 10.3 I have stated the impact of the players' outside options conditional on the relative magnitudes of z_i^* and w_i ($i = A, B$), where the former is the SSPE share of each and every cake to player i when neither player has any outside options, while the latter is player i's 'average' outside option.[16] However, it should be noted that since (for each $i = A, B$)

$$z_i^* \gtreqless w_i \quad \text{if and only if} \quad V_i^* \gtreqless E_i,$$

the impact of the outside options may be stated conditional on the relative magnitudes of V_i^* and E_i ($i = A, B$).

Proposition 10.3 shows that the outside option principle, which was discovered in the context of one-shot bargaining situations, is valid in the context of repeated bargaining situations. In particular, the players' outside options influence the SSPE if and only if some player's outside option is strictly greater than her SSPE payoff.

Remark 10.7 (Opting out on a period-by-period basis). It is implicitly assumed above that if a player opts out in a RBS, then the players' relationship is terminated *forever*. This makes sense in many repeated bargaining situations. For example, divorce (typically) means that the couple

---

[14]Notice that $w_B > z_B^*$ implies that $w_A \leq z_A^*$.

[15]Since $w_A + w_B < \pi$ and $z_A^* + z_B^* = \pi$, it is not possible that $w_A > z_A^*$ and $w_B > z_B^*$.

[16]It is possible to interpret w_i as the share of some *alternative* cake that player i obtains (every τ time units) when and if the players terminate their relationship.

have terminated their marriage forever. However, in some repeated bargaining situations it may be possible for the players to opt out on a 'period-by-period' basis: that is, a player could opt out in any given period, but subsequently the players continue their relationship (with the option to opt out again for one period). For example, consider a bilateral monopoly market for some input in which the seller and the buyer have the opportunity to engage in a sequence of one-shot transactions. Furthermore, suppose that the seller always has the option to sell the input to some alternative buyer at some fixed price, and the buyer always has the option to buy the input from some alternative seller at some fixed price. In this RBS the seller and the buyer may choose to trade with these alternative traders in any given period, but subsequently return to trade with each other. I now argue that the impact of outside options in such a RBS is as stated in Proposition 10.3. Consider the following amendment to the extended repeated bargaining model studied above (which formalizes this 'period-by-period' opting out): when a player opts out (after the rejection of an offer of a partition of some cake), player i immediately obtains a payoff of w_i ($i = A, B$), and then τ time units later the two players return to bargain over the partition of the next cake. Assuming that $w_i \geq 0$ and $w_A + w_B < \pi$, it is straightforward to show that Proposition 10.3 characterizes the unique SSPE of this amended model.[17]

10.4.1 An Application to Firm Provided General Training

Consider a repeated bargaining situation in which, in each period, a firm and a worker can produce a quantity of output $f(I)$ after they reach agreement over that period's wage, where $I \geq 0$ denotes the amount of *general* training provided by the firm at the beginning of the RBS.[18] Furthermore, while bargaining over the wage rate (in any period) the worker has the option to quit working for this firm, and instead work for another firm at an exogenously given wage rate $v(I)$. If she exercises this option, then the firm

---

[17]The argument is similar to that contained in the proof of Proposition 10.3, except that it should be noted that in any SSPE player j's payoff from not accepting any offer is now $\max\{w_j + \alpha_j V_j^*, \delta j V_j^*\}$.

[18]The worker is assumed to be credit constrained, and, hence, cannot provide any such training for herself.

earns zero profit. Assume that the two players have a common discount rate $r > 0$, and that $f(I) > v(I)$ for all $I \geq 0$.

I apply Proposition 10.3. For any $I \geq 0$, the wage rate in the unique (limiting, as $\Delta \to 0$) SSPE is

$$w(I) = \begin{cases} f(I)/2 & \text{if } f(I)/2 \geq v(I) \\ v(I) & \text{if } f(I)/2 < v(I). \end{cases}$$

Hence, for any $I \geq 0$, the firm's equilibrium profit per period is

$$\Pi(I) = \begin{cases} f(I)/2 & \text{if } f(I)/2 \geq v(I) \\ f(I) - v(I) & \text{if } f(I)/2 < v(I). \end{cases}$$

Letting $c(I)$ denote the cost to the firm of providing I units of general training before the RBS unfolds, it follows that the amount of firm provided general training I^* (where $I^* \geq 0$) maximizes the firm's net total profit, which is

$$\frac{\Pi(I)}{1 - \alpha} - c(I),$$

where $\alpha \equiv \exp(-r\tau)$. Assuming that $c'(0) = 0$ and $f'(0) > 0$, it follows that if $f'(0) > v'(0)$ then $\Pi'(0) > 0$. Thus, the firm will provide a *strictly* positive amount of general training if the first unit of such general training increases the marginal product of the worker more than it increases the worker's wage rate at the other firm.[19]

As is well known (since Becker (1964)) this conclusion does not hold in a competitive labour market — since in such a market the competitive equilibrium wage rate is equal to the worker's marginal product. That is, in such a market $w(I) = v(I) = f(I)$, and, hence, the firm in a competitive labour market will provide *no* training in general skills.

The *first best* level of general training I^e maximizes $f(I) - c(I)$. It is clear that in general (with appropriate assumptions on f, v and c) $I^* < I^e$. Thus, although (when wages are determined through bargaining) the firm will provide *some* training in general skills, she does not provide it at the efficient level.

---

[19]It should be noted that $f(I)$ — and not $f'(I)$ — is the marginal product of the worker.

10.5   The Role of Long-Term Contracts

I now study the role of long-term contracts in the context of the archetypal repeated bargaining situation in which a seller and a buyer engage in an infinite sequence of one-shot transactions. Before the RBS unfolds, the following sequence of events take place at 'dates' 1–3.

At date 1 the buyer and the seller have the opportunity to write a long-term contract that specifies the terms of trade of each and every one-shot transaction to be encountered. I shall elaborate on the details of such a long-term contract in Sections 10.5.2 and 10.5.3. It is worth emphasizing here that a long-term contract commits the parties to trading on the terms specified in the contract — in the sense that when trade occurs either party can choose to enforce that it take place on the terms specified in the contract. However, trade can occur on terms that differ from those specified in the contract if and only if *both* players agree to do so.

Whether or not a long-term contract is signed at date 1, at date 2 the players simultaneously choose their respective *investment* levels I_B and I_S, where $I_i \geq 0$ ($i = B, S$). The cost to player i of investing an amount I_i is I_i, which she incurs at date 2. Then, at date 3 the state of nature is randomly realized, where Θ denotes the finite set of possible states of nature, and $\gamma(\theta)$ the probability that the state is $\theta \in \Theta$.

The buyer's reservation value v for a unit of the input depends on I_B and θ, and the seller's unit cost of production c depends on I_S and θ. They are written as $v(I_B; \theta)$ and $c(I_S; \theta)$. It is assumed that for any $\theta \in \Theta$, v is twice continuously differentiable, strictly increasing and strictly concave in I_B, and that c is twice continuously differentiable, strictly decreasing and strictly convex in I_S. The appropriate first-order and second-order derivatives with respect to the investment levels are denoted by v', v'', c' and c''. For simplicity, but with some loss of generality, I assume that for any I_B, I_S and θ, $v(I_B; \theta) > c(I_S; \theta)$ — that is, gains from trade always exist.

At date 4 the RBS begins to unfold. The buyer requires a single unit of the input every τ ($\tau > 0$) time units. As such the RBS involves a sequence of one-shot transactions. The instantaneous profits to the buyer and the seller respectively from trading a unit of the input at price p — given that at date 2 the chosen investment levels are I_B and I_S, and at date 3 the realized state of nature is θ — are $v(I_B; \theta) - p$ and $p - c(I_S; \theta)$. The players have a common discount rate $r > 0$, where $\alpha \equiv \exp(-r\tau)$.

If no long-term contract is written at date 1, then the sequence of prices at which trade occurs is determined via bargaining in the manner described by the repeated bargaining model studied in Section 10.2. That is, the players negotiate the price of the input when the buyer requires it. On the other hand, if a long-term contract is written at date 1, then depending on whether or not the contract is 'complete' — a notion that is discussed in Section 10.5.2 — the players will either trade at the price specified in the contract or renegotiate and trade at some other price.

In addressing the role of long-term contracts, attention will focus on the extent to which such contracts affect the players' incentives to invest at date 2. As such it is useful to define the *first best* investment levels, which are the investment levels I_B^e and I_S^e that maximize the difference between the expected present discounted value of the gains from trade in the RBS and the total cost of investment. That is

$$(I_B^e, I_S^e) = \arg\max_{I_B, I_S} E_\theta \left[\frac{v(I_B; \theta) - c(I_S; \theta)}{1 - \alpha} \right] - I_B - I_S.$$

Thus, (I_B^e, I_S^e) is a solution to the following pair of equations

$$E_\theta[v'(I_B; \theta)] = 1 - \alpha \quad \text{and} \quad E_\theta[-c'(I_S; \theta)] = 1 - \alpha. \qquad (10.5)$$

10.5.1   Equilibrium Without a Long-Term Contract

I first characterize the unique (limiting, as $\Delta \to 0$) SSPE on the assumption that the parties do not write a long-term contract at date 1. For any I_B, I_S and θ, the unique (limiting) SSPE of the repeated bargaining model at date 4 is characterized in Corollary 10.2 with $\pi = v(I_B; \theta) - c(I_S; \theta)$ and $r_A = r_B = r$. In this limiting equilibrium trade occurs immediately in each and every bargaining situation at the same price, which is denoted by $p^*(I_B, I_S, \theta)$. Corollary 10.2 implies that the equilibrium profits from each transaction to the buyer and the seller are respectively defined in (10.6) and (10.7) stated below

$$v(I_B; \theta) - p^*(I_B, I_S, \theta) = \frac{v(I_B; \theta) - c(I_S; \theta)}{2} \qquad (10.6)$$

$$p^*(I_B, I_S, \theta) - c(I_S; \theta) = \frac{v(I_B; \theta) - c(I_S; \theta)}{2}. \qquad (10.7)$$

Hence, the trade price

$$p^*(I_B, I_S, \theta) = \frac{v(I_B; \theta) + c(I_S; \theta)}{2}. \tag{10.8}$$

I now derive the Nash equilibrium investment levels chosen at date 2. For any pair (I_B, I_S), the expected equilibrium payoff to player i $(i = B, S)$ is

$$E_\theta \left[\frac{v(I_B; \theta) - c(I_S; \theta)}{2(1 - \alpha)} \right] - I_i.$$

Hence, a Nash equilibrium pair of investment levels (I_B^*, I_S^*) is a solution to the following first-order conditions

$$E_\theta[v'(I_B; \theta)/2] = 1 - \alpha \quad \text{and} \quad E_\theta[-c'(I_S; \theta)/2] = 1 - \alpha. \tag{10.9}$$

It follows by comparing the equations in 10.9 with those in 10.5 that the Nash equilibrium investment levels will be strictly less than the first best investment levels — that is, $I_i^* < I_i^e$ $(i = B, S)$. Each player under-invests relative to her first best investment level because she only receives one-half of the (average) expected marginal return from her investment. The other half is negotiated away to her opponent at date 4. Thus, when the long-term relationship between the buyer and the seller is governed by an infinite sequence of short-term contracts, the parties have poor incentives to undertake relationship-specific investments that enhance the expected gains from trading within the relationship.

10.5.2 Equilibrium With a Complete Long-Term Contract

Now suppose that at date 1 the parties write a long-term contract that specifies a price *contingent* on the realized state of nature. That is, the long-term contract specifies the price p as a function of θ. Thus, if the buyer chooses I_B, the seller I_S and the realized state of nature is θ, then the contract states that they trade the input at price $p(\theta)$.

This type of contract can be enforced by a third party (such as the courts) if and only if the realized state of nature is *verifiable* by the courts. It is not sufficient (for the enforceability of the contract) that the realized state of nature is *observable* by the buyer and the seller. When it is possible for the courts to verify the values of all variables upon which the parties wish to condition the price, it is said that the parties are able to write a *complete* long-term contract. In the next section I explore the role (if any) of *incomplete* long-term contracts.

Fix an arbitrary complete long-term contract $\langle p(\theta) \rangle_{\theta \in \Theta}$ such that for any $\theta \in \Theta$, $v(0; \theta) - p(\theta) \geq 0$ and $p(\theta) - c(0; \theta) \geq 0$. Many such complete long-term contracts exist given my assumption that gains from trade always exist. Since $v' > 0$ and $c' < 0$, it follows that for any $\theta \in \Theta$, $I_B \geq 0$ and $I_S \geq 0$: $v(I_B; \theta) \geq p(\theta)$ and $p(\theta) \geq c(I_S; \theta)$. Hence, given the complete long-term contract, whatever the investment levels chosen at date 2 and whatever the realized state of nature, at date 4 each player will prefer to trade at the contracted price rather than not to trade. Consequently, for any pair (I_B, I_S), at date 2 the expected payoffs to the buyer and the seller are respectively

$$\frac{E_\theta[v(I_B; \theta) - p(\theta)]}{1 - \alpha} - I_B \quad \text{and} \quad \frac{E_\theta[p(\theta) - c(I_S; \theta)]}{1 - \alpha} - I_S.$$

Hence, a Nash equilibrium pair of investment levels $(\widehat{I}_B, \widehat{I}_S)$ is a solution to the following first-order conditions

$$E_\theta[v'(I_B; \theta)] = 1 - \alpha \quad \text{and} \quad E_\theta[-c'(I_S; \theta)] = 1 - \alpha. \tag{10.10}$$

It follows by comparing the equations in 10.10 with those in 10.5 that the Nash equilibrium investment levels — given the complete long-term contract — are equal to the first best investment levels. This is because each player receives the full (average) expected marginal return from her investment. Thus, when the long-term relationship is governed by a complete long-term contract, the parties have excellent incentives to undertake relationship-specific investments.

10.5.3 Equilibrium With an Incomplete Long-Term Contract

The assumption made in the preceding section that the realized state of nature can be verified by third parties (such as the courts) is not particularly realistic. For a variety of reasons — such as those due to the complexity and multidimensionality of the state of nature — it is often too costly to write a state-contingent contract in a sufficiently clear and unambiguous manner that it can be enforced. In this section I therefore assume that the realized state of nature is *observable* to the buyer and the seller, but not *verifiable* by the courts. As such the parties cannot write a long-term contract in which the price is conditioned on θ. For similar reasons, it is assumed that the contracted price cannot be conditioned on the investment levels chosen at date 2. It is said that such long-term contracts are *incomplete*.[20]

Suppose, nevertheless, that the parties do write an incomplete long-term contract at date 1, which is a constant price p. Thus, for any chosen investment levels and any realized state of nature, the contract specifies that if trades occurs, then it occurs at price p. However, either player can choose not to trade. The cost to a player of refusing to trade is zero, since the courts cannot verify which party refused to trade if trade does not occur, or alternatively, that the courts do not wish to enforce trade. For example, in the absence of slavery, courts do not force an employee to work for an employer.

Fix an arbitrary incomplete long-term contract p, investment levels I_B and I_S, and state of nature θ. If the following two inequalities hold, then trade occurs in each and every one-shot transaction at the contracted price p

$$v(I_B; \theta) - p \geq 0 \quad \text{and} \quad p - c(I_S; \theta) \geq 0. \tag{10.11}$$

These inequalities ensure that each party prefers to trade rather than not to trade. Now suppose that one of these two inequalities fails to hold.[21] This implies that one of the two parties prefers not to trade *at the contracted price p*. Since (by assumption) there are no penalities for not trading, she will refuse to trade. In which case each player's profit per period is zero — ignoring the costs of investment (which are sunk). But this is not *ex-post* efficient, since $v(I_B; \theta) > c(I_S; \theta)$. That is, if the parties were to *renegotiate* the price and agree on a price p' such that $v(I_B; \theta) > p' > c(I_S; \theta)$, then each player would earn a *strictly* positive profit per period. Therefore, since it is *mutually* beneficial for the parties to renegotiate the trade price, they will indeed tear up the (incomplete) long-term contract and renegotiate.

Suppose that in this eventuality (when one of the two inequalities in 10.11 fails to hold) the parties do not write a new long-term contract, but now

---

[20]For an excellent discussion on the reasons for contractual incompleteness, see Hart and Holmstrom (1987).

[21]It should be noted that since (by assumption) $v(I_B; \theta) - c(I_S; \theta) > 0$ for any I_B, I_S and θ, at least one of these inequalities must hold.

the sequence of trade prices are determined as in the repeated bargaining model. Hence, the price (in the unique limiting SSPE) at which trade occurs in each and every transaction is given by (10.8).

Hence, at date 4 the equilibrium expected payoffs to the buyer and the seller are respectively

$$\begin{cases} (v(I_B;\theta) - p)/(1-\alpha) & \text{if } c(I_S;\theta) \le p \le v(I_B;\theta) \\ (v(I_B;\theta) - c(I_S;\theta))/2(1-\alpha) & \text{otherwise} \end{cases}$$

and

$$\begin{cases} (p - c(I_S;\theta))/(1-\alpha) & \text{if } c(I_S;\theta) \le p \le v(I_B;\theta) \\ (v(I_B;\theta) - c(I_S;\theta))/2(1-\alpha) & \text{otherwise.} \end{cases}$$

For each pair $I = (I_B, I_S)$, define the set $\Gamma(I) \subseteq \Theta$ as follows: $\Gamma(I) = \{\theta \in \Theta : c(I_S;\theta) \le p \le v(I_B;\theta)\}$. Hence, given the arbitrary incomplete long-term contract p, the expected payoffs at date 2 to the buyer and the seller respectively from an arbitrary pair (I_B, I_S) are

$$E_{\theta\in\Gamma(I)}\left[\frac{v(I_B;\theta) - p}{1-\alpha}\right] + E_{\theta\in\Theta/\Gamma(I)}\left[\frac{v(I_B;\theta) - c(I_S;\theta)}{2(1-\alpha)}\right] - I_B \quad \text{and}$$

$$E_{\theta\in\Gamma(I)}\left[\frac{p - c(I_S;\theta)}{1-\alpha}\right] + E_{\theta\in\Theta/\Gamma(I)}\left[\frac{v(I_B;\theta) - c(I_S;\theta)}{2(1-\alpha)}\right] - I_S.$$

Consequently, given the incomplete long-term contract p, a Nash equilibrium pair of investment levels (I_B^{**}, I_S^{**}) is a solution to the following first-order conditions

$$E_{\theta\in\Gamma(I)}[v'(I_B;\theta)] + E_{\theta\in\Theta/\Gamma(I)}[v'(I_B;\theta)/2] = 1 - \alpha \tag{10.12}$$
$$E_{\theta\in\Gamma(I)}[-c'(I_S;\theta)] + E_{\theta\in\Theta/\Gamma(I)}[-c'(I_S;\theta)/2] = 1 - \alpha. \tag{10.13}$$

It follows by comparing equations 10.12–10.13 with the equations in 10.5 that in general there is under-investment: $I_i^{**} < I_i^e$ ($i = B, S$). Thus, when the players sign an incomplete long-term contract at date 1, each player's equilibrium investment level is in general less than her first best investment level. However, by comparing equations 10.12–10.13 with the equations in 10.9 it follows that in general each player's equilibrium investment level when an incomplete long-term contract is signed at date 1 is greater than her equilibrium investment level when no long-term contract is signed at date 1. Therefore, although incomplete long-term contracts do not in general achieve first best investments, the parties will prefer to sign such a contract rather than not signing any long-term contract.

A main message that emerges here is that long-term contracts can have a beneficial role in those repeated bargaining situations in which the parties have the opportunity to engage in relationship-specific investments that enhance the value of the RBS — notwithstanding the possibility that such contracts will necessarily be highly incomplete.

10.6 Reputation Effects

A player's *reputation* for being a particular *type* of bargainer may have a significant impact on the bargaining outcome. Consider, for example, a seller whose unit cost of production is low, but who has a reputation for having a high unit cost of production — by which I mean that the buyer attaches a high probability to the seller's unit cost being high. With such a reputation the negotiated price will tend to be relatively higher than it would be were the seller not to possess such a reputation. As another example consider a union that is weak in the sense that its members are unlikely to support and endure a long lasting strike, but which has a reputation for being strong — by which I mean that the firm attaches a high probability to the union being strong. With such a reputation the negotiated wage and the other terms of employment will tend to be relatively more attractive to the union than they would be were the union not to possess such a reputation.

A host of questions arise concerning the role of reputations on the bargaining outcome, including the following. What actions can a player take in order to build (and maintain) a reputation for being a particular type of bargainer? What are the costs of such actions, and what are the benefits from acquiring such a reputation? Under what circumstances would a player build a reputation?

Below I briefly consider such questions in the context of a simple repeated bargaining model in which a seller and a buyer can trade a unit of some input in each period, and the seller's unit cost of production is her private information — it is either high or low.

10.6.1   A Perfect Bayesian Equilibrium in a Simple Model

In each period t (where $t = 0, 1, 2, \ldots$) a seller and a buyer can trade a unit of some input. The seller's unit cost of production c is her private information, while the buyer's reservation value v is known to both players. This asymmetry in information is modelled as follows. Before their relationship begins in period 0, the seller's unit cost of production is randomly drawn from the following binary distribution: with probability α ($0 < \alpha < 1$) the unit cost of production $c = 1$, and with probability $1 - \alpha$ the unit cost of production $c = 0$. The seller knows the realization of the random draw, but the buyer does not.[22] It is assumed that $v > 1$, which implies that gains from trade exist with probability one.

In each period t, the buyer makes a price offer p_t to the seller. If she accepts it, then trade occurs, and the profits obtained by the buyer and the seller in this period are respectively $v - p_t$ and $p_t - c$. However, if the seller rejects the price offer, then trade does not occur in this period, and each player obtains no profit in this period. In either eventuality the game then moves to period $t + 1$. The discount rates of the buyer and the seller are respectively r_B and r_S, where $r_B \geq 0$ and $r_S > 0$.

I now construct a perfect Bayesian equilibrium (PBE) that illustrates the main point of this model. Consider the following pair of strategies. The seller accepts a price offer p in any period if and only if $p \geq 1$, whether her unit cost of production is high ($c = 1$) or low ($c = 0$). Letting μ_t denote the probability the buyer attaches in period t — before making her offer — to the seller having a high unit cost of production, the buyer's pricing strategy is as follows: if $\mu_t > 0$ then she offers $p_t = 1$, and if $\mu_t = 0$ then she offers $p_t = 0$.

The buyer's *posterior* beliefs consistent with Bayes' rule — given the above described pair of strategies — are as follows: (i) if $\mu_t = 0$ then $\mu_{t+1} = 0$, (ii) if $\mu_t > 0$ and $p_t \geq 1$ is rejected/accepted then $\mu_{t+1} = \mu_t$, (iii) if $\mu_t > 0$ and $p_t < 1$ is rejected, then $\mu_{t+1} = \mu_t$, (iv) if $\mu_t > 0$ and $p_t < 1$ is accepted, then $\mu_{t+1} = 0$.

I now verify that the above described pair of strategies is a PBE. The high cost type of seller has no incentive to deviate from this strategy. Fur-

---

[22]The buyer only knows that the seller's unit cost of production is a random draw from this binary distribution.

thermore, given the seller's strategy, the buyer has no incentive to deviate from her strategy. The key issue is whether or not the low cost type of seller can benefit from a one-shot (unilateral) deviation in which she accepts (in any period t) a price offer $p_t < 1$. If she deviates and accepts such a price offer, then her profit in period t is p_t and her profit in any period after (and including) period $t+1$ is zero. On the other hand, her payoff by conforming to her proposed strategy, and thus rejecting this price offer, is $\delta_S/(1 - \delta_S)$, where $\delta_S \equiv \exp(-r_S)$. Hence, if $\delta_S/(1 - \delta_S) > 1$, then she does not benefit from such a one-shot deviation.

In summary, therefore, the above described pair of strategies and buyer beliefs is a PBE if $\delta_S > 0.5$. Thus, provided the seller is sufficiently patient, there exists a PBE such that along the equilibrium path the buyer's price offer in period t (for all $t = 0, 1, 2, \dots$) is $p_t = 1$, which is accepted by the seller. The buyer has no incentive to deviate from this equilibrium price path — no matter how small α might be — because of the credible threat made by the low cost type of seller to reject any price offer $p < 1$.

Notice that in this PBE the buyer's and the seller's per-period profits are respectively $v - 1$ and $1 - c$. In contrast, it may be noted that with perfect information — that is, when the seller's unit cost c is known to the buyer — there exists a unique subgame perfect equilibrium (SPE) in which trade occurs in each period on price $p = c$. Thus, with perfect information, all the surplus from trading in each period is obtained by the buyer. In particular, the seller (whatever is her cost) obtains no profit. This observation illustrates the potentially significant role that reputation effects can have on the bargaining outcome.

10.6.2   Further Remarks

It is easy to show (by construction) that the model studied above possesses a multiplicity of other PBE.[23] Clearly further research is required here to narrow down the set of equilibria in this type of model. It may be noted that Hart and Tirole (1988) and Schmidt (1993) have studied the *finitely* repeated version of this model — that is, with the assumption that the relationship between the seller and the buyer lasts a finite number of periods, say N.

---

[23]The construction is based on the following idea. A price path is supported in a PBE by the threat of reverting to the PBE described above were the buyer to deviate from it.

They show that the model has a *unique* PBE which converges, as $N \to \infty$, to the PBE characterized above.

It goes without saying that the model studied above is very simple in many respects. There is considerable scope to extend and amend it to better understand the role of reputations in repeated bargaining situations. For example, an interesting extension would be to assume that the buyer (also) has private information (about her reservation value).

I conclude by noting that there is much need for research into the fascinating topic of the role of reputations in repeated bargaining situations. More models need to be constructed and studied, both in the abstract and motivated by specific real-life bargaining situations. For example, I would argue that a union that goes on a costly strike during the current year's wage negotiations does so partly to build a reputation for being strong, where some of the benefit from such a reputation is obtained during *next* year's wage negotiations. It remains a challenge to construct plausible models of such phenomena.

10.7   Notes

The repeated bargaining model studied in Section 10.2 is based upon Muthoo (1995b). For an alternative repeated bargaining model, see Groes (1996). The application to dynamic capital investment considered in Section 10.3 needs much further work. In particular, the analysis of the Markov SPE of the model awaits characterization.

Felli and Harris (1996) and Leach (1997) study repeated bargaining models in which the sequence of bargaining situations are interdependent. The former paper considers a situation in which a worker and two competing firms bargain in an environment in which the worker accumulates some specific (payoff-relevant) information. The latter paper, on the other hand, considers a situation in which a firm and a union bargain in an environment in which the firm chooses whether or not to accumulate inventories. However, in order to simplify the analysis, Felli and Harris (1996) adopt (respectively, Leach (1997) adopts) the (strong) assumption that in each period the two competing firms make (respectively, the union makes) take-it-or-leave-it-offers to the worker (respectively, firm). Nonetheless, both papers derive some interesting results.

The application to firm-provided general training is based upon the analyses in Acemoglu and Pischke (1999).

The analysis in Section 10.5 is inspired by the work of Hart and Moore (1988). For an excellent introduction to the subject matter of incomplete contracts and their role in long-term relationships, see Hart and Holmstrom (1987, Section 3) and Hart (1995). For further references to the large literature on the subject, see the survey by Malcomson (1997). For an analysis of short-term (complete) contracting in long-term relationships, see Crawford (1988).

The finitely repeated version of the model studied in Section 10.6 has been studied by Hart and Tirole (1988) and Schmidt (1993) — the former also address the role of long-term contracts in this setting. Although the finite-horizon assumption is problematic and has been criticized in this book, these papers contain some useful, and insightful, techniques of analyses and messages. It may be noted that there is a large literature on reputation effects, but — with the exception of Hart and Tirole (1988) and Schmidt (1993) — not in the setting of repeated bargaining situations. Nevertheless, the techniques and insights from that literature should prove useful in future research on the role of reputations in repeated bargaining situations. For an excellent introduction to that literature, see Fudenberg and Tirole (1991).

11   Envoi

11.1   Introduction

The theory developed in the preceding chapters contains some fundamental results and insights concerning the role of some key forces on the bargaining outcome. It cannot be overemphasized that the focus of this theory is on the *fundamentals*. Indeed, in the first stage of the development of an understanding of any phenomenon that is precisely the kind of theory that is required — one that cuts across a wide and rich variety of real-life scenarios and focuses upon their common core elements.

This objective to uncover the fundamentals of bargaining has meant that my study has centred on some basic, elementary, models. That is how it should be. However, it is important that we now move beyond the fundamentals, in order to develop a richer theory of bargaining. With the theory just developed providing appropriate guidance and a firm foundation, it should be possible to construct tractable and richer models that capture more aspects of real-life bargaining situations. At the same time, future research should continue to develop the fundamentals; not only should we further study the roles of the forces studied in this book — especially the study of models in which many such forces are present — but we should also study the role of other forces that have not been addressed in this book (some of which I mention in Section 11.2).

It is worth acknowledging that the role played by the game-theoretic methodology in the development of the theory described in this book has been crucial. I would like to suggest that notwithstanding the justifiable criticisms of this methodology — which I touch upon in Section 11.3 — research in the further development of the theory and application of bargaining should continue to employ these methods. This methodology still provides (and it will continue to do so in the foreseeable future) the best set of tools currently available to formalize the richness of real-life bargaining situations, and generate (in a relatively tractable manner) some useful and insightful results. However, as I briefly argue in Section 11.3, research should also (at the same time) proceed on developing new types of models of bargaining, based upon a different set of tools (which are currently under development).

I conclude this envoi (in Section 11.4) by offering some comments on the role that bargaining experiments might play in the further development of bargaining theory.

Before proceeding, however, I would like to make a general point concerning the modelling of specific real-life bargaining situations. It appears to me that, in many contexts, applied theorists have not yet developed models of bargaining that adequately and persuasively capture the essentials of the bargaining situations that interest them.[1] It should be understood that bargaining theory is there to *guide* on how best to construct bargaining models of real-life bargaining situations, and not to supply readily made such models; it is meant primarily to provide the fundamentals.

11.2   Omissions

I begin by identifying two topics that have been studied in this book, but where there is room for much further productive research (using the game-theoretic methods employed in this book).

The first topic concerns *repeated bargaining situations*. The analyses in Chapter 10 have only just scratched the surface of the complexities that

---

[1]For example, I believe that we still do not have a plausible and persuasive model of union-firm wage and employment negotiations. Roberts (1994) is an improvement over the models that one tends to find in the labour economics literature, which seem to omit some key aspects of such negotiations.

characterize repeated bargaining situations. This is a topic of some considerable importance, and research should be motivated substantially by the many real-life repeated bargaining situations. The various types of linkages that often exist amongst the sequence of bargaining situations — but which, with the exception of the application in Section 10.3, were not studied in Chapter 10 — are key elements of real-life repeated bargaining situations. They need to be emphasized, and their roles studied, in future research. The role of reputations, and reputation building and maintenance, in repeated bargaining situations (briefly touched upon in Section 10.6) is clearly an important force that we have hardly any deep understanding of.

The second topic concerns *bargaining tactics*. In Chapter 8 I focused entirely on one type of tactics employed by bargainers. There is room, no doubt, for much further research on the role of such commitment tactics, which may perhaps proceed by enriching the models studied in that chapter. But, in order to develop a deeper understanding, we need, in particular, to develop models in which the processes through which players attempt to make commitments stick are made explicit. That is, of course, a more challenging enterprise. And, of course, the study of other types of tactics employed by bargainers needs to be put on to the research agenda.

11.2.1   Non-Stationary and Stochastic Environments

A weakness of the theory developed thus far is that the bargaining environments modelled are stationary and deterministic. Although these assumptions have been useful in order to develop some of the fundamental results in a simple manner, we should now study models based on non-stationary and/or stochastic environments that characterize many real-life bargaining situations. For example, in the context of union-firm wage negotiations, a firm's market share might significantly decrease after (and if) the union has been on strike for, say, two weeks. This introduces a non-stationary element in the structure of the wage bargaining process that may have a significant impact on the bargaining outcome — for a preliminary analysis of this type of consideration, see Hart (1989).

There is a small literature that has made some inroads on this issue from a theoretical perspective, which includes Binmore (1987), Merlo and Wilson (1995), Groes and Sloth (1996), Cripps (1998) and Coles and Muthoo (1999).

However, as will become clear from reading these papers, a lot more research needs to be done, especially from an applied perspective; we ought to study bargaining models motivated by the specific types of non-stationarity and/or randomness found in real-life bargaining situations — as is, for example, done in Hart (1989).

11.2.2 Multilateral and Coalitional Bargaining

In this book I have focused entirely on bilateral bargaining situations — that is, bargaining situations involving two players. However, many important and interesting bargaining situations involve three or more players. The reasons for this omission are two-fold. Firstly, because of the primacy of bilateral bargaining situations — they are the more basic, and the more prevalent in real life. And, secondly, and this is partly related to the first reason, the literature on multilateral and coalitional bargaining that uses the (strategic or non-cooperative) game-theoretic methodology employed in this book is extremely small (albeit growing) and under-developed. Having said so, this is clearly an important area for future research.

An important, and rather fundamental, new element that rears its head in bargaining situations with three or more players — but which is non-existent in bilateral bargaining situations — is that players might consider forming coalitions. This element makes the modelling of such bargaining situations somewhat tricky. A theory of such bargaining situations should not only determine what each player gets individually, but also determine which coalitions will and will not form. It should thus, in particular, model (in the extensive-form) the processes through which the players consider whether or not to form a coalition.

Consider, for example, an extension to the exchange situation described at the beginning of Section 1.1 in which there is another buyer who also values the house at £70,000. In modelling this three player (one seller–two buyers) bargaining situation, one should allow for the possibility that the two buyers might consider forming a coalition, and then bargain with the seller over the sale of the house in some way that takes into account the side-deal they have made. At the same time, perhaps while the buyers are negotiating the terms and structure of their coalition, the seller may have the opportunity to approach one of the two buyers and negotiate to sell the house to her — a strategy intended to prevent the formation of the buyers' coalition. Clearly, such factors need to be considered when modelling bargaining situations with three or more players.

There is indeed a rich set of issues that arise here which are absent from bilateral bargaining situations making the construction (and study) of tractable, yet plausible, models somewhat tricky. I suggest that the development of a theory of such bargaining situations should be pursued hand-in-hand with the development of applied models specifically tailored to fit specific real-life bargaining situations. This may help the former, since real-life bargaining situations often have, to some extent, established mechanisms through which coalition-formation takes place.

Consider the extension of Rubinstein's bargaining model (which was studied in Chapter 3) in which N players (where $N \geq 3$) bargain over the partition of a *single* cake of fixed size according to an alternating-offers procedure. It has been shown by Avner Shaked that the model possesses a multiplicity of subgame perfect equilibria, provided that the time interval between two consecutive offers is sufficiently small — see, for example, Osborne and Rubinstein (1990, Section 3.13) for a precise description of this result. This result — which concerns a basic multilateral bargaining situation (in the absence of any coalition-formation issue) — has been a source of frustration in the development of a theory of multilateral bargaining. One particular recent resolution is contained in Krishna and Serrano (1996). But, their model and results depend on a somewhat strong assumption (which is the subject of discussion in section 8 of their paper). There is, indeed, room for much further research on such multilateral bargaining situations.

Chatterjee, Dutta, Ray and Sengupta (1993) study a model of coalitional bargaining. It is a generalization of Rubinstein's alternating-offers model in which N players bargain over both what coalitions to form and what each individual gets in each such coalition. Although they derive some interesting and useful results, much research on modelling coalitional bargaining is desperately required.

Issues of coalition-formation naturally arise when, for example, a single firm bargains with more than one worker. Shaked and Sutton (1984) study a model of such a situation on the strong assumption that the firm only requires a single worker — and, furthermore, disallow (by assumption) the workers from forming a coalition.[2] We still await — especially for the sake of labour economics — for a plausible extension/generalization of the Shaked and Sutton model to the case in which the employment level is endogenously determined. Issues of coalition formation ought to figure prominently in such a model.[3]

Although it is convenient to disallow coalition-formation when modelling bargaining situations involving three or more players — and this may be justified when studying some real-life bargaining situations — future research ought to focus attention on this issue.

It may be noted that bargaining and matching models of large markets also rule out (by assumption) coalitions from being formed. For an excellent introduction to that literature, see Osborne and Rubinstein (1990, Part II). Most of this literature assumes that sellers and buyers are randomly matched in pairs to bargain over the price at which to trade. Hence, it is not possible for a group of sellers, say, to organize and form a coalition.[4]

11.2.3 Arbitration and Mediation

The role of arbitrators and mediators on the bargaining outcome is another area that needs much research. The distinction between them is important. While arbitrators impose an agreement, mediators facilitate the reaching of an agreement by the players. There is a large literature on arbitration — see, for example, Crawford (1981) for a brief survey. But most models in that literature do not give the players sufficient opportunity to negotiate an agreement on their own. Models in which the players negotiate in the shadow of an arbitrator are hard to come by — in such a model the players would call upon the arbitrator when, and if, they jointly agree to do so. For

---

[2]Hendon and Tranes (1991), Jehiel and Moldovano (1995), and de Fraja and Muthoo (1999) also study a one seller–two buyers bargaining situation and also disallow (by assumption) the buyers from forming a coalition. The first of these papers studies the effect of differing buyer reservation values, the second the effect of externalities between the buyers, and the third the effect of asymmetric information.

[3]Things will obviously get complicated when one considers the interaction of such imperfect labour markets with oligopolistic product markets. For an early attempt, see Davidson (1988).

[4]For a bargaining and matching model in which sellers and buyers are not matched randomly, but in which coalitions are also ruled out (by assumption), see Coles and Muthoo (1998).

two such models, see Manzini and Mariotti (1997) and Compte and Jehiel (1998).

Turning to mediation, it seems to me that mediators do play some role in some real-life bargaining situations, such as when a married couple are facing difficulty reaching agreement. For example, a mediator may help co-ordinate the players' expectations when at least one of the players possesses private information on some variable. Ponsati and Sakovics (1995) explore the impact of mediation on the efficiency of the outcome in a bargaining situation with asymmetric information.

11.2.4 Multiple Issues and the Agenda

When there is more than one issue over which the players may negotiate, the agenda may be important. The agenda not only specifies the order and details of negotiations, but also the issues that will and will not be subject to negotiations. Exploring the role of the bargaining agenda, and how players might manipulate it, is an interesting and important area of research, especially given that many real-life negotiations (such as trade negotiations) involve multiple issues. The literature on this topic is small (albeit growing) — see, for example, Fershtman (1990), Bac and Raff (1996), and Lang and Rosenthal (1998).

11.2.5 Enforceability of Agreements

The issue of the enforceability of the agreements struck via bargaining is an important one — as has been implicitly raised when I introduced the notion of the incompleteness of a long-term contract in Section 10.5.2. With the exception of the analyses in Sections 10.5.2 and 10.5.3, I have implicitly assumed throughout the book that the agreement struck is implemented, in the sense that each player fulfils her part of the agreement. Presumably this assumption may be defended by an appeal to a contract that is enforceable via the courts. However, in many bargaining situations (for a variety of reasons) this cannot be taken for granted — notwithstanding the presence of third parties (such as the courts).

The point is that players in real-life bargaining situations will be (and, indeed, are) influenced by the issue of which agreements can and cannot be enforced (either through third parties, or in a self-enforcing manner). Hence, the enforceability of agreements ought to play some role in determining the bargaining outcome. This should be explored in future research.

11.3   Thorny Issues

The theory of bargaining developed in this book is based upon the Nash equilibrium concept and its refinements (namely, the subgame perfect, Bayesian Nash, and perfect Bayesian Nash equilibrium concepts) — in the sense that the outcome of a bargaining situation is an equilibrium of some bargaining game. An implicit notion which underlies these equilibrium concepts is that the players are somewhat rational. Especially since there are *bounds* on the rationality of humans, it is important and interesting to define such bounds and explore their role on the bargaining outcome. Although this ought to be a main topic for future research in bargaining theory, it is not an easy topic to study. The basic problem lies in the construction of (tractable and persuasive) models of boundedly rational players that formalize such bounds on the rationality of humans, and which can be applied to study bargaining situations. Rubinstein (1998) contains many interesting ideas and tools that should prove helpful in constructing appropriate bargaining models with boundedly rational bargainers.[5]

An attractive (and fairly tractable) methodology that has already been used to explore the role of boundedly rational players on the bargaining outcome is provided by evolutionary game theory and learning models.[6] The handful of papers include Young (1993), Ellingsen (1997), Binmore, Piccione and Samuelson (1998) and Poulsen (1998). As will become evident from reading these papers, there is considerable scope for the development of this type of bargaining model. Such models should complement the models based on the game-theoretic methodology used in this book. Furthermore, the role of (bargaining) norms and emotions — and there would appear to be a role for them in real-life bargaining situations[7] — may be fruitfully explored using this type of model.

---

[5]For an interesting discussion of some of the issues that such models ought to address, see Bazerman, Gibbons, Thompson and Valley (1998).

[6]Recent textbooks on these methods include Weibull (1995), Samuelson (1997) and Fudenberg and Levine (1998).

[7]See, for example, Elster (1989).

In order to use the game-theoretic methodology — as I have done in this book — the rules of the bargaining process have to be precisely and unambiguously specified, since only then can one specify the extensive-form that underlies the bargaining game. This can be problematic. Although bargaining situations are games, it is often the case — as is briefly mentioned in Chapter 7 — that these rules are either only partly specified and/or ambiguous. Some type of methodology based upon and/or adapted from the methods of evolutionary game theory and learning models could perhaps be used to fruitfully model bargaining situations without the need to precisely and/or unambiguously specify the rules of the bargaining process.[8]

11.4   On the Role of Experiments

I now offer some comments on the role that bargaining experiments might play in the further development of the theory and application of bargaining.

It is instructive to first re-emphasize the nature of the theory developed in this book. This theory concerns the fundamentals of bargaining; it is meant to provide an *understanding* of the roles of the main forces (or, variables) on the bargaining outcome. It should therefore be judged on such terms — that is, on the extent to which it helps us to better understand the roles of various forces on the bargaining outcome.[9] Furthermore, from an applied perspective, this theory should help in the construction and study of models of economic and political phenomena that are (partly) characterized by bargaining situations.

It cannot be over-emphasized that the theory developed in this book does not purport to generate falsifiable predictions *à la* Popper — and indeed it cannot do so, since some of its key ingredients (such as the rationality of the players — which is implicitly embodied in the equilibrium concepts employed) are neither observable nor controllable. As such this theory cannot be tested by an appeal to experimental or field data. Besides, as stated above, that is not its purpose.

A primary role of bargaining experiments should be to make new discoveries about bargaining — for example, to identify new forces that may

---

[8] For a most stimulating discussion of the issues raised in this section, see Kreps (1990b).

[9] For illuminating discussions of what constitutes better understanding, see Kreps (1990a, pp. 7–10) and Rubinstein (1998, pp. 190–194).

have a significant impact on the bargaining outcome. In that way bargaining experiments can help in the further development of the theory of bargaining.

It is worth noting that since the subjects of such experiments are humans (whose unobservable reasoning processes may differ from what may be implicitly implied by the use of game-theoretic equilibrium concepts), experimental observations and discoveries should help in the construction of *descriptive* models of bargaining. Such models should complement the game-theoretic bargaining models studied in this book.

Most of the bargaining games experimented on so far have been finitely repeated versions of Rubinstein's model — with much attention being focused upon the ultimatum game (which is described in Section 7.2).[10] It may be noted that too much discussion has centred on the observation that subjects in many of these experiments tend to behave in ways that differ from what is indicated by the theory developed in this book. In view of what I have said above about the nature of this theory, I fail to appreciate the significance of this observation (and much of the discussion of it). On the other hand, some of the discoveries provided by such experiments (such as on the effects of deadlines) are to be welcomed. Indeed, motivated (partly) by the experimental studies on the effects of deadlines, Ma and Manove (1993) construct and study a game-theoretic bargaining model that explores, and provides some understanding of, the role of deadlines on the bargaining outcome. This is an illustration of the potentially important role that bargaining experiments can play; they can help stimulate the construction and study of new (and useful) game-theoretic models of bargaining. This, in turn, would improve our understanding of the determinants of the bargaining outcome.

A basic limitation of bargaining experiments comes from the difficulty of controlling variables that relate to the subjects of the experiments. These subjects are not atoms, or chemicals. These subjects are humans, who — no matter what they might say in an experimental set-up — will bring into the experiment their life experience, expectations, perceptions, norms, moral principles, and — most important of all — their reasoning processes. As such there is little hope (at least in the foreseeable future) of generating falsifiable predictions from both game-theoretic and descriptive models of bargaining. Therefore, the focus of bargaining experiments should be on

---

[10]For an excellent survey of the literature on bargaining experiments, see Roth (1995).

making new discoveries about bargaining, which would then feed into the further development of the theory of bargaining.

References

Abreu, D. (1988), "On the Theory of Infinitely Repeated Games with Discounting," *Econometrica*, 56: 383–396.

Abreu, D. and F. Gul (1999), "Reputation and Bargaining," *Econometrica*, forthcoming.

Acemoglu, D. and J. Pischke (1999), "The Structure of Wages and Investment in General Training," *Journal of Political Economy*, forthcoming.

Akerlof, G. (1970), "The Market for Lemons: Qualitative Uncertainty and the Market Mechanism," *Quarterly Journal Of Economics*, 89: 488–500.

Ausubel, L. and R. Deneckere (1989), "Reputation in Bargaining and Durable Goods Monopoly," *Econometrica*, 57: 511–531.

Avery, C. and P. Zemsky (1994), "Money Burning and Multiple Equilibria in Bargaining," *Games and Economic Behavior*, 7: 154–168.

Bac, M. and H. Raff (1996), "Issue-By-Issue Negotiations: The Role of Information and Time Preferences," *Games and Economic Behavior*, 13: 125–134.

Basu, K., S. Bhattacharya and A. Mishra (1992), "Notes on Bribery and the Control of Corruption," *Journal of Public Economics*, 48: 349–359.

Bazerman, M., R. Gibbons, L. Thompson and K. Valley (1998), "Can Negotiators OutPerform Game Theory," in J. Halpern and R. Stern (eds.), *Debating Rationality*, Cornell University Press, Ithaca, New York.

Bebchuk, L. (1984), "Litigation and Settlement under Imperfect Information," *Rand Journal of Economics*, 15: 404–415.

Becker, G. (1964), *Human Capital*, University of Chicago Press, Chicago.

Binmore, K. (1985), "Bargaining and Coalitions," in A. Roth (ed.), *Game-Theoretic Models of Bargaining*, Cambridge University Press, Cambridge.

Binmore, K. (1987), "Perfect Equilibria in Bargaining Models," in K. Binmore and P. Dasgupta (eds.), *The Economics of Bargaining*, Basil Blackwell, Oxford.

Binmore, K. (1992), *Fun and Games*, D.C. Heath and Company, Lexington, Massachusetts.

Binmore, K., M. Piccione and L. Samuelson (1998), "Evolutionary Stability in Alternating-Offers Bargaining Games," *Journal of Economic Theory*, 80: 257–291.

Binmore, K., A. Rubinstein and A. Wolinsky (1986), "The Nash Bargaining Solution in Economic Modelling," *Rand Journal of Economics*, 17: 176–188.

Bolt, W. and H. Houba (1997), "Strategic Bargaining in the Variable Threat Game," *Economic Theory*, 11: 57–77.

Bulow, J. and K. Rogoff (1989), "A Constant Recontracting Model of Sovereign Debt," *Journal of Political Economy*, 97: 155–178.

Busch, L., S. Shi and Q. Wen (1998), "Bargaining with Surplus Destruction," *Canadian Journal of Economics*, forthcoming.

Busch, L. and Q. Wen (1995), "Perfect Equilibria in a Negotiation Model," *Econometrica*, 63: 545–565.

Carlsson, H. (1991), "A Bargaining Model where Parties make Errors," *Econometrica*, 59: 1487–1496.

Chang, R. (1995), "Bargaining a Monetary Union," *Journal of Economic Theory*, 66: 89–112.

Chatterjee, K., B. Dutta, D. Ray and K. Sengupta (1993), "A Non-Cooperative Theory of Coalitional Bargaining," *Review of Economic Studies*, 60: 463–477.

Chatterjee, K. and L. Samuelson (1990), "Perfect Equilibria in Simultaneous Offer Bargaining," *International Journal of Game Theory*, 19: 237–267.

Chaudhuri, P. (1992), *Joint Ventures and Bargaining*, Ph.D. thesis, Indian Statistical Institute.

Chaudhuri, P. (1994), "Firm Size and Pricing Policy," Jawaharlal Nehru University, mimeo.

Coase, R. (1972), "Durability and Monopoly," *Journal of Law and Economics*, 15: 143–149.

Coles, M. and A. Muthoo (1998), "Strategic Bargaining and Competitive Bidding in a Dynamic Market Equilibrium," *Review of Economic Studies*, 65: 235–260.

Coles, M. and A. Muthoo (1999), "Bargaining Equilibrium in a Non-Stationary Environment," University of Essex, mimeo.

Compte, O. and P. Jehiel (1998), "When Outside Options Force Concessions to be Gradual," C.E.R.A.S., Paris.

Crawford, V. (1981), "Arbitration and Conflict Resolution in Labor-Management Bargaining," *American Economic Review Papers and Proceedings*, 71: 205–210.

Crawford, V. (1982), "A Theory of Disagreement in Bargaining," *Econometrica*, 50: 607–637.

Crawford, V. (1988), "Long-Term Relationships Governed by Short-Term Contracts," *American Economic Review*, 78: 485–499.

Cripps, M. (1998), "Markov Bargaining Games," *Journal of Economic Dynamics and Control*, 22: 341–355.

Davidson, C. (1988), "Multi-Unit Bargaining in Oligopolistic Industries," *Journal of Labor Economics*, 6: 397–422.

de Fraja, G. and A. Muthoo (1999), "Equilibrium Partner Switching in a Bargaining Model with Asymmetric Information," *International Economic Review*, forthcoming.

de Meza, D. and B. Lockwood (1998), "Does Asset Ownership Always Motivate Managers?: Outside Options and the Property Rights Theory of the Firm," *Quarterly Journal of Economics*, 113: 361–386.

Ellingsen, T. (1997), "The Evolution of Bargaining Behavior," *Quarterly Journal of Economics*, 112: 581–602.

Elster, J. (1989), *The Cement of Society*, Cambridge University Press, Cambridge.

Evans, R. (1989), "Sequential Bargaining with Correlated Values," *Review of Economic Studies*, 56: 499–510.

Felli, L. and C. Harris (1996), "Learning, Wage Dynamics and Firm-Specific Human Capital," *Journal of Political Economy*, 104: 838–868.

Fernandez, R. and J. Glazer (1991), "Striking for a Bargain Between Two Completely Informed Agents," *American Economic Review*, 81: 240–252.

Fershtman, C. (1990), "The Importance of the Agenda in Bargaining," *Games and Economic Behavior*, 2: 224–238.

Fudenberg, D. and D. Levine (1998), *The Theory of Learning in Games*, MIT Press, Cambridge, Massachusetts.

Fudenberg, D., D. Levine and J. Tirole (1985), "Infinite-Horizon Models of Bargaining with One-Sided Incomplete Information," in A. Roth (ed.), *Game-Theoretic Models of Bargaining*, Cambridge University Press, Cambridge.

Fudenberg, D. and J. Tirole (1991), *Game Theory*, MIT Press, Cambridge, Massachusetts.

Gibbons, R. (1992), *Game Theory for Applied Economists*, Princeton University Press, Princeton, NJ.

Groes, E. (1996), "Asymptotically Finite Repetition of Rubinstein's Bargaining Game," Institute of Economics, University of Copenhagen, mimeo.

Groes, E. and B. Sloth (1996), "Sequential Bargaining Theory with Decreasing Discount Factors," Institute of Economics, University of Copenhagen, mimeo.

Grossman, S. and O. Hart (1986), "The Costs and Benefits of Ownership: A Theory of Vertical and Lateral Integration," *Journal of Political Economy*, 94: 691–719.

Grossman, S. and M. Perry (1986), "Sequential Bargaining under Asymmetric Information," *Journal of Economy Theory*, 39: 120–154.

Gul, F., H. Sonnenschein and R. Wilson (1986), "Foundations of Dynamic Monopoly and the Coase Conjecture," *Journal of Economy Theory*, 39: 155–190.

Haller, H. and S. Holden (1990), "A Letter to the Editor on Wage Bargaining," *Journal of Economy Theory*, 52: 232–236.

Hart, O. (1989), "Bargaining and Strikes," *Quarterly Journal of Economics*, 104: 25–44.

Hart, O. (1995), *Firms, Contracts, and Financial Structure*, Oxford University Press, Oxford.

Hart, O. and B. Holmstrom (1987), "The Theory of Contracts," in T. Bewley (ed.), *Advances in Economic Theory*, Cambridge University Press, Cambridge.

Hart, O. and J. Moore (1988), "Incomplete Contracts and Renegotiation,"

Econometrica, 56: 755–786.

Hart, O. and J. Moore (1990), "Property Rights and the Nature of the Firm," *Journal of Political Economy*, 98: 1119–1158.

Hart, O. and J. Tirole (1988), "Contract Renegotiation and Coasian Dynamics," *Review of Economic Studies*, 55: 509–540.

Hay, B. and K. Spier (1998), "Settlement of Litigation," in P. Newman (ed.), *The New Palgrave Dictionary of Economics and the Law*, Macmillan Reference Limited.

Hendon, E., H. Jacobsen and B. Sloth (1996), "The One-Shot-Deviation Principle for Sequential Rationality," *Games and Economic Behavior*, 12: 274–282.

Hendon, E. and T. Tranes (1991), "Sequential Bargaining in a Market with One Seller and Two Different Buyers," *Games and Economic Behavior*, 3: 453–466.

Hindriks, J., M. Keen and A. Muthoo (1998), "Corruption, Extortion and Evasion," University of Essex, mimeo.

Holden, S. (1994), "Bargaining and Commitment in a Permanent Relationship," *Games and Economic Behavior*, 7: 169–176.

Jehiel, P. and B. Moldovano (1995), "Negative Externalities May Cause Delay in Negotiations," *Econometrica*, 63: 1321–1335.

Kambe, S. (1999), "Bargaining with Imperfect Commitment," *Games and Economic Behavior*, forthcoming.

Kreps, D. (1990a), *A Course in Microeconomic Theory*, Princeton University Press, Princeton, NJ.

Kreps, D. (1990b), *Game Theory and Economic Modelling*, Oxford University Press, Oxford.

Krishna, V. and R. Serrano (1996), "Multilateral Bargaining," *Review of Economic Studies*, 63: 61–80.

Lang, K. and R. Rosenthal (1998), "Multi-Issue Bargaining with Perfect Information," Boston University, mimeo.

Leach, J. (1997), "Inventories and Wage Bargaining," *Journal of Economic Theory*, 75: 433–463.

Luce, D. and H. Raiffa (1957), *Games and Decisions*, John Wiley and Sons, New York.

Lundberg, S. and R. Pollak (1993), "Separate Spheres Bargaining and the Marriage Market," *Journal of Political Economy*, 101: 988–1010.

Ma, C. and M. Manove (1993), "Bargaining with Deadlines and Imperfect Player Control," *Econometrica*, 61: 1313–1339.

Malcomson, J. (1997), "Contracts, Hold-Up, and Labor Markets," *Journal of Economic Literature*, 35: 1916–1957.

Manzini, P. (1999), "Strategic Bargaining with Destructive Power," *Economics Letters*, forthcoming.

Manzini, P. and M. Mariotti (1997), "A Model of Bargaining with the Possibility of Arbitration," Working Paper No. 374, Economics Dept., QMW College, London.

Mas-Colell, A., M. Whinston and J. Green (1995), *Microeconomic Theory*, Oxford University Press, Oxford.

McDonald, I. and R. Solow (1981), "Wage Bargaining and Employment," *American Economic Review*, 71: 896–908.

Merlo, A. and C. Wilson (1995), "A Stochastic Model of Sequential Bargaining with Complete Information," *Econometrica*, 63: 371–399.

Muthoo, A. (1990), "Bargaining Without Commitment," *Games and Economic Behavior*, 2: 291–297.

Muthoo, A. (1991), "A Note on Bargaining Over a Finite Number of Feasible Agreements," *Economic Theory*, 1: 290–292.

Muthoo, A. (1994), "A Note on Repeated-Offers Bargaining With One-Sided Incomplete Information," *Economic Theory*, 4: 295–301.

Muthoo, A. (1995a), "A Bargaining Model with Players' Perceptions on the Retractability of Offers," *Theory and Decision*, 38: 85–98.

Muthoo, A. (1995b), "Bargaining in a Long-Term Relationship with Endogenous Termination," *Journal of Economic Theory*, 66: 590–598.

Muthoo, A. (1995c), "On the Strategic Role of Outside Options in Bilateral Bargaining," *Operations Research*, 43: 292–297.

Muthoo, A. (1996), "A Bargaining Model Based on the Commitment Tactic," *Journal of Economic Theory*, 69: 134–152.

Muthoo, A. (1998), "Sunk Costs and the Inefficiency of Relationship-Specific Investment," *Economica*, 65: 97–106.

Myerson, R. (1979), "Incentive Compatibility and the Bargaining Problem," *Econometrica*, 47: 61–73.

Myerson, R. (1991), *Game Theory: Analysis of Conflict*, Harvard University Press, Cambridge, Massachusetts.

Myerson, R. and M. Satterthwaite (1983), "Efficient Mechanisms for Bilateral Trading," *Journal of Economic Theory*, 29: 265–281.

Nandeibam, S. (1996), "Bargaining in Partnerships," University of Birmingham, mimeo.

Nash, J. (1950), "The Bargaining Problem," *Econometrica*, 18: 155–162.

Nash, J. (1953), "Two-Person Cooperative Games," *Econometrica*, 21: 128–140.

Osborne, M. and A. Rubinstein (1990), *Bargaining and Markets*, Academic Press, San Diego, California.

Osborne, M. and A. Rubinstein (1994), *A Course in Game Theory*, MIT Press, Cambridge, Massachusetts.

Perry, M. and P. Reny (1993), "A Non-Cooperative Bargaining Model with Strategically Timed Offers," *Journal of Economic Theory*, 59: 55–77.

Phelps, E. (1961), "The Golden Rule of Accumulation: A Fable for Growthmen," *American Economic Review*, 51: 631–643.

Ponsati, C. and J. Sakovics (1995), "Mediation is Necessary for Dynamic Efficiency in Bargaining," UAB (Barcelona), mimeo.

Ponsati, C. and J. Sakovics (1998), "Rubinstein Bargaining with Two-Sided Outside Options," *Economic Theory*, 11: 667–672.

Poulsen, A. (1998), "An Evolutionary Analysis of Bargaining," University of Essex, mimeo.

Reinganum, J. and L. Wilde (1986), "Settlement, Litigation, and the Allocation of Litigation Costs," *Rand Journal of Economics*, 17: 557–566.

Roberts, K. (1994), "Wage and Employment Determination through Non-Cooperative Bargaining," STICERD Theoretical Economics Discussion Paper No: TE/94/274, London School of Economics.

Roth, A. (1995), "Bargaining Experiments," in J. Kagel and A. Roth (eds.), *Handbook of Experimental Economics*, Princeton University Press, Princeton, NJ.

Rubinstein, A. (1982), "Perfect Equilibrium in a Bargaining Model," *Econometrica*, 50: 97–110.

Rubinstein, A. (1985a), "A Bargaining Model with Incomplete Information about Time Preferences," *Econometrica*, 53: 1151–1172.

Rubinstein, A. (1985b), "Choice of Conjectures in a Bargaining Game with Incomplete Information," in A. Roth (ed.), *Game-Theoretic Models of Bargaining*, Cambridge University Press, Cambridge.

Rubinstein, A. (1991), "Comments on the Interpretation of Game Theory,"

Econometrica, 59: 909–924.

Rubinstein, A. (1998), *Modeling Bounded Rationality*, MIT Press, Cambridge, Massachusetts.

Rubinstein, A., Z. Safra and W. Thomson (1992), "On the Interpretation of the Nash Bargaining Solution and Its Extension to Non-Expected Utility Preferences," *Econometrica*, 60: 1171–1186.

Rubinstein, A. and A. Wolinsky (1985), "Equilibrium in a Market with Sequential Bargaining," *Econometrica*, 53: 1131–1150.

Samuelson, L. (1997), *Evolutionary Games and Equilibrium Selection*, MIT Press, Cambridge, Massachusetts.

Samuelson, W. (1984), "Bargaining under Asymmetric Information," *Econometrica*, 52: 992–1005.

Schelling, T. (1960), *The Strategy of Conflict*, Harvard University Press, Cambridge, Massachusetts.

Schmidt, K. (1993), "Commitment through Incomplete Information in a Simple Repeated Bargaining Model," *Journal of Economic Theory*, 60: 114–139.

Shaked, A. (1994), "Opting Out: Bazaars versus 'High Tech' Markets," *Investigaciones Economicas*, 18: 421–432.

Shaked, A. and J. Sutton (1984), "Involuntary Unemployment as a Perfect Equilibrium in a Bargaining Model," *Econometrica*, 52: 1351–1364.

Spence, M. (1974), *Market Signaling*, Harvard University Press, Cambridge, Massachusetts.

Spier, K. (1994), "Pretrial Bargaining and the Design of Fee-Shifting Rules," *Rand Journal of Economics*, 25: 197–214.

Sundaram, R. (1996), *A First Course in Optimization Theory*, Cambridge University Press, Cambridge.

van Damme, E. (1991), *Stability and Perfection of Nash Equilibria*, Springer-Verlag, Berlin, second edition.

van Damme, E., R. Selten and E. Winter (1990), "Alternating Bid Bargaining with a Smallest Money Unit," *Games and Economic Behavior*, 2: 188–201.

Vincent, D. (1989), "Bargaining with Common Values," *Journal of Economic Theory*, 48: 47–62.

Wang, G. (1998), "Bargaining over a Menu of Wage Contracts," *Review of Economic Studies*, 65: 295–305.

Weibull, J. (1995), *Evolutionary Game Theory*, MIT Press, Cambridge, Massachusetts.

Wolinsky, A. (1987), "Matching, Search and Bargaining," *Journal of Economic Theory*, 42: 311–333.

Young, P. (1993), "An Evolutionary Model of Bargaining," *Journal of Economic Theory*, 59: 145–168.

Index